Sustainable Family Farming and Yeoman Ideals

Within the frame of family farming, this book offers a longitudinal study of the Castra district in North-West Tasmania from first European settlement to the end of the twentieth century. It draws upon historical sources for yeomanry characteristics from Britain, Canada, the USA, New Zealand and Australian mainland colonies to show how these characteristics were persistently supportive of family farming.

Surveying farming communities over several generations, this book explores a range of topics including colonial surveying practices, settler families' motivation, attributes and demographics, the role of Methodism, the ways children were inculcated into yeoman farming enterprises, the role of women as companionate wives and the political participation of farmers in the public sphere. The book also offers a new perspective of three commonly held myths of settlement failure: the settlement of retired Anglo-Indian military and civil officers in the 1870s, the settlement of soldiers on small farms after the Great War and the claims that the ideal of yeoman family farming was anachronistic to capitalist commodity production. The book draws from a wide selection of previously underused primary source materials, including oral histories from current and past residents, to provide a comprehensive overview of an important aspect of rural Australian history.

The book is a valuable contribution to Australian historiography and will be a useful resource for students and scholars of rural history, social history, environmental history, colonialism and sustainable agriculture.

Dr Rena R. Henderson is Adjunct Researcher of rural and social history at the University of Tasmania. After various roles in Tasmanian and national community organisations, she returned to academic study drawn by the unique history of the rural area where she lives.

Sustainable Family Farming and Yeoman Ideals

1860 to 2000 in North-West Tasmania

Rena R. Henderson

LONDON AND NEW YORK

First published 2021
by Routledge
2 Park Square, Milton Park, Abingdon, Oxon OX14 4RN

and by Routledge
605 Third Avenue, New York, NY 10158

Routledge is an imprint of the Taylor & Francis Group, an informa business

© 2021 Rena R. Henderson

The right of Rena R. Henderson to be identified as author of this work has been asserted in accordance with sections 77 and 78 of the Copyright, Designs and Patents Act 1988.

All rights reserved. No part of this book may be reprinted or reproduced or utilised in any form or by any electronic, mechanical, or other means, now known or hereafter invented, including photocopying and recording, or in any information storage or retrieval system, without permission in writing from the publishers.

Trademark notice: Product or corporate names may be trademarks or registered trademarks, and are used only for identification and explanation without intent to infringe.

British Library Cataloguing-in-Publication Data
A catalogue record for this book is available from the British Library

Library of Congress Cataloging-in-Publication Data
Names: Henderson, Rena R., author.
Title: Sustainable family farming and yeoman ideals: 1860 to 2000 in north-west Tasmania/Rena R. Henderson
Description: New York, NY: Routledge, 2022. | Includes bibliographical references and index.
Identifiers: LCCN 2021036204 (print) | LCCN 2021036205 (ebook) | ISBN 9781032135588 (hardback) | ISBN 9781032135571 (paperback) | ISBN 9781003229841 (ebook)
Subjects: LCSH: Family farms – Australia – Tasmania. | Rural families – Australia – Tasmania. | Tasmania – History.
Classification: LCC DU198.C37 H46 2022 (print) | LCC DU198.C37 (ebook) | DDC 338.109946/5 – dc23
LC record available at https://lccn.loc.gov/2021036204
LC ebook record available at https://lccn.loc.gov/2021036205

ISBN: 978-1-032-13558-8 (hbk)
ISBN: 978-1-032-13557-1 (pbk)
ISBN: 978-1-003-22984-1 (ebk)

DOI: 10.4324/9781003229841

Typeset in Times New Roman
by Apex CoVantage, LLC

Acknowledgement to Country

The lands of North-West Tasmania that are the setting of this book are *lutruwita* (Tasmania) Aboriginal land, sea and waterways. I acknowledge, with deep respect, the traditional owners of this land, the palawa people.

The palawa people belong to the oldest continuing culture in the world. They cared for and protected Country for thousands of years. They knew this land, they lived on the land and they died on these lands. I honour them and pay my respects to elders past and present and to the many Aboriginal people that did not make elder status and to the Tasmanian Aboriginal community that continue to care for Country.

Our Island is deeply unique, with spectacular landscapes of bushland, wilderness, mountain ranges and beaches. It is a privilege to stand on Country and walk in the footsteps of those before us.

Contents

List of Figures	viii
Measurements	ix
Introduction	1
1 The Castra Association 1864 to 1873: 'A home in the colonies'	18
2 Castra land and Anglo-Indian ownership	45
3 Development of Castra farms and institutions 1880–1910	63
4 Closer settlement in Castra	88
5 Soldier settlement in Tasmania and Castra	108
6 Succession and inheritance in Castra families, 1900–2000	137
7 Childhood and youth in Castra	156
8 Women play their part – tradition and change	180
9 Men and their land – doing what was best: 1880–1980	199
Conclusion	230
Acknowledgements	234
Abbreviations	235
Bibliography	236
Index	269

Figures

0.1	Map of Devon and Adjacent County	2
0.2	First Leven Bridge and Dial Ranges	4
1.1	Segment of Proposed Tramway Plan to Castra	29
1.2	Portrait of Lieutenant-Colonel Andrew Crawford	33
1.3	Crawford Family Farm, Deyrah, Central Castra c. 1880–1890	44
2.1	Ritherdon Lot, Dooley's Plains Survey Plan	49
2.2	Macnee Lot, Dooley's Plains Survey Plan	50
2.3	Shaw & Shaw Lot, Leven Survey Plan	51
2.4	Wilson Lot, Central Castra Survey Plan	52
2.5	Various lots, Leven Survey Plan	53
2.6	'Diagram of Actual Survey', Lewis Lot, Castra Parish	55
2.7	St. John Crawford Lot, North Motton Survey Plan	59
5.1	Division of Rockliff Estate 1920	124
9.1	Bingham Family Home and Dairy Enterprise	214
9.2	Henry Johnson's Preston Descendants, 1996	226

Measurements

For most of the period covered in this history, relevant measurements are pre-metrication areas and pre-decimal currency. Even as acres changed officially to hectares, the generation of farming folk interviewed still think and talk of 'acres' and geographic features like 'the ten-foot track' just as old property and place names persist. For those reasons, I have maintained the 'old ways' throughout but offer the following comparisons for readers more familiar with the new.

Land area was measured in acres, roods and perches.

1 acre = 4 roods; 1 rood = 40 perches. 1 acre = 10 square chains (area). For example, survey plans might show '88 A. 3 R. 5 P', i.e. 88 acres, 3 roods, 5 perches.

1 square mile or section = 640 acres. Thus 320 acres = a half section and 160 acres = a quarter section (in the colonial era, these were both common areas for small farms).

Distance was measured in miles, rods and chains.

1 mile = 80 chains. For example, survey plans show standard road reserves of 10 chains wide.

1 chain = 22 yards = 66 feet = 100 links (the latter used by surveyors for measuring land). For example, 160 acres might measure 56.70 chains by 28.25 chains, so links enabled an early decimal system.

In Chapter 2, survey plans show how areas were adjusted to maintain accurate measurements when roads were inserted or altered.

Length was in yards, feet and inches. 1 yard = 3 feet = 36 inches.

Money was measured in pounds, shillings and pence, shown as £, /- and d, thus, £5 10/6d.

£1 = 20 shillings 1 shilling = 12 pence. Rough decimal comparison meant £1 = $2, but comparisons in history are irrelevant unless comparing, for example, a task costing £16 per week that later reduces to £10, as labour became more available. Comparative prices are relevant in Chapter 5.

Introduction

The intimate connection of yeoman ideals to family farming was a fundamental part of the history of Australian agriculture almost from the earliest time of European occupation. The long history of yeomanry and the associated notions of pioneering agricultural work on small farms and independent subsistence arrived from England with the First Fleet and Governor Phillip, whose royal instruction was to 'proceed with the cultivation of the land' (25 April 1787. HRA 1914, Vol. 1, 15 quoted by Shaw, 1 in Williams 1990). Ever since, the crucially important contribution made by small family farms to Australia's economic growth was based on their large families that provided labour for sustainable agricultural output. The cultural importance of family operated farms continues to arouse supportive responses to media stories like drought or flooding, indicating widely held positivity towards farmers and their communities well into the present century (Lloyd and Malcolm 1997, 59).

Historian John McQuilton argued that the concept of the yeoman ideal in both Australia and America gave primacy to land ownership as the true key to wealth; small-scale agricultural production stimulated permanent settlement and engendered 'independence in spirit, self-sufficiency and democratic values'. He made a connection with Frederick Turner's 'frontier thesis' of 1893, but suggested that earlier 'powerful champions' of the ideal had included Thomas Jefferson and Ernest Gibbon Wakefield (McQuilton 1993, 32).

In this book, I examine whether that intimate connection between the institution of family farming and yeoman ideals still endures, using the case study of the family farming community of Castra in North-West Tasmania. Starting at first European settlement there, this rural social history extends forward to the end of the twentieth century. Such a long timespan was essential to demonstrate that yeoman ideals in self-sufficient family farming were the motivating force for settlement success and that these ideals remained strong over several succeeding generations, lasting in some families to 2000 and beyond. Castra and its farmers provide an example of the success and endurance of the yeoman ideal.

The setting

In North-West Tasmania, the parish of Castra is 50,000 acres of forest and agricultural land that extends from the Leven River eastwards to the Wilmot River, a

DOI: 10.4324/9781003229841-1

2   Introduction

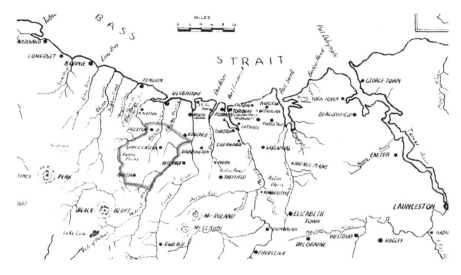

Figure 0.1 Map showing Castra Parish (marked) and major north-flowing rivers.
Source: James Fenton, *Bush Life in Tasmania* 1891, opposite page 12.

tributary of the Forth River. It encompasses large rural villages that developed at Gunns Plains, Preston, Upper Castra and Nietta. The area is located between 14 and 20 miles south and inland from the coastal town of Ulverstone. When Ulverstone was only a collection of cottages and land grants, it was known as Leven after the Leven River on the coastal banks of which it grew.

As seen from Figure 0.1, the Leven is one of five large rivers that flow northward into Bass Strait between Emu River in the west and Tamar River in the east. The others are the Rubicon meeting Bass Strait at Port Sorell; the Mersey flowing into the sea between Formby and Torquay, later amalgamated to form Devonport; the Forth meeting the sea at Leith; and the Blyth flowing out at Heybridge.

The county name was Devon; from 1856 it had one representative in Parliament. Following the 1870 *Electoral Act*, in 1871 it was divided into Wellington (west of Emu Bay/Burnie), West Devon (encompassing my area of interest) and East Devon (from Devonport to the Tamar), each having one Member of Parliament. By 1885, population had grown sufficiently for five members to represent the North-West Coast (Townsley 1956, 69).

The hinterlands of West Devon contain several ranges of low mountains dominated by Black Bluff (4,383 feet/1,336 metres high), which drains north-west into the Leven and east into tributaries of the Forth River. This was snow-covered from July to October each year in the childhoods of elders interviewed and was still the case up to the 1980s (Binks 1980, 15).

Rainfall averaged from 30 inches (750mm) along the coast to over 70 inches (1800mm) along the mountain ranges, where dense wet sclerophyll forest began to yield to moorland (Stokes 1969).

Introduction 3

Sporadically, there were areas of undulating high plains and river flats, where trees were more thinly distributed in sharp contrast to the remainder that was dense 'bush' or so-called 'scrub' and thickly growing trees, enormous in height and girth. The dominant species were eucalypts, E. *obliqua* (stringybark), E. *ovata* (yellow gum), E. *viminalis* (white gum) and E. regnans (swamp gum) in the damp valleys (Stokes 1969). A close undergrowth of Sassafras, Musk, Dogwood and fern trees among others completed the picture (Calder 1860; News 1860b). Prior to European occupation, the rivers had heavily treed, steep-sided valleys, with strong year-round river flow through them. All except the Leven were dammed for hydroelectricity in the later twentieth century.

Tasmania has attracted comment about its benign and healthy climate since its occupation by Europeans in the early nineteenth century. In 1902, New Zealand legislator and diplomat Pember Reeves described Tasmania as:

A valuable colony not much smaller than Scotland, and, like Scotland, a land of cliff and mountain, lake and forest, with precipitous coasts and peaks that rival the Grampians [in Scotland] in height . . . . . Its latitude is Italian and its climate more resembles that of Brittany . . . . All that is useful in English flora will grow, and most of it does grow, in Tasmania.

(Reeves 1902, 19–20)

Wood wrote that Tasmania's geological composition 'exerted a big influence on lives and occupations' because the varied relief allowed a wide range of crops and economic activity, from timber-getting, agriculture, dairying, orchards and 'pasturing' (1923, 11). In the volcanic period, lava flows formed sheets of basalt in Tasmania's North-East and North-West that decayed to form 'wonderful chocolate soils' and remained as hills through which streams carved their courses (Wood 1923, 20–21). These were described in 1860 as 'almost uniformly of a red colour and are of considerable depth, varying from about four to eight feet in thickness, the choicest land being most thickly timbered' (Calder 1860).

Situated about 41–42° south, Tasmania had 'a cool maritime climate of distinct seasons' with shorter winters and longer summers than the British colonists' experience of the 'mother country'. This climate was long-touted as conducive to good health by the many who particularly advocated it for recovery from tropical India (Reynolds 2005, 458; Walker 2011). Regular winter rainfall and generally hot dry summers with the moderating influence of the sea breezes is the typical experience in the Castra district. The topography and climate are important underlying themes in this history.

Tasmania's North was identified in what Warwick Frost called Australia's 'wet frontier' of high-rainfall forests that stretched from the tropics of Cairns' hinterland down the Dividing Range of eastern Australia to Gippsland, the Otways and King Island into Tasmania. Although timber-getters had made early incursions, farming settlement in the forests was slow to take off before the 1870s (1997, 19–20). The lands of Castra were another type of frontier – an agricultural one that

4 *Introduction*

Figure 0.2 Dial Ranges and first bridge over the Leven River, 1866 (Calvert 1879).
Source: *Illustrated Australian News*, August 2, 1879. Object 135882586. National Library of Australia.

contrasted with the 'pastoral frontier' that developed in Australia's South-East from the 1860s and in Tasmania from the 1830s.

Devon's identity as an agricultural community was already evident from its early population figures; just over 3,000 in 1857 grew to 5,416 by 1861, 572 of whom were land-owning farmers, 1099 were farm labourers and only 43 were shopkeepers or businessmen (Pink, 1990, 104). Women and children may have represented most of the remaining 1,714. The 1870 census recorded place of birth; the majority (3,583) were Tasmanian born, either before 1851 or as children of early immigrants arriving after 1851. From Great Britain and Ireland, there were 2,197, 82 from mainland colonies and 62 from Germany and North America (Census 1870). Town directories from 1890–1891 to 1941 confirm that farmers predominated over 'labourers' and 'other settlers' in feeder communities of Ulverstone and North Motton in earlier years until post offices opened in Castra's villages of Upper Castra, Gunns Plains, Preston, Preston South and Nietta (Wise 1890 to 1941). The figures recorded reflect changes referred to in later chapters.

The striking eye-level view of river and mountain range seen by the 1860–70 pioneers features in Figure 0.2. The Leven bridge opened in September 1866, improving access to Penguin, the next settlement west along the coast. On the left bank called Nicholson's Point, the larger house was the first house on the Leven recorded by surveyor James Scott in November 1851. The distinctive peak is called Mount Gnomon (Scott 1851; Devon Map 90, AF396-1-702). It was the subject for Tom Roberts in 1899, painting the Dial Range from the Ulverstone Wharf.

This book bridges an identified gap in rural histories that extend across the colonial period up to the end of the twentieth century. Also importantly, it refutes opinions that the yeoman ideal was an anachronism by the time of Australia's Federation in 1901. I examine how characteristics intrinsic to the yeoman ideal served settler communities very satisfactorily, because it encouraged people to create strong kinship-linked families and develop connected-ness to land they owned. This was achieved through common interests and associations that developed ties binding residents together in stable, enduring ways over generations – even through two world wars, the Depression and the agricultural crisis of the late twentieth century.

It is not a new idea that people and communities are held together by intangible 'webs of association' and 'the everyday fabric of connection and tacit cooperation' identified by Adam Smith in 1776, de Tocqueville in 1840 and Durkheim in 1897 (Halpern 2005, 3–5). Each farming community develops uniquely depending on the character, motivation and ideals of its individuals. Such ties take time to develop in newly settled frontier areas. Primary family ties grounded in life on a family farm are key from the start, but, before long, the needs of social contact, religious practice and neighbourly reciprocity must be satisfied in the interests of survival. How were those connections created? What were the common bonds the early settlers shared and did they help in times of inevitable adversity? How did ownership patterns connect settlers to the land and locality? How did the society sustain ties in the early years to support the establishment of institutions? How did families manage generational change and durability of the farm and the family through succession and inheritance? Answers to these questions are addressed in chapters that focus on the various ways people approached settlement on this land from the colonial period of the 1860s through to the early 1920s settlement of soldiers after the Great War, and how yeomen families managed their aspirations to hand on their land to family members or to help them establish themselves independently.

The conceptual framework of continuity and change is used to take a deeper look at aspects of farming families' lives during the twentieth century. I evaluate the endurance of the yeoman ideal through tangible evidence of family ties, neighbourly relationships, business and economic arrangements, and religious and political allegiances. I consider how concepts of gender impacted on family decisions about farm succession and inheritance. Continuities are contrasted with the effects of changes in family size and aspirations, and in land usage and farm size. Economic survival strategies demonstrate how family farmers adapted from self-sufficiency to capitalist commodities and engaged in self-help and political participation to benefit both their family and their enterprise.

6   *Introduction*

My study is a rural history with an uneasy fit somewhere between regional and local history. So, where does it sit? In time, it is not limited to the pioneering phase of the late nineteenth century, though this was common in academic histories of Australian rural regions, according to Davison and Brodie, writing *Struggle Country* in 2005. They were critical of the paucity of historical attention to twentieth century rural history even when authors professed to cover two centuries of European settlement. Citing recent publications, they suggested the twentieth century seemed like a 'postlude to the pioneering era' (ix–xvi). Congruent with their title and tone, the twentieth century histories they highlight are tragic tales of adversity and failure, like Marilyn Lake's *Limits of Hope* (1987), which receives more attention in a later chapter.

Regional history has a long tradition that has experienced high points. McCarty argued that regional history of the 1960s had 'emerged as one of the most interesting areas of Australian historical writing' ((McCarty 1978, 88). He highlighted the now-classic works by Kiddle (1961), Buxton (1967), Walker (1966), Waterson (1968) and Hancock (1972), agreeing with Hancock's proposition that each new study had shown variety in both regional characteristics and historical approaches. These early works were mostly about pastoral areas that each formed a 'formal or homogeneous region', but other types of regional history were important too. He defined a functional region as 'a town or city and its hinterland' affected by 'a significant economic, social or political relationship', such as Hirst's important 1973 study about Adelaide and its relationship with country South Australia (McCarty 1978, 92). Another type is 'the history of a group of related regions', arguably applying to any Tasmanian history with its distinct regionalism (Reynolds 1969b, 14–28). One less-explored version was a country town and its hinterland, like Tom Griffiths' lauded study of Beechworth (Griffiths 1987). McCarty's later theorising that an 'inland corridor' linked interior settlements and towns would significantly influence two books aimed at broadening ideas of inland Australia (1980). These essay collections picked up themes of environmental, aboriginal, social and cultural histories with newer topics feeding debates like ecological, farming and societal sustainability (Mayne and Atkinson 2008, 2011).

Previously, Weston Bate had weighed into the discussion, arguing that 'regional history without some geography is like a boat without a rudder' (1970, 106). He consistently argued that towns were an essential ingredient to rural histories due to their 'pervasive influence in the district' (108). Bate also saw that local history of a locality could 'carry the torch' for regional history (118). In a way, that resonates with the Puritan approach to development in (American) New England in small market towns that were also promoted in settling New Zealand. They were expected to be 'servants of productive farming districts rather than dominant masters' and factory production should serve the growth of agricultural wealth (Brooking 1996, 82–83). Endorsing this idea and because my study centres on the rural Castra community, I approach from the opposite perspective – it was its hinterland settlements and people that influenced Ulverstone's growth from an un-named cluster of cottages to a thriving commercial and transport hub. Bate's description of local history fits well with Mayne's position that 'micro-histories'

Introduction 7

of 'ordinary people' with their aspirations and experiences all contribute to Australia's 'social landscape' and is applicable to my work (2011, 2–4).

Laverty also endorsed 'competent local histories' to provide helpful secondary sources for regional historians. His main call was for greater integration of city and regional histories that pay particular attention to inter-relationships with wider hinterlands. Following his main theme, he criticised regional histories that overly focussed on land settlement without integrating local towns with hinterland activities, citing Bate's work on Ballarat that integrated the provincial city with its regional context and their common evolution (Laverty 1995, 103–38). Both Buxton's Riverina study and Meinig's 1970 study of South Australia were applauded for demonstrating that integration. Laverty criticised the 1960s regional histories mentioned for seldom extending into the twentieth century and ignoring or underplaying their towns' contribution to their hinterlands.

I agree that geography is especially relevant to rural histories. Outstanding physical geographical features of region, or hinterland and town, influence the shape of a functional history. For example, Tasmania's many distinctive characteristics stem from it being an island (see Solomon 1972; Harwood 2011). When the prevailing topography tends to dictate the way people make use of the land, that becomes its defining characteristic. Such characteristic images inform stereotypes that evoke 'romantic' or nostalgic notions; thus, our image of *pastoral* land is of thin tree cover on undulating grasslands; our image of *forestry* is densely packed trees going up hills to the rocky margins of growth; our image of the yeoman *agricultural* landscape is of a patchwork of fields with potatoes, poultry or pig-keeping within visible fence lines or hedges not far from a farm homestead such as typified by the physical landscape of small-scale yeoman farms in Western Australia (Tonts 2002, 106).

Regional boundaries may be either politically or physically loosely defined, especially when they fade away into unexplored or unalienated land. McCarty argued that evolving boundaries were more fitting for longer period studies because they reflected historically relevant changes. Pertinently, he emphasised that writers of regional social history are principally interested in the people, their social identity and unity, their pride in their customs and their distinctiveness, but their history still needs to relate to a wider setting and have its broader significance explained (McCarty 1978, 92).

Rural life seemed to have been somewhat overlooked by historians in the previous 30 years, according to Darian-Smith in 2002, the gap being filled by social scientists analysing regional and rural change (2002, 92). Classic oft-cited Australian sociological studies are Alston in 1995 and Dempsey in 1990 and 1992. Historical geographers Powell and Davidson were the exception. They wrote about two aspects of rural history – people and land – in a study about Australian family farms (Lees 1997, 1–13). The 'agrarian' ideal, equated to yeomanry, represented 'small-scale farming enterprises owned and operated by individual families' (Lees 1997, 1–13). Lees showed that this concept was adopted and mediated

8 *Introduction*

by farmers' varied experiences across Australia's differing climatic and soil zones, and that it was promoted by those in political power.

Davidson gave an overview of the crucial process of land policy and tenure, and the ways each colony used their policies to encourage selection of Crown Lands by small farmers. He stated that single family farms have always been the main type of Australian agricultural unit, later generally supported by government policy because they achieved flexibility in daily decision-making compared with managed corporate-owned farms (Davidson 1997, 15–16, 29, 37–40, 53). How this was manifested in Tasmania's colonial land policy is examined in relation to Castra's genesis.

Historical geographers, including these two men, have written of the political attraction and the implications on the ground of Australia's approach to the yeoman ideal. Roberts (1924) identified 1884 as the start of emphasis on the small farmer in Victoria and South Australia. The suggestion is that it lost its appropriateness for this continent due to climatic changeability and over-exploitation (Powell 1988; Davidson 1981). While I accept their proposition in connection to drier mainland Australian states, I argue that their view was much less appropriate for agriculture under North-West Tasmanian soil and climatic conditions – this area is still very different to most agricultural practice on our continent. I also contend that proliferation of a 'rural idyll' by city-based writers is a myth used to espouse the idea of country-mindedness to urbanites that never had any connection to the lives of yeoman family farmers, wherever they farmed (Davison 2005, 1.1–1.15).

Writing from a Tasmanian base, it is appropriate to mention different themes in Tasmanian rural history since the 1990s that extended into the early twentieth century. These include Breen recounting the history of the Deloraine area (2001), Cubit considering the differing constructs of nature in the Central Plateau (2001), Haygarth collaborating on works about mountain huts (2016) and the history of rural youth (2018), Bardenhagen exploring the German peoples of Lilydale in the Great War (1993) and Rootes, who has produced works about Tasmanian local government (2004, 2008). Alexander has written several municipal histories (2003, 2006, 2012) that tend to focus on their urban centres and allocate less space to rural life, though these would count as regional histories using Laverty's criteria.

When a history of Victoria was mooted about 1980, Bate and Aveling proposed a three-volume thematic social history called *The Victorians*. In 'Settling' (Vol. 2), Dingle described a mob of selectors on the steps of Parliament in Melbourne in August 1860 clamouring for 'A Vote, a Rifle and a Farm', the last of which was most important to satisfy their post-gold-rush desire to settle down as yeomen farmers (1984, 58). According to him, the meaning of the yeoman ideal was seldom articulated because of the assumption that everyone understood it, so its interpretation varied in ways that would impact on Victoria's agricultural policymaking and development for many decades. The idea of small areas of land that families could live on, rear animals and grow food for their own consumption without paying labour or being exploited by employers arrived with English

Introduction 9

radicals attracted by gold rushes. Before long, widespread unrest about the squatters' power and landholdings came from many quarters, and the yeoman ideal was adapted to fit the different objectives of merchants, investors, land-hungry potential farmers and liberal-minded politicians. For the politicians, it was important for selectors of 320- or 640-acre lots to have families who could manage with their own labour in line with the yeoman ideal, deemed vital because 'a class of rural labourers would run counter to the spirit of the yeoman idea' (Dingle 1984, 61–64). Thus, the family enterprise was 'the foundation stone of the selection era' by 1890 (76). The spread of yeoman farms to regions north of the Dividing Range and into Gippsland were the 'turning point' in Victoria's agricultural history (102–30). Prior to Federation and driven by his need to boost population, Victorian Premier Thomas Bent was still anxious for 'agriculturalist producers to settle using the real wealth from the soil to add to national wealth' (Frost 1983, 196). This exemplified political attitudes to the value of the yeoman farming model.

Religious leaders in the 1880s believed that Queensland's 'moral health' was supplied by the rural yeoman, 'a stabilizing force' against urban radicalism, because, according to Archbishop John Dunmore Lang, 'a man with . . . land is unlikely to become a socialist or political' (Lang 1892). Lang was a Presbyterian clergyman and politician who promoted education, immigration and was an anti-transportation advocate believing in land reform. Following his ideals, political advocates pressed for legislation to enable agricultural interests and the yeoman ideal (Lang 1861 cited by Waterson 1968, 103–4).

In New South Wales' northern rivers sugar-growing districts, a yeoman class of settler was favoured in 1870 because they settled permanently. Large plantation owners supported a land policy for small holdings, believing yeomanry cane-growers would accept smaller profits in return for landownership. This strategy, according to a local newspaper of the 1870s, resulted in the highest density and level of influence of yeoman settlers in the colony. In 1871, one editor was advocating for any regulations to help establish 'a sturdy yeomen class', but, by 1877, he was less satisfied by their increasing political strength that 'ignored every other class of settler's interests' (News 1870, 1871, 1877a).

The value of Dingle's book lay in unequivocally stating the significance of the yeoman ideal as a motivating force right across Victorian society. But then he argued that selectors behaved as if the land was an exploitable resource, meaning that they did not fit the yeoman ideal under which land was seen as a legacy to be cared for and protected (74–75). Where did the interpretation of the yeoman ideal come from and why might it manifest differently to its advocates?

Yeomanry and the qualities of the yeoman ideal

To answer the question about its origin, it is instructive to identify the characteristics of yeomen that informed the yeoman ideal. Trevelyan, in his mammoth classic *History of England*, argued the 'yeoman motif' infused a 'potent and life-giving force' to English thought, literature and politics from the Hundred Years' War through to the Industrial Revolution. He wrote that 'yeoman was used for

10 *Introduction*

a free peasant farmer, irrespective of whether his land was freehold or held on lease, until the late 18th century', and neither villeins nor landless labourers were yeomen (Trevelyan 1973 (1926), 275). The yeomen farmer benefited most after early enclosures as his methods improved, enabling him to give work to 'the humble' and avoid constant quarrels over shared commons; yeomen broke down the old structure of medieval lord and villein. Writing at the Civil War's outbreak, Thomas Fuller described the yeomanry as 'an estate of people almost peculiar to England. France and Italy . . . hath no points between nobility and peasantry' (quoted in 516). Yeomen freeholder and leaseholder farmers became identified as part of the 'middling' sort as small independent agricultural producers (Neale 1981, 74).

Interest in English social hierarchy led to three major national surveys over time; Gregory King (1688), Joseph Massie (1759) and Patrick Colquhoun from 1801–3 based on the 1801 (first) census (Hay and Rogers 1997, 19–21, 26–36). Yeomen farmers were hard to isolate because large and small freeholders and farmers were separate categories. In 1688, Gregory King estimated that 50 per cent of English farmers were owners (Rae 1883, 546–65). Two-hundred years later, the yeomanry had declined so much that it drew attention to major property redistribution, and Gray (1910, 293–94) cited Rae as the first historian to importantly consider their decline. Using contemporary sources, Rae convincingly showed 1815 as the year disaster struck for yeomen farmers. While gaining from high grain prices and demand during the War with France (1793–1815), their numbers had grown through the so-called 'terramania' land-grab in the Midlands and Yorkshire. From 1815, they were under pressure as prices dropped and the newly mortgaged yeomen did not have the inherited asset of land to fall back on and keep them going; rents continued rising for yeomen tenant farmers, especially in corn lands (Snell 1985, 193). Large fortunes made in local and colonial trade competed promptly for any available land. But by the 1870s, agricultural prices collapsed again, due to low production costs in North America of grain that was gradually supplanting local produce (Boyce 2020).

Newby (1987) wrote that the 1873 New Domesday Survey, promoted by Lord Derby to rebut claims of limited land ownership in Britain, actually confirmed the few elite landholders; however, it also divided landholders into aristocracy, gentry and yeomen with holdings of between 100 and 1,000 acres, who prospered during the mid-Victorian period (60–61, 71). Evidence to the Duke of Richmond's Royal Commission of 1881 indicated decline was more widespread than previously supposed, identifying Lincolnshire as the yeoman's last stronghold by 1880 (Gray 1910, 325). The yeoman small-holders of Lincolnshire were found to have suffered least of all farmers and were more resilient against cheap food imports (Thirsk 1957).

In spite of emigration appearing to offer a solution to their problems, Rae argued that:

> The yeomen seldom sold to make better; they sold to save bad becoming worse. They relaxed their hold upon land slowly, and against their will. The

Introduction 11

land is the charter of their personal independence, and the foundation of all the hope and security of their life . . . the small farmers belong [to a class that is] unspeculative, and, indeed, averse to speculation.

(Rae 1883, 556)

He affirmed that investment in their land was more attractive and satisfying than a bank deposit. They valued being masters of their own fate, growing their own crops in their own way, not answerable to anyone for their votes. Beckett (1977) found that Yorkshiremen were strongly rooted in independence and conspicuously industrious and economic; Westmorelanders were 'very impatient of insult or oppression' and expected respect from their superiors (567–81).

Ambiguities arose over the term yeoman, also used for copyholders and tenant farmers. Beckett identified differences in eighteenth-century Cumbria, where tenant farmers styled themselves as yeomen, because, under a distinctive northern land law, they held, or could inherit, 'customary tenure' with a title deed that was virtually freehold. Two thirds of Cumberland land were held this way, always owner-occupied. Yeomen farmers on larger holdings still existed there with rising prosperity by the late 1870s (Beckett 1982). As elsewhere, 'by-employment', meaning off-farm employment, was significant to their survival; blacksmiths, carpenters, tanning, salt-making and coal mining, and shipping in the coastal counties. Wealthier yeomen acted as executors for others and as stewards or bailiffs for the large estates. The 1861 census increased concern about the yeomanry's displacement there and rising land accumulation by 'greater magnates', and radical calls for land reform were strengthened (Beckett 1982). This parallels similar discontent over the squatters' stranglehold at about the same time on potential agricultural land suitable for subdivision for yeoman farmers in Australia's mainland colonies.

Thus far, the *English* yeoman farmer has been characterised as forming the middle level between labourer and lord, conservative in practice, averse to speculation and wary of change. Their families were industrious, often with extra artisanal skills and flexible about by-employment. They were proud of their status as independent farm landholders.

Trevelyan noted that the yeomen, craftsmen and 'small gentry', used to living in substantial villages of the Midlands and south-east, were among the great majority of migrants to New England (North America) up to 1640, in response to religious and political conflicts. Their Puritan faith combined 'self-help and economic individualism with residence in large village groups' to form new communities (520). He claimed their hardiness and survival against their new challenges contributed to ideas of democracy, religious tolerance and 'the frontier spirit' of American history (Trevelyan 1973 (1926), 522–27). This brings me to examine sources about American yeomen (Appleby 1982, 833–49; Fields 1985, 135–39; Ford 1986, 17–37; Atack 1988, 6–32; Wilkison 2008), and whether, as settlers in the New World, they developed different attributes. According to Webster's 1828 *Dictionary*, yeoman was 'a common man, or one of the plebeians, of the first or most respectable class; a freeholder, a man freeborn'.

12 *Introduction*

Appleby wrote about the American post-revolutionary period when 'yeomanry' described freehold farmers, who she called 'ordinary farmers'. Similarly, others used 'plain folk'. She traced the 30-year boom in agricultural produce after the Revolution ended in 1783. Ordinary farmers gained an unusual advantage in benefitting from demand in English and southern European markets. Those owning between 75–100 acres were able to increase surpluses of Indian corn, wheat and animals using only their own and family labour, using access to market by wagon or riverboat, without risks associated with dependence on cash crops of hemp or tobacco as in Virginia and North Carolina from the 1760s (Appleby 1982; Risjord 1973, 30, 225).

A farmer himself, Thomas Jefferson's vision of 'democratic agrarianism' was a unique combination of agrarian philosophy from Europe grafted onto American democratic ideology (Lees 1997, 3). It grew from his intimacy with ordinary farmers' concerns and the triple combination of mixed farming, overseas trade and the 'golden era' of grain growing. 'Farmer' was the word for the new future; 'planter' was the word of the past. Opening new lands for them, emphasising products from family farms, linking economic freedom to political democracy, all formed part of a rational agrarian vision that stressed how yeomanry farmers tangibly contributed to political and economic national advantage. Committed to good stewardship himself, Jefferson believed that an educated yeoman farmer who managed the land carefully was the key to America's future, so an effective educational system was a means to develop leadership in common men. Economically independent farmers were less likely to be dominated by 'aristocratic or demagogic influences' in government (Kenyon 1971, 985–89). Jefferson's name continues to be synonymous with yeomanry and agrarianism wherever it is discussed (Brooking 2019, 69). Family farms were integral to American agrarianism:

> It assumed that the nation needed a large number of family farms, each endowed with the resources required for families to lead good lives. It stressed the importance of landownership. It insisted that a family farmer (who in most cases was male) must not be obligated to others such as landlords, must be free to do what he wished with this land and its products but should have no more land than his family could use. And family farmers deserved large roles in government and special attention from it.
>
> (Kirkendall 1987)

Hahn's study of the yeomanry of Georgia from 1850 found that both men and women protected their independence, abhorring the idea of hiring workers or using slaves; their 'egalitarian instinct' did not agree with rule over others. Farmers, mostly landowners, grew crops and livestock to the level of self-sufficiency with a few acres of cotton to either sell to buy what they could not produce, or to spin and weave at home. Those who had a trade served local needs as well as farming (Fields 1985, 136). These people were living life much as we have seen the yeomanry in England. Tenants gradually saved to buy their own land.

Introduction 13

Farmers had networks of exchange with local stores, ties that bound households together through mutuality and reciprocity that mediated unequal relationships. From 1850, this way of life was under pressure from increasing population and land needed to assist sons into farming. The civil war added further impositions, demonstrating their lack of political power because the planters held the power and advanced their own agendas (Fields 1985, 137).

As common land rights disappeared and Emancipation occurred, these yeoman farmers were forced to engage with capitalist commodity production of cotton-growing, thus losing their independence and mutual support mechanisms, becoming eventually 'tools of the merchants' and, in Texas, loss of commons created more dependence on lenders and landlords (Wilkison 2008, 165). Australian farmers experienced this process during the 1980s, when commodity prices fell below the cost of production and processors dictated the price to producers, particularly in the sugar industry. Increasing powerlessness and poverty in Georgia's yeoman farmers planted the roots of Southern populism and its challenge to entrenched political power (Fields 1985, 136–39).

In Texas, the traditional religious and cultural ties, and 'habits of mutuality' that had sustained the rural yeoman community up to the 1870s, started to fragment due to combined effects of intra-state migrants increasing population, new railroads and national market access, which increased land prices beyond the reach of 'self-sufficient, but cash-poor, Texan yeomen' (Wilkison 2008, 4–5). The yeoman perception was that tenancy was only for the young getting established. Land ownership was seen as a 'badge of independent, mature manhood' and when this changed it qualitatively changed the 'plain folk way of life'. Wilkison wrote, 'within one generation, . . . under cotton's aegis, many would come to know the new poverty of propertylessness', as a majority of yeoman farmers were reduced to tenancy and its accompanying 'geographical mobility'. Increasing poverty was evidenced by reduction in farm-family personal wealth (e.g. milking cows, hogs, machinery, wagons etc.) over 40 years (Wilkison 2008, 35–41).

Ford (1986) focussed on South Carolina to look at the effect on the yeomanry of the move to capitalist commodities. Echoing Rae's English analysis, 'safety-first agriculture' there in 1840 combined with the ethic of self-sufficiency that prevailed among the 86 per cent of farmers who were yeomen. But, wary of growing dependency on cotton, by 1859 they were receptive to politicking that promoted the idea of a slave-holders' republic and secessionist ideals. A clear pattern emerges across the south of landowning farmers badly affected by capitalist commodity production, losing out socially, communally and economically, and sometimes becoming pawns of big moneylenders. Their lifestyle was under threat, in much the same way that English yeomanry had experienced after 1815.

Was it the same for yeomen in the Northern states? Atack looked at the period after the Homestead Act of 1862 that granted 160 acres free to those who cultivated them for five years. English laws of entail and succession no longer applied by 1830 and land was available to the general masses (1988, 14). Owner-operated farms increased, promoted early by federal land policy. Farm ownership varied across the northern half of America, but tenancy grew almost everywhere. The

14   *Introduction*

difference seemed to lie with wealth, yeoman farmers having the accumulated capital value in their land as well as a 'superior income stream' (24). He concluded that rising tenancies from 1860 to 1920 indicated lack of capital and increasing land prices rather than lack of aspiration (32).

In summary, *American* yeomanry was characterised by mixed farming, using family labour generally, on farms of average 75–100 acres, self-sufficiency in labour and produce, supported by community networks of mutuality and reciprocity. They embraced landownership and wanted land for their sons; those able to keep land over generations accumulated capital gain in their land. We saw their identification with politics as a response to powerlessness.

In Australia too, Buxton, in the Riverina, and Bolton, in North Queensland, both discovered that yeoman settlers were politically alert and willing to represent their interests to politicians (Buxton 1967, 189, 191, 210; Bolton 1963, 146, 299, 302–5). However, both their studies contrast with those reviewed because their yeoman farmers operated a virtual monoculture environment, significantly different to those in England and in both the American North and South where the regimen of mixed farming with a focus on self-sufficiency in foodstuffs for livestock and family was the prevailing similarity.

In Tom Brooking's 2019 study of the yeoman ideal's longevity in *New Zealand*, he argued that it 'lasted longer and achieved greater hegemony' there than in Australia, Canada or the United States (68). Part of the reason was the domination of simple commodity production by family farmers despite the adoption of greater mechanisation and chemical and fertiliser use, generally perceived as linked to industrial farming. In addition to highlighting 'yeowomen' and their farming partnership role, he emphasised factors across the period that made the difference, such as substantial political influence, leaders who were farmers, support of the Farmers' Union, their asset gains during boom years, and their response to the recession of the 1920s. Brooking took his study into the twenty-first century, predicting 'glimmers of hope' in ways to manage current agricultural challenges and social perceptions of farming connected with land custodianship. This definite echo of the Jefferson ideal matches the 'philosophy of kaitiakitanga, or guardianship', a feature of Maori communal ownership (75–91). His study presents support for the durability of the yeoman ideal in Castra and ways in which it was sustained.

Returning to Dingle's point that understanding of the yeoman ideal was assumed, the range of characteristics I have identified helps to shed light on that assumption. The long history of yeomanry in England and America meant that immigrants from either country who came for mining opportunities across Australia well understood the status and appeal of the yeoman's life on land he owned and worked with his family. The diggings provided some men with the capital to get started. Bolton identified this in North Queensland and Pike referred to the diggers' race for land in South Australia (Pike 1962). Later, mining in Tasmania's West helped fund some of the 1880s settlers into Castra.

Taking a different perspective was Belich's 2009 study about the 'settler revolution' that happened between 1815 and 1915. 'Booster literature' provoked movement of emigrants to new frontier lands across the Anglo world. There were examples of a so-called 'paradise complex' in materials about New Zealand, Canada and America that encouraged people seeking a promised land to look towards those new frontiers. Belich argued that 'settlerism' promoted 'a freehold family farm' because of the perception that the shared desire of 'common emigrants' was to attain land of their own and become yeomen freeholders. To those in power, their being poor mattered less than being moral, sober and hardworking (Belich 2009, 152–54; see Tonts, 2002, 103–15). However, settlers were often prepared to compromise by taking on tenancy or a leasehold, using their capital to develop their farm and house; 'the potential yeoman' wanted 'independence from masters, not markets'. The yeoman ideal became personalised, evidenced from letters to family (often wives) in England from American, Canadian and Australian migrants that showed the strong ties and loving relationships sustained by absent loved ones (Snell 1985, 9–14).

Who supported the yeoman ideal in Australia? Politicians were the most important people whose assumptions about the yeomen ideal and yeomanry attributes affected land settlement policies nation-wide. They needed their populations and economies boosted and saw the answer in the yeomanry's reputation of industriousness, conservative values, productivity and stability. When the press counterpoised the yeomen as morally superior and physically stronger than radical urban elements, this acted to endorse land policies designed to establish small farmers and the attempt to subdue the powers of squatters and large pastoralists. Scholars consistently considered the political appeal of the yeomanry (Powell 1970, 1985, 1988; for all states, Roberts 1924; for Tasmania, Meikle 2011, 2014).

Merchants and storekeepers were also influential in support of yeoman settlers because increased density of people held prospects of profits and a stable demand in contrast to pastoralists' itinerant labourers. Their businesses benefitted by offering credit and bartering produce (Waterson 1968, 164–81).

This review of yeomanry and the manifested yeoman ideal in Anglo societies has revealed a prominent theme – the transition from self-sufficiency to capitalist commodity production in a global economic system, and the influential effects of markets, politics and governments. In later chapters, I investigate how that process translated in the agricultural environment of Castra.

The yeoman ideal has been shown to be intrinsic to family farming, typified by the idea of the ties that bind – the shared beliefs – that link people together in settler societies. In rural societies, these ties were endorsed by Protestant church attendance, occurring often in hymns like 'Blest be the tie that binds' by John Fawcett, written in 1818, and reinforced in Methodist evangelism of the early twentieth century by Reverend W. G. Taylor (Wilson 2011, 404). This key idea is highlighted in themes addressed in following chapters.

Chapter 1 sets Castra's origin into the context of land settlement policies. The yeoman ideal was pressed hard politically in the quest to encourage population and productivity growth, so Colonel Andrew Crawford's proposal to encourage long-served Indian officers to retire in Tasmania gained Government approval.

16 *Introduction*

I argue that Crawford implicitly subscribed to the yeoman ideal evidenced by his intentions and actions.

Chapter 2 examines surveying from state to local level because surveyors' practices played such a significant part in frontier land settlement and survey decisions had long-lasting implications. I delve deeply into the way Castra was divided into 320- and 160-acre lots, followed by a qualitative examination of Valuation Rolls to analyse the longevity of ownership by the Anglo-Indian purchasers. My data makes a positive connection to the yeoman ideal and repositions perception of failure of Crawford's Castra Association.

Chapter 3 moves to the 1880s period when demand for land by sons of small farmers in other areas of Devon was the stimulus for a new wave of farming selectors. I research their backgrounds and motivations and introduce the earliest members of several multi-generational families who settled in Castra. Early development of community assets for religious, educational and social activities demonstrates support of the yeoman ideal and exemplify the Protestant work ethic.

Chapter 4 and Chapter 5 focus on two forms of settlement exercised by the Tasmanian government following examples set elsewhere. First, closer settlement filled spaces of potential agricultural land unalienated in 1906 with purchasers. This was followed by settlement of soldiers after the Great War from 1917 onwards as government lessees. The success or failure of both these schemes have occupied historians across the world. Three areas of Castra were used for closer settlement. The ideology that yeoman farmers were politically, socially and economically advantageous provided motivation for closer settlement and it continued to resonate when the problem arose of resettling thousands of Great War returnees back into civilian life. The social agenda to enable men to go farming as a reward for their efforts in service overwhelmed the basic yeoman premise of private landownership and was adapted to fit with mixed results in consequence. I look in depth at more than 30 cases of soldier settlers approved to lease Castra farmlands to consider the validity of the yeoman ideal to this constituency. I show convincingly that the oft-cited story of failure was untrue in Castra. The returning soldiers embraced the ideal of a family farm of their own and eventual ownership (for many) supported by strong kinship and community ties.

Chapter 6 addresses how the aspiration of yeomen farmers to hand on their land to family members or help them establish themselves independently occurred in Castra families through various farm transition strategies of succession and inheritance.

Chapter 7 fills a gap in historical work about rural children's lives. So often they are included in women's rural history almost in passing. Local biographies and personal interviews permit focus on ways children themselves were incorporated into the yeoman family farm labour structures, how work was integrated into their daily routine and how they gained a sense of belonging in place and nature. Sporting and other social activities in adolescence highlight community activity that sustained the ties binding families together as well as helping courtships that interwove kinship relationships. Eventually, locally available social interactions

Introduction 17

became limited by the move to smaller families and the fewer children were encouraged to broaden their interests and ambitions beyond the family farm.

Chapter 8 explores the lives of the 'yeowomen', as Brooking called them. Since agriculture has typically been seen as masculine and because there is a gap in literature about Tasmanian countrywomen, I wanted to give value to their contribution. They were pivotal to the yeoman ideal as producers of 'everyday' income for family needs while the farmer supported the farm business. Those activities were impacted in the transition from simple production to capitalist commodity production, and how this issue was resolved in Castra is explored. I argue consistently that they were partners with their husbands in the family enterprise (contrasted with characterisations as 'helpers'), in decision-making over inheritance and their management of house, homestead production and family social life as well as being prolific mothers. Women were critical to creating the 'social glue' that bound the farming community together from the 1880s onwards. This was their endorsement of the yeoman ideal.

Chapter 9 examines how Castra farmers pursued their political interests in the public sphere locally and in State and Federal arenas. Exercising political influence and participation was another characteristic of yeomen farmers, achieved through membership of organisations, being politically alert and willingly weighing up change carefully. The Castra community originated several significant political figures and many others who actively added their backing to campaigns and organisations supporting their agricultural interests, demonstrating yet another link to yeomanry characteristics. Their adoption of by-employment, as Beckett called it, and ways they had of working together formed an important part of the yeoman ideal.

My aim was to explore Castra's uniqueness as an insightful window into comparable rural settlement communities in colonial-origin locations with temperate-forest environments. I sought to reframe ideas about the yeoman ideal to show that family farming was sustainable beyond self-sufficiency and well able to adapt to the capitalist agricultural economy over the twentieth century.

For centuries people were motivated by the desire to produce food and occupy their own land – an intrinsic facet of the yeoman ideal best exemplified by farming families. Professor Brooking's timely work about yeoman family farming in New Zealand tells me that mine is not a cry in the wilderness. Future researchers may cast another eye over the social history of other rural locales in the Anglo world to build on this work.

1 The Castra Association 1864 to 1873

'A home in the colonies'[1]

This history of yeoman family farming in Castra started with a somewhat different dream of a rural future for a group of family men who shared the common experience of living many decades in India as officers in the Indian civil and military service. The architect of this dream was Lieutenant-Colonel Andrew Crawford, who came to settle in the 1860s as a 58-year-old family man and lived out his vision as a farmer until his death at 84 in 1899. Despite good intentions, some Government backing and his total commitment to the dream, it had mixed success as we shall see. But it laid the groundwork for younger yeoman farmers to arrive within 20 years to buy and create their own dream of self-sufficient mixed farming assisted by various adaptations in Tasmania's land regulations.

Without Crawford openly expressing yeoman ideals of land ownership and self-sufficient farming, his plan effectively advocated it with a unique twist – a contingency fund to establish community assets. His plan was directed towards British officers and high-ranking civil servants who had long service in India like himself and usually retired in their fifties. In the nineteenth century, 'Anglo-Indian' was used to refer to officers who served in British India and their family members who may have been born in India, like Crawford's children. He had discovered a love of Tasmania he wanted to share and some Crown Land in the forested North-West that held promise for a new agricultural community. He decided to call the land Castra, a military camp in Latin, and created the 'Castra Association' to put the plan into action. The Tasmanian Government listened receptively to Crawford's ideas, which came when it was using immigration to boost development of productive farmland. For a Parliament dominated by members owning large pastoral properties, built upon free convict labour in other parts of Tasmania, the idea presented no particular threat and, perhaps more importantly for the perennially cash-strapped Government, it did not appear to cost anything and it might have achieved its aim of attracting farmer settlers. Parliament agreed to the allocation of 50,000 acres of unalienated Crown Land to the scheme.

Tasmanian land settlement and Anglo-Indian connections

By 1823, Commissioner John Thomas Bigge had spent two years conducting a Commission of Enquiry into colonial agriculture and trade for Earl Bathurst,

DOI: 10.4324/9781003229841-2

the Colonial Secretary (Bigge 1823). Under examination in Van Diemen's Land (VDL) in 1820, Deputy-Surveyor George William Evans explained to Bigge how land grants were allotted (Jones 1989). It was Evans who advised that applications were generally accepted only one day in June annually and about long delays in receiving approvals back from Sydney, New South Wales (NSW) (Hurst 1938). The lengthy, awkward process of handling applications between the two colonies encouraged inconsistencies and unsatisfactory practices in the way land was distributed, and Bigge believed there should be regulatory guidance rather than discretionary decisions. He recommended that emancipated convicts and their adult sons should have preference for small cultivation acreages near towns, that is, 30 acres for a single male, 50 acres for a married male and ten acres for each child at time of grant, ten years free of taxes and quit rents on condition of residence, cultivation and improvement. Other British subjects could be granted larger areas. These recommendations indicate his appreciation of the role small farmers played in providing food for colonial towns, an idea that resonated with the British understanding of the yeoman ideal. This was also the early post-Napoleonic-war period when the yeomanry and tenant farmers were under financial stress at home. He would have been unlikely to suggest these measures if he had any doubt about their reception by Bathurst.

Bigge discovered an exception was made for persons arriving from India if they proved they had capital as well as intention to settle permanently in VDL when they represented themselves to the Lieutenant-Governor. Those likely to absent themselves (such as sea-going men) were refused grants until they returned to reside, a practice with which Bigge agreed, noting, however, the need for prompt surveying lest the 'monied settlers' dissipated their funds while they waited.

Having gained an understanding of the local survey demand and the advantages for it to be accomplished locally, Bigge strongly recommended that a 'surveyor-general' be appointed in each colony (NSW and VDL) accountable to the local governor or lieutenant governor, and each should have additional assistants. This took effect after he left. He thought road surveying was more properly run under district commissioners, who also applied road repair levies.

Bigge's report showed that ex-military Anglo-Indians received special treatment, because some had already been granted about 40,000 acres of land in the vicinity of the Derwent, Shannon and Clyde rivers. This questionable special treatment had included free grants of thousands of acres, convict workers and local military protection, a process resulting in wealthy estates and a 'landed gentry' (Reynolds 1969a, 63–64; Pink 1990, 65).

Many more Anglo-Indians responded to publicity in India. Books were written by three men who had visited the colony around 1829 – John Henderson (1832), Captain T. Betts (1832), and Augustus Prinsep with his wife Elizabeth, who published his letters in 1833 after his death at sea in 1830. The Prinseps had been merchants of indigo, salt and nutmeg since the eighteenth century, and Augustus Prinsep's brother Charles, Bengal's advocate-general, owned land in northern Tasmania. Henderson particularly aimed to encourage officers from India to settle

20   *The Castra Association 1864 to 1873*

in Australia's colonies instead of retiring to England. That two of these books were published in Calcutta points to recognition of their appeal.

Anglo-Indian Henry Cornish wrote a series for his employer, the *Madras Times*, after a visit in 1870, which continued to feed that interest, evolving into a book, *Under the Southern Cross*, in 1880. News reports were a staple commodity to and from India. The Anglo-Indians had their own newspapers and periodicals that articulated their own views and cultural identities that were often new hybrid ideas and interests not embodied in Indian and British press (Cadell 2003). This would provide ready access to Crawford's target audience. Correspondence, both business and personal, was also very important, especially when wives followed their husbands to the colony, or husbands depended on them for business correspondence between Tasmania and India.

Due to Lt.-Governor Arthur's liberal attitude over new grants and extensions of existing land grants and their small townships, such as Richmond, where Crawford had family connections, occupation was concentrated between Hobart and Launceston and their major river valleys such that little land was available by 1830. For the next 20 years, settlement intensified into lands to the east and west of this line that would have implications when the push came to sell lands and encourage settler immigration (Burroughs 1967, 91–92). Prestige and acceptability were accorded to officers of the army and navy, and 'masters of merchantmen and persons of respectable connections', demonstrating that status was very significant and that new immigrants in the era of colonial settlement had to be of the right type (West 1852, vol. 2, 445). This factor was in Crawford's favour and may well have opened doors to new Anglo-Indian settlement in due course.

The process of colonial land allocation was an ongoing dilemma for the Colonial Office after 1825. Edward Wakefield's *A View of the Art of Colonization* (1849) about 'systematic colonisation' found acceptance because it fitted the trend of policy development of the time. Belich's account of the 'settler revolution' argued that Wakefield was 'riding a wave of public opinion', indicating an even wider resonance (2009, 147). Clarke argued that it fed into a combination of British lack of knowledge about colonial conditions and well-established prejudices about convict exiles being dispersed beyond the reach of morally civilising influences from schools and churches. Colonial Secretary Viscount Goderich, Earl of Ripon, established Regulations in 1831 that 'intended to rationalise British land and emigration policies and to ensure concentration of settlement in compact agricultural communities' (Clarke 1977, 124–25, 128; see Burroughs chapter 2). There would be no more free land grants and no more imposed commitments to cultivate. Land was to be sold at auction without credit available since it was thought to have enabled unwarranted alienation between 1825 and 1831. In Van Diemen's Land, Burroughs wrote of 'wasteful liberality' caused as Governor Arthur took advantage of sabotaging the Regulations by giving away about 'a quarter of a million acres' that year following two already generous years (92–93, 144).

Both the House of Commons Committee and the Land and Emigration Commissioners held that all land except in towns should be sold at a fixed price of £1 per acre, but this took no account of varied land quality and proximity to a town.

The Castra Association 1864 to 1873   21

Scott identified several men who quickly lodged applications near Melbourne and profited handsomely (1925, 178–79). Burroughs highlighted the 'enduring weakness of imperial practices' that expected these conditions to apply in all the colonies, and administrators in both Western Australia and VDL objected to what was an overly high price in their colonies. In NSW, speculators took advantage of the surveying situation and, without even seeing the land, could resell before survey and make massive profits, causing the Government to spend well above its means on the bonanza from selling land (Burroughs 1967, 212–23). When Governor Gipps arrived in Sydney, he refused to allow this to continue. Lord Russell took over as Colonial Secretary and enacted the *Crown Land Sales Act* 1842, under which all land was to be sold by auction with a minimum (not a fixed) price at £1 per acre. Half of the land sales revenue had to be spent on immigration and the rest on public works (Scott 1925, 178–79). Here was early evidence of the linkage between public infrastructure advancement and immigrant encouragement.

Tasmania gained responsible Government in 1854 and land settlement decisions then could be tailored to its local conditions. Like NSW yeoman farming districts of Narrandera and the Riverina, Tasmania already had a mixed farming economy based on sheep and wheat. But this happened in the Midland areas' lightly wooded plains occupied by landed gentry families, who would never have considered themselves yeomen. In the late 1840s, pastoralists had extended into the south-west and northwards from the inland lakes towards the Van Diemen's Land Company lands (Burroughs 1967, 339–40). What scope was there for Tasmania to extend settlement to Tasmanian native-born men and immigrants onto small farms fitting the yeoman ideal of self-sufficiency?

Advance of settlement to the North-West

Along the north-western coastline of Tasmania, mid-nineteenth century development depended very much on shipping access to the many northward flowing rivers from the Tamar near Launceston to the Emu River in the north-west. The hinterland between the Mersey River and Emu Bay (now Burnie) was hilly, covered with dense scrub and tall trees, land that had been rejected by the VDL Company surveyors in the 1820s as not justifying the effort of clearing even with its cheap convict labour (Skemp 1964, xi). The surveyors' quest then was for native grasslands, with few trees – plains of native grass and white grass – suitable for sheep. Found in the upper Mersey River, Surrey Hills and Middlesex Plains, they were appropriated by the Company for summer grazing. Binks suggested these plains and the more commonly occurring button grass plains 'were undoubtedly fired frequently by Aboriginal hunting parties as they drove wallaby and emu' (1980, 19).

After exploring with Alexander Clerke and Edward Carr Shaw in 1839, James Fenton was the first settler west of the Forth River in 1840, initially attracted by coastal marshlands, but eventually forced by saltiness to tackle the dense forest on the chocolate soil slopes nearby (Fenton 1891). Here he pioneered ringbarking in Tasmania, a method that was endorsed by Henry Widowson writing in 1829 as

22   *The Castra Association 1864 to 1873*

'the general mode of clearing', although, in the pastoral districts of the 1820s and 1830s, the cheapest way previously to get rid of the tree 'encumbrance' was to cut one half through and let it fall against a row like dominoes (Bonyhady 2000, 81–83). The stumps left after 'girdling' or 'ringing' made the method controversial because it was thought they were more trouble to remove (Atkinson 1826 cited by Bonyhady, 84–86). But, as heavily forested northerly Tasmanian districts were settled, this practice was effective because of the potential to grow grass or crops in spaces around dying trees before they fell over and could be burnt. This was not Fenton's only legacy – after 40 years of living at Forth, he wrote his reminiscences about the settler life, recollections of the North-West's indomitable pioneers, his many friends and contemporaries, thus providing posterity with 'a mine of information' (Skemp 1964, xvi). Long-term results of mass deforestation caused disquiet from the 1870s in NSW (Stubbs 1998). But in North-West Tasmania the timber's value was soon realised and harvesting for use and sale became the settlers' initial focus. Nineteenth-century photographs of early town settlements and pioneer farming lands are characterised by backdrops of skeleton trees *en masse*. Photographs available of settler landscapes show typical features of Castra farms – high-quality post and rail fencing – in addition to what looks like a substantial house built from farm-harvested timber (*Weekly Courier* 1913, 21, images 1–2).

Communications between early communities of the 1850s at Port Sorell, the Mersey, the Forth and the Leven mouth all depended upon small coastal boats like the *Titania*, a small screw steamer, to connect with Launceston and markets at Port Phillip, because there were no roads, just bush tracks created by settlers themselves, and no bridges over rivers. Lack of roads was a problem that became more obvious after 1851.

Hoping to deter many colonial youths from leaving to join the mainland gold rush in 1851, the Government passed the Pre-Emptive Land Right regulations that Fenton described as 'so liberal that in two years all known agricultural land in Devon was alienated' and back-country lots of up to 640 acres could be selected with no payment due until the survey was completed, which stimulated speculative selection (86–87). Fenton himself took up 640 acres back from Manning's Jetty (on the Leven River). There was much speculation and some reselling at £5 per acre. Fenton tells of selling his 640-acre bush block for £2/10s. per acre in 1855, £1800 with a cash deposit of £800, but the land was surrendered to him when the land value dropped when the law tightened up (101–2). This could have been typical of the time.

Increasing demand in developing agricultural areas and fast-growing townships made the provision of a local surveyor based in Devon a necessity. Altogether some 90,000 acres across the North-West were taken up by speculators, large landowners and merchants from the Midlands, Hobart and Launceston, and some were leased to tenant farmers in smaller lots (Stokes 1969, 5–6). Some took up options on land along the foreshore in the Leven area, as large as 640 acres, both east and west of the Leven River, with no intention of occupying them. For example, the first was taken up in 1853 by E. J. Beecraft at 'Badger's Plains',

Ulverstone township's first name, later sold to a man who let to small tenant farmers, while he took over management of Dr Cornelius Casey's Irish immigrant tenants at Balmacargie, Forth (Fenton 1891, 101, 103; see Gardam 2000, 79–82). Close examination of early plans will reveal the large number of 500-acre and larger lots, most of whom were lessees (often speculators) across the most northerly part of the plan.

Surveyor-General Calder requested from Britain 16 Royal Sappers and Engineers to come to Tasmania to carry out trigonometrical surveys in August 1851. One was Surveyor George Melrose based at Devon's administrative centre in Port Sorell in 1854 to 1855. Calder took the opportunity of the land rush to have township reserves created at Torquay and Formby, each side of the Mersey mouth and Latrobe some miles up-river, and put some of the town lots up for sale. About the same time, Melrose surveyed town lots for sale in Hamilton-on-Forth, while, in 1854, surveyor James Scott was authorised by the Devon Road Trust, formed in 1852, to survey roads to link coastal township reserves, so then trees were cleared and useable roads were begun.

Fenton and others were benefiting from the Victorian building boom and good prices paid for straight-grained, durable eucalypt hardwood from forests all along the North-West, where access to navigable rivers made transportation feasible. Products in demand were weatherboard palings, staves, billets, posts, rails and other cuts cut by bush farmers and skilled fallers and splitters, using bullock teams to haul the huge split logs to mills and then timber to waiting ships (See Joyce 1846, 67). Record prices that were still less than in Victoria helped to consolidate the financial situations of many pioneer farmers at this time, with some acquiring more land, as Fenton did (Lot 364 500 acres) on coastal land between the Forth and Don Rivers. This he rented out to tenants in small 50-acre allotments, which they could clear, sell the timber and start cropping (Pink 1990, 96–97).

A new *Waste Lands Act* 1858 had provisions particularly suited to encouragement of a 'sturdy, hard-working, respectable yeoman class' of small proprietors whose farms would emulate the green fields and neat farmhouses of England (Stokes 1969, 359). It allowed the general public to select Crown Land for £1 per acre on long interest terms. Tasmania was the first colony to address the need to offer credit, and this resulted in a general fall in value of speculative lots that were not earning.

Because Melrose was posted to NSW, in March 1856 James Monahan Dooley was appointed as District Surveyor based at Forth. Dooley, his wife Alice and three children under nine years had arrived in Launceston in December 1855 in the *Black Swan* (Denholm 1980, 10–11, 14).

Problems in coping with demand for surveys came to light in enquiries by Select Committees of 1861 (HAJ Vol.VII, No.161) and 1862 (Vol.VII, No.111). Having already worked in the Huon in 1860 and from Launceston in 1864 as North-East surveyor when Dooley was working in Devon, surveyor Richard Hall was sent to Devon about 1864. Richard and wife Harriett arrived from Yorkshire on the *Montmorency* in Launceston in June 1855; they were proposed by Henry Rockliff of Sassafras as labourer and wife, £22 each. But that category may have been a

24   *The Castra Association 1864 to 1873*

ploy to avoid immigration constraints, and Rockliff may have known them or their families in Yorkshire to offer sponsorship. Rockliff would also have been aware about delays in surveying since he was adroit at land purchasing (CB7/12/1/5, book 8, 16–7). The Pre-Emptive Rights Regulations had resulted in an obstacle to earlier farming settlers in the Gawler area because there was no coast access without trespassing over dense, scrubby, uncleared land and up-river access in the Leven was limited by shallows. This problem attracted disapproval in a newspaper report about Devon. Fenton, as Justice of the Peace, was presiding over nearly 100 appeals against the 1860 Devon valuation roll revision. Mention was made of the opening of 'Mr Gunns new country at Leven'. Editorial opinion was that, if the 'Hobart pre-emptive right gentry' would send tenants for their blocks, it would benefit them and add to public convenience. Fenton was qualified to express an opinion when he referred particularly to a 640-acre block sold to eight settlers who discovered the old splitters road they had been using was blocked and the owner refused permission to cross his land (News 1860a). Fenton later described the situation as 'positively wicked' of the authorities to sell land without road access (104).

By 1860, some 60 miles of road and bridges over the Mersey, Muddy Creek (at Port Sorell), Don and Forth Rivers had been built from Deloraine (Denholm, 41). This encouraged farming people to come from that district and beyond to take up settlement opportunities created when speculative land reverted to the Crown as conditions were not fulfilled. The Government reviewed the situation of lands under Pre-Emptive Rights, extending periods of credit under sections 74 and 75 of the *Waste Lands Act* 1863. Dooley himself had 400 acres unpaid in 1864 near the Mersey River. Similarly, Alexander Clerke was still 'purchasing on credit' two adjacent lots (Lot 700 320 acres and Lot 701 640 acres) along the Forth's banks (HAJ Vol. XI, 1864, No.104; see Land District Chart, LIST).

Selection by genuine pioneer bush farmers proceeded on lots up to 320 acres on easy terms, and Leven River's eastern shore-land was reserved for town growth in Scott's 1851 plan. Ulverstone was officially proclaimed on 22 February 1861 (Pink, 228–30). The town and its main streets were surveyed in September that year (Dooley 1861, AF721/1/735). In July that year, Dooley sent Calder a list of 65 settlers attracted by the *Waste Lands Act* in the district noting that the 'country is taking off a good deal . . . large numbers of old hands [meaning emancipists] establishing themselves in the country districts' (Dooley to Calder, LSD72/1/3).

Surveyor Dooley was kept busy surveying his district from the Tamar to the Emu River and from Bass Strait south to the Meander River; for example, Blythe River, 1862 (AF395/1/22); Ulverstone south, 1865 (AF398/1/676). In 1865, Fenton joined Dooley and Calder in inspecting reported land discoveries in Leven River upper reaches for agricultural potential, after which Calder provided a frank description of travelling difficulties in the back-country (Calder 1865; News 1867b). These lands appeared to have been identified by Surveyor Peter Lette and Ronald Gunn, Deputy Commissioner of Crown Lands, in the summer of 1859 to 1860, and reported to both Houses afterwards (HAJ Vol. XI, 1860, No. 11; LCJ Vol. XI, 1860, No. 14). Based on this, Calder estimated that 'there was about 150,000 acres of land that may be matched against anything in the world for excellence' (Calder to Gibson, HAJ Vol. IV, 1859, No. 89). After Dooley marked a bridle track from Ulverstone via North Motton, Calder's party eventually found 'a beautiful dry, level plain of what seemed [to Fenton] to be about fifty acres of clear land, covered with a closely cropped sward of kangaroo grass' (Fenton, 114–16). Fenton believed that Gunn had reported seeing no visible signs of charcoal that would have indicated regular bush fires from either natural or Aboriginal sources on this land, but a close reading of Gunns Report (HAJ Vol. XI, 1860, No. 11) does not demonstrate clearly that he and Lette came as far north as the land later named after him. They were on the Middlesex Plains, rode towards Mt Roland and Mt Claude, over that range and downhill to the upper Mersey River, close to Hellyer's early route (Fenton, 117).

About 1861, Dooley, Fenton's next-door neighbour at Forth, told him about finding 'an extensive open country, surrounded by good agricultural land'. Providing a clear description of this land that would become integral to Crawford's Association, Fenton wrote:

> It is easy to imagine how gratified a man must feel who has been out for days exploring through dense scrubs to come suddenly upon a beautiful undulating expanse of country quite clear of the everlasting forest that intercepts his progress in every direction. Dooley's Plains stand up prominently on rising ground, with a gently undulating surface, but the herbage upon it was of little use for pasture. At first sight it looked like a closely cropped sward of grass. The soil is red-brown and wanting in some chemical property for agricultural purposes; at least that was my impression when I saw it . . . . I visited Dooley's Plains in company with the late Mr Hugh McLusky, surveyor, and Colonel Crawford, when that gentleman first went to view the promised land for Indian officers. There were four of us on horseback and a very rough track it was to the plains. I believe we were the first equestrians who imprinted a horseshoe (emblem of good luck) on Dooley's Plains. The Principal plain was a mile in length, varying in width from half a mile to less. It lies about midway between the Wilmot and the Leven [rivers], at an altitude of 1300 feet above sea-level, parallel with Gunns Plains and only a few miles off: but the descent must be very considerable to the latter as there is a difference of 1100 feet in the elevations.

> (Fenton, 117–18)

Dooley made a huge impression on development by publicising the potential of inland areas that eventually became known as North Motton, Preston (the village situated in the northern part of Dooley's Plains), Castra and Gunns Plains, and recommended that roads be established to assist the spread of settlement (Pink, 230). Dooley's communications with the Lands and Surveys Department show that, from 1856 to 1868, he travelled widely on foot and horseback through wilderness in all weathers (LSD24/1/1). Following the enactment of the *Waste Lands Act* 1863, Dooley made a significant report in December 1863 on

26 The Castra Association 1864 to 1873

potential agricultural areas in Devon, as Government attention was being directed towards benefits from small farming. Eventually, his first recommendation was Gunns Plains with 3,000 to 4,000 acres, then Blythe River, ten miles inland from Heybridge, with at least 5,000 acres, and then the Vale of Belvoir adjoining the Middlesex Plains and Surrey Hills, already granted to the VDL Company. Calder advised Parliament that this area had been reported on by Hellyer and Fossey about 1828. Dooley endorsed 4,000 acres at Gunns Plains and a further 2,500 towards Eden town reserve; he estimated mileage cost of a road to access the sea, but noted that pre-emptive rights allotments hemmed in the line of road, and settlers there would need 'a good road' (HAJ Vol. XI, 1864, No. 19, p. 4).

Entries from Dooley's correspondence to Calder relevant to the Castra history occur on 14 February 1865, reporting his preparation of plans and stations for the 'Ulverstone Tramway', and then on 13 June, referring to forwarding plans for the 'Leven Tramway' and on 6 August, the most suitable spots for settlement in Ulverstone, Blythe, Wilmot and Leven (Denholm, 42–46). The first two plans refer to the proposal for a road or tramway (the 'Plank(ed) Road') from the Leven River wharf at Ulverstone continuing southwards to the emerging settlements in the rural hinterland. On 21 August, *The Public Works Act* 1865 was enacted with attached schedules 2 and 3 relating to the Ulverstone Tramway (£10,442) and to bridges over the Forth (£2,000) and Leven (£4,000), indicating Calder's interest and commitment to the tramway Dooley had described.

The original map was drafted by W.C. Piguenit for the Survey Department from Dooley's work to show the proposed route of the Plank Road in relation to the land proposed for settlers from India. This may have been prepared at the request of Colonel Crawford, because a large fold-out copy formed the frontispiece of his 'Letter to the officers of H.M. Indian Services' (Crawford 1865). Dooley also prepared a six-page report of costings to clear land on 30 June 1865 that became Appendix 4 to the 'Letter'.

Crawford and his association

Lieutenant-Colonel Andrew Crawford was a man with interesting personal history and past experiences, which inspired him to form the Castra Association. Born in 1815 into a generational family of naval men in Devonport, the naval suburb of Plymouth, Devon, England, he decided to join the East India Company at the age of 18 (Stilwell 1969). He served 38 years in various regiments and was involved in many campaigns. During this period, he regularly published articles in local Anglo-Indian newspapers. At 25 years old, in 1840, he married Matilda Frederica, the third daughter of Major Samuel Carter of the 16th Regiment. Her sister had married Captain David Ogilvy of the Bengal Army and they had arrived in July 1837 from Calcutta (News 1837), to settle at 'Inverquarity' near Richmond. About 1847 to 1848, the Crawfords spent a leave visiting the Ogilvys and Matilda gave birth to Ellen, their fourth child, attended by Dr J. Coverdale, Deputy Registrar and ex-Indian officer.

Crawford travelled quite widely in Tasmania on this holiday and bought some land at Richmond he called Belmont. As Ogilvy had been one of those earlier settlers arriving between 1830 and 1850, it is likely the idea of settling in Tasmania was discussed. Nevertheless, when Crawford retired in December 1861, he and his family returned to England for two years. After that experience, he decided to bring Matilda and their children to Tasmania in 1864 to live at Richmond where Ronald was born.

The 1857 Indian Mutiny and its suppression were disasters for British India, importantly due to it wounding British goodwill and confidence. From then, the way of life for Anglo-Indian military and civil officers changed under the new structure of the British Raj. The East India Company closure had disappointed Crawford and many of his fellow old officers, causing much discontent, mainly because previous expected pensions of £3,000 or £4,000 were no longer paid. Positions in the new Imperial Indian Services became highly competitive and continued to be phased out as the Government streamlined administration and decreased uncontracted white officers that later affected Edward Braddon (Pink 2001, 5). These concerns were still prominent in 1878 in the preamble to his letters to the *Statesman and Friend of India* that referred to 'the eyes of "old Indians" turning to the colonies so their children will find room for themselves instead of struggling for existence in the fierce competitive mill in England' (Braddon, June 14, 1878).

Crawford started to work on his idea for the scheme to encourage those disaffected officers and civil servants to consider retiring to Tasmania, being well able to describe conditions they would face on return to English life and lack of opportunities for their sons and daughters there. His developing ideas became a 65-page booklet containing his own address to his 'old comrades and those of all "the Services" who may be contemplating retirement', as well as a collection of valuable information and useful documents he believed would assist them to make the right decision for their families' future (Crawford "Letter," 1–29, and its Appendices, 31–54, August 15, 1865). The Anglo-Indian press proved useful in spreading the word, because it actively followed conditions in other British colonies (Bayly 2012).

As mentioned, Crawford had been up to the North-West, met James Fenton and been escorted around the lands now opening up for alienation between the Leven and the Wilmot Rivers. Crawford selected extracts from Surveyor-General Calder's own detailed report of his excursion to lands between the Mersey and the Leven, written for the Government. These comprise three pages of direct quotation, in which Calder extolled the district he had seen because it contained soils and forests unsurpassed in Tasmania. His report was aimed at providing the Government with a 'clear idea of the value of the district' with descriptions of harbours and climate, before he proposed expenditure to open lines of traffic costing several thousands of pounds (Calder in "Letter," Appendix 3, 37–39; see News 1860b). Calder had described the forests, noting that their density had not deterred old hands (emancipists) from clearing at a lesser cost in recent years than previously; he mentioned 'scrubbing' and 'ringing' as much easier techniques

28   *The Castra Association 1864 to 1873*

that would clear land over three seasons. The Northern Counties had invariably the most thickly timbered land and his surveyor's reports (Richard Hall) assured him that settlement was proceeding most rapidly in them. Fenton's ringbarking method had obviously become completely accepted within 20 years.

Appendix 4, 40–1 was a compilation of Mr Dooley's Report to the Surveyor-General dated 30 June 1865. It was a suggested program of work through the year for the new settler with costs estimated for everything; 'a rude hut', not more than £5, a barn for about £10, pigsty and fowl house about 30 shillings each, and so on. To provide evidence for his estimates and calculations, he sourced agricultural settlers inland of Port Sorell at Sassafras and Fossil Bank, which had been heavily forested before settlement. Two examples were costs incurred by Henry Rockliff, who cleared four acres in 1863, and James Smith, who cleared 12 acres in 1864, followed by the financial outcome of their crops grown on those acres the following season. In the late 1850s, Henry Rockliff and his brothers had set the example of tackling forest-covered land and swiftly engaged in agriculture, which encouraged other Sassafras settlers. James Smith had been operating a coach service between Torquay to Deloraine, calling at Latrobe and Whitefoord Hills from December 1858 for about four years that may have funded his land purchase at Fossil Bank on the route (Ramsay 1980, 210). Crawford himself added a note about the potential sale of charcoal, pyrolignus acid and tar from timber conversion using distillation to offset clearing costs (45).

Crawford included two more Appendices. Appendix 5, 46 laid out the retail price of provisions as of 31 December 1863 and 1864 and average wage rates for farm labourers, ploughmen, shepherds, gardeners and female servants. Appendix 6, 47–51 was an abstract of several sections of the *WLA* 1863. It provided full information about the legal parameters of buying Crown Lands of different classes, sale by auction or exchange through private contract to purchase, conditions of payment and granting of land under the *Real Property Act* 1862, and the Road Fund that was funded by 'one-fourth' of the Land Fund, paid at the rate of 'sixpence for every shilling raised by assessment in each District'.

While Crawford was writing and assembling his 'Letter', Parliament approved the construction of the 16-mile tramway shown on the Plan in Figure 1.1. It was proposed to run from the Ulverstone Wharf through settled inland districts of Kindred and Abbotsham (east of North Motton and the Gawler River) past the un-inhabited Town Reserve of Eden (now near Sprent). It would continue southwards into the un-alienated 'superior' land that Crawford had chosen for officers he hoped to inspire, with a number of locations of plains, two eastward tramway branch lines towards the Wilmot River, and outer limits marked 'unsurveyed'.

In April 1865, Crawford wrote a lengthy exposition of his Castra Association to Colonial Treasurer Charles Meredith, in Hobart (included in Appendix 2, 32–35). He wrote that his 'predilection' for a colonial life was well-known amongst brother officers, who had asked his advice about Tasmanian retirement. He rued the deprivation of officers' ability to sell their commissions to obtain capital for a new 'career' due to changes in the Indian Service. He 'most earnestly deprecated the idea of any gentleman plunging alone into the backwoods, however tempting the situation', and made the point that, by being a 'body of gentlemen,

The Castra Association 1864 to 1873   29

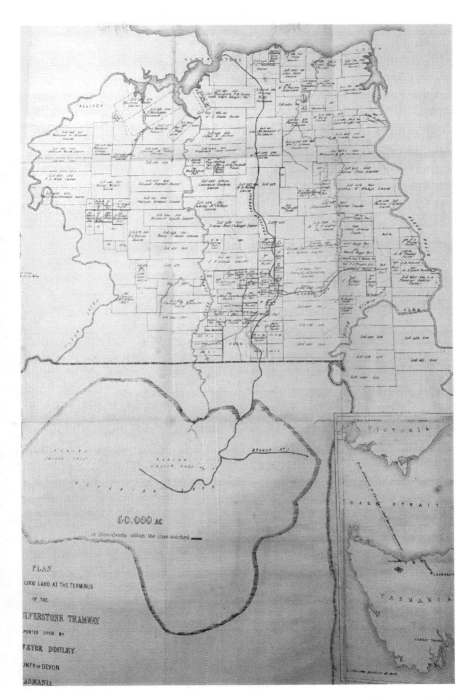

Figure 1.1 A segment of the large map described showing the proposed Tramway (Plank Road) in black from Ulverstone town reserve.

Source: Lithograph by W.C.Piguenit. 1867. Hobart: Government Printer, Tasmanian Archives. Photograph by Stefan Petrow 2020.

30   *The Castra Association 1864 to 1873*

sending their Agent [himself] ahead of them as their pioneer and supplying him with funds, [they] would soon change the aspect of the wilderness, and convert to their own benefit, as well as to the advantage of the country at large, tracts of land that are now absolute barriers to progress' (Crawford to Meredith reproduced in 'Letter', 34).

He feared that speculators, hearing of the scheme, would rush to secure land to resell profitably as interest rose, because he personally could not supply deposits for the 32,000 acres of land that he sought for 100 officers. He asked for the 'kind assistance of Government' to keep the 'land-jobbers' out. To enable this, he asked for a reservation of the area only as protection against 'intruders', pointing out that he was not asking for favours or free land, as had been offered to officers and soldiers as inducements to settle in the colonies of New Zealand and Queensland. Crawford was quite clear his pamphlet set forth 'the advantages I conceive may be gained by Officers settling here *in a body*' (Crawford's emphasis) (Crawford to Meredith, April 8, 1865). Ten days later he wrote again, clarifying his claim about not asking for favours. He stated his choice of the 'particular line of country' that he had 'mentally selected' had been 'greatly influenced by understanding that Government proposes' to construct a tramway from Ulverstone, benefitting other settlers on its way to his location, obviously knowing the works had been approved (Crawford to Meredith, April 18, 1865). Meredith responded with news that the Government believed Parliament should sanction his request and asked for details of the land (Meredith to Crawford, May 20, 1865). Crawford described it in as much detail as possible for unsurveyed land. He estimated it at about 80 square miles or 50,000 acres, some 22,000 of which was of superior quality, an opinion probably from Dooley or Fenton, both qualified to judge by experience (Crawford to Meredith, July 29, 1865). By now we can see that Crawford was demonstrating his commitment to present his officers with his every step by including all these correspondences.

The 'Letter's' final pages (52–54) detailed the cost of survey and of the Grant Deed for various acreages, and a copy of his handwritten letter of 30 October 1865 to the Secretary of the Royal Society of Tasmania, James Wilson Agnew, asking him to present his 'Letter' to the Fellows for their support of his efforts to encourage 'a valuable class of settlers in considerable numbers' to contribute to the 'moral and material development of the Colony'.

Crawford intended 100 shareholders to each take up 320 acres at double (£2/acre) the Government price, allowing establishment of a fund for community amenities like church, parsonage, schools and roads. Planned provision of such amenities was the unique twist in his version of the yeoman vision. Each purchaser was expected to choose his own land and survey would confirm that selection. It was a plan for a settlement community of men who were looking for constructive retirement as yeoman farmers, not as ex-Indian 'gentry', perhaps echoing past lives growing up as sons of the British 'middling sort' and aware of the status that better-off yeomen held there.

Crawford's 'Letter' was published as a 65-page pamphlet in Hobart Town on 23 October 1865, and circulated in Madras and Bombay, where, according to the

Madras Times, 'Colonel Crawford's now widely circulated and much read Tasmanian pamphlet caused a sensation amongst the Indian services' (News 1866b). The result of this enthusiasm was 'prodigious correspondence with men considering joining his flag' and even a letter in the *Madras Times* confirming the truth of Crawford's claims for his 'scheme for amateur bush life' (News 1866c). The 'Letter' went to a third edition by 1874, confirming enduring interest by Indian officers in stations all across India. What was needed next was Government's tangible support, and this may have encouraged Crawford to move his family from Richmond to New Town in Hobart in April 1866. This brought him nearer to Tasmania's Parliament and men of influence including the Fellows of the Royal Society. While there, Matilda gave birth to their eleventh and last child, Hugh Sewell Crawford, in 1867.

A Select Committee Report advising about possible amendments to the *Waste Lands Act* 1863 was considered in Parliament on 1 October 1867, the most relevant recommendations being that a separate bill be prepared for Indian settlement of lands in the District of Castra and lots would be limited to 320 acres maximum (HAJ Vol. XV, 1867, No. 65). According to the Editorial in the next day's *Mercury*, some members of Parliament believed that neither Government nor legislature should encourage in any way retired officers to come, in case they would be blamed when attempts to 'colonise' failed and the men would come looking for Government reparation. The response was that Crawford already had applications and was satisfied with the land, having inspected it twice, and absolved the Government and legislature of any further responsibility. Attorney-General William Lambert Dobson was reported earlier as having suggested the settlement would be 'simply a refuge for the destitute', but, when reminded about this, he declared it had been a slip. Opinion was that, if the officers failed to 'speedily convert [the land] into a flourishing settlement', it would be their own fault. They would need to be guided by Colonel Crawford, particularly in the matter of bringing wives and children with them so as not to be overly discouraged at the start. (News 1867b).

A few days later the Government thought it should not impede Crawford's way in the scheme, though John Helder Wedge, MHA Huon, thought the reservation was 'unfair to others' and Thomas Yardley Lowes, MLC Buckingham, opposed the bill because he knew some Anglo-Indians who had been ruined on their land. Colonial Secretary Richard Dry (also Premier) pointed out that the ten shillings for every acre spent on the tramway would make the land valuable very soon, and supported the bill (News 1867b).

On 11 October 1867, two Acts of Parliament were passed; the *Immigration Act* 1867, which amended the 1855 *Act* to specifically allow fare-paying persons from Europe or India to request 30 acres, plus 20 acres for his wife and ten acres for each accompanying child, within 12 months of arrival in Tasmania. The second was the *Land for Settlers from India Act* 1867, in which the preamble refers to 'representations made to the Government of Tasmania that certain persons are desirous of coming from India to Tasmania for the purpose of forming a settlement at Castra in the County of Devon'. The Governor was authorised to reserve an area for three years 'not exceeding fifty thousand acres, situate [sic] at Castra

32 *The Castra Association 1864 to 1873*

near the River Leven in the County of Devon, for the settlement of Europeans who may come or intend to come from India for the purpose of settlement' (S.1, 7). Section 3 also stated that the Government would spend ten shillings for every acre selected on roads and bridges, once at least five thousand acres had been selected. This Section was critical to the Association and the Government would have cause to be reminded of it often in future.

Further reinforcement of the project came in a letter on 25 November 1867 from Colonial Secretary Richard Dry to Edward Clive Bayley Esquire, Secretary to the Government of India. This was formal notification of the former Government passing the two relevant *Acts*, enclosing copies of them, as well as 498 copies of Castra reservation material. Because it was 'the wish of this Government that the course adopted by the Tasmanian Parliament and its motive shall be made fully known throughout the whole of British India', he asked that all possible steps be taken to 'insure attainment of this object'. He pointed out that all Tasmanian unoccupied lands were also open for selection if migrants preferred another district. He would mail 1,200 further copies the next month for distribution to every regiment, civil station and to every Authority 'throughout the three Presidencies'. Although Dry had recently taken over action on this project, after Whyte and Meredith lost the election in late 1866, this endorsement indicated his policy during his Premiership to open up lands in the North-West up the Mersey valley and the coastal districts. His defence against criticism was the need for land for Tasmanian farmers' sons and for English and Scottish migrants (Reynolds 1956, 140).

Once news of the Acts being passed reached India, some officers in Bombay formed a group called Castra & Co. with Charles Heathcote as Secretary, which wrote regularly directly to the Government to check on progress of the tramway that had been promised in 1865. Tenders for the first four miles from Ulverstone to Castra, including three chains near the jetty levelled and metalled, the remainder to be slabbed and rubbled at the ends of the slabs, had been let during 1868 (first four miles and jetty work, £3,332) and in 1869 (from 4th to 8th mile, and from 8th to 11th mile terminus, £1,249). These went to a local storekeeper at River Leven, James Alfred Fogg, collaborating with his brother-in-law, George McDonald Jr. The funded work was clearly for a plank (slab) road, not a tramway (News 1868a, 1869a).

Calder advised Castra & Co. in July 1869 that the funds set aside would soon be used up, and would only be sufficient for eight miles of the track from Ulverstone, when Castra land started at the ninth mile (Stilwell 1992). This situation had a negative effect on Indian interest, and some detractors had already started. One described 'small settlers' as 'poorest, least reputable members of [a] society where there is a larger mixture of convict blood than even in New South Wales' and showed sardonic disdain for Crawford's 'Eden in a state of jungle and forest', claiming the improbability of making profits from agriculture to compete with the squatters in Victoria and New South Wales ('Englishman' 1866b). Crawford did his best to counter the controversy, by staying in touch with Indian supporters and writing letters of rebuttal such as to the *Mercury* on 18 August 1866. He wrote that he already had 'a goodly collection of extracts from English, Indian and colonial

Figure 1.2 Portrait of Lieutenant-Colonel Andrew Crawford.

Source: J.W. Beattie, Photographer, Hobart. *Cyclopedia of Tasmania* 1900. Vol. 2, 282. NS5030/1/1. Tasmanian Archives.

newspapers in support and against [his] proposed system of immigration', and he was happy that overall support seemed predominant. He wrote that Colonel Shaw, who was presently 'advancing the cause of temperance around Ayr', thought he might induce emigration to Tasmania of mechanics, artisans and labourers from overcrowded parts of central Scotland after seeing Crawford's 'Letter'. Lt. Col. Fulton particularly supported him through the press and Castra & Co. publishing positive letters sent from Crawford (Fulton/Crawford Letters, 2 January 1866 to 21 November 1874). The portrait in Figure 1.2 was probably taken before Crawford came north.

34   *The Castra Association 1864 to 1873*

In 1870, Crawford moved his family up to Hamilton-on-Forth to give his whole attention to opening the district with roads and clearing operations. His son Alexander reminisced about this journey when elderly. The family sailed from Hobart to the Forth River with their furniture on the schooner *Scamore*, catching a shark and heaps of couta en route, an exciting experience for him as a ten-year-old (News 1949c). In 1870, there was very little habitation in Ulverstone – a hotel, a store and bridge across the Leven much as we saw in Figure 0.2, with a police station adjacent, and John Frith's house opposite. Frith was employed by the Public Works Department in charge of roads and bridges.

Before Crawford left Hobart, he wrote to the Minister Henry Butler, MHA Brighton, requesting an extension, after the first payments in July 1870, for lots selected for his clients, pointing out that lengthy delay in getting surveys done had used most of the reservation period. Crawford noted that a further 4,140 acres had been requested on top of the 6,631 acres already paid to be surveyed, and 490 acres in free grants given. He requested an extension of a further year to 10 October 1871 (Crawford 1870; HAJ 1870, Vol. XX, 1870, No. 106). This was when Richard Hall was surveying nearly 7000 acres. By 1871, in a letter to the *Times of India*, he wrote of illustrious visitors taken to see the progress, of the road to Castra going ahead and of a 'good road line' going into Gunns Plains between the Gawler and the Leven Rivers.

Support did come from some quarters. Major Arthur Vincent Dumbleton, who had just retired from the 21st Hussars and was then going to Tasmania, chaired a meeting of Castra & Co. on 10 May 1869, at which the reduction in acreage price was announced. Crawford still hoped buyers would 'bestow' one-sixteenth of their land for the amenities proposed. Crawford received a vote of confidence 'for his untiring energy towards so much advantage to men of the Indian Services'. A full report was printed in the *Times of India* on 25 May 1869, reprinted in *Mercury* 14 July 1869. Later that year, Dumbleton's letter to Fulton at Raipore discussed his practical experiences of clearing having settled on his 180-acre lot at Torquay near the Mersey River. He wrote that Indian Officers coming to Tasmania 'could not do better than go to Castra', but added that single settlers would do better to settle in 'more civilised parts', even though the private sale prices were £4 per acre compared to Government rates (Dumbleton 1869). He also bought 210 acres at the southern end of the Gunns Plains valley, and mentioned that potential use of the Leven River, if large timber was cleared from it, would avert dependence on a road. The Castra & Co. covering letter announced it now had '22 members, requiring between 5,000 and 6,000 acres' and more expected every month (Castra & Co. to *Times of India,* December 3, 1869, Dumbleton's letter attached).

In 1869, Lt. Colonel Michael Shaw attempted to identify reasons for the slow uptake by Indian officers of Castra land, suggesting natural hesitation (is it too good to be true?), being capital-poor and depending on their pay, rose-tinted memories of 'home' and children in education in England, and lack of game for the 'inveterate sportsman' in Tasmania to suit the ex-soldier. He himself, having

The Castra Association 1864 to 1873 35

already settled on the Mersey near Latrobe, a growing commercial town, had no sympathy with those nay-sayers, writing:

> I should consider location among persons of their own mode of thought, in a rural habitation, and with their children all around them to a climax superior to the amassment of splendid fortunes. Money is not able to provide for the rising generation a way of life giving such faithful promise of a happy future, in a rural location in *The* most salubrious climate in the world. But a beginning is required for Castra. When this takes place there will be a rush.
>
> (Shaw to Boyer, July 7, 1869)

Another positive opinion came through another letter to the *Times of India* from a Tasmanian-born officer of long-standing, Lt. Colonel William Vincent Legge, who wrote of Castra:

> I have a far better opinion than many have of the scheme. Let our Indian friends know they must not come out to make money, but to find an opening for their sons who are willing to labour, and to wait, with eyes open and willing hands, and I do not think their moderate expectations will be disappointed.
>
> (Legge to *Times of India* 20 June 1871)

Meanwhile, in 1873, Crawford's adult sons, Edmund (born 1851) and Montague (born 1852) built a bark hut and started to clear the land he had selected at Castra. They built a cottage on the farmland they called Deyrah to which the family moved in early 1878. By this time, they had a gravel road they could use for carts, '70 acres cleared and grassed, an orchard planted and a six-roomed cottage' that was later extended to fit the whole family. Crawford had developed 'a nucleus of stock' to take to Deyrah from their rented farm base at Forth and was already asserting that he had been 'far happier and more profitably employed than I could possibly have been in England, whilst I have never had occasion to put the children or myself on short commons' which he believed may not have been true for those 'cleaving to Cheltenham or Bath' in 'the customary groove' (Crawford to *Times of India,* December 21, 1877). Crawford and his wife Matilda stayed there until his death in 1899.

Early in 1873, Crawford became more vexed over delays into Castra parish by road, but the Government was in a state of flux (Stilwell 1992, 20; Reynolds 1956). Thomas Chapman, MLC Buckingham, became Colonial Secretary in August 1873, and about May 1874, he visited Devon with other Members and expressed interest in the Castra Association. So, Crawford responded with a six-page letter on 1 August 1874 recapping the Government's commitment to Indian settlers, the delays to surveying caused by winter weather conditions, and the Association's extension. The resultant selection of 9,700 acres plus 800 acres in free grants was made by Anglo-Indian immigrants through

36 *The Castra Association 1864 to 1873*

his 'personal exertions, and vested in the hands of gentlemen who will bring into the country, for expenditure here, an annual aggregate income, pay and pension, of certainly not less than £10,000'. He then cited difficulties transporting essentials only by packhorse or on men's backs, due to the impossibility of bringing a dray to Castra without risk of overturning. Regarding poor access to Gunns Plains and Dooley's Plains, they were 'virtually excluded from improvement'. He was requesting the assistance granted to his purchasers under *Act* of Parliament. His 'respectful request' here was for credit to the Castra Association of the £1,000 paid to Government in respect of 2,500 acres in the West Gawler area, 'to be devoted to completion of a road specifically for their district' (Crawford to Chapman, August 1, 1874, in NS1383/1/1). This seems to imply that he would then arrange for the work to be done on the Association's behalf.

Crawford continued, 'Without roads, these forests will remain but the grave of the hopes and bodies of the brave men struggling to conquer them. With practicable highways they would soon yield first their vast stores of valuable timbers to the merchant and then their soil to the plough'. He questioned whether the principle embodied in local public works was giving aid to companies to build railways and bridges, but not for extending ordinary roads for landholders (News 1874). To provide evidence of lands selected, he attached a two-page addendum of the 52 purchasers' names with amounts of both purchases and free grants. Based upon Crawford's list, I collate evidence about these persons in the next chapter to find where their land was situated and how long they were owners, even if not simultaneously occupiers.

A successful association – or not?

As we saw from the 1840s and 1850s when settlers were extending north-westwards overland into the districts of Port Sorell, Sassafras and the Mersey, lack of roads to get to ports in pioneering districts was a huge handicap. And so it was for the Castra Association, something Crawford foresaw as essential for progress from the very beginning when he was taken to the land by Fenton. He had also emphasised the need for access to Colonial Secretary Meredith. Hardly surprising then was his disappointment at the postponement of the tramway completion. This decision was off-putting for some contemplating the Castra Association plan, and the outcome was obvious to Crawford, as indicated in his letter to Chapman. It was not until the mid-1880s that this road was metalled (Pink 1990).

Yet *Walch's Tasmanian Guide Book* of 1871 (194–5) was extolling the lands of Castra for its variety of timbers, the grassy plains opening to 'patches of surpassing beauty' and 'two bridle tracks in different directions' to reach Castra – perhaps not for the faint-hearted tourist! Reference to the 'abominable roads' to Castra was made in an article published in the *Bombay Gazette* in July 1880 by an anonymous purchaser of 160 acres at the 'Castra Settlement', in which he wished to 'put Castra in its true light before the Indian public' (News 1880a). He argued that

The Castra Association 1864 to 1873   37

benefits of being able to 'retire and enjoy their pensions comfortably' on 'fertile, healthy country' had to be weighed up against the fact that,

> Indian officers have been so long accustomed to Indian habits that the necessity for self-help becomes a difficulty too great to be surmounted, and when the facts are taken into consideration that Castra is 14 miles from the nearest township . . . and the district covered with forests through which the sun's rays hardly penetrate, the benefits are neutralized by the discomfort . . . . When I state that the track is in some places as steep as one in six, but when to this needless steepness of gradient is added the execrable state of the so-called road, winding as it does through innumerable mudholes two and even three feet in depth, it is only surprising that loads can be got up at all.

> (News 1880a)

He told of his procurement of house timber from a sawmill seven miles away, which took a team of six bullocks two days to bring that distance. He thought that if Crawford was to write 'his pamphlet' after recent years' experiences, he would be less 'jubilant' in tone and 'confine himself to the advantages Tasmania offers as to healthiness of climate and beauty of scenery', because 'Indian officers cannot make a living out of their farms in Castra' (News 1880a).

But Crawford did not lose sight of the road quality dilemma and the people whom he represented. He submitted a letter and petition in 1879 to Parliament advocating for the funds that were promised to be spent after 5,000 acres were sold actually be applied to the roads in West Castra (Dooley's Plains) and for the line of road marked out by Surveyor Frith in 1872 to be completed. He pointed out the 'genteel progress' and additional Crown Land sales that had accrued to the Government when five miles of road had been made in the North Motton parish (HAJ Vol. XL, 1879, No. 91).

Putting aside the road problems, was there evidence of success of Crawford's Association? I argue that there was success in some respects and a failure in terms of actual residence and agricultural activity by Indian Officer purchasers that meant not all the communal assets Crawford proposed were built. One measure of success was his effort to persuade Indian Officers to migrate to Tasmania, whether to Castra or to other land in the county of Devon or beyond.

Under the *Immigration Act* 1867, European and Indian immigrants who paid their own way to Tasmania still had some advantageous conditions regarding land acquisition and grant after five years residence in Tasmania, regardless of where they selected land (Calder, November 20, 1867). Some of the 52 purchasers at Castra also bought land elsewhere in Devon, just as Dumbleton did. Lt. Colonel Shaw bought land on the Mersey near Latrobe in addition to his lot at Gunns Plains, and also eventually built a house called Molenda on Castra Road in 1872 (now heritage-listed). Here he constructed one of the first coastal grain mills, Union Mills, operated by his son Thomas, who lived in a cottage on the same farm (News 1896). Other Anglo-Indians were attracted to settle, like Major-General

38 *The Castra Association 1864 to 1873*

William Lodder, who built Lonah, a classic stone Georgian-style house, between Ulverstone and Penguin in 1877.

Stokes wrote that Anglo-Indians were people 'who by virtue of their education, forthrightness and love of organisation became accepted as leaders by the small farmers in a most unusual alliance for the bludgeoning of the government and betterment of the community', both aspects that receive more attention in later chapters (Stokes 1969, 77). Some used their advocacy as Stokes alluded and were significant contributors to the broad Devon community. An outstanding example is Edward Nicholas Coventry Braddon, who, at only 48-years-old and having lost his Indian employment through amalgamation, decided to buy a small run-down 48-acre property above Forth in 1878. Crawford's 'proselytizing activities' were thought to have been persuasive to the Braddons and others, and Braddon did his best in turn to encourage and inform other possible settlers, that being the main purpose of his series of 30 letters sent for publication in the *Statesman and Friend of India* (Braddon and Bennett 1980).

Braddon and his wife were encouraged by nearness and social mixing with other Anglo-Indians like Dr John Dundas, Captain Sage and Colonel James Robert Fulton and his family, who had also bought two lots on the Leven River (Morell 2011, 33). Some held seats in State Parliament, like Braddon, MHA West Devon 1879–1888, 1893–1901 and Premier from 1894–1898 and 1899, and in Federal Parliament from 1901–1904 (Bennett and Bennett 1979, 30, 57–58). Crawford was an early local resident MHA for West Devon in 1876–77. Crawford, Dumbleton and Dr Arthur Young, among other community notables like James Fenton and Henry Rockliff, were all Justices of the Peace in 1877, while Dumbleton was President of the Cricket Club and Dr Young presided over the Devon Institute, and Crawford was on both Boards of the Castra Road and Ulverstone Schools (Walch 1877b, 232). Alexander Crawford, one of Crawford's sons, and Dr Young were both volunteers in the West Devon Company. Stilwell suggested it would be hard to find a local cause that did not include active Anglo-Indians, especially in prominent roles, like Crawford who was President of the Devon Agricultural Society for years in the 1870s and 1880s. He asserted that the Anglo-Indian society was quite a closed social group, a factor that supports Crawford's plan that they could all work together to mutual advantage at Castra (Stilwell, 24).

Anglo-Indians were active in the Forth and Ulverstone communities, and in organisations with a wider focus, like the Road Trusts of Devon and Forth, the Ulverstone Farmers' Club and the Forth Cricket Club. Local rifle clubs and country sports days were supported through leadership positions. Their education and past experiences in Indian service had certainly fitted them for leadership, commitment and responsibility, highly desirable qualities that benefitted the rapidly developing Devon communities of small farmers and businessmen.

Crawford's legacy to North-West Tasmania was the name 'Castra'. It was used for the municipal Parish created on Castra Association land, and Castra and Upper Castra, long-lasting village community successes, perhaps unseen by Crawford himself, who died before the huge family farming development advances of the early twentieth century.

The Castra Association 1864 to 1873   39

Another aspect of success is harder to measure precisely. Success came from the huge publicity that Crawford's efforts attracted in persuading Indian Officers to migrate to Tasmania, whether to Castra or to other land in the county of Devon or beyond. His 'Letter' was so widely circulated in the Anglo-Indian press over several print runs, which meant that Tasmania with its healthy climate and beautiful scenery was being promoted to a group of influential, widely travelled people, a 'valuable class', as Crawford believed, that would benefit Tasmania if they came to settle, bringing their skills and money. In the same way that his Association was well publicised, he may have read or heard about Edward Wakefield's Company's colonising attempts in New Zealand around 1840 and slightly later planned settlements of associations supported by the Church of England at Canterbury and the Free Church of Scotland at Otago (McAloon 2002, 17–19; Arnold 1981, 16, 355–56). The choice of the name Castra *Association* was arguably deliberate. We cannot know how many of his 'Letters' made their way to England and exerted persuasive pressure on potential immigrants, perhaps including the activities of Colonel Shaw in Scotland. What is more certain is that his efforts would have helped cement the colony's new name Tasmania, adopted in 1856, through interest in his vision in the Western and South Australian colonies and other Anglo societies.

From my reading of Crawford, I am convinced he was a far-sighted man with initiative and vision; he may well have been charismatic, because he was certainly able to persuade; he was comfortable dealing with Government and high-ranking public servants, and confident that he had made his best possible effort to achieve a worthwhile outcome for his adopted country. He demonstrated very clearly his real understanding of the needs of immigrants. This may have grown through meeting other friends of the Ogilvys and Dr John Coverdale, Richmond doctor for many years, but born in Kedgeree, Bengal in 1814, who probably attended Crawford's wife in her pregnancy. The family's two years in England on limited income had developed his appreciation of challenges that returning after decades in India presented a family man with many children, such as 'life divested of most of its enjoyments', unable to mix in society, travel or reciprocate hospitalities. He knew the problems associated with advancing his sons by a Commission or paying premiums into business partnerships. He understood the Indian lifestyle after 30 years, the institutional environment of colonial service where accommodation, servants, regimental support and fellowship were taken for granted, and its contrast with English life 'on limited means and little support' (Crawford, 2–3).

Crawford was 58 when he returned to Tasmania, and the question of work for one's self and a good future for immigrant sons form a strong thread throughout his 'Letter'. He also realised being a pioneer in the wild forested areas he had in mind was not for the faint-hearted, and, because of this, he believed that new immigrants to the colony would benefit from the affinity and strengths of being in a community of like-minded people, with similar challenges, but also similar experiences and background – the ties that bound them together.

He went to some lengths to caution the fullest, most careful consideration of immigration and pointed out the 'real advantages to tempt the settler' to Canada,

40 *The Castra Association 1864 to 1873*

the Cape, Natal, Queensland, New South Wales and Western Australia (the latter three all with a 'semi-torrid climate'), Victoria (a 'long hot summer'), and New Zealand ('healthy, bracing atmosphere, but not so far advanced in civilization as Tasmania'). In consequence, 'an Indian Officer's choice is between New Zealand [opened to settlers in 1830] and Tasmania, and [he] gave preference to the latter' (Crawford, 7). The delightful contrast of the Tasmanian climate to the 'relentless and unwearying sun, hot winds, mugginess as of a vapour bath, prickly heat, &c'. of the Indian experience, that Braddon described, was clearly a major factor in his mind (Braddon 1878, Letter 1).

A Utopian plan – or not?

In literature about utopian communities, schemes such as Crawford's are often included. Historians use 'intentional communities' to describe living and working arrangements formed by a group of usually unrelated persons united voluntarily by a sense of common purpose (Claeys 2011, 130; Bill Metcalf 2008, 49). Utopianism scholar Bill Metcalf made the claim that the Castra community:

> Would recreate the idyllic life of the Indian Hill Stations, with imported workers doing all the hard labour, and numerous servants to attend to the needs of the fortunate members, who would enjoy a life of genteel culture and gentlemanly recreation. Incredibly, Castra got underway near Ulverstone in 1874, but soon collapsed.
>
> (Bill Metcalf 2008, 56)

Explaining about the Castra Association and Tasmania, he misquoted Crawford, writing 'they collectively establish a semi-utopian community . . . continu[ing] the privileged life they had enjoyed in India, . . . rich land, good hunting . . . and servants to do all the menial work', none of which is contained in the 'Letter' (William Metcalf 2008, 5, 7). Building on Stilwell's assessment about communal settlements being 'doomed to failure', Metcalf argued that Castra failed 'as a semi-utopian capitalist, elitist community' (2008, 8). In paraphrasing Crawford's 'Letter', he used the phrase 'elitist utopia' (2008, 5 n.17). Metcalf also claimed Crawford was 'well-read in utopian literature', without any evidence other than Crawford's insertion quoting John Robert Godley's 'moral theory of emigration' that supported a 'remove from one part of the empire to another' (Crawford, 2–5). Godley, devout Church of England follower, started Wakefield's Christchurch settlement but died in 1861; Crawford may have read his writings to source this quotation (Hensley 1990, 303–4). This quotation hardly supports a utopian concept, and Metcalf was wrong to include the Castra Association in his 'a litany of failure' in Tasmania, but may have been influenced by being told of local belief in failure by Ulverstone Museum volunteers met during research.

In Claeys' *Searching for Utopia* he reminded us of Titus Salt's British workers' village, Saltaire in 1850, and Robert Owen, 'the founder of British communitarian socialism', who worked to improve working and living conditions for his New

The Castra Association 1864 to 1873 41

Lanark Mill workers from 1800–1825 (130, 121–22, 132–33). These and others he cited shared an element of control over workers and their labour, whilst ostensibly 'improving' their lot.

It has been suggested that Owen and Wakefield, as contemporaries, shared utopian ideas because they 'looked for regeneration of man by returning him to the land in newly developing countries' (Clarke 1977, 126; Claeys, 132–33). But whereas Owen searched for lower-class independence, Wakefield 'hoped to force them into dependence and subordination' (Clarke, 126). There was no resonance of these ideas with those of Crawford, although 'an agricultural community based on the English yeoman farmer' enthused those Wakefieldian supporters who saw colonial potential in this manifestation (Clarke, 125).

While 'intentional community' can validly be applied to Crawford's scheme, I argue against any link to utopianism or even altruism, another oft-linked concept, because it is very clear that his scheme was founded on a pragmatic assessment of opportunity for income and potential for capital asset accrual through land for sons in his own family as well as those of others. What Crawford presented was his twist on the yeoman ideal. Fairburn described a similar possibility of a peaceful, rural idyll, with independence that came from owning land, building a home and a living within a like-minded social group that gained traction in New Zealand during the same years (1989, 20–22). This idealised vision has helped to sell migration from England to various places in the 'new world' not only in the nineteenth century.

The communal villages planned for the Castra and Crawford town reserves were not intended to be utopian – Crawford's vision was for self-supporting villages with jointly owned common land for essential rural facilities, where settlers' needs would stimulate commercial opportunities like general produce stores, sawmills, dairies, blacksmiths and wheelwrights. There is a strong resonance with the concept of traditional English village structure, the style of which Crawford and his comrades would have remembered from their youth.

Crawford made his scheme seem feasible and attractive, presenting his vision of a collaborative community of similar people with all amenities for a good life that they had contributed to creating on land they would own for themselves and families. The critical ingredient was reasonable tracks to the lots, especially early on when access was essential for goods in and out. Bullock drays were the usual heavy transport and they needed good, well-drained tracks, especially in this area of high winter rainfall.

So why did the scheme *appear* to fail after all Crawford's energetic support? Shaw's knowledge of Anglo-Indian circumstances made his analysis perceptive. Idealised images of 'home' (England) competed with the vision Crawford presented and involved taking a risk with a family in tow. Without doubt, the well-publicised news in Indian papers from detractors about the deplorable tracks would not have been encouraging. Castra & Co. were already losing members by mid-1869 because nothing had started; 'two or three gentlemen have lately gone to Tasmania, and would have joined the Castra community if it had been started', but went elsewhere for an immediate start (Castra & Co., May 10, 1869). Edward

42   *The Castra Association 1864 to 1873*

Braddon made no bones about the volume of unsolicited and uninformed negative advice, and allusions to his and his wife Alice's madness about their Tasmanian dreams in the late 1870s (Letter I, May 6, 1878, 122).

Another situation applied to the Fulton family, who arrived from India to Forth in 1871. Major James Fulton himself was delayed for years, a circumstance that may not have been unique. He had a wife and ten children, and Crawford was acting as his agent as well as being a close friend and neighbour at Forth. Writing from Bangalore in 1873, he was about to be promoted to a Commandantship and felt he could not leave India until he had paid out Government loans on the land. He corresponded monthly with his family and was a great advocate of the Association. He supplied the *Times of India* with Crawford's letters for publication, which explains why names are deleted in the reprints (e.g. Fulton to Crawford, August 18, 1873, NS1383/1/1).

Shortage of female Anglo-Indian sources makes it difficult to evaluate the perspective of wives and adult daughters, especially when Tasmanian bush life contrasted dramatically with genteel society life of an Anglo-Indian 'lady'. Elizabeth Fenton's diary (1828) provides an earlier idea of adjustments women made leaving India. She agreed to leave because of prevalent fear of cholera and expecting her first child. Cholera continued to be an underlying issue for decades and the subject of regular newspaper reports (News 1866a). Australia's climate and potential economic prosperity from free land grants were the main attraction (Pos 2014, 35–36). Letters were influential in persuading friends and, in Calcutta, lawyer Charles Prinsep urged them to go to Van Diemen's Land, extolling its advantages. She arrived in 1829, delighted with Hobart's landscape, bringing her four-month-old daughter born en-route in Galle (Ceylon). Servants brought from India provided help, and by 1830, the family moved to bushland acreage in the Derwent Valley. She wrote admiringly about 'birds, trees and wildflowers and lovely weather'. The farmhouse was very run down and dirty, and she 'had to draw on all her resources to manage', but was philosophical about the difficulties and hardships compared to her Indian life, believing she would count her blessings when things went well (59). Her husband, Michael Fenton, a typical example of the Anglo-Indians discussed earlier, was granted two free properties, and served in the Legislative Council from 1840, so he was often away from home. He brought out 18 Irish families to work on his great estate, Glenora. He and Elizabeth made a family home for 50 years at Fenton Forest, he dying in 1874 as 'the old Captain' and she two years later. Elizabeth's descendant, Pos concluded that Elizabeth, based on her documents and diaries, was 'not a silent partner in their business affairs' (83–84). This hints at a companionate relationship between them.

Braddon was a rare source in his observations about women and regularly referred to himself and his wife Alice as 'we'. Once they settled at Forth, he wrote light-heartedly about his challenges collecting wood and his wife's in cooking, both 'roughing it thoroughly', and her nervousness initially about cows that turned out to be docile. Alice was encouraging and he quoted her opinions. Their two locally sourced servants were appreciated for their hard work (Letter XV, July 1878, 173).

The Castra Association 1864 to 1873   43

Another contemporary source was Theophilus Jones, who moved with his family to Tasmania in 1877 after nine years in the Bombay Pilot Service. He combined freelance work as a travelling correspondent for the *Mercury* with insurance agency, writing articles aimed at Tasmanian readers and potential immigrants by describing life experiences of ordinary folk (Haygarth 2011). In 1885, he described his travel along Castra Road and to Deyrah, which sheds light on Castra farm life and life for ladies from India. With understanding, he wrote:

> The ladies, or many of them, used to conventionalities and gaiety of station life in India, and the easily obtained native service, do not like our bush and the conditions of life it necessitates. No man or woman should dream of tackling colonial life . . . unless the parental instinct is sufficiently strong to cheerfully surrender [what] is really hollow and artificial for the sake of their children's welfare. The Colonel's place, 320 acres good land and general surroundings is a better exemplification of his pet project than a thousand arguments.
>
> (Jones, Article 32 in Archer 2015, 173–75)

Jones' detailed description noted Crawford looking younger than his 70 years, the place was neat and developed with horses, cattle and sheep, the dwelling set in a beautiful flower garden, the meal of Indian delicacies and home-grown meat, fruit and vegetables from the orchard and garden, and evidence of a maid, cook, gardener and other farm labourers. Hugh and Robert were in London for school, one 'sturdy robust young fellow' (Alexander) helped his father with managing the farm and 'somewhat voluminous paperwork' and others were variously employed. The Crawfords had an impressed officer from Afghanistan visiting (175). Jones' reports could be deliberately flattering (Haygarth, 55). Even so, he described a settled, comfortable, spacious life typical of the yeoman ideal that contrasts sharply with the British suburban alternative, and adequate financial ability to send his boys overseas for education. Crawford took on a traditional yeoman role by acting as an agent (or steward) for prospective owners and later was listed as absentee owners' Tasmanian contact in the valuation rolls.

Castra's lack of progress was probably due to Tasmanian factors. Crawford's idea was ahead of its time because, unluckily, it coincided with difficult financial years for the Government caused by a long depression that reduced finances for the road programme (Townsley 1955, 36). Parliament was over-represented by landed pastoralists with 17 out of 32 members of the House of Assembly, and nine out of 16 of the Legislative Council from the south-east quarter of the island, who saw no advantage in north-western development (Blainey 1954, 69). These, and other factors discussed earlier, meant that a relatively modest area of land was actually secured by Anglo-Indians in Castra; almost 11,000 acres were selected from the reserved 50,000 acres that remained the Parish of Castra. Although J.R. Scott (one of the Indian buyers), disillusioned with Crawford's management, claimed that Crawford 'was unfitted for the task he undertook, and failed completely if results be the test' (News 1880a), Stilwell argued that the

Figure 1.3 Crawford Family Farm, Deyrah, Central Castra c. 1880–1890.
Source: *Cyclopaedia of Tasmania* 1900 Vol. 2, 282. NS5030/1/1. Tasmanian Archives.

'scheme did not prosper partly because of the temperament of the Anglo-Indians and partly because the Government did not honour its undertaking to construct roads' (Stilwell Papers NS1383/1/1/).

For the man of vision wanting a good life for his sons and a good husband for his daughter Ellen (born 1848) (who married a squatter from New South Wales in Hobart in 1870) while enjoying active retirement, Crawford seems to have succeeded unquestionably. He demonstrated the possibility of the yeoman ideal for others who made their 'camp' in Castra even if this had to wait for another decade or so. Figure 1.3 is the only known visual record of the home that Jones visited and described, because a fire sadly destroyed it and all his papers.

Note

1 Edward Braddon, his articles' title in the *Statesman and Friend of India*, (Calcutta, 1878).

2 Castra land and Anglo-Indian ownership

As we saw previously, there is a history of doubt about the success of the Castra Association. My research of the valuation rolls over a long period, charting how long each Anglo-Indian purchaser owned their lot has highlighted the need to reassess those claims of failure held by historians as well as local Ulverstone residents interested in local history. My findings suggest there was more Anglo-Indian involvement with agricultural progress than implied by simply focussing upon Colonel Crawford's activities.

In the history of settlement across the Anglo-world, land suitable for agricultural settlement was crucial because each colony needed to create a regime of self-sufficiency as a defence against the tyranny of distance from a remote 'mother country'. Land was a 'trust and a resource not to be squandered' (Brown 1980, 15). Settlers set their sights on land that would provide 'wood, water and hay', but not so much wood as to preclude running livestock swiftly without much laborious clearing (Murchie, Allen, and Booth 1936). Colonial administrators perennially faced political problems in addition to raising revenue from sales of Crown Land. One instance was inspection of imposed residential conditions. Another was assessing the value of labour or material improvements. Quit-rent, the ancient payment made to the British Crown, was imposed in all British colonial lands, even on free land grants, and enforcement and collection was difficult (Petrow 2001). In New Holland in 1814, Governor Macquarie regarded it as a discouragement to settlers (Roberts 1924, 21). Obstacles occurred from inadequate surveying skills and capacity for the volume of lands granted. All these problems were experienced in colonial Canada as well as New Holland and Van Diemen's Land (Roberts 1924, 79).

Other problems could arise when selections involved boundaries irrespective of topographic features like hills and rivers, and regulations for siting townships were mandated, as in the American state of Illinois, where school reserves were always central in the town reserve regardless of unsuitable boggy ground (Woods 1822, 273). Reeves reflected that the 'Land Question', as he termed it, had been a 'vital and living issue in public affairs, the real dividing line of parties, and key to more manoeuvres and intrigues than any other' from the start of European settlement in Australia (1902, vol. 1, 193).

DOI: 10.4324/9781003229841-3

46 *Castra land and Anglo-Indian ownership*

Land surveying was thought to be the oldest mathematical art, deriving from ancient Egypt, and accurate measurement underpinned land title as the foundation of the world's wealth (Gillespie and Staley 1887, iii). Its application for colonisers of new frontiers was indispensable, a quality often taken for granted even to the present day. Who acquired land, how they acquired it, and how much was acquired, shaped each colony's development. Survey decisions affected the social structures of the colonisers, institutional arrangements of control and effect on indigenous populations. 'Matters cadastral' identify a 'social and economic unit of land' owned by individuals in 'comparatively small' lots defined on a plan of survey (Brown 1980, 14–15, 24–26). No less important were the changes wrought on the land itself and ways that settlement altered the landscape. An obvious example was the practice of ringbarking.

Survey and surveyors in Van Diemen's Land and Tasmania

In 1820s Van Diemen's Land, little of the known land was agricultural, except for home-produce gardens on pastoral estates or small farms near major centres. The majority of grants of Crown Land were made to pastoralists through favouritism, Governor's patronage, scurrilous manipulation of pre-emptive rights and 'dummying', and much of that land was not occupied or developed (Reeves, 238–39; Eldershaw 1962, xiv). Following formal separation from NSW in 1825, Lieutenant-Governor Arthur appointed Commissioners of Survey and Valuation to conduct a thorough review of settled lands. They had four responsibilities: to create divisions based on the English model of counties, hundreds and parishes, such that counties were divided into 1600 square miles, containing hundreds of one hundred square miles, each with four parishes; to set general valuations of settled and unoccupied land; to make reserves for town sites, roads and public uses; and to reserve lands for support of clergy and schools (Eldershaw, pp. xiii-xiv). At that point, about one-third of the island was settled, but they did include more areas despite 'intractable wilderness of dense mountain and forest' and horrendous conditions, particularly during winter weather of snow, hail and rain (Jones 1989, 46–47). English county names were copied too – Buckingham, Cornwall, Dorset, Devon, Somerset, Cumberland and a salute to Wales – Glamorgan, Pembroke and Monmouth.

The Journals of the Commissioners' Reports were detailed and well-considered, particularly about inequities in setting a general valuation of land for each parish that failed to reflect variation in soils and topography (Eldershaw, xiii-xiv). They regretted the lack of a complete island geographical survey, due to insufficient surveying staff to handle demand (McKay 1962, 121). They also visited small farms, often making complimentary reports of gardens and livestock management by wives of men with Government posts away from the farm. Female grantees and wives ran small yeoman-style farms close to major centres, where they sold produce in very similar practice to contemporary hard-working tenants on British farms (Morgan 1991, 27–29). However, Commissioners were concerned that small land grants to impecunious ex-convicts and

Castra land and Anglo-Indian ownership   47

settlers created potential for exploitation by 'larger unscrupulous neighbours' (Jones 1989, 51).

Following the 1823 Bigge Report, survey matters moved from the Governor to that of a Surveyor-General. Land valuation matters have always been significant to the Government because the surveyors' practice of recording features and attributes, and setting an appropriate value for each selection served the primary purpose of raising revenue for the Government (Meikle 2014). Grants of Crown Land and Australian terms of tenure were governed by English law. Tenure, that is, to a 'man and his heirs' was the term used about grants of Crown Land (Brown, 24). By the time Tasmania commenced responsible Government in 1855, the administration of land settlement matters followed well-established processes.

Tasmania's society comprised of two main groups. One was the pastoralists or 'landed gentry' who already owned huge estates mainly in the Midlands and upper Derwent and wielded great political and administrative power (Reynolds 1969b, 16). The worry about unscrupulous neighbours was still evident in the 1861 Report on the *Waste Land Act*, when Captain William Langdon, MLC Derwent, told a Select Committee that the pastoral gentry of Hamilton were prepared to pay large prices to guard against 'small proprietors' purchasing land, because they did not want ex-convicts or even yeoman farmers living in their midst (HAJ Vol VII, No.161, 6–7).

The second group comprised small farmers (often tenants or time-served emancipists) and their sons, and the working population of labourers, civil servants, small businessmen or tradesmen, described by the Government as 'humble men' (HAJ Vol. VIII, 1862, No. 111; Meikle 2011, 3). For farmers to move from tenant to freeholder, or for new rural immigrants, terms of purchase were as important as accessibility to land on which to make a living. Tasmanian Governments were preoccupied for many decades with three land management issues: the combined objectives of gaining financial and population growth benefits from Crown 'waste lands'; perennial demands for better road access to yeoman selectors' lots; and measures to avoid regulatory abuses.

The *Waste Lands Act* 1858 followed accepted practice in granting tenure to Crown Land by mandating that land for selection had to be unoccupied, not listed for sale, and not previously held under 'Depasturing' or 'Occupation' leases. The maximum lot size was 320 acres and only one could be bought by each applicant, until this was amended in 1859 to allow multiple purchases to a maximum of 320 acres (*WLA* 1859, s.13 and s.19). Pastoral lands reverting to the Crown when leases fell due facilitated survey into auctionable lots that were advertised in the *Hobart Town Gazette*, even though this risked flooding the market during depression times when the Government sought all possible revenue.

Land-jobbing and speculation, with 'clever trickery and patient evasion', was a continuing concern for Governments from the 1820s to the 1880s. Robson believed as much as half the free grant acreage in Van Diemen's Land before 1830 was because of evading the law (1983, 199; Reeves 1902, 210–11). Public dissatisfaction with speculative behaviour was already evident when Colonel Crawford

48 *Castra land and Anglo-Indian ownership*

addressed it during his negotiations with Surveyor-General Calder. Attempts to avert this led to more stringent conditions being incorporated into land legislation. Grant of ownership consistently depended on material and labour improvements and a home built and occupied by the owner, until a change in those occupancy conditions was recommended in a bill to both houses by a Select Committee (HAJ Vol. XLIV, 1883, No. 130, and LCJ, No.112). This removed the owner's personal residence clause and changed it to allow for a tenant or servant to reside, which obviously favoured owners of large multiple holdings.

Early Tasmanian Governments were keen to support British immigrants as a yeoman class of settler and provided favourable payment terms through its framing and administration of successive *Waste Lands Acts*. This aim was sustained by Premier Braddon in later years (News 1886), although, in the 1860s, incomers from the mainland and New Zealand were excluded from land grants (Meikle 2014, 321–22). Terms and conditions focussed on encouraging family farmers to make a productive life in the yeoman tradition. Described as the 'agrarian ideal' in South Australia, this aim was also shared by NSW, Victoria and Queensland Governments between 1860 and 1870, who saw multiple advantages in encouraging 'the small man on the land', seeking people who would settle and be agriculturally productive. In those states, the survey came first, with road access for each individual farmer and carefully situated town reserves for provision of 'cultural, educational and religious facilities'. Michael Williams argued that intensifying land distribution hinged on 'the elusive factor of credit' (1975, 75–76).

Tasmania shared the objective but differed in the process. To select a Crown Land lot, the intending settler chose from a list of available land at the local District Surveyor's office. After visiting the desired area, the applicant settled boundaries of his selection and made application for it. Under the *Waste Lands Act* 1863 s.19, eight steps (briefly described here) had to be undertaken and complied with:

- an eligible class of land;
- written application to the office of the Department of Lands;
- selector applicant to check if officially eligible;
- deposit the survey fee of £4 or £5 for 50 acres depending on whether heavily wooded or not;
- selection is then surveyed as quickly as possible;
- when the plan is received, selector pays deposit; £12 under 1863 *Act* and £1.13.4d under the 1868 *Act;*
- selector makes contract with Commissioner;
- selector may take possession and occupy for as long as instalments are paid regularly and he fulfils residence conditions of s. 2 of the *Act;* and
- s.5 of the *Act* decreed that half the purchase money is to be reserved for roads in the vicinity after 1,000 acres have been taken up.

To keep their grant, purchasers needed to comply with the various conditions in the *Act* under which they were granted (Oughton Papers undated, UHM.).

Castra Association lands

In the case of the 50,000 acres set aside for the Castra Association, the lots were chosen mostly by Crawford acting as agent for the Indian officers who wanted to buy within those acres, but who may not have left India. There were three particular areas to which Crawford gave preference, all within the parish of Castra and subsequently surveyed by Richard Hall. These were the area of central Castra where he bought (Plan AF396/1/673), the area on the eastern side of the Leven River in what would become Gunns Plains (Plan AF396/1/671) and an area between those at Dooley's Plains (Plan AF396/1/672), hereafter referred to as 671, 672 and 673.

I examined these three original survey plans of 1870 and 1871 to discover who purchased land under the *Indian Settlers Act* or received free immigrant grants. While some marks on the plans record subsequent changes to land ownership, the original markings' clarity has made this possible. Richard Hall surveyed these three portions of the Castra Parish using numbered Field Books. After completing the survey, the plans were drafted to display common graphic features, replicating those used on the 1826 Land Commissioners' maps. Graduated grey-blue shading of contours indicates hilly ground, blue creek lines have direction arrows, flat grassy areas were outlined and slight yellow-shading marked 'Plain', patches of green tree shapes showed heavy forest and road reserves were shown in pale brown (later changes were red); in addition, Hall's recommended value was notated. Examples of these features plus purchasers' first and second names in full, and the *Act* under which the land was selected are shown in Figure 2.1.

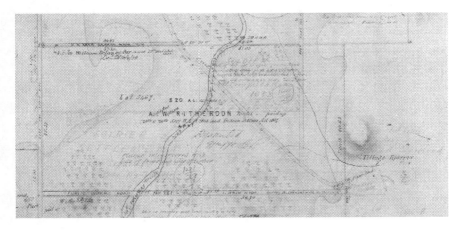

Figure 2.1 Extract showing Lot 5467 of 320 acres, Augustus William Ritherdon Purchr. paid up (*19th & 29th Sec*^{s}. *W. L. A. 1863 and Indian Settlers Act 1867*) Value £1 per acre. AF396/1/672. Tasmanian Archives.

50   *Castra land and Anglo-Indian ownership*

Beyond the inked lots, there is often pencilled notation of the neighbouring purchaser or 'Crown Land' that provides more information. In Figure 2.1, just visible in the right-hand corner is a useful note, 'Village Reserve' and (faintly) 'Lot 6026, E. H. [Ernest Henry] Crawford, 200 acres', which links the Dooley's Plains and the Castra survey plans and shows the location of the intended village of Castra. Surveyor Hall specifically noted on 671 and 672 that 'sufficient roads have been reserved'. This notation reflected the requirements of the *Waste Lands Act* No. 3, 1865 s.9 and No. 4, 1867 s.2 that, in a proclaimed agricultural area, 'when a road or tramroad was marked out, laid to or through such area, the said area shall be divided into lots respectively containing not more than One hundred and sixty acres, and having a frontage on such road'. This section responded to the difficulties experienced following the pre-emptive rights period where owners of land fronting a road prevented access to owners of land behind. Further, the amended 1867 *Act* mandated that 'before any lot is disposed of in any area, a road shall be marked or laid out through each such area to a Cross Road, or to some place of shipment or navigable river', a very clear indication that dissatisfaction in this matter had received acknowledgement and amendment.

Lot 7272 on Plan 672 shown in Figure 2.2 is the most northerly lot in Dooley's Plains. It was bought by Henry Macnee, Conductor of the Ordnance Department, Bombay, who would live out his post-Army life in the Hobart area, working as a music teacher (Macnee 1877). It was sold to William Elliot, who was farming at North Motton about 1898 or 1899, probably as an investment or for the timber. In early 1901, it was bought by James Robert Peebles, and is still owned and occupied by Peebles descendants. When Henry Macnee bought it, it was 160 acres, a rectangle 70 chains east-west and 23 and a half chains north-south, making an area of a quarter of a square mile (640 acres equalled a square mile). The solid red N-S line on the right is the route of the eventual railway, the centre line marked

Figure 2.2   Extract showing Lot 7272, 160 acres to Henry Macnee. AF396/1/672. Tasmanian Archives.

with little crosses is Hall's original road reserve closed formally by 'Gazette on 12.8.13' and the next left solid red line is the amended 'public works road'. It can be seen that the standard for a rural road reserve was one chain wide, i.e. 66 feet or 22 yards. The survey date is clear, '1st August 1870' and Hall described it thus: 'The west portion of this lot is steep and hilly, the other part is level good land. It is heavily timbered and covered with musk, dogwood and other scrub. Value £1 per acre'. The understorey plants identified were characteristic of wet sclerophyll forests. The steep hilly part is heavily shaded, and a creek (eventually called Preston Creek) runs between the contoured shading with two waterfalls marked, one inside and one just beyond the boundary. These came to be called Preston Falls and Delaney's Falls, named because William Delaney bought the adjacent lot to the west of Preston Creek, noted in pencil on the large plan.

To provide an example of other descriptions, I have chosen two other Castra lots. The first is Lot 7606 on Plan 671 shown in Figure 2.3. It was purchased by Michael Maxwell Shaw, Bombay Army retired, and Thomas Shaw, his son. This comprised 100 acres, bought under 'Immigration Certificates, 7th Sec. 31 Vic. No. 26' and had the Leven River as a boundary on the west. Hall described it as 'ten acres of inferior soil on this lot, the remainder is all good and level; all but the plain is heavily timbered. Worth £1 per acre'. Although they were both eligible under the *Indian Settlers Act*, they chose to use their Certificate entitlement as fare-paying immigrants to acquire this land. Certificates, issued to persons not receiving Land Orders, allowed 30 acres for the fare-payer, 20 acres for his wife, and ten acres for each child within 12 months of arrival, under the 19th Sec. *Waste Lands Act* 1863. In the November 1871 Valuation Roll, the Shaw's ownership had been split 70/30 (acres). Another point of interest in this extract is the survey completion date. It took about six weeks from commencement.

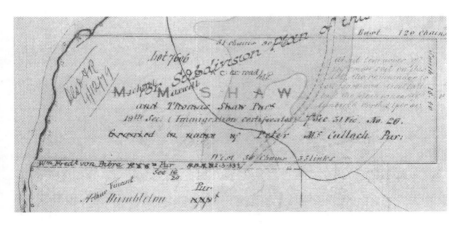

Figure 2.3 Extract showing Lot 7606. 100 acres to M. M. Shaw and T. Shaw. AF396/1/671. Tasmanian Archives.

The second lot was Lot 7902 on Plan 673, purchased by John Hatton Wilson, Civil Engineer, Jubbulpore, India. It was 320 acres, bought under the '19th Sec. W. L. A./63 and *Indian Settlers Act* 1867' and shown in Figure 2.4. It had a western boundary to the West Gawler River, and Camp Creek running north-south across the middle of the lot. One road reserve intersected diagonally then ran along the northern boundary with the next lot. Hall described it as '100 acres . . . hilly and second-class land, the remainder is . . . generally of a fair description of soil, heavily timbered and well-watered'. The northern neighbour was Andrew Crawford, on Lot 9756 of 320 acres, annotated 'sale completed on 15 November 1872'.

Typical trees identified in the descriptions were light wood, dogwood, white gum, stringybark gum, and scrub, 'ferntrees' and ferns. The size of the large trees was not specified. 'Open grass and ferny plain' is used to refer to lots on Dooley's Plains, and the steep slopes running from there down into the Leven River area are described as 'inferior or useless from being excessively steep' and heavily timbered.

Figure 2.5 of Plan 671 demonstrates the way that lands were transferred among the Anglo-Indians and, also, what happened in the case of death of the original purchaser. Lot 10093 was only 81 acres, with frontage to the river, and purchased by John Alexander Shaw, Surgeon in 4/5 Royal Artillery, Tanghoo. It was extracted from Lot 7024 that had been 515 acres, purchased (paid up) by George

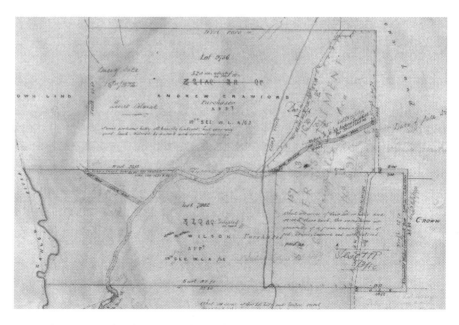

Figure 2.4 Extract showing Lot 7902 to Wilson and Lot 9756 to Crawford. AF396/1/673. Tasmanian Archives.

English, but granted to John Newbold Wilson as 320 acres, less nine acres for road reserves. All three men were buying under the 19th and 29th Secs. *Waste Lands Act* 1863 and *Indian Settlers Act* 1867.

Figure 2.5 also provides an example of transfer of ownership. Lot 7292, the most northerly lot of Plan 671, was 258 acres purchased by James Robert Fulton, but this was later granted to his wife Eliza Jane, and split into two east-west lots: one of 109 acres (less road) and 149 acres (less road) becoming Lot 11248, possibly the outcome of his application for 150 acres free land for him, his wife and ten children (Fulton 1868). Colonel Fulton commanded the 23rd Mounted Native Infantry at Bangalore when this land was selected, but he died in 1875 while on leave from India, a sad outcome for the family that waited so many years for their husband and father to pay off his land loans working in India. His family decided to settle at Leith, near Forth, in a house called Park House that was built for Eliza with pension money from the Imperial Government. His second son, also James Robert, managed his father's interests while he was based at Leith; his diaries are an interesting mixture of his work on the Leven land, managing his mining investments, personally repairing equipment and supervising his men (Fulton Junior Diaries 1882–1901). He left for Queensland in 1882 to follow up business with

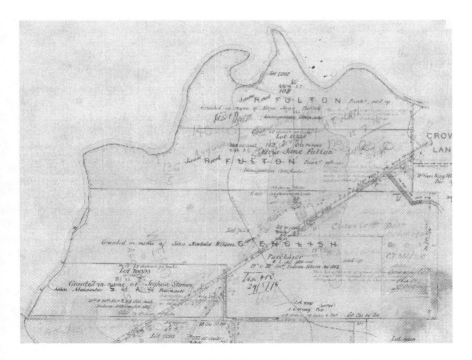

Figure 2.5 Extract of Leven Lots 10093, 7024, 7292 and 11248, various persons. AF396/1/671. Tasmanian Archives.

54 *Castra land and Anglo-Indian ownership*

relatives, so the transfer of ownership to his mother protected her local interests, and she became the grantee having lived in Tasmania longer that the mandated five years. She remained at Park House until death in 1898 (News 1898d).

There is, incidentally, a newspaper cutting from the *Government Gazette* of 21 May 1935 affixed to the Dooley's Plains Plan that announces the revoking of the original road reservation over the Greenfield Lot 7288. This demonstrates the durability of these original plans used by the Surveys and Lands Department. As such, they repay close inspection for what they disclose about the intricate details of changes in landownership and for other small surveys, such as when Richard Hall surveyed one acre of land donated to the school/hall for South Preston on 16 July 1907 by William Delaney.

Detailed information about each selection was of course important to purchasers, many of whom could not view their land in person. It also reinforced Crawford's credibility in conveying to them an appraisal of the land in question by a trusted Government official. Nevertheless, it seems clear that the information was mainly to provide the colony's Government with yardsticks for classification of land, sale price and rateable value, and enabled extrapolation of potential or expected income.

Richard Hall was especially concerned to ground the value he gave the land in a detailed description of its attributes of economic value while making the survey. In this, he was following precedents set in the 1820s by the colony's Land Commissioners, and those that informed Surveyor-General Calder's reports of the 1860s, which were used by Crawford in his 'Letter'.

The work of Tasmanian surveyors was affected by adoption of the Torrens system of land title registration, developed in the 1850s by Robert Torrens, who became Registrar-General in South Australia in 1858 (Roberts 1924, 229). Following a visit to Tasmania in 1861, he drafted the *Real Property Act* 1862, based on his enacted law in South Australia (Petrow 1992, 167–81). The system of registering title deeds had been the responsibility of the Supreme Court Clerk from 1858, but this 'simple and cheap' system attracted exuberant press support, the *Examiner* telling its readers of its great benefits in landed property dealings, though Petrow showed that opinion was divided between northern and southern lawyers (News 1862, 180–91). Even so, the *Act* took effect from 30 June 1862, and the Launceston Agent was Ronald C. Gunn, the highly regarded public servant. The obvious advantage to surveyors was the registration of land based on boundary marks, the absence of which in the past had caused problems. Another change under this *Act* was that all land transactions were to be supported by a certified surveyor's diagram (Jones 1989, 165).

From 1870, standards of qualifications and regulation over produced work demanded tighter professional control, and Hall was chosen as one of four members of the new Board of examiners in 1883. In this year, surveying and public works became two parts of the Department of Lands and Works under a Minister, and in 1884 Charles Sprent (whose name was later given to the expanding Castra village centre just on the northern Parish boundary) became Deputy Surveyor-General. Sprent was responsible for *The Crown Lands Guide* published under Ministerial authority and available through booksellers and Lands offices in May 1884 (News 1884a). He supported his 'New Regulations' for surveyor's guidance and use by the general public. The professionalisation of land surveyors raised their status and contributed to probity, after they were disallowed from accepting private work while Government employees (Jones, 172, 176, 178; News 1884a; Brown 1980, 191–92).

Rigour of accurate surveys for purchasers of small lots was even more important than for pastoralists whose operations ranged widely. The very nature of farming on small acreages depended on collaboration and good neighbourliness, so any form of dispute over fences or boundaries would have been socially unproductive. The onus was on selectors to conform to boundaries, and it was not until 1908 that Parliament formalised legal rights and responsibilities in the *Boundary Fences Act* 40 of 1908. Professional survey back-up staff, with computation, plotting and drafting skills (all compulsory examinable subjects), and an inspection regime proved their value, particularly when land transactions continued to be a critical part of Government activities and revenue-raising (Jones, 176, 178). Figure 2.6 is an example of this intricate attention to detail. It displays a typical

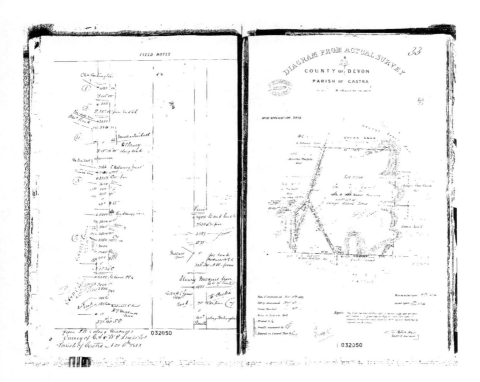

Figure 2.6 Survey Diagram, 6 November 1883.

Source: Base image reproduced with permission of TASMAP (www.tasmap.tas.gov.au) ©State of Tasmania.

56 *Castra land and Anglo-Indian ownership*

two-page Diagram of Survey. Field notes started at the bottom of the page and made associations with landmarks and other alienated lots. The right-hand section is the plan identifying intersections with neighbours. The fractional number 26/33 is the filing system; the upper number is the field book page, the lower is the specific survey.

At the bottom of the plan can be seen the new system in action – actual dates for: the date of instruction; survey commenced; survey finished; plotted by; finally examined; and entered on general plan. The 'Report' is couched in similar terms to those we examined earlier and relates to soil, topography and vegetation. George Alfred Lewis was the original grantee of this 200-acre lot in Preston.

Another occasion illustrating the robustness of the Government concept of 'free selection' occupied Deputy Surveyor-General Edward Albert Counsel (appointed in 1889) at the end of the century. This is clear in his letter concerning claims made by the President of the Surveyor's professional organisation in his annual address. President Fincham claimed 'very serious past (and perhaps continuing) waste of money in road locations in newly settled areas' and the 'system of laying roads around square boundaries of surveyed towns' (Fincham 1898). Counsel's written rejoinder was published in *The Surveyor*, May 1898, 235. He was taking issue with two items – road surveys and town planning – that reflected badly on the administration of the Crown Lands Department. He thought it 'a fine idea' to lay out roads before settlement to avoid the need to realign, but that was against the Government's free selection policy. The issue of town boundary roads took no account of the topographical constraints in Tasmania that often made this impractical, in contrast to practices in other colonies, and justified his adherence to the rule that no gradients in excess of 1 in 12 were to be planned. Straight boundary roads were only laid out after the local District Surveyor reported agreement.

Investigation of valuation rolls for Anglo-Indian selections

What does an investigation of the valuation rolls reveal about how long the Anglo-Indian purchasers kept their selections? Is there any indication of the level of development undertaken before they were sold or of more land nearby being available for settlement to settlers who would start actively to farm?

To answer these questions, I used Crawford's list of 52 purchasers to extract names of Anglo-Indian landowners who were subject to payment of Government taxes (rates) based on various rateable categories. The selected valuation rolls for the Castra Parish were for the years 1871(2), 1872, 1878, 1880, 1881, 1882, 1883, 1886, 1890 and 1895 (*Hobart Town Gazette*). Each entry has two columns about people, one identifies the Proprietor (or owner) and the other identifies the Occupier (or tenant/lessee). It is obvious if they are the same person. Most properties were categorised initially as 'land', but by 1878, this changed to 'unimproved land', and then any improvements such as 'hut and land' or 'cottage and land' or

Castra land and Anglo-Indian ownership   57

'cottage and farm' were listed. Improved land attracted a higher taxable value (TV); for example, in 1878:

Unimproved land	320 acres	TV £10
Cottage and land (non-resident)	320 acres	TV £13
Cottage and farm (resident)	320 acres	TV £12

I followed the entries for Anglo-Indian purchasers over the years noted earlier. The results from this research confound the myth of failure. Eleven of the original 52 landowners appearing on the rolls for 1871 were still there on the 1895 roll, that is, 24 years later. Another four of them owned the land for 19 years, four for 15, one for ten and one for nine years. Arthur Dumbleton is a further example: he started in 1871 with 210 acres, until about 1879 when he sold 200 acres, and kept the remainder unimproved until 1895, retaining interest in his Leven riverfront lot in Gunns Plains for 20 years from his various homes east of the Mersey (perhaps it was a summer picnic/fishing spot). A total of 22 Anglo-Indian purchasers kept their land and paid their dues on it for a substantial period by any standard. And when the other 30 owners decided to sell after fewer years, it opened up the possibility of access for other settlers with farming and timber-getting in mind. From these results, we can see yet another way that Castra was not a 'utopian community' because there was no restriction on who could buy the Anglo-Indian lots once they were put up for sale.

Some settled on the land quickly. An original from 1871, General G.A. Fulton had established by 1878 his farm and cottage called Hielands, no doubt echoing his Scottish origins. He resided there until 1883, when he rented to George Nichols until 1886 and moved to Forth to probably retire. Colonel Crawford moved into Deyrah, his Castra house and farm in 1881 (according to the official record), and he also purchased on behalf of the Castra Association 200 acres in 1886 that were still attracting taxes in 1895. Colonel Charles Heathcote held his land in Upper Castra from 1872 and built a house that he occupied until 1895, when the property was rented to John Wright, the forerunner of a significant local family. Henry Macnee built a hut with a brick chimney on his block, and in one year's roll, he was recorded as resident in Leven, Ulverstone's early name. Once he found work in Hobart, perhaps it was used for holidays, but it provided the first shelter for the Peebles family later.

One of the younger Anglo-Indian officers, Colonel Henry Watts Stockley, Crawford's northerly neighbour, was committed to settling in Castra; he bought 320 acres in 1878, by 1883 he had built a house, called his property Thatcham, after a small town three miles from Newbery, Berkshire UK, and purchased a further 160 acres of unimproved land. This last was let go by 1890, but another 49 acres were added to his estate. In 1895, he rented both Thatcham and the 49 acres to James Robertson, who became the occupier. Robertson operated the farm as a dairy farm, producing milk for the Sprent creamery, then making cheese for the west coast demand, as he continued to improve land and new buildings, achievements that attracted praise from a newspaper correspondent in 1898 (News

58 Castra land and Anglo-Indian ownership

1898c). Stockley still owned the 369 acres 30 years later when it was offered to the Closer Settlement Board in 1908 and 1909 (see Chapter 4).

Colonel Henry Lionel Charles Bernard bought by 1878 a 320-acre lot on which he had a 'cottage and barns' called Dunley, after a small village in the Malvern Hills, Worcestershire UK. This was rented for a while to George Nichols and reoccupied by him in 1886 until 1895. Meanwhile, his two sons, Henry Lionel Charles Junior and George Claude Bernard bought their own unimproved lots of 132 and 50 acres, respectively, in 1883, and George added 214 acres in 1895. Unfortunately, the valuation rolls of this era do not provide accurate locations, so one cannot tell if those purchases were adjacent to or even the same as their father's land, as the last purchase may have been, only that they were in the same parish. The Colonel, whose address for rates notices over some years was in New Town (Hobart), died in 1911 and his obituary pointed to his value to Tasmania because he initiated and established a corps of country rifle clubs at the invitation of the Tasmanian Government and commanded the state's reserve force until his retirement in 1888 (News 1911d).

Colonel John Hutton Wilson bought in 1871 320 acres and arrived in 1882 from India. This passed to his wife and was sold between 1890 and 1895. Their fourth child of six, John Newbold Wilson, mentioned earlier, bought his own 320 acres in Gunns Plains in 1880 and still owned that lot unimproved (though he may have used it or let it in a way that did not attract higher rates) in 1895, while based in Penguin with his mother. By 1898, he was having sawn timber harvested by a Sheffield contractor for building with and was occupying a three-roomed hut 'built since 1892 or 1893' and farming 'in a small way', potatoes, mangolds, swedes, beetroots and carrots and had cut 15 tons of oat hay (News 1898c). This is clearly another instance of successful outcome for an Anglo-Indian in yeoman farming.

Two of the originals, Robert Cameron Henchy and James Henkel, lived locally (Ulverstone and West Devonport); both kept, but had not improved, their lands by 1895. Grazing or timber harvesting themselves or by sub-letting would have been unlikely to attract a category of 'improved' but may have yielded income to off-set the taxes.

The final category of long-term owners is those who appear not to have come to Tasmania, because Colonel Crawford was recorded each time as their agent. These were John Henry Bedford, Henry Evelyn Coningham, Mrs Mary Alice Mead, the widow of Colonel Mead, and Lieutenant-Colonel D. Grant. They may also have come to a different part of Tasmania and were happy for Crawford to continue as their local agent. These absentee owners are the evidence relied upon by those who have suggested that the Castra Association was a failure (Stilwell 1992; Metcalf 2008b; Cornish 1880, 328). But investigation of the valuation rolls not only reveals extended ownership, but also that, for some fathers, Crawford's original concept of establishing a good life and a future for their sons, albeit with hard toil, became a reality. The Bernard and Wilson family have already been mentioned. Andrew and Matilda Crawford had a large family, only two of whom were daughters. They brought six children with them from England and two more

Castra land and Anglo-Indian ownership 59

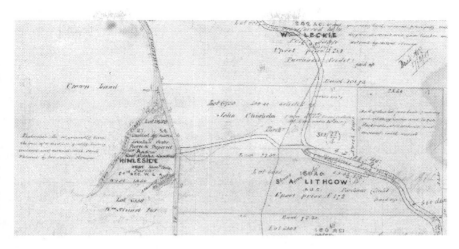

Figure 2.7 Extract. Robert St. John Crawford, Lot 9489, 27 acres. See also Leckie and Lithgow Lots. AF396/1/676, 1872. Tasmanian Archives.

sons were born in Tasmania (Crawford 1877b). Hardly surprising, then, that the Crawfords were so concerned in the 1860s with the need to set up their own sons and the sons of Crawford's associates for a good, if not wealthy, life as self-sufficient yeoman farmers.

There is evidence of Crawford's actions in regard to his own sons. As early as 1878, in Ernest Henry Kinleside's twenty-first year, 200 acres were bought in his name (noted on Figure 2.1). In 1890, Alexander, then 30 years old, acquired 192 acres plus 19 acres from Mrs Wilson, on which, in 1898, he was profitably fattening sheep and cattle and growing cocksfoot grass for seed (News 1898c). Also in 1890, Hugh, then 23, bought 30 acres; their father bought another 320 acres too (which may have been either Ritherdon's or MacGregor's Anglo-Indian lots). The 1872 Survey Plan for southerly North Motton lots in Figure 2.7 shows land in the diagonal junction of the Gunns Plains Road with what is shown even then as the 'road from Castra to Ulverstone' (AF396/1/676). This 27-acre Lot 9489 was granted under a Location Order to Andrew Kinleside under the *Immigration Act* 1867, s.7, then his name was deleted to show Robert St. John Crawford, granted under an Immigration Certificate (Crowley 1954, 104). There must have been a (family/friendship) connection between Crawford and Kinleside since Ernest was given his name. Robert's marriage to Helena Aitkenhead of a Devonport family was noted in the newspaper at New Year 1889 (News 1889a) and they remained living locally.

Also on this Plan are two more Anglo-Indian purchasers: Lieutenant-Colonel William Leckie, Lot 6007, 242 acres (Upset price £254, dated February 1881); and Surgeon Stewart Aaron Lithgow, 160 acres (Auction price £172, bought in April 1873) who were not included in the valuation roll research. Crawford claimed that he had encouraged the sale of these lots following his active

60   *Castra land and Anglo-Indian ownership*

representation over the improvement of the road from Ulverstone to North Motton that opened up interest in West Castra lands. The improvement possibly stemmed from a petition tabled by Mr Braddon in Parliament in 1880 on behalf of 158 'landed proprietors and residents of East and West Castra and Old Gawler Roads and vicinity thereof' (JPPP, Vol. XXXIX, 1880, No. 68).

Another value of close analysis of these valuation rolls is to gauge the point at which pressure for smaller lots of land with agricultural potential from yeoman farmers began to occur. Settlement was starting to fill up the available countryside in areas all along the North-West of Tasmania and increased demand came from both tenants anxious to become freeholders and established farmers to expand. As the Castra data clearly illustrates, from 1884 to 1886 the demand for land rose in the Parish with 36 new purchasers plus Colonel Crawford's 200 acres for the Association. The lots varied from 30 acres to just around 100 acres with the exception of W.B. Smith of Sassafras (224 acres) and E.T. Shadbolt, who occupied his 315 Castra acres. Shadbolt's farm and progress were described in 1889 by an unnamed newspaper correspondent – 'additions to the dwelling house', and 'three years ago planted six acres of apple trees' now beginning to fruit. His farm was 1,300 feet above sea level, 'with a fine view of the estate of Colonel Crawford and Sons, those *persevering pioneers* of west Upper Castra' (my emphasis). He also mentioned J. Wright leasing General Heathcote's estate (News 1894b). Two of the largest lots, 101 and 99 acres, were selected west of Dooley's Plains on a road eventually carrying their name by brothers Samuel and Alfred Reid, starting an unbroken line of ownership to the present day.

Surviving data for 1890 shows a further 68 new owners were added, but by this time there was much more variation in the size of the lots, mostly under 100 acres. What is also noticeable is the location of the owners that ranged from as distant as Sassafras, Devonport and Northdown, and as close as Abbotsham, Sprent, Gawler and North Motton. This confirms that the Castra area had become recognised by farming folk for its potential, both for timber resources on unimproved land and for subsequent cropping on deep red soils. For distant buyers, the pattern of renting to tenants as a means of clearing unimproved land had been practiced since the 1850s, and Castra Parish lands offered attractive means of diversification and the expansion of holdings when no closer land was available.

In 1890, the important general storekeeping business, Messrs G. and A. Ellis, based in Ulverstone and eventually Sprent and Preston, appears as owner of 15 lots, many of which are 50 or fewer acres. Their stores sold goods essential for farmers who could run up debt against future income. This may mark the time the Ellis's started taking land in lieu of payments from people who could not afford to repay, a well-known practice among local residents (Ken Brown 2018). But the Ellis's also owned three large lots in Gunns Plains, 320, 270 and 100 acres, which were more likely business investment properties, that may have been tenanted and supplied products to their stores.

The final year, 1895, of the data investigated here shows a continuation of the pattern of purchasers for small acreages, and four small ten-acre lots were sold in the Crawford township-reserve near the northern parish boundary towards Sprent.

Castra land and Anglo-Indian ownership 61

However, five Anglo-Indian lots of 320 acres had changed hands since 1890. Two of them had houses and farms already; one in Dooley's Plains was owned by William Lade of Scottsdale but rented to Colonel Crawford, perhaps for adult sons working the farms. Two others had owners at Forth and Latrobe and were unoccupied. Altogether there were another 51 new owners, and 19 of these had land just either side of 50 acres, which was still a realistic size to create a self-supporting mixed farm for a family. This was just as Dr Arthur Young, the Anglo-Indian who settled in Torquay, had predicted in his letter to Castra & Co., Bombay, in 1872, quoting a Mr Watson:

> With a small farm of 40 or 50 acres, an income which in England would give a man with a family the barest subsistence, will here afford all the necessities of life in abundance, with a healthful, and to those fond of agricultural pursuits, an interesting occupation. . . . Mr Watson says, now he knows the ways of the country, he finds living costs next to nothing.
>
> (Young 1872)

Later this was endorsed by J.R. Scott, writing in 1876 as 'Anglo-Indian', to the *Times of India* recommending to other Indian officers that the purchase of a 'farm of, say, one hundred or fifty acres . . . [will be] quite large enough to begin with'. He was enthusiastic enough to include a fine description of the equable climate and copied a table of the mean temperature at Hobart and five other global centres on similar latitude to back up his remarks. He reminded readers of the value of immigration certificates too.

Small farms set the pattern for the expansion of settlement and development of mixed cropping and livestock during the next few decades, which had ramifications for the newly developing community. The increasing numbers of large families among the settlers fuelled demands for institutions like churches, schools and post offices. It also put pressure on the Government to provide all-weather roads with metalled surfaces better suited to horses moving goods to market in the increasing farm traffic.

To conclude, the evidence from valuation rolls confirms that, for the Anglo-Indians who actually came to Tasmania and took possession of the land set aside on their behalf, some of Colonel Crawford's vision for them came true. As he had advised, they came to a beautiful part of Tasmania, blessed with good soils and pleasant climate. Those who persevered, as he did through the strictures of inadequate road development caused by the financial doldrums of the 1870s, became part of the expansion and development of agriculture and an increasing demand for agricultural land. The valuation rolls bear that out. Some of those families, through their sons (and probably daughters, too, through marriages), started dynasties, descendants from which became part of the fabric of Tasmania, and they had opportunity for active roles and financial comfort in the community. When Crawford died in 1899, he had witnessed many changes since 1865 and had actively championed the cause of development for the part of Tasmania he loved. His obituary writer claimed he was the only Anglo-Indian left at

62 *Castra land and Anglo-Indian ownership*

Castra, which was not true – he obviously disregarded Crawford's and others' adult sons as Anglo-Indians (News 1899a). Fenton described Crawford as 'a gentleman worthy of all praise for the great good he has done for West Devon as a pioneer in the backwoods' (Fenton 1891). The *North West Post* of 9 February 1899, 2, described him as 'the very type and model of an English gentleman and soldier'. He was not without neighbours or friends who regarded him highly. He was happy with his 'comfortable' life, 'far happier and profitably employed' creating a mixed farm in a parkland setting, the planted legacy of which we see in Figure 2.7, than would have ever been possible in England. Alexander was farming a 200-acre estate near his father (Lot 11428). Ernest's 200-acre farm was nearby probably worked with the other farms (Lot 6026, both gazetted 18 May 1877 on AF819/1/45). Cheese-making was a good alternative when poor roads precluded fast access to the coast and Alexander had enjoyed learning cheese-making and accreditation from Victorian dairy expert McCormick, under the auspices of the Council of Agriculture. G. and A. Ellis sent a sample of 'Deyrah Cheddar' to the *Mercury* in Hobart, publicised as 'manufactured by Alexander Miller Crawford of Deyrah, Castra, intended to meet the requirements of those who prefer a small, good cheese made from milk mixed with cream from the previous setting' (News 1894a). His father's vision and farm had acted as a springboard for his sons' progress just as he had hoped.

This chapter has assessed the contribution to settlement by the original Anglo-Indians through the analysis of survey plans and valuation rolls over two decades. The evidence they provide of duration of ownership challenges the received verdict that the venture can be considered a 'failure'. Looking beyond the Crawford family, other families with connections, sons who went farming and other Devon lands purchased not far from Castra, as in North Motton and Sprent, this is all evidence of durable success in the face of huge access difficulties that only started to improve in the last two decades before Federation. Historians have noted that elders of pastoralist families who had held positions of high political and social power were almost all gone by the 1880s (Reynolds 1969a). This was also true for older Anglo-Indians like Crawford himself. The field was open for smaller mixed farming settlement emphasising the yeoman ideal. The scene is set to meet families who created the Preston Castra community and their aspirations to follow yeoman farming on their new selections.

3 Development of Castra farms and institutions 1880–1910

The advantages of yeoman characteristics in settlers in the North-West forested areas were reinforced by the small farmers who settled in Castra from the 1880s, when many Anglo-Indian properties were changing hands. The lives of the farms and families that grew on them over several generations demonstrate the traditional model of the yeoman ideal in self-sustaining family farming. The valuation rolls of 1886 and 1890 disclosed that 114 new selectors took up Castra land of between 30 and 100 acres. As well as established properties being bought, selection continued to fill the Crown Land gaps into the early twentieth century. In 1899, for example, Alfred T. Pillinger, the Crown Lands Commissioner, advertised Crown Land lots in Devon for sale offering credit of a quarter of the price, permitted under the *Crown Lands Amendment Act* 1895 Ss. 6–7. Indicative of small lots available locally were 29 acres 1st class rural land for £22; 18 acres Leven Town reserve (southern Motton) for £25; and 9 acres Crawford Town reserve fronting Ulverstone main road for £15, all more directed to attract rural labouring families rather than farmers (News 1899b).

New settlers to the northern area called Preston came from the migrant generation of farmers who had selected land during the 1850s and 1860s in the Leven (Ulverstone) hinterland at Gawler, North Motton and along the Plank Road towards Sprent. Young adult members of their large families – single men and young couples – were in the 1880s vanguard, but gradually word spread about opportunities through established agricultural areas in the eastern reaches of Devon around Sassafras, where the expansionist settlement pattern had been established three decades earlier. There, the pioneer frontier had offered opportunity to enterprising men and allowed 'more ruthless, more able colonists to create small but prosperous estates' that are discussed more later in this chapter (Roberts 1977, 171).

The Anglo-Indian lots in Dooley's Plains appeared large enough to present new opportunities for mature farmers with years of experience and family labour to help them, and potential land for their maturing sons. Three families in this group were the Peebles family, the Johnson family and the Brown family, whose patriarchs, James Robert Peebles, Henry Johnson and Arthur William Brown, arrived in Castra in the first decade of the twentieth century. Because their descendants have remained established and farming to 2021 in Preston, the history of these families grounds my analysis of the persistence of yeomanry

DOI: 10.4324/9781003229841-4

64 *Castra farms and institutions 1880–1910*

characteristics over the century. What was the background of these three men? Where and how did they gain their farming experience? And what was their motivation in coming to this area of relatively little cleared land with the prospect of years of hard toil ahead?

To answer these questions, a good place to start is with the commission agents who handled farm listings. J. Sturzaker's Castra land agency advertised farms and other properties for sale or rent in 1887 (News 1887c). In Leven, Robert Robson advertised 'farms of all descriptions for sale' in 1887, having established his business as early as 1877 (News 1887a). Two Crawford Brothers operated the Ulverstone Land and Commission Agency in 1884 and 1885; by 1887, they had two sites as general storekeepers and commission agents, in Ulverstone and Redbourne, their farm on the Castra Road (News 1884b, 1885, 1887f). A new agency, C.A. Jarvis & Co., opened in 1887 in Ulverstone's main street for auctioneering and land commissions (News 1887e).

Land agents naturally made extensive use of newspaper advertising. For decades, a variety of newspapers were published across Tasmania, some three times a week and others weekly. Their viability was determined by readers' interest in advertisement pages, as well as news content and being reasonably priced. For example, the weekly *Tasmanian*, published on a Saturday in Launceston, was sixpence in the late 1880s, but reduced to threepence in 1895, and when the *North Western Advocate* became daily, it cost a penny. Parliamentary proceedings were published from 1860 in the Hobart-based *Mercury*. The main northern paper, the *Examiner*, started from 1842 as a weekly, then tri-weekly until 1877 when it became daily; the same publishers created the *Weekly Courier* from 1901 that carried a glossy insert filled with pictures of people and events that remain a wonderful fully digitised historical record of early twentieth century Tasmania (TA). *The Tasmanian* carried, amongst other content of general and farming relevance, parliamentary proceedings sent by electric telegraph, allowing northern residents to keep track of their local members' contributions. Launceston also had the *Cornwall Chronicle* from 1835 to 1880 and the *Daily Telegraph* from 1883 and in Formby (later Devonport) the *North West Post* was published from 1887 to 1916; the *North Western Advocate and the Emu Bay Times (NWAEBT)* started tri-weekly then daily from West Devonport in 1899; the West had the *Zeehan and Dundas Herald* from 1890 to 1922, which catered to mining interests (see more in Russell et al. 2009; Tasmania 269–74, 316). Throughout Tasmania, newspapers were available through local stores and post offices in established and fledgling communities such as those in the North-West. Newspapers had a wide readership because public schooling expanded following the passing of the *Public Schools Act* in 1868. The focus on basic reading and writing in schools, plus encouragement from Protestant churches and Sunday schools, meant that literacy was widespread (Jackson 1987, 11; see Claydon 2019).

A regular feature in North-West newspapers was its reportage of agricultural progress in hinterland districts, often as substantial farm-by-farm articles by 'travelling representatives', often anonymous, but the *NWAEBT* published Richard Hilder's journeys in 1908. One featured properties and activity along Castra Road

Castra farms and institutions 1880–1910 65

through Abbotsham, Spalford and Sprent and on to Central Castra via Colonel Crawford's Deyrah and to Alex Crawford's farm further south (News 1898c). Historians of the colonial period onwards identified that clippings were enclosed with letters to relatives and friends located overseas or on the mainland, either as encouragement to come or return to Tasmania, and to sustain distant connections. In Britain, the *Manchester Weekly Times* was open to printing letters from Tasmanians about life here and published up-dates about migration to Tasmania, like costs, terms and legal changes (News 1854a, 1866d, 1867a). Rising literacy among British working people from 1870 extended their aspirations and widened horizons especially about migration (Belich 2009, 47, 50; Newby 1987, 120–21, 135).

Newspapers were attractive for both Tasmanian and inter-colonial Government advertisers, such as land advertised by the South Australian Crown Lands Commissioner (News 1888b). International news, market prices and shipping movements were valued content. Land agents like Robson, the Crawfords and Jarvis & Co. kept standing advertisements with the *Launceston Examiner* in 1887, but were keen to move their advertising as more locally based newspapers opened. When the *North West Post* started in 1887, the Crawfords transferred their advertising to it, offering their services as a butchery and cash buyers of fat cattle and sheep. Ulverstone's value to its hinterland consumers is evidenced in these advertisements of diverse services.

The 1880s northern Castra settlers were drawn to unalienated land by considering the soil colour, the type of scrub and trees and its access to water, before they started the 'painful process of clearing by axe', and battling forest and 'insidious bracken' using fire (Harper 1954, 185). Many of them chose land that shared a boundary with family members, like three brothers, William, James and George Lewis, because of collaborative advantages. However, purchasers in the early 1900s of the larger southerly lots surveyed in 1870 and 1871 were more separated from neighbours. This was characteristic of frontier settlements, where individual settlers were isolated until others arrived to establish denser distribution, but it was also more usual in Ireland, Scotland and Wales (Newby 1987, 142). Eventually these consolidated as 'open' villages, forming clusters around crossroads or along a main through-road (Hudson 1969, 366, 381). Despite the practice of colonial surveyors setting aside village/town reserves, as Richard Hall did for Castra, Leven and Crawford, these were not always suited to experience on the ground. Both Sassafras and Preston share the fact that their villages were unplanned, simply developing as areas were populated and in response to residents' needs – Sassafras from the late 1860s and Preston 30 years later (Friends 1988, 45). This feature of Preston's development would later have important implications for the siting of community assets and infrastructure.

Agricultural heritage and expertise

The first thing the three families had in common was agricultural inheritance brought from yeoman farming areas of Britain. Mixed farming, that is, a

66 Castra farms and institutions 1880–1910

combination of cropping and livestock, had been practised successfully in the eastern part of Tasmania's Devon County since European settlement began in the 1840s in lightly wooded coastal areas from Port Sorell to Wesley Vale and North-down (Ramsay 1980, 45–55). As settlers selected further inland and started clear-ing forest around Thirlstane, Green Creek and Sassafras – either selling or using the timber felled – they continued mixed farming based on their previous experi-ences near Deloraine. There, farming families had been in that part of northern Tasmania long enough to understand climatic conditions, potential of the soils in heavily timbered land and regularity of higher rainfall.

Those new areas were nearer the coast and Port Sorell on the Rubicon River, which attracted Deloraine land owners because they needed access to sea trans-port to expand their own activities, and tenant farmers were looking for land owned by absentee landowners, some of whom had secured large lots under the pre-emptive rights; for example, brothers Henry and George Rockliff bought their first 500 acres at Sassafras (Friends 1988, 9; Fenton 1891, 112).

This coast-ward movement extended the Deloraine settlement system based upon a few freehold farmers and many more tenant farmers (Breen 1990, 25–26). For example, the valuation rolls for Sassafras, Forraberry Parish, show that one selector, Robert Beveridge, bought 640 acres to occupy in 1859. Fifteen months later it was a farm called Falkirk after his home in Scotland; by 1861, he had let to other Scots; 80 acres to Alexander Mong and 60 acres to Robert Peebles, the original migrant patriarch of one of the families investigated here (*HTG* 1859, 1860, 1861). Henry Rockliff was another. He had been the manager for his rela-tive, Henry Reed at Wesley Dale, Chudleigh (near Deloraine). He bought lots of 100, 404 and 202 acres in 1860, and within nine months, owned a further 490 acres, occupied by six tenants, James Foster, Patrick Glarman, Henry Gor-don, Andrew Moatt, Edward Rouden and John Shaw, with houses on acreages, four on 100 acres, one on 60 acres and the sixth on 30 acres. By 1864, Henry Rockliff brought his large family to the farm he called Skelbrook, eventually developing a flour mill there, and becoming a prominent farmer and landlord in the district (Friends 1988, 39, 122). Rockliff and his two sons developed his farms using several employed labourers living on site, like Samuel Skemp who, in 1882, went to work for him for 'ten bob a week and keep' for a year to 'learn the ropes' while waiting for his brother to join him from Britain to start out on their own (Skemp 1952, 28). By 1870, Rockliff owned a steam threshing plant that travelled around with additional seasonal labour, some of whom were added to the permanent workforce to continue the clearing of trees and stumps. The Port Sorell Collector reported that the plant's 'usefulness is very much limited' because poor district roads often made moving it impossible (Skemp 1952, 43; *Statistics of Tasmania, 1870*).

Development depended upon entrepreneurial men like the Rockliffs, father and sons, who exploited opportunities to expand their land holdings with the help of labour from immigrants and tenant farmers, whose work on the land benefitted them in the long term. One notable example was the 1700-acre Thirlstane estate of William Sams that had a succession of lessees (Ramsay, 52–53). This pattern

Castra farms and institutions 1880–1910   67

echoed the three-deck (or Newby's tripartite) social and structural changes in agricultural England occurring from the mid-eighteenth-century (Mathias 1969; see also Newby 1987). British freehold yeoman farmers had already been the middle rank of rural families for over a century, sometimes acting as stewards for large estates while working their own mixed farms (Beckett 1977; Rollison 1992). Under this developing class structure, landowners concentrated on management and were less involved with hands-on farming. They sought the best rent from the ablest men of skill and capital, so their land had to be attractive to the best class of farmers (Newby 1987). Yeoman tenant farmers were understood as 'the true entrepreneurs' controlling 'the most productive unit of capitalist enterprise, the farm' (Beckett 1977, 573). In England, good tenants were a favoured category because their capital was not tied up in land so they withstood recessionary times, and they often expanded through 'commercial acumen' and advantageous marriages (Newby, 17). Small wonder that settlement histories of the United States, Canada, New Zealand and colonial Australia highlight how desirable this immigrant class was – entrepreneurial yeoman farmers with skills, initiative and finance (Dawson and Younge 1940, 11–14; Arnold 1994, 118; McIntyre and Gardner 1971; Woods 1822; Raby 1996; Waterson 1968; Tonts 2002; Dingle 1984).

'Labouring peasantry', the lowest level of the tripartite system, provided manual labour, supported by wages, whether daily or annually hired, but prey to the precarious nature of farming work, accompanied by difficult living and working conditions and often poverty that prevailed longer in Ireland, Wales and the Scottish Highland areas (Mathias 1969, 61; Newby, 17). Women and children were also part of this labouring strata as key field workers, usually in seasonal aspects like harvesting and gleaning, and inside workers as dairymaids and domestic servants (Valenze 1991, 143; Kitteringham 1975, 73–138). Snell argued that they bore the brunt of structural changes that drove women and children into gang work to make up for reduced work, wages and rising rents from the 1830s (1985, 124–25, 155–59). They were the source of emigrants who were assisted or bonded to cater to the colonial need for farm labourers, dairymaids and domestic servants (Haines 1997, 23).

Across this structural spectrum, exposure to prospects opening up in the colonies came via the 'traffic in goods, people and ideas' from relatives or the popular press, and Newby argued that migration was more influential in raising living standards of farm workers than local unionism (135). Not only landless people or those fearing 'encroaching poverty' or loss of status due to mechanisation of rural trades or artisanal skills were drawn to the possibilities, but also those with accumulated means and expertises (Rollison 1992, 7, 11; Breen 1990; Haines, 21).

British agriculture had been adjusting to agrarian capitalism and rationalising to become more productive commercially to cater for expanding urban markets, accompanied by a slow trend towards larger farms (Williams 1973, 185). Many immigrants to Sassafras from rural arable regions of Scotland, including Robert Peebles, Robert Beveridge, Alexander Mong and Alexander Robertson, another early Sassafras pioneer, would have experienced these changes to agricultural production. They were well advanced in the Scottish Lothians and Perthshire by

68 *Castra farms and institutions 1880–1910*

the 1850s, where strategies to maintain soil fertility were improving. One was planting a ley, a pasture sown and ploughed in to grow a crop, on a significant proportion of arable land (Henzell 2007, 4). Large farms in these regions 'achieved the highest standard of mixed farming', while Scottish farming as a whole 'provided excellent training for those intending to settle in new countries of the world' (Symon 1859, 162). Many early Scots settlers attracted favourable mention by Roderic O'Connor, one of the VDL Land Commissioners in 1826 to 1828, for quality improvements, imported stock and farming proficiency, as well as residing on the farm and engaging in tillage as against pastoralism (Macmillan 1967, 124–25). In central Scotland, there was well distributed use of water-powered threshing mills, cornmills and sawmills, often using the same stream. They enhanced productivity while relieving horses of monotonous work. Extra threshing mills offered farmers multiple gains (Dallas 1970, 134–37).

Henry Rockliff and his brothers George, Francis and John, originated from Kirk Smeaton, in Yorkshire's West Riding (Ramsay 1980, 56–58). Echoing the changes in Lowland Scottish agriculture, the evolution of changing practices in that area was reflected in these men's expertise and experiences. Yeoman farmers were men of high status (Beckett 1977, 567–81). Landownership was part of that *cachet*, the key to supremacy of the 'natural order' in rural society. Roberts observed that, in Britain, although capital was important, 'land has always been the source of economic and political power' (1977, 197).

Further south in England, changes taking place were also important for productivity. The rotational practices of mixed farmers referred to usually as the 'Norfolk four-course sequence' (wheat, turnips, barley and red clover) provided better livestock food supply and nitrogen-fixing legumes that improved soil fertility. Fertilising fields with accumulated manure from over-wintering in yards and sheds recycled nutrients from grazed fodder crops (Henzell, 3–4). English Protestant gentry spread these ideas across the Irish Sea as landlords of Irish estates, thus spreading knowledge to the labouring peasants there (Kee 1972, 152–53, 396).

Experience of these agricultural practices and crops brought by immigrants from Norfolk, Scotland and Ireland, who arrived in Devon, Tasmania from the 1850s onwards, spearheaded their adoption in the colony. Immigrants were engaged for mixed farming operations around Sassafras, or as tenant farmers in the Forth and Don areas near Devonport. Their experience with well-established British practices was 'an invaluable part of the colonial inheritance' and enabled farmers to adapt to farming realities of soils and climate and cope with 'trials and tribulations' in their new environments (Henzell, ix). Around Deloraine and in the North-West, rotation was the trend where soils were suitable for grain and (winter-grown) root crops, and it suited small, previously heavily timbered farms. The move away from fallow land was evident in Deloraine (Easteal 1971, 143–45). An additional outstanding advantage North-West immigrant settlers had was familiarity with a seasonal climate more favourable to winter cropping than Britain that required less adaptation than northerly mainland colonies, where droughts, semi-arid or tropical conditions often prevailed (Jones 2017).

As British farms consolidated, smaller landowners or tenant farmers could sell up and migrate with capital to invest in Tasmania's relatively cheap land. It also provided farmer entrepreneurs around Sassafras with a model for consolidation. This is illustrated by several Sassafras examples. The Norfolk-born William Howard cleared his own 200-acre lot while continuing his lease on another. In western Sassafras, Irish-born Michael and Patrick Roche purchased several lots between 15 and 90 acres after arriving in 1843, while Patrick Pettit from Longford, Ireland acquired two small lots, 50 and 58 acres, apart from each other, which he farmed for 25 years surrounded by neighbours all with small 50-acre farms (Friends 1988, 36–37). By 1880, newly elected Edward Braddon MHA was touting Devon as the 'first agricultural district in the colony' when supporting road expenditure to farms (Braddon 1880 in HAJ Vol. XXXIX, No. 68). Larger landowners continued to need labourers and families who would not be enticed away by mining and who might become good tenants for their expanding estates. One solution was finding promising local family farmers like Henry Johnson and his wife Sarah as tenants. The other solution provides the common link shared by the other two families featured in this work – free immigrant settlers from Britain.

Attracting free immigrants had been a concern from the earliest days of Van Diemen's Land. Henry Widowson, agent for an Agricultural Society from 1825, was advocating migration to British farmers in 1829. Captain Butler Stoney was so impressed by what he saw visiting Tasmania in the 1850s that he published a book to show 'the British public the present condition and state of the island'. He admiringly referred to the 'free born sons of Britain [who] have flocked to [Tasmania's] shores, carrying with them the noble characteristics of the mothercountry, and their unceasing perseverance and industry adding to the lustre of their race'. He wanted to 'make known advantages offered by this colony as a field for emigration' (Stoney 1856, v–vi). Both Widowson and Stoney were advocating migration to yeoman farmers, who could be expected to exploit opportunities available while perpetuating social and agricultural structures of the old country in the new. Just as important as these was the plethora of Scottish publications in the late 1830s, cited by Macmillan, which were avidly read by 'the Scottish reading public' and informed the inflowing emigrant settlers (1967, 311–25). In 1859, Melbourne-based William Fairfax published his *Handbook to Australasia*, and eulogised Tasmania's 'most liberal land system in Australia', highlighting its North-West agricultural settlement opportunities with potential for selling timber and potatoes from the Mersey to Circular Head (1859, 116).

Broeze (1982, 235–53) showed the crucial role during the 1830s and 1840s played by private colonisation companies and shipping entrepreneurs, who saw advantage in supporting imperial policies of assisted immigration and influenced government policy through lobbying, delegations and approaching interested politicians. Additionally, private individuals, often with financial interests in Australia, worked with local clergy or benefactors to combine philanthropy with self-interest. Broeze argued that 'active participation of private enterprise' was 'vitally necessary' and without it the imperial government would have only been able to regulate, but not execute, their policies. The British debate over who should pay

70 Castra farms and institutions 1880–1910

for its excess population to emigrate and ease domestic difficulties was active at the end of the 1840s, with Lord Grey supporting those going to North America in preference to Australia, because the British Government had paid nothing for over 1.34 million people to go there that decade (*Hansard*, 10 August 1848 cited in Burroughs 1967, 274–75).

The link between revenue from Crown Land sales and subsidising colonial emigration continued to be an issue during the growing demand from Australian colonies for independence from imperial administration. The Immigration Committee in 1847 favoured raising funds for assisting the labouring poor to emigrate, but not by taxing the 'distressed inhabitants of Great Britain' so that 'the already rich in NSW' might benefit from more labour and get richer (Thomas Eliot in Fitzroy to Grey, 29 September 1847, C.O. 201/384).

Lord Grey's *Australian Colonies Government Act* 1850 (England) was passed and granted, which expanded opportunity for the colonies to develop their own constitutions as well as extending the franchise to every £10 householder (Pike 1957, 416). Manning Clark saw that admission of 'the populous masses to a fair and well-regulated share in making the laws' was a safeguard against 'democratic' turbulence and 'red republicanism' (Cathcart 1995 (orig.1962), 242). Very soon afterwards, the post-1851 exodus from Tasmania to the Victorian goldfields brought the question of attracting new immigrants to Lieutenant-Governor Denison's Government's attention (Shaw 1961,116). Agents were set up in Britain to find prospective migrants and Immigration Agents were appointed to check and record arrival details (Pearce and Cowling 1975). There were only three years, 1853, 1855 and 1857, when more people arrived in Tasmania than left it. Difficulties could arise because, by the time immigrants arrived after a three- or four-month journey, seasonal demand would often have passed. When ships arrived in January, that was ideal for harvesting in Tasmania.

The immigration link for our Preston families started in the 1850s and demonstrates the way colonists were prepared to help themselves. Colonists formed societies and appointed agents to go to rural districts in England and Scotland to hold meetings and circulate information pamphlets. Tasmania and Western Australia depended on societies or shipping agents to recruit emigrants because it was more economic than appointing Government agents in Britain (Haines 1994, 226). Reverend Benjamin Drake, a Congregational minister, was chosen as agent for the Launceston Immigration Aid Society. Drake was to go to agricultural regions in Essex, Norfolk and Suffolk where he had worked for years, and recruit and send 80 families plus single adult emigrants from there (Dowling in News 1854b). Drake was to distribute a 'document about the Colony and its future prospects' written by Lieutenant-Governor Denison and to attract the waged manual agricultural workers who might not be encouraged by local gentry or Commissioners (perhaps because they were too good or useful to lose) (Fenton and Walker 1884, 261). Advances would cover the tickets and outfits required for the voyage. They were to be told it would be hard toil but with good prospects after a few years (Ramsay, 65–67). The *Whirlwind* with 330 bounty immigrants arrived in April 1855, followed by the *Southern Eagle* with the balance of the families.

Castra farms and institutions 1880–1910   71

These families all pioneered North Motton and were Methodists (Passenger List, CB7/12/1/4 Book 12, TA).

Another was St Andrew's Immigration Society, founded in 1854 (Learmonth Collection 185-, TA). Joseph Bonney, Perth (Tas.) farmer, volunteered his services as agent to promote migration out of Liverpool. He was to seek men from the Highlands as shepherds and women as farmers' servants, and from the Tweed valley, the Lothians and Fife in central Scotland, indoor servants and skilled ploughmen. Bonney recruited emigrants for the *Commodore Perry* to go to Launceston, and the *Ocean Chief* to go to Hobart on the Hobart Town Immigration Society's behalf (Green 1990/91, 161–62). St Andrew's introduced about 1,200 Scots including 200 Highlanders on an indentured Bounty Scheme, under which they each signed to agree to repay proportions of the deposit and compulsory outfitting costs (Haines 1997, 237). Jane Mong, who married Robert Peebles, was one of these immigrants (more further in this chapter), but she could have been nominated under the Friends and Relations Regulations by her relative David Mong, already living in Sassafras.

Between 1854 and 1882, the Bounty System was the principal way immigrants were assisted, because it appeared to offer the chance of attracting the most desirable people (Richmond 1957, 339). Supported by the Tasmanian Government from 1854, it allowed Tasmanian residents to nominate friends and relatives at £3 per adult male or £5 per family passage cost. Nearly 5,000 had arrived under this system by 1860 (Pearce and Cowling, 14–15). Many Norfolk families, including members of the family connected to the Preston Browns, were among these. Along the North-West coast, these society emigrants gained a reputation for character and industry, and would provide leaders for their communities over coming decades, in spite of quite humble origins (Pink 1990, 104–5). Surveyor Dooley described them as 'eminent for probity, energy and industry' and a gentleman-farmer, Edward Shaw, at Port Sorell, observed that 'almost all were men of the labouring class who had saved their wages to settle on the land' (Evidence, HAJ, Vol. VIII, 1862, No. 111, 12–13). By 1872, the preponderance of small farms in the North-West led the customs collector to call it 'emphatically the land of the cockatoo or peasant farmer' (HAJ, Vol. XXIII, 1872, No. 2, 188). They typically lived as frugally and self-sufficiently as they could, with pigs, poultry, sheep, dairy cow, garden, orchard and bees and help from their wives and children, with any money reinvested in the farm. Pink suggested the 'spud cockies' constituted an 'industrious yeomanry' that 'successfully pioneered one of the most diverse rural areas' in Australia (Pink 1990, 105–7).

Emigrants from Britain and Ireland had a high level of literacy indicating levels of education and skill that encouraged self-selection because they could read the publicity and newspaper advertising. This is borne out by immigration records that show skilled tradesmen, like blacksmiths, and artisans, like ploughmen and millers, brought their literacy and useful skills with them and dairymaids too, all from the labouring classes (Richards 1999, 345–59). Some were older craftsmen whose skills had been replaced by industrial production in Britain, like shoemakers from Leicester (Williams 1973, 188; *Whirlwind*, CB7/12/1/4, Book

72   *Castra farms and institutions 1880–1910*

12). Predominantly, government immigrants were male, but female cooks, house-maids and general servants provided a substantial proportion, reflecting demand in both urban and rural areas (Crowley 1954, 106; Alford 1984). For a brief period between 1854 and 1855, immigrants whose fare was wholly paid by the Government were indentured to a 'competent employer' if they could not repay the cost within 14 days of arrival; the employer paid half up front, and the rest within a year, with authority to deduct instalments from the immigrant's wages over two years (Pearce 1975, 14).

Positions for arriving immigrants were sought through notices inserted into the *Hobart Town Gazette* by the Board of Immigration Office announcing the expected arrival of an immigrant ship, including names and employable skills of those aboard. One example announced 112 female immigrants expected from London; their occupations were mostly housemaids, cooks, dairy, laundry and nurse maids. People wishing to hire applied in writing, choosing servants from the list (*HTG* 22 January 1861, 137).

Immigrants who had worked with sheep in the English northern counties and northern Scotland would have had more attractive skills to offer the pastoralists in the Tasmanian Midlands, Victoria and South Australia. But immigrants to Devon from arable areas like those from central Scotland, who settled around Gawler, or from Norfolk, who settled in the Penguin, North Motton and Kentish areas, or from Ireland, who went to the Don and Forth hinterlands, would have been more drawn to the potential of arable farming, often starting off as labourers or tenant farmers. The Norfolk and Scottish farmer immigrants coming to Devon in the late 1850s were praised 20 years later in the *Devon Herald* (11 September 1878, 2) for their success in their 'agricultural life on freehold estates'. Another strategy that advantaged both farmer and new immigrant labourer was that adopted by Skemp, who chose to work 'living in' on the farm, specifically to learn local skills and farming methods (Skemp 1952, 28).

James McCulloch and his family of eight, original settlers in 1859 in the Leven hinterland, migrated from Scotland in 1855 and worked for four years near Hagley between Launceston and Deloraine. They bought and settled on 'a square mile of land at Upper Gawler' (640 acres), between Gawler and Abbotsham, adjacent to the Gawler River (see Hall's sub-dividing survey of November 1869, AF396-1-668). They were Clarence (Clarrie) McCulloch's great-grandparents, and their descendants spread widely into other districts, including Preston (McCulloch 1998).

By the mid-1860s when Colonel Crawford was promoting Castra selection, settlement had expanded south from the coast through Gawler, Abbotsham and Spalford, all located along the Plank Road. George Henry Wing's brother James and John Robertson and his family, all originally from Wymondham, Norfolk, had taken up land between Abbotsham and Spalford. Because of this connection, in November 1873 James and John met the steamer at Leven bringing the Wings from the Derwent and helped them, their three young boys and baby to their selection at Abbotsham (Wing 1873–75). Wing's diary demonstrates the value of friendship and collective effort in the very early settling process. The Robertsons

Castra farms and institutions 1880–1910   73

gave them food and shelter while they cut a road into the land. Wing wrote of help received from Andrew McCulloch, Joshua Stone and Tom Bingham. Two of the Wing boys, George Henry Jnr and Ebenezer (Eb), would take up land in Preston a decade later. The McCullochs brought their Scottish heritage and the Wings and Robertsons brought theirs from Norfolk to the Leven hinterland; their knowledge of farming would prove to be a springboard for subsequent generations.

Similarly, through their migrant parents, Preston pioneers brought their heritage as first-generation Tasmanians brought up to know North-West Tasmania as their birthplace and place of belonging. As Mackintosh wrote about pioneers in the Canadian prairies:

> The men and especially women . . . brought with them not only physical strength, some knowledge and some capital, but also familiarity with institutions in other places, social attitudes and habits, bits of civilisation from a great variety of regions and countries . . . . New ways of life were forged . . . institutions borrowed from older communities or invented to meet new needs.
> (Foreword in Dawson and Younge 1940)

Kee highlighted the sense of ambivalence typified by Irish migrant settlers' feelings towards their mother country, that they sought 'somehow to reconcile an affection for the ties which bind them with impatience at the restraint these place on freedom of action' in their new home (Kee 1972, 29). Kiddle observed in western Victoria that colonising squatters 'tried to recreate the Old World they had lost, but despite themselves, they founded and helped build a new society'. Those few who returned to Britain found themselves out of kilter with their past life, being 'rooted in the new country' (Kiddle 1961, 511). This resonates with the experience of the Anglo-Indian families who went to Britain to retire and discovered they, too, were out of kilter with the social milieu there. Reynolds argued that the descendants of Tasmanian immigrants of the earlier nineteenth century were less likely to leave during the 1870s depression because they 'were no longer sojourners willing to walk away from their homeland . . . . For better or worse they had become Tasmanians' (Reynolds 2012, 171).

Previously, we saw that retired Anglo-Indian officers had little or no experience such as described earlier to bring to their endeavours, but the focus here is on people who *did* have the heritage, motivation and, most importantly, farming experience when they came to Preston. In so doing, they committed themselves and their families wholeheartedly to creating new homes and farmlands for ensuing generations to benefit from in their turn, just as Crawford himself did, and as Widowson had predicted 80 years earlier (1829, xiv–xv). Their attitude toward mobility and willingness to move for better prospects, especially for their sons, was characteristic of the pattern set by yeomanry in Northern America, New Zealand and other mainland colonies (Fahey 2011a, 97–108; Kiddle 1961, 24–25; Buxton 1967, 286–87; Belich 2009, 226–28; Lower and Innis 1936, 148). For them, and many other immigrants who arrived in Tasmania and elsewhere in colonial Australia, there was no going back, only moving forward.

74 *Castra farms and institutions 1880–1910*

The first generation of Preston case study families

This examination of three yeoman farming families, who moved into the Anglo-Indian area of Dooley's Plains in the earliest years of the new century, provides two examples of the way agricultural heritage and immigration links coalesced. The third case demonstrates the drive for land ownership and land for sons that motivated a long-time tenant farmer. Each family has been succeeded by generations of farmers on Castra land, who were still engaged in agriculture in 2000, and remain there in 2021, further attesting to the durability of the yeoman ideal.

1) The Peebles family

James Robert Peebles was a first-generation Tasmanian. Robert Peebles, his father, had travelled with his older brother James (no.600) to Tasmania on the *Commodore Perry* arriving in Launceston in April 1855 (CB7-12-1-12). Robert (no.676) declared his occupation as a ploughman who could read and write. Born in Scotland in 1832, Robert was 23 years old and went to Sassafras to work (probably) for Robert Beveridge. By 1861 at 52, he had rented 60 acres of farmland from Beveridge and on 31 May that year he married Jane Mong at Sassafras (RGD37/1/20 no. 339). Jane had arrived from Glasgow on the *Indiana*, arriving on her 31st birthday in Launceston on 24 April 1860 (CB7/12/1/9). Born in Montrose, she travelled on a single bounty ticket and was a dairymaid. Her immigration had been arranged through the St Andrew's Immigration Society. James Robert was their first child born in 1862, followed by two brothers and a sister. This first Peebles family remained at Sassafras, eventually buying an 80-acre farm previously owned by James Grant. The couple both died in the mid-1890s and were buried in Sassafras (Friends 1988).

When James Robert married Margaret Mason at Barrington near Sheffield in July 1888, his occupation was farmer and hers was 'daughter of farmer' William Mason (RGD37/1/47 no. 886). They continued to live at Sassafras and started a family. In 1890, James Robert and brother David bought adjoining blocks of land at Sassafras, 93 acres for James and 105 acres for David. James and Margaret had nine children prior to 1900, eight sons and one daughter, while living at Sassafras. When she was expecting her tenth baby and William, their eldest, was about 12, the family moved to Preston to the 160 acres of land previously owned by Henry Macnee, the original Anglo-Indian grantee, which his widow sold to William Elliot, owned briefly before selling to James Robert (Valuation Roll, March 26, 1901). He and Margaret went on to have another four children after Ruby was born in April 1901 during their first few months.

James was nearly 40 years old when he decided to move away from Sassafras. By this time, both his parents had died, and he had a large family of sons in an agricultural area that had little available land for expansion. He may well have been motivated by the chance to start on new ground while he was still young

Castra farms and institutions 1880–1910   75

enough to tackle the challenges of land clearing, and the possibility of a better living off the larger farm to springboard his sons as they grew up. His whole life up to that point had been spent living, learning and executing mixed farming practices on his father's and his own farm, which he sold to Peter Rockliff. He already understood the value of landownership and the Scottish ideology relating to inheritance may well have been an additional driving force for seeking better opportunities in Preston (Barclay, Foskey, and Reeve 2007, 36). Coming to higher altitudes in Preston, there was potential for better rainfall for crops, particularly in spring, in addition to the inherent value of the timber still on the land (Gordon (Bub) and Robert Peebles, 2018).

When he sold two acres for the new combined school in 1912, some trees on that block measured over seven feet across at the sawing level (Education File No. 915/11). While the family made do living in Macnee's hut, he built a substantial timber home for his family on a rise above the road with a good prospect over much of his land and a north-facing front verandah. Across the width of the back of the house was a long room with a large table able to seat up to 18 people, as it needed to for this family that would eventually number 16. Its size was testament to dimensions of timber available on the land and was still in use up to 1958.

Richard Hilder, a West Pine yeoman farmer well qualified to pass judgement on what he observed, wrote about his regular 1908 sorties into hinterland agricultural areas. He recorded that James Peebles had partly cleared his 'excellent quality' land and had oats, hay, swedes, potatoes and dairying all combined on his farm, the typical mixture of yeoman farming. Hilder was invited to share the Peebles family hospitality and remarked upon the healthy appearance of theirs and the many other large families that he had met in the Preston district (News 1908a). Summing up the value of family farming, he wrote:

> Why, at the house of Mr. J. Peebles, who kindly entertained me to tea, there were no less than 19 at table – Mr. and Mrs. Peebles, 11 sons and three daughters, a little boy staying with them, the grandfather, and myself! I dropped suddenly on this interesting family on a Saturday evening and though 16 miles from Ulverstone town, a tidier, better behaved, more active, and healthier household party would be hard to find. This is the parent class who need encouragement by our Tasmanian Government, for are they not adding an asset to our State of incalculable value?

2)   The Johnson family

Henry Johnson's background has been the subject of considerable research by family members, but what information is available has been difficult to corroborate. Although Henry's origin and life-story growing up is unclear (he was apparently born in the mid-1850s, probably in Tasmania, and his family celebrated his birthday on 5 August), he eventually got work as a farm labourer

76 *Castra farms and institutions 1880–1910*

in the Deloraine district. This included three years working for farmer George Burgess at nearby Brady's Plains. Here he met Sarah Ann Burgess, the youngest of 11 children. They married in her home there in 1877. They started their large family with a son, William, born in 1878. His birth was registered at Port Sorell with the local registrar, but by 1883, the children were recorded as born at Sassafras (Banks 1999). Henry worked for George Rockliff when they arrived in the Sassafras district, until he became his tenant on 100 acres for over 25 years (Valuation Roll 1888). When he asked if he could buy the farm that he had worked so long, Rockliff refused. This started Henry Johnson's search for land, and about 1902, he decided to buy 120 acres of undeveloped bush that was most of Ritherdon's Anglo-Indian Lot in Dooley's Plains for his family, near the Castra town reserve on the original track to central Castra past Deyrah. A 50-acre farm in Sassafras was large enough to provide an income at that time for a large family, so this larger amount of land would potentially do even better. It was covered in trees when he bought it, and out of the timber, he built the house and sheds for the farm, as well as posts, sleepers and palings to sell (Tas Johnson, grandson 2017).

The Burgess family history tells the story that Henry began building the house sleeping under a large tree at night, a tree that was left growing in his memory, a regular talking point for the family (Lohrey in Banks 1999, 69). Gollan (hereafter Georgie) Johnson, his grandson, showed me a photo of the house that Henry built that lasted out the twentieth century. His brother Tas clearly remembers their grandfather. He told me that, 'Henry had a reputation for being able to do anything with wood – he could make furniture and fine work as well as outdoor timberwork, and he enjoyed it' (Tas Johnson 2017).

By 1902, Henry's first son, William, was in his mid-twenties and the next surviving son, Harty John, was 18. There were more younger sons growing up, so Henry was motivated by the need to invest in land nearby for his sons as the farm became established and the boys grew up. In their years in Sassafras, both Henry and Sarah shared a commitment to the Sassafras Baptist Church, undergoing baptism at the Latrobe Baptist Tabernacle in 1892. Both their Baptismal Certificates to mark the occasion were shown to me. Their acceptance of the small doctrinal differences between Protestant denominations explains his new alliance to the Preston Methodist Church as its first Steward and as lay preacher too (Jackson 1987, 78).

Above all, it was Henry's agricultural experience gained from the years of farming at Sassafras that was the essential ingredient for his future success. Having been a tenant for so long, he knew that tenants only gained income and experience, but never the solid asset that land provided. Georgie Johnson believed the Rockliff family went guarantor for Henry's first purchase. This story is plausible because of evidence that the Rockliff brothers bought Greenfield's Anglo-Indian 320-acre lot and had 70 acres scrubbed and under grass in 1899 (News 1899d). They advertised in 1904 for tenders to scrub 30 acres and to buy all blackwood logs at a thousand-foot rate (News 1904f).

Castra farms and institutions 1880–1910 77

2) The Brown family

Several members of the Brown family have been farming in Preston for up to five generations, and the youngest member farming is in his mid-twenties (2020). This young farmer is a direct descendant of Arthur William Brown, the first of his family to buy farming land in Preston (Brown 2018). Since that time, farming has been the occupation of choice for the men in this family line. The current patriarch, Kenneth Albert Brown, is a member of the third generation, born in 1938, Arthur William's grandson. Ken can remember his great-grandmother, Elizabeth Brown nee Brett, who died in Ulverstone in 1943 at 103 years. This is her history too.

The Brown family story begins with William Brown, the first of his family to live in Tasmania. He was born in 1835 at Rougham, near King's Lynn, Norfolk. He married Elizabeth Brett in May 1864 in Launceston, where he was working as a gardener and she worked as a servant (RGD37-1-23 no. 452). Elizabeth was born at Hockham, in the same Norfolk area. Their first child, Ellen, was born in Tasmania, but the next two children, Agnes and Elizabeth, were born in Victoria. According to the family story, Arthur William was 'born at sea' in April 1874 (probably *en route* from Victoria) as his birth was registered in Launceston. The next sibling, William Alfred, was born at North Motton in February 1875. Another son, Herbert Wilfred, was born in October 1877 in Melton, Victoria, but the family returned to North Motton to farm and bring up the children there, probably to be near Elizabeth's family already established at North Motton.

In the 1899 Valuation Roll, William Brown was Occupier of 101 acres on Dooley's Plains Road. This meant they were living in North Motton's southernmost part before Barren Hill and would have seen traffic passing to and from Preston's new areas. By 1903, they owned 55 acres with a house on Allison Road near North Motton (VR 1903, 2164). Both William and Elizabeth Brown died in the district, he in 1911 and she in 1943.

Elizabeth's immigration story started when she was 18 in Norfolk. She came with her father, William Brett, his second wife Mary Ann, their other children and her married brother, Isaac Brett and his wife, also Elizabeth. They had migrated together on the *Southern Eagle* in 1857 on Bounty tickets 474 and 475 (CB7-12-1-12-00155, 146). After four years at Bishopsbourne, near Launceston, the rest of the family took the opportunity to settle in newly opened-up North Motton in March 1866, soon after Elizabeth's marriage to William Brown. The extended Brett family were the first settlers along with Nathan and Sarah Brothers, John and Elizabeth Marshall, John and Ellen Hudson, and James and Maria Hudson, who were also from Hockham, Norfolk, arriving on the *Whirlwind*. An excellent account written on the 66-year anniversary of their arrival was written by 'G.W.E.', a self-described 'member of the first muster', noting that the first Methodist minister, Rev. W.H. Walton, arrived with the first selection contingent six months earlier (News 1932c). He went on to build a Primitive Methodist Church and parsonage either side of Penguin Creek, both still surviving and in use (Fenton, 113–4).

78   *Castra farms and institutions 1880–1910*

Isaac and Elizabeth Brett also lived the rest of their lives in North Motton and brought up a large family of seven. Bretts Road underscores their significant contribution to North Motton's community, which bolstered expansion into Preston, Castra and Nietta, as those lands opened up. Until such institutions were established in Preston, North Motton was essential for church, school, post and newspapers.

Arthur Brown and his two brothers were brought up learning and observing farming practices on their father's farm that was nearer to Ulverstone wharf so they knew about selling farm products. The soil was very similar to Dooley's Plains and the climate only slightly different due to lower altitude. These Brown boys and their Brett cousins, growing up in the late 1870–1880s, were looking to farm on their own account and lands opening up just over the Barren Hill provided those opportunities, especially with family connections to John Porter, George Wing Junior's neighbouring farmer already established near Barren Hill.

Arthur and William Brown became major land holders in the North Motton parish, often listed as Proprietors under 'A.W. and W.A. Brown' in the Valuation Rolls when other people, often family members, were listed as Occupiers. In 1896 Arthur married Ada Annie Porter of Preston and they started their large family in North Motton. They had 14 children, nine girls and five boys. Before long, Arthur was first to make the move to Preston, starting a farm at South Preston (VR 1903, 100 acres). It was their seventh child, and third son, Albert Hedley, born 14 August 1905, who became father of the generations that still farm in Preston.

Again, the Bretts and the Browns exemplify benefiting from elders' knowledge of Norfolk farming practices combined with expertise in North Motton's land and agricultural conditions. This combination demonstrates that the Brown brothers' entrepreneurial risk-taking was hedged by more advantages than simply rent. By investing in land and becoming landlords of family tenants who were potential collaborators in farming, this presented benefits from reciprocal labour and shared machinery, motivated by creating solid security for their families.

Getting settled from 1880

Looking at the experiences of these and other contemporaries making a new start on the land, one can only speculate on their priorities. In contrast to life nearer the coast, the altitude of Preston and Dooley's Plains was likely to bring frost and snow and ground needed to be cleared of trees and prepared for crops to go in for the following season. While wives would be wanting shelter for the family, the men would also be considering important construction of sheds and barns for livestock, especially their horses, bullocks and cows, and the imperative of obtaining necessary building materials probably from the land, a dilemma of priorities discovered in other Anglo-colonial areas (see Osterud 2012). To provide insight into

Castra farms and institutions 1880–1910   79

the process, we have the advantage of George Henry Wing Junior's own writing in the 1880s about how he progressed at 19:

> I was eleven when I came to the Leven . . . . I selected 50 acres of land at North Motton [what became Preston], where the nearest farm was 2½ miles away. The country intervening was very rough and broken [Barren Hill], and properties were connected by only a bush track. The first thing after the land was surveyed in 1881 was to clear enough scrub to put a camp on – this camp being made of bark stripped from the trees. After scrubbing about five acres, it was left for some months to dry, and was then burnt, grass being sown on the land between the trees.
>
> In the second year, I cleared about 20 acres. On some of this land I put crops and potatoes. After piles of trees were burnt, I sowed oats and covered them with a hoe – known as 'chipping in' – and it took about a week to do an acre. As the land became more cleared, the plough could be used.
>
> (Wing quoted in Roake 1928, 19)

This process of incremental clearing would continue for decades to come; the pace of clearing would depend on available labour and the imperative to get vital crops planted. In between, in Wing Jnr's case, he gained income from work at the Mt Bischoff mine. The burning season was after February, hottest month then, though fire was a frequent danger, often caused by lightning. In hindsight, one wonders how prevalent lightning strikes were on the enormous skeleton trees just waiting to fall after ringbarking. Wing Jnr made his permanent home in 1884, the first permanent resident in that northern part (News 1999a).

For permanent settlers, food supplies were critical in the very early period. Poultry could provide readily accessible meat and eggs and could thrive free ranging in the bush. It is likely the wives that brought fowls with them for immediate advantage as poultry were usually their domain. But 'a good fowl-house at night' was needed that was 'proof against the depredations of the little spotted animal known as the Native Cat [or quoll] (*Dasyurus viverrimus*) that has a decided *penchant* for chickens' (Just 1892, 43). The distance and time it took for a provisioning trip to Ulverstone made it an irregular event. The women needed all their acquired skills in household management and organising children to help in any way they could during the settling-in process, something already seen with Elizabeth Fenton in the 1830s and Alice Braddon in the 1870s. Women's and children's work would always be a real advantage to each family in the yeoman farming tradition.

The Official Handbook of Tasmania for settlers describes three dwelling types with lists of necessary materials and labour for each (Just 1892, 43). First, the bark hut like Wing Jr. built; then, the slab hut – a stronger timber-framed construction, roofed with shingles split from stringybark trees; the third was built with palings, thin split planks of wood about four feet long, early forms of today's weatherboards but unchamfered. Chimneys were built of field stone held together by clay.

80   *Castra farms and institutions 1880–1910*

It was suggested that a four-roomed dwelling with nails and some labour would cost between £10 and £20 at 1892 prices. In 1890 there were three brick-making businesses in Ulverstone struggling to keep up with demand (News 1890b). So by 1900 brick chimneys that were outside on small farmhouses could be constructed within bigger houses. Internal brick chimneys and basalt field stone were used as foundations and perimeter. Photographs of Johnson's and Peebles' homes illustrate the style and 'built to last' quality employed by these early families, and both show there was money as well as good quality raw materials available (both had chamfered boards that needed extra work). Peebles' was occupied until 1958, replaced by a smaller brick and tile house, and Johnson's until about 1980. This same building style was used for the schoolhouse built in 1912 with two internal brick chimneys.

Soil potential was demonstrated by the 1880s settlers. Allan Chisholm, who bought 75 acres from the Ellis Brothers in 1890, Edward Delaney who arrived in 1886, John Porter and the Lewis brothers all about 1883, were already growing potatoes, oats, turnips for fattening cattle and hay. In 1888, there were 136 occupied farms near what became Sprent, 69 in North Motton (that included northern Preston) and 37 in Castra parish including Dooley's Plains, Gunns Plains and Castra villages, all in Anglo-Indian territories (Apex Club 1952, 17). By 1900, 18 farmers were established in Preston, but over in Upper Castra there were 22, a reduction from 43 in 1890, perhaps reflecting the adjustment as Anglo-Indians aged and retired off-farm, like General G.A. Fulton who lived at Forth (Town Directory 1890, 1900; Val. Roll 1890).

The *North West Post* reporter, returning to Wing's homestead in 1899 after nearly 20 years, was able to remark that 'far and wide the whitening trunks of the dead giants of the forest arise out of green pasture fields' in the farmland nearby. Wing showed him his 'rat-proof grain store, well-filled awaiting a rise in the grain market'. This report described the traditional, archetypal yeoman farm, making the point that farmers in Preston did not 'believe in having all their corn in one bushel, but go in for a little grazing and dairying, and grow a little fruit' as well as keeping a small herd of sheep. George Wing's sheep were cross-bred Lincoln-Leicester and his milk cows were crossbred Ayrshire-Durham. He also had pigs, some of which were pure Berkshires, bred from the New Town Government Farm stock (News 1899d). In 1887, Wing's father, George Wing Senior, then in his 60s, and his family moved to the Preston farm from Abbotsham (News 1999b). By 1908, Hilder was reporting upon 'exceptional quality of soil for grass and corn', 'good and abundant' potato crops and 'vigorous clearing' of 'very heavy' timber on properties under development from Preston to Dooley's Plains. He visited Ed Delaney's farm next to the first shop, Wing's, where he was preparing land for 'Praties' with a team of bullocks. Hilder wrote: 'I urged more early planting than was usual in this locality, and found Mr Delaney in defence of his own policy quite as dexterous with his tongue as with his bullock whip, and [I] found considerable difficulty in holding [my] own on this occasion'. He had no hesitation about Preston being the best district that he had 'traversed' with even better prospects. Central Castra's 'good chocolate soil cultivation and green

Castra farms and institutions 1880–1910 81

pastures abounding . . . presented a fine spectacle from a farmer's point of view' and Upper Castra showed 'good country again with very fine farms hereabouts' (News 1908a).

A Nichols photograph in *Weekly Courier*, 23 July 1914 (insert 3, 2) serves to show the size of trees that the early settlers of Castra had to clear contrasted against bullocks and men, and stacking them for burning indicates there was no shortage for conversion to useable timber for building.

Development of communal assets – churches, schools and store

It was soon obvious that some community infrastructure would make life easier, especially as more and more families had taken up land towards the west as far as Gunns Plains properties and far to the south, into the realms of muddy tracks, as described by the *North West Post* correspondent who, in 1899, went to the furthest reaches of settlement and then wrote feelingly about the absolute necessity of roads to be properly made for these new settlers (News 1899d). Complaining must have borne fruit since Hilder was able to travel on 17 miles of metalled road from Ulverstone to Cullen's mail coach terminus opposite the first central Castra road by 1908.

Spiritual and cultural needs were not neglected and helped to develop and sustain the spirit of community from the early years, although northerly Preston and southerly Dooley's Plains and Gunns Plains and Castra to east and west were somewhat geographically separate. Churches followed the pattern already established in North Motton, which had Methodist worshippers from 1877 and St John's Church of England from 1889 (Grant n.d.). In Sassafras, the first Baptist church on Skelbrook (1865) and the Wesleyan (1876) had each been built by congregation members, the former replaced in 1900 (Friends 1988, 39). Rather than families travelling to North Motton, from 1890 Preston's Anglican services were held in Frank Chisholm's farm close to Barren Hill until the Church of England had been built on land donated by Edward Delaney next to the shop. Chisholm continued to conduct the Sunday school (Roake, 19).

In the east, a Church of England church-cum-school had started in 1871 at central Castra. It is reasonable to assume that Crawford was integral to this building because he provided the site and probably contributed finance, staying true to his communal commitment to local residents and also for the use of his large family (AF396–1–673). Years later, according to 'a former splitter', Crawford was pivotal in helping to raise funds and gather tenders for a new church in the growing centre of Castra on the Plank (Castra) Road (News 1889c, 1890a, 1890e). Articles or reports in the newspapers referred to this settlement as Castra up to 1891, when it was renamed Sprent after James Sprent, who surveyed the North-West from 1842 and became Surveyor-General from 1857–1859. This explains why, when Fenton was writing his memories in 1891, he referred to Sprent. The new church was called St Andrew's Church of England and was dedicated by Bishop Montgomery on 31 October 1890 at a hugely attended full-day gala event

82 *Castra farms and institutions 1880–1910*

of sports, cricket, bazaar and chopping as well as the service. Colonel Crawford donated the font to celebrate his and Matilda's wedding anniversary, inscribed: '3rd October 1890. A thank offering from Lieutenant-Colonel Andrew Crawford, H.M. Indian Army, and Matilda Frederica, his wife, on the fiftieth anniversary of their wedding day'.

Another local myth is that the Sprent area was originally to have been called Eden; but again the newspapers provide clarity based on their contemporary knowledge and observations. Between St Andrew's and its adjacent small building sites, cut up by Ulverstone doctor and MHA and developer, Dr John McCall, and the Crawford town reserve was the farm called Eden Grove, occupied by Mrs George Gould Snr., with her son's and three more farms going southwards (News 1888a).

At Castra's western edge, St Mary's Church of England opened in Gunns Plains in 1900, followed in about 1907 by another new church-cum-school, four miles further south at Lowana (South Gunns Plains), which had between 25 and 30 school-age children attending in 1908 (News 1900b, 1908e). This figure indicates large families among the 20 or so farmers in the valley, and there were two overseers, probably employed on the Henry brothers' farms, but few labourers listed (*Town Directory*). At the eastern edge in Upper Castra, there was already a public hall and state school in 1908, and the Church of England, built to match the one at Sprent, was ready for consecration by the Bishop on 30 May 1915 (News 1908a, 1915b). The stimulus for the use of church buildings as schools in Forth and Leven parishes came from long-time minister at Penguin Church of England, Reverend Wilfred Earle (Henslowe 1978).

In 1900, with help from James Lewis, the first school in Preston was started in the Church of England with one teacher (News 1900a). Lewis had obtained school furniture made at the Hobart Gaol, and the building was lined throughout with pine and altered to suit this use (Henderson 2016). His and Sarah's youngest three-year-old Thomas (Tom) was admitted to make up the numbers and justify the government-paid teacher (Dot Bellinger, great-niece, pers. comm. 2019). By 1904, it had 22 pupils attending (News 1904a). This grew to 34 by 1911.

In Preston, James and Margaret Peebles hosted Methodist services at home until the first Methodist church, a Home Mission, was built and opened in October 1902 about three miles further south than the Church of England (News 1902a). William Delaney had bought Lot 7287, Coningham's lot, and he donated one acre next to the road on which to build the church (see AF396–1–672). This building received large contributions from James Peebles, Mrs Ada Cullen nee Tongs (wife of Thomas) and William Delaney, amongst others. Henry Johnson was the first church steward until 1907 when James Peebles took over until his death in October 1929. At the Jubilee service in 1930, more early Church events and people were recalled from the first years; Mrs Frederick Tongs was the first organist, followed by her daughter, Mrs Elsie McCulloch (Clarrie's mother); the first baptism was Pearl Cullen and the first wedding was Sarah Johnson, one of Henry Johnson's daughters, to Peter J. Marshall, a Gunns Plains farmer (News 1930a).

Castra farms and institutions 1880–1910 83

Soon, it became clear that the northerly school was inadequate for the growing number of children, because of the huge increase in farming families from 18 in 1900 to 64 farmers, no labourers and only seven residents of other categories in Preston and South Preston (*Town Directory* 1914). There was lobbying for a new school and two sites were proposed. The Ellis site was two miles from the Barren Hills and under a mile from the village centre. The Delaney site was at the southern end known then as South Preston. The core problem was that the mandated distance for children to attend school was by then two and a half miles, but the growing Preston population was spread out south along the main road. Which was the best site to accommodate the majority of children?

The choice was a situation that was unique in the history of Castra because it became the source of community tension that blew up in a very public forum, a succession of letters 'To the Editor' from 1903–4. After a public meeting by Inspector Brockett at which a show of hands favoured the Ellis site, the local Board of Advice was joined by William Delaney, which exacerbated difficulty over the choice and gave rise to claims of unfair influence. Brockett changed his decision, but James Lewis, a supporter of the Ellis site, wrote that this would be an 'injustice' to the residents at the northern end who would be forced to consider opening a private school with 'not less than 20 scholars'. Delaney's response used distance to argue his case and was dismissive of Mr Lewis's 'insinuations'. The schooling of 66 children along the distance was at stake from a population of 307 persons. These two men argued back and forth in this public forum in very heated fashion. Delaney even challenged Lewis to a wager in front of justices to prove who was telling the truth about events – Preston's version of a duel! One local voice of sanity, George Wing, pointed out that the majority of children were only a 20 minutes' walk from either site. Petitions were sent to the Minister from both men, Lewis taking the part of the district's unmarried residents who might need a school eventually, and Delaney's 'landholders and residents of Preston' not wanting the decision favouring his site altered (Education, File 915/11). The solution was to run a school in the Methodist Church as well as the northern school in the Anglican.

This was done and it started in March 1905 with over 30 pupils, but as selectors with families spread further south, that number soon grew. The *Weekly Courier*, 7 April 1906, 23, 1, shows the weatherboard church/school with a neat paling fence surrounding it, a fence that 'used an exorbitant amount of wood and labour' but was probably feasible in this wooded district (Pickard 2005, 31). The background shows the original height of the ring-barked trees that were growing on Delaney's land. The government-employed teacher, Frederick Augustus Finch, stands with the children. Finch had previously been a teacher at Ulverstone State School and Librarian for the Ulverstone Farmers Club (News 1892). His high standing in education circles would later make him a reliable source in consultations over establishing a central school some years later.

Small farms were being taken up by families, many of whom already had children and more children continued to be born. Both existing church-cum-schools had been built by community members at their expense and labour. Fees from

84 *Castra farms and institutions 1880–1910*

parents contributed to the teacher's salary, which was scaled according to the academic level of the pupils. State-wide calls over a number of years argued for free state schooling that led to a Ministerial Statement in 1900, which the Minister of Education Stafford Bird presented to the House of Assembly, describing various teacher categories related to a schools' grading. Higher salaries for male compared to female teachers are obvious. The overall estimate of additional cost to the State was £15,000 per annum. The Minister asked the House rhetorically who would pay this amount. General taxation? 'Are taxpayers willing to pay that price in order that State School Education may be entirely free?' The answer then was obvious, because it was not until 3 December 1908 that free state schooling occurred (JPPP 1900, Vol. XLII, No. 65).

The demand by Preston residents along the seven miles or so of settlement in 1911 for a government-paid building was hardly surprising in light of them having already paid for buildings and fees as well. By then, the number of school-age children had grown to 82 throughout the combined district, with 49 at South Preston school in one room. There were even more younger children foreseeably needing schooling, so community pressure grew for larger schools, built and wholly financed by the Government. J.W. Yaxley wrote a letter making the point that residents had already had to 'buy a Post Office and Telephone' and were anxious not to have to 'buy a tin-pot school at South Preston' based upon understanding from Inspector Davis that room and board would be only paid by the department if sufficient pupils could be guaranteed. Signatories from the top school were Will Simpson, W.E. Gillam, C.M. Campbell, W.J. Hutton, W.L. Gillam and Yaxley with other signatories from South Preston (Letter to Whitsitt 1912, 915/11). The detailed history leading to the establishment of one large 'central' school has been written elsewhere (Henderson 2016).

What I noticed in researching the churches is that northern Preston, central Castra and Gunns Plains were occupied mainly by people belonging to the Church of England. Those who settled Dooley's Plains and the areas south of Rifle Range Road were more likely to be Methodist or Baptists like the Johnsons. There appears no particular evidence to explain why, with the possible exception of Crawford's church; adherence to the established church among Anglo-Indian service personnel was most likely.

When George Wing Senior decided in 1903 to open Preston's first store on his son's farm about half a mile south of Barren Hill, it was a timely innovation. It was next to the newly built Church of England building and opposite James and Sarah Lewis' house, The Pines. It provided the essential service of an agricultural agency and a northern meeting place, when people came for newspaper and mail collection as well as goods, even though it was a few miles north of Dooley's Plains. The exchange of surplus produce so integral to yeoman farming areas began to be a possibility. Newspapers and postal services operated from there for a few years until 1908. George Wing died in 1909, aged 82 years. The store was run by Mrs Lee after Wing Snr's death until it need to be removed in about 1912 along with the Church of England because they were in the way of the railway line (News 1910d) (more in Chapter 9). In the *Weekly Courier* of 7 April 1906

Castra farms and institutions 1880–1910 85

(25, 2) the store's photograph has Wing Snr on the porch with possibly his son beside him. The simple building has unchamfered boards, no visible chimney and it seems unlikely that a dwelling was intrinsic to the store; my feeling is there was a separate house, or George Jnr's was large enough to accommodate his parents.

The post office operated from Sarah Lewis's house prior to the store opening. In 1908, the post office moved back to her house into a purpose-built extension and the telephone was installed in 1909, at which time a photograph was taken of the whole family of nine children with parents and horses (Phil Lewis, grandson, personal collection). Robert, the tenth, was born in 1911. The post office still operated from there in 1926, when John Dunham was reminiscing about the Preston pioneers (News 1926g). Sarah continued it until she died in 1942. Her eldest daughter, Sally, helped her and kept it going until her death in 1945 (Phil Lewis, nephew, pers. comm. 2016). The house still exists in 2021.

John Dunham was a pioneer of Preston himself. He owned Anderson's Anglo-Indian lot between Peebles' and William Delaney's lots, and, as well as farming and owning the first traction engine in the district, he set up a sawmill there. It was conveniently located for timber needs in Preston and Dooley's Plains and was operating when Hilder passed through in 1908.

In Tasmania from the 1890s into the early 1900s, wherever there were pockets of vacant Crown Land, blocks were being sold for small farm settlement, and this occurred throughout North-West Tasmania. Increased interest in farmland would not have come just from population growth, but may also reflect the ending of the 1890s depression and mining income providing 'small' people with funds to set-up a yeoman life of self-sufficiency (Reynolds 2012, 189). From about 1903, this was true of the lands in the Castra parish, the North Motton parish areas of Preston and the valley in Gunns Plains. As basic elements of churches, schools and post offices developed, village centres began to form around them in Gunns Plains, central Castra, Upper Castra and Nietta. O\bviously anticipating demand from residents, a mail coach service between Ulverstone, Sprent, Upper Castra, Preston and North Motton was advertised by Messrs Rowland and Kenner in 1904 (News 1904c). Thomas Cullen's mail-coach service mentioned earlier would have replaced this in Preston.

Other institutional improvements

Probably motivated by his keenness to create civil and social amenities in Castra, Crawford had instigated the formation of the Independent Order of Odd Fellows Loyal Jubilee Lodge No. 9 and Dr McCall examined candidates for office. Fortnightly meetings at the school were reported in *The Tasmanian* (News 1887d). Robert Crawford was an office bearer. Forty members expressed interest in joining (News 1887b). Crawford also had a hand in creating the Albert Hall, perhaps named to honour the Queen's Consort.

A Show Society had grown out of a meeting to form the Ulverstone Farmers' Club in 1879 with an initial membership of 35. The President was Colonel Warner, a Castra Anglo-Indian settler. The first 'Grand Agricultural Spring Show'

86 *Castra farms and institutions 1880–1910*

was held on 8 December 1880, featuring classes for all farm animals, machinery, implements and 'skilled labour', meaning wood cutting. All except wood-cutting was free to enter subject to £1 membership subscription already paid (News 1880b, 1881; Centenary Brochure 1996). The range of classes is ample evidence of the style of yeoman farming that included all livestock, although obvious omission of poultry indicates its male-focussed schedule in those early years.

Wood chopping continued to feature at agricultural shows across Tasmania and served to demonstrate the skill and fitness of young rural men. Special events continued to draw countryfolk to Ulverstone, until hinterland villages grew large enough to support their own associations. Ulverstone was the centre of championship wood-chopping and sawing for many years, actively encouraged by Hubert Allen Nichols, who had been a keen axeman in his youth, learnt while clearing scrub at Blackwood Park, his Castra home. He wrote the rules for the United Australian Axemen's Association, and its competitions attracted entrants competing for world titles from across the Commonwealth (News 1940e).

Following tradition in Britain and India, sports involving horses was recognised early as a recreative activity. A popular sports day was arranged at Castra in 1888, on loaned private land, which included chopping and sawing, running races, horse jumping in which Crawford brothers took first and second prizes and a shooting gallery, which had also been popular in India (News 1888c, 1890b). Such events were followed by a ball with dancing till daybreak. These entertainments became annual events across country Tasmania, and also provided opportunities for young men and women to meet one another and perhaps make matches.

As an addition to the church-cum-school at South Preston, by 1906 William Delaney had built a 'fine roomy' hall somewhat behind the school 'in which numerous gatherings were held from time to time' adjacent to a recreation ground, also on his land. This was where races and sports were usually held, and visitors came to picnic under the trees (News 1906c). Catering for weddings and other events was made easier once the 'central' school freed up the building in 1913. The wedding here of one of John and Mary Ann Dunham's four daughters, Ruby, to Morton Linthorne Butler of Penguin on 19 December 1917 is a photographic record of fashions and a uniformed soldier reflecting contemporary events (Jason Butler, descendant, 2015).

Community leadership

It is easy to see the importance to this developing community of valuable contributions of land, materials and labour to create buildings to satisfy its needs and to inspire mutuality among residents to pitch in and help. The other essential ingredient was always leadership, and Castra district had a number of significant men filling that role from the earliest years. Colonel Crawford was the most notable. George Wing Senior's store provided the essential service of a northern meeting place. Thomas Cullen, whose wife Ada donated to the Methodist Church, established a store by 1908 on his farm opposite the junction of Rifle Range Road (along Ritherdon's E-W boundary, which became the turning point for goods delivery wagons and would later have a post office to service the southern settlers). He ran a thrice-weekly coach service between Ulverstone and South Preston by 1911 (*Walch's Almanac* 1911, 384). William Delaney was a man of significance and philanthropy, pivotal in establishing the South Preston school not least to serve his own large family and his interest in other Preston-based associations and events. Even the unique school dispute was a passionate effort, as was James Lewis's, to do his best to improve educational provision and reduce the walk for local children. By supporting both Church of England and the Methodist Church, he demonstrated the same quality of egalitarianism that appeared in practical Protestant religious observance elsewhere in Australia, where it was not uncommon for early buildings to be shared with other denominations (Jackson 1987, 32–33). On Delaney's Dooley's Plains farm, his relative affluence is apparent from his family and home, located on a rise well into the property, already well established by 1906 (*Weekly Courier*, April 7, 1906, 23, 3).

Some have written of hard times in the early years (News 1999b). That claim was not unique to the Castra parish, nor even to Tasmania. Settling in untouched, unalienated forest was a recipe for hard toil and patience as young George Wing attested. But development of mineral finds at Mount Bischoff near Waratah and the mining work that ensued provided income to bridge the gaps of time waiting until scrub could be burnt and early crops sown and harvested. The example set by the 1880s settlers clearly demonstrated the yeoman ideal, especially if the description of George Wing's farm after 20 years could be regarded as typical. The potential of the land was evident for the three pioneer patriarchs who came years later to choose and settle their new purchases. These men and their wives and others of the same period had expectations of a village life with its institutions, based upon their previous experiences elsewhere. They were prepared to contribute by forming binding ties and future community on what was already there. In these ways, they typified the yeomanry we read about in the Introduction, sharing and working with neighbours, yet remaining their own masters. We know so little about the wives of this era in Tasmania except through official records, but we can reasonably assume they were committed to the new family venture of creating a farm and a future, even when as close to giving birth as Mrs Margaret Peebles. The women's contribution receives more attention in Chapter 8.

Meanwhile, pressure was building in the Government to boost the whole State's agricultural productivity by breaking up large under-used estates to create smaller farms, following mainland states and New Zealand. Closer settlement, as this movement was called, is examined in the next chapter.

4 Closer settlement in Castra

This chapter and the next are closely linked by their association with land programs – closer settlement and soldier settlement; the major difference between them is that settlers in the first were from the general population, and in the second they had served in the imperial forces during the Great War. Here I follow the land ownership theme and the continuing story of the yeoman family farming ideal, which was deeply embodied in the concept of closer settlement in New Zealand and other states of Australia, and to a lesser extent in Canada. How was closer settlement viewed in Tasmania and Castra, why was it adopted and how did the media and external sources influence political decisions?

As farming families on small farms gradually filled the Crown Land gaps in northern Tasmania and in Castra in particular, the closer settlement concept there was misplaced. People who bought their own land were widely believed to have more staying power in the development stages and more committed to a longer-term future than those who were tenants. Evidence from some Castra closer settlement supports this, leading to a conclusion that closer settlement's lack of appeal owed much to widespread belief in the yeoman ideal of landownership with direct, independent control, in contrast to tenancy with a Government landlord and what that entailed legally from a tenant's point of view.

Canada, New Zealand and closer settlement

Because settlement of small farms in the prairie lands of Canada had a similar development process and timeline from 1872 onwards as North West Tasmania, it is relevant to consider ways the Dominion Government dealt with filling land gaps between homesteads, as small 160-acre farms were called. Was the philosophy of making long-term Government loans to settlers adopted, matching Australia? By 1904, in the prairie provinces, a combination of factors were addressed, first in response to the 'tide of immigration' and consequent high demand for land from new migrants, and second, from existing farmers who, with increasing mechanisation, realised they needed more land to stay economically viable (Murchie, Allen, and Booth 1936, 87–88). Russell (2012) showed that farming families in Ontario pushed hard for new land to satisfy demands for their next generation and were encouraged to move westwards into Manitoba, the

DOI: 10.4324/9781003229841-5

neighbouring prairie state. The Government enacted two methods to cope, offering pre-emptive rights to existing farmers to acquire additional land adjacent or opposite their properties providing they complied with cultivation conditions on both their original holding and the new block. New settlers who moved to more settled communities could buy under the same terms, but were not obliged to live on the land. Government financial support was limited to a low price per acre and three-year repayment terms for both categories of buyers. Murchie, Allen, and Booth (1936, 87–88, 192–203) describe the Swan River Valley in Manitoba as hilly with mountains to the north and south interspersed with a level valley plain and very fertile agricultural land. The first settlers arrived in 1898. In a nice comparison with Castra and other Devon districts, the area was heavily forested but progressively cleared for agriculture, and settlers gained income from forests before their cropping eventuated. Over 80 per cent of farmers were owner-operators, purchasing under Canadian homesteading laws. These easy provisions continued until 1918 and meant that settlement went ahead quickly and particularly benefited British settlers making homestead purchases under the latter category. Until 1919, the Canadian Government supported a policy of land-ownership of farms from 160 acres to 640 acres because it provided permanence and stability of citizens who had 'a permanent stake' in their community, countering the migratory rural workforce elsewhere. It was also thought that better productivity and effectiveness was more likely from owners than from tenants who were three to four years older before acquiring ownership (Murchie, 195). However, the post-war demands of returning soldiers would change the Government's position.

New Zealand's new law on land tenure was touted in the Tasmanian Parliament in 1901 as an example of closer settlement that Tasmania would do well to follow (News 1901a). This referenced the Liberal's Minister for Lands, John McKenzie's success in passing *The Land for Settlements Act* 1894 that was based on the principle of retaining state ownership of land to avoid losing the value to the nation of increases in land values over time (Brooking 1996, chapter 7; Stewart 1909a). It allowed for lands purchased to be split into small farms and leased under Land Purchase Commissioners (Stewart 1909b, 144).

Much of New Zealand's best land was locked up in large underworked freehold estates, and the 'land-hunger' from aspiring small farmers to exploit the advantages of refrigeration exerted pressure on the Government to break up the land monopoly (Condliffe 1959, 199). The idea of retaining land by the state had been supported by two previous land ministers, but always defeated by the landed estate owners in the Legislative Council, because there was no right to purchase, only a right of renewal of lease (Stewart). McKenzie's acquaintance with the 'evils of land monopoly' by freeholders in the Highlands of Scotland fuelled his 'obsession with closer settlement' (Stewart, 85; Condliffe, 200). As a farmer himself, McKenzie accepted the premise that tenants would not have the same commitment to productive land as they would if they were owners, echoing the ideology championed in Canada. He had included tenure known as 'occupation with right to purchase' after ten years occupation. But in the committee stage, a 999-year

90 *Closer settlement in Castra*

lease on a fixed rental was inserted, to which he 'reluctantly agreed', because it claimed the advantage of leaving farmers' capital available for improvements (Condliffe, 205).

Stewart, a Crown Lands Commissioner, noted that these 'eternal leases' were popular since their advantages were obvious – 640 acres first class or 2,000 acres second class land practically freehold without capital outlay (85). Condliffe wrote that the new land system was 'a bad bargain for the State' because rental returns did not increase and it had little influence on development, with only about 5,000 tenants on two and half million acres by the time of its repeal in 1907 (Condliffe, 205–6), although Stewart cited 1.122 million acres costing £5.217 million, including roads and development costs (Stewart 1909b, 145). Brooking's research revealed 225 estates, 1.297 million acres, 5,560 settlers contributing over 20,000 persons (246). From 1907, future 999-year leases were abolished and replaced by a 33-year reappraisal of rent that was 5 per cent on the land's capital value to allow also for surveys and roads. The concept of national retention of 'the unearned increment in the land' was originally aimed at providing money that could be applied to beneficial community uses. From his viewpoint, writing in 1909, Stewart saw little evidence of success, but his main concern related to the large Government loans with high interest payments not off-set by gains from land leases/rents (Stewart 1909a, 88).

From his 1950s perspective, Condliffe argued the breakup of the landed monopoly and its economic deadlock was effectively managed through McKenzie's vigorous administration of his land policies that were coherent and fulfilled his conviction of 'the right of a farming peasantry to have access to the soil' (208). Taking advantage of leasehold to get started as prices and land values rose, thousands of successful farmers eventually took up the option to acquire their farms' freehold. There was long-lasting national benefit from another aspect of the legislation; McKenzie's advances of cheap capital plus expert advice and instruction through the Department of Agriculture were of 'unchallenged usefulness', because the whole community gained from increasing agricultural productivity and lowering costs, and because they were designed to raise small farmers above marginal income levels (Brooking 2019, 75).

Brooking presented a different view of McKenzie's and the Liberal's activities (1992, 78–98). Citing the enormous areas of 'busted up' Maori lands, most of which took place in the 1890s, he showed how that process facilitated massive accumulation of Crown Lands for splitting into small yeomen farms and also led to 400,000 acres of private purchases. While the Liberal Government extolled the virtues of the family farmer and agriculture as a moral and economic basis for development (Premier Ballance owned *The Yeoman* newspaper), closer settlement was being accomplished by buying Maori lands (Brooking 2019, 74). The 'double irony', as Brooking put it, was that, in hoping to avoid the 'horrors of the highland clearances', McKenzie 'effectively dispossessed Maori' and lost the chance to develop 'a truly bicultural society' (1992, 97–8). The last big land grab was done by the Reform Government in 1912, but they paid more than twice the amount the Liberals did with their early advantage (1992, 80–81).

Mainland Australian experiences

There is an obvious contrast between the original aim of the New Zealand laws, designed to retain Crown Land asset value as well as enabling land access to 'peasant' farmers', and the aims of Australia's mainland states. Over decades, various iterations of Selection Acts had failed to produce 'stable rural communities and a class of contented settlers' based on the yeoman ideal (Waterhouse 2005, 30). Roberts made the point that 'an earth hunger' existed in all colonies in the late 1800s, and demand by 'distressed artisans and intending settlers' could not be met, since the best land had been alienated into large estates, much of which was not being put to productive use. One instance was the Hunter district where 227,000 acres, owned by 14 persons, had cultivation on only 331 acres within reasonable reach of the metropolis. Demand matched the politically perceived need for increased rural population, and a solution appeared to be voluntary repurchase of land from owners for subdivision. This was the genesis of what became 'closer settlement' land policy, denoting 'intensive settlement' where small farms were near markets and other employment (Roberts 1924, 356, 358).

Closer settlement using publicly funded financial support to assist settlement on easy terms and conditions to small tenant farmers was widely supported as an alternative effort to increase productive use of land, while continuing to support the yeoman ideal. Severe economic depressions at the end of the nineteenth century led politicians to think that rural families had a better chance of surviving such times 'with free board and home-grown food' rather than being unemployed and troublesome in the cities (Connors 1970, 74). In addition to worryingly low population growth, outward migration drift back to Britain occurred between 1901 and 1905. Closer settlement opportunities provided the inducement of State Government assistance to new migrants to counterbalance these trends in the three major mainland states. Families on the land were seen as not only a 'productive force', but also as 'politically stabilising' rural electors that would counterpoise growing urban radicalism. Government ambitions for a 'white, settled yeomanry' melded with settlers' aspirations to settle at the 'lowest up-front cost'. This concept gained traction in Britain and New Zealand as well as in Australia (Connors, 75; Orwin and Whetham 1964, 332; Brooking 1992, 78–98; Keneley 2002, 365).

Other scholars looked at sources of support for closer settlement. In Victoria's western districts, Keneley found pressure came from rural town tradesmen and professionals, who saw better business potential in many small farming families in contrast to the often-absentee owners and low staffing levels of the few large pastoral estates adjacent to town (2002, 365). Cameron argued that Queensland politicians had a 'grandiose vision' to create an agrarian yeomanry of independent family farmers growing maize, vegetables, fruit and grains to intensify rural densities and make better use of rural wasteland, an objective of the closer settlement ideal that went back to the 1860s. Support came from enfranchised liberal townsmen, who believed their hip pockets as well as their 'political and social ideals' would be satisfied servicing more selectors. Not only this group, but the working class in Queensland also endorsed closer settlement as a means of countering the

92 *Closer settlement in Castra*

dominance of large British pastoral companies and the political and economic power of the squattocracy (Cameron, 06.4). Tonts (2002) found political support too as Western Australia governments actively encouraged yeoman settlers after the Royal Commission on Agriculture was held from 1887 to 1891 to promote economic development through small-scale enterprises. They were seen as practical, self-reliant agriculturalists who settled permanently, a social class of farmers who would create mixed-enterprise farming on 'not too much land'. Their 'inherent qualities' were admirable and suitable, and 'cheap credit' should be available to avoid going to commercial money-lenders (103–15).

Williams saw closer settlement in the context of nation-changing and world-changing events. He highlighted the impetus of post-Federation optimism about Australia's future, and underlying concerns about implications of the Japanese victory in the Russo-Japanese War in 1905. Both events tended to focus political attention on consolidating continental hold over its assets against possible threats from the Asian 'yellow peril', whether real or imaginary, by intensifying agriculture and, consequently, settlers and productive land (1975, 92, 99). He argued the basic objective of promoting rural settlement 'for its own sake' had not changed over the previous century. Closer settlement, followed later by soldier settlement, continued that objective, aided by growing Governmental appreciation of the broader economic advantages of providing better services to rural areas in support of efficient farming. Williams agreed it was a successful strategy when righting past wrongs of the mainland Selection era, but admitted it proved to be a costly project not least because of infrastructural spending. Nevertheless, this could be vindicated when wealth and prosperity were being created by expanding agricultural production into new land areas and diversity of outputs (93).

Water was always one of the first concerns for settlers anywhere, either by irrigation or by draining low-lying land. Irrigation projects in the Murray and Murrumbidgee areas were seen as 'a holy grail for Governments seeking answers for those wanting land and profitable farms' (Linn 1999, 114). Along the Murray riverlands, fruit growing developed, and dairying took off in the drained swamp lands of the lower Murray (Williams 1975, 93). Broome et al. in *Mallee Country* (2020) pointed out it was selectors who had already amassed up to 30 years of experience and with good supplies of family labour that succeeded in Victoria's Mallee closer settlement in the 1890s, despite difficulties with water scarcity and drought (110–11). There is an echo here of the experiences farming families brought to Castra from elsewhere in Devon.

Settlement 'for its own sake' – a social effect – was gradually being replaced by political and economic imperatives as Australian agriculture recovered from the 1890s depression. All mainland states passed closer settlement acts between 1891 and 1901, and once fully operational, they aimed to repurchase land suitable for agriculture near enough to markets to satisfy the growing population (Waterhouse, 30; Reeves 1902). Land was acquired by diverse means: voluntary purchase of large estates, purchase at auction, and compulsory purchase, the latter particularly where land was located near railways (Waterhouse). Using specially established Advisory Boards to assist the relevant State minister in decision-making,

Closer settlement in Castra   93

Governments used the opportunity to cut large pastoral leases down into smaller lots for mixed farming, especially when available transport methods meant they were within reach of metropolitan markets. Sometimes, land resumed for irrigation occurred where wheat crops were failing from drought or rabbits (Pike 1962).

Reflecting on closer settlement history across Australia, Henzell suggested one major reason for its importance to Governments was a 'strong belief in the social value of yeoman farmers, which in Australia translated into small family farms' (2007, 63). This belief was reinforced widely by persistently held 'ruralism', a philosophy that pitted the country against the city. In his classic work, Williams wrote that the country epitomised socially and morally superior life (1973, 281–83). Metaphors describing farmers as 'the backbone of the economy' or 'the lifeblood of the nation', for example, were persistently used by rural press and farmers' leaders and politicians in America and New Zealand as well Australia (Brooking 1996, 82). But, in sub-dividing land, there was 'a near universal tendency to go too far' by making blocks too small for a reasonable living, thereby sacrificing economic efficiency, challenging the land's potential and causing resultant human distress (Henzell 2007, 64; Keneley 2002, 363–79).

Linn focussed on the concept's riskiness because so many settlers were under-financed and unprepared for challenges they would face. He highlighted its high cost of £34 million spent on 2.7 million acres for more than 12,000 families by 1914, which, for each family, averaged over £12 per acre, 225 acres and about £2,700, a result he called a 'vast amount of land and money' that apparently failed to include cost of borrowing or agricultural advice (Linn 1999, 114). The contrast seems immense compared to New Zealand, where McKenzie paid six shillings and fourpence average per acre for his first 3.1 million acres of farmable Maori land, but for land bought in the breakup of landed estates, he paid an average of £4 4s per acre (the landed gentry obviously gained there). The Reform Government's 'high price' was still only £2 6s. average per acre (Brooking 1992, 78).

On the other hand, Waterhouse highlighted claims of its success in the early twentieth century, particularly on Queensland's Darling Downs, where mixed farming took off. This success was endorsed by Cameron, showing that most of the growth between 1906 and 1920 was in the south-eastern districts. The widespread 1890s hardships of depression and drought were replaced by dairy industry expansion and higher value agricultural production on land that previously only had sheep (Waterhouse 2005, 31).

In Tasmania, once Castra lands were released from their exclusive reservation in the early 1870s and things started to improve economically from about 1877, there was more interest in land on the eastern side of Castra, approaching along the Plank Road through Sprent village. Some miles further south at a higher elevation, Upper Castra developed with small farms and cottages on either side of the Plank Road, which ended then at Blackwood Park, early home of Hubert Nichols.

By 1886, a sufficient amount of acreage had been settled for an extension of the road to be surveyed for a further seven miles south (AF398-1-731). This included a 200-acre Nietta town reserve about three and a half miles along. The 1886 Plan showed five unalienated lots of 320 acres that may have been ear-marked for

94 *Closer settlement in Castra*

Castra Association purchasers, but not taken up. According to a detailed newspaper report in 1894 of changes over the previous year, about 350 acres at Nietta had been scrubbed and grassed which, because of its '1300-foot elevation' and cooler climate, enjoyed 'luxuriant pasturage during summer and autumn'. Another farm had 90 acres under grass and fruit trees. The elevation had enabled development of a dairying and cheesemaking industry, particularly by John Forsyth Wright Senior and wife Emma, daughter of George Lewis in Preston, who leased General Heathcote's original property, Rawleigh at Upper Castra (News 1894b).

Other original Anglo-Indian farms there had changed hands; Colonel Bernard's Dunley was bought and much improved by Arthur Pedley, and Blackwood Park was bought by Charles Fogg, who had embarked on major fencing and clearing improvements. In 1894 road construction of the seven miles was nearly finished, which provided a 'road suitable for carts' for the 23 miles from Ulverstone to Nietta. Much of this area was natural dense forest, and its distance from the coast had impeded development until the road facilitated travel. By 1903, three families had settled at Nietta (News 1894b). The number of occupied farms in Castra, including Nietta at this stage, was growing to 54 by 1914. So not only were agricultural improvements proceeding on the early Anglo-Indian farm lots, but also villages centred in the newly selected lands were progressing, supported by road improvements.

One important advantage to the settlement process was access to sawn timber, which made it quicker to build a dwelling and avoided the labour of splitting, and it was used to build schools and churches. Sawmills operated frequently through the Castra forests towards Nietta and gradually south into Loongana. A photograph exists of the first Upper Castra sawmill in the very early 1900s operated by the Bott family. Many family-run sawmills were very prone to fire loss but were then rebuilt (Robinson, private collection).

Nietta was not the only area where demand for new, uncleared land was pushing development further south. Along the North-West, inland of the coastal settlements, small farms were being created out of dense forest. These hinterland farms were supported by coastal townships at Burnie, Wynyard and Ulverstone, where services expanded, such as sawmilling and port facilities, as well as attracting population to serve increasingly diverse social and commercial needs (Blainey 1954, 114). Demand for undeveloped farmland was mirrored by interest extending from Launceston into the North-East, particularly at Scottsdale where farmers benefited from railway access to markets via Launceston (65). One North-West example was the Anglo-Indian family of George Easton, who sent his two sons, John and George Junior, to travel ahead to their selection of a 210-acre virgin forest lot at Upper Flowerdale, south of Wynyard, in 1879 (Mercer 1978, 71–95). The North-Eastern example is that of Samuel and Rowland Skemp, who selected land at Myrtlebank beyond Lilydale in 1883. Samuel wrote three articles for prospective migrants entitled 'Settling in Tasmania' about their bush life and extra paid work obtained that were published in *Manchester Weekly Times* to which they subscribed (1, 8 and 15 March 1890). Henry Reynolds noted extension of small acreage selections to create orchards in the heavily forested Huon district (2012,

Closer settlement in Castra 95

189–90). By 1900, the production of apples, pears and berry fruits there added to the value of Tasmanian small farm products, such as potatoes, cheese, butter and fruit in the North-West, which was then its most productive region (191).

Demand for produce was stimulated in two significant ways. Blainey suggested first that the relatively large population living in West Coast mining districts created a demand for food because the cold wet climate there did not suit food cropping. Second, the cessation of inter-state trade barriers following Federation re-opened previously closed markets. He also noted that the 21 per cent rise in men working in agriculture from 1891 to 1901 accompanied a rise in cropping acreage from 168,000 to 233,000 acres, signalling that cropping was still labour intensive in this period (1954, 68).

But this data also indicated the politically desirable trend towards agriculture as opposed to pastoralism. In light of this demand-fuelled expansion by aspiring small farmers who perceived potential returns from their land and labour, the concept of Government-supervised and Government-funded closer settlement would seem to have been somewhat irrelevant in Tasmania and certainly in the North-West, North-East and Huon forested areas. Why did the Tasmanian Government adopt it?

As noted earlier, the Tasmanian Government was aware of closer settlements' attraction to the mainland colonial Governments from about 1890 and was observing those developments (Pike 1962, 30–33). There was talk in the late 1890s of the Government purchasing under-used land to improve productivity, evidenced by an enquiry in the House of Assembly on 11 July 1900. Dr Edward Lodewyk Crowther, MHA Queenborough, enquired of Premier Elliott Lewis if any steps had been taken to resume suitable estates for sub-division and closer settlement as promised on 3 November 1899. Lewis responded that no suitable estates had come on the market so far that year (News 1900c).

Public as well as political interest was aided by regular news articles, often about inter-state occurrences, and editorial comment in the newspapers, especially the Hobart *Mercury* since it carried reports of Parliamentary activity and would have been essential reading for people with political or commercial interest in Government decisions. A few examples follow.

On 13 July 1900, editorial comment stated that the New South Wales Premier 'favours very strongly closer settlement on Crown Lands and the establishment of a State Bank to utilise Trust funds'; on 11 August, it was reported that two estates near Warrnambool, of 5,400 and 4,000 acres, were under offer to the Victorian Government for closer settlement purposes subject to inspection by the Premier and the Minister of Lands (News 1900d). By 1905, the positive tenor had been replaced by a more cautionary note when the Tasmanian Closer Settlement Bill was being discussed. The *Mercury* editor warned about a never-intended situation in Victoria that was a result of a poorly drafted section of its *Act*. The Government had discovered that over £500,000 had been used over the previous five years to build working-men's houses in Melbourne (News 1905a). The same newspaper issue had an item about a New South Wales ex-MLA admitting to taking a Government commission of £5,554 for a closer settlement land purchase.

96 *Closer settlement in Castra*

Later that month, there was a reprint of a Sydney *Daily Telegraph* interview with William Redmond MP, an Irish Nationalist of over 20 years, in which he spoke of the *Irish Land Purchase Act* 1903. Twenty million pounds had been spent to create a 'peasant proprietary' by resuming large estates and grazing runs in the west of Ireland in order to increase small holdings for a better livelihood above subsistence. It was not working because landlords were not selling and there was no provision for compulsory purchase; they were only selling when the price was high enough. The landlord and tenant had to agree a deal and the Government would lend the tenant the money at a fixed annual interest rate. At the end of about 68 years approximately, the tenant or his descendants would own the land as 'absolute owners'; this was seen as the 'greatest incentive to work and thrift – the sense of ownership' and that 'direct ownership of land makes a people much more satisfied' (News 1905b). The full replication of this interview appears to be alerting local parliamentarians of the advantages of ultimate ownership and the perils of not including compulsory purchase arrangements; both these insights were taken up in Tasmania as I explain later.

When Premier Lewis, MHA for Richmond, moved the second reading of the *Lands for Settlement* bill to purchase private lands in 1901, he commented on the precedents already established by New Zealand in 1892, Queensland in 1894 and Victoria in 1898, and the New South Wales Government currently considering a closer settlement bill; all of these shared the objective to promote settlement and increase production. Emphasising his support, he went on to cite specific developments in New Zealand and Queensland and their investment potential to date, arguing that 'Tasmania would do well in following the example set' (News 1901a). William Propsting, MHA for Hobart and Leader of the Opposition, also supported the bill because Crown Lands of good quality were less available, and benefit to new settlers would 'confer a benefit also on the State as a whole'. John Hope, MHA for Devonport, made the salient point, probably based on his local knowledge, that, where the lands were 'further back', the bad condition of roads affected the land price (News 1901a).

Minister for Lands, Edward Mulcahy, MHA for Hobart, suggested that, in addition to suitable land, 'the right class of settler was required' because 'there was a deep-seated feeling in the hearts of people to secure a home for themselves, which was their very own for ever'. He was cautious about creating misconceptions in the public mind about what the bill would achieve and was keen to avoid dummying that had already occurred on good lands in some areas. This was the practice of a sham purchaser working on behalf of an anonymous buyer to that person's advantage. Potential purchasers who were prohibited for reasons such as speculation or no intention to reside employed this tactic. Carmichael Lyne, MHA for Ringarooma, thought the main objective was to increase settlement close to railways, but that care should be taken in selecting land and settlers so as not to lose taxpayers' money; he thought proximity to rail and ports would attract plenty of yeoman farmers and he supported the bill (News 1901a).

Editorial commentary made a few days later about parliamentary discussion over this bill was somewhat scathing of different members' contributions to

Closer settlement in Castra 97

the debate, while pointing to the contribution made by Hope, 'a practical bush farmer', who had seemed to advocate compulsory purchase of currently unused lands and the need for better roads. Frank Archer, MHA for Selby, did not think it was such an urgent matter compared to other measures, and was ambivalent about the bill's value. Though it received general support, the bill went to committee for further work (News 1901a). The bill was passed into law on 13 December 1901 and allowed for a Board of Commissioners to be established to negotiate with landowners, oversee valuation processes and prepare statements about possible purchasers for Crown Land.

On 17 June 1902, the first meeting of the Board of Land Purchase Commissioners was held, at which Chief Secretary George Collins, MLC Tamar, introduced the *Lands for Settlement Act* and noted that a similar *Act* was in force in New Zealand (News 1902b). He hoped Tasmania would benefit from partially open lands being eligible for closer settlement, including underused estates capable of cultivation but not yet exploited. Land near railways would be most attractive, and land suitable for dairying would supply Tasmania's needs. He referred to expanding market potential under Federation, considering successful competition in barley and hops, crops well suited to Tasmania's climate. He realised New Zealand was Tasmania's strongest produce competitor, which was why he had 'devised' a new closer settlement plan. Board members could see benefits in increased rail freight income and land taxes. The Premier's letter expressed the hope that immigration of 'desirable families' from 'the old country' would be increased as another beneficial outcome. Surveyor-General Edward Albert Counsel accepted the vote for him to be appointed chairman (News 1902b).

By 1903, following a state election, the *Mercury*'s editorial strongly endorsed the need of the new Ministry to increase Tasmania's population by inducing immigration onto Crown Lands as a priority. It argued that those lands in the North-West that may be only partially cleared would still be in great demand based on the current high productivity of potatoes that were in great demand in mainland markets. It continued the public debate over the issue of closer settlement, where cutting up large estates might be a means to attract farmers from Victoria; Legerwood in the North-East was an example cited (News 1903b).

It is likely that the Tasmanian Government was following events in New Zealand as the implications of their Act's perpetual 999-year lease, with no right of purchase, became clear; these had been part of the Tasmanian *Lands For Settlement Act* 1901. But in the *Closer Settlement Act* 1906 S. 28(i) and S.35(i), these critical clauses were amended; the length of lease was reduced to 99 years and lessees' right to buy their farms after ten years occupancy was included. These changes attracted relatively little debate, except the clause that would give the Minister compulsory purchase rights, which John Dennistoun Wood, MHA for Cumberland, thought was 'unnecessary and inadvisable' from the bill's first reading (News 1906b). As the son of an army officer-grantee at Bothwell, he typified the response of landed members of the Legislative Council that excluded the clause on two occasions, attracting comment even in South Australia (News 1907a).

98 *Closer settlement in Castra*

By early 1907, news of these changes were canvassed in New South Wales, particularly mentioning the purchase of 15,000 acres of the Cheshunt estate, cut into 58 farm lots of between 30 and 120 acres, with a school, church, country store and telephone in Deloraine (News 1907d). These examples are a small indication that the concept of closer settlement for yeoman farmers was engrossing the media intra-state and across the Tasman. An element of 'boosterism' was illustrated by another article written to entice Victorian farmers to go to New South Wales or even Queensland, where their capital could do 'incomparably better' than their place in Victoria (News 1907a).

The 1906 *Act* allowed for a Closer Settlements Fund and establishment of the Closer Settlements Board (CSB) to take responsibility and report annually to Parliament. The following year, Government tried to get support for compulsory purchase, failing again, but was successful in passing the *State Advances Act 1907*, which created the Agricultural Bank of Tasmania in 1908 'to promote the occupation, cultivation and improvement of the agricultural lands of Tasmania' by assisting people who selected Crown Land to develop farms. This function was later extended to permit lending for various farm purposes and later, in 1920, for dwellings, which made those loans available for soldier settler lessees too. The CSB operated in close collaboration with the Agricultural Bank, which provided the finance for its operations.

The issue of compulsory purchase was actively debated throughout 1910 with signs of support from all political sides and opposition being worn down; in July, Richard Charles Field, Anti-Socialist member MHA for Wilmot, admitted he had always been an opponent, but 'thought it must come'. James Belton, MHA for Darwin (the new NW electorate in 1903), felt it was the Government's duty to assist settlers and 'keep them there', and that its powers should not be limited. Edward Mulcahy, Liberal MHA for Wilmot, with past experience as Minister for Lands, spoke of two relevant principles: first, a 'universally admitted principle', that ownership carried responsibility to make best use of the land, and second, 'private interests should not interfere with public welfare' or 'stand in the way of general good' (News 1910b). According to Labour MHA for Bass Charles Richard Howroyd, closer settlement had to contend with aggregation of properties, but the Minister for Lands, Alexander Hean, MHA for Franklin, said settler properties would be big enough to compete successfully with 'big men'. There was support for tenants to become freeholders because it was accepted across the world that 'they proved to be the best', according to Herbert James Payne, Anti-Socialist MHA for Darwin. Benjamin Watkins, ALP MHA for Darwin, declared that the work put in by both parties to arrive at a solution for the issue of compulsory purchase of estates had paid off, because it was the first time in Parliament's history that a 'measure was carried through without division' (News 1910b). So it was that Tasmania adopted compulsory purchase (*Closer Settlement Act* 1911 Sections 8, 9 and 10).

In 1910 while the debate was ensuing, only nine farms were made available and the least amount of acreage was purchased, illustrating the difficulty the CSB had in operating without that instrument. From Tasmanian data published by the Commonwealth Government, the average purchase cost of each available farm

Closer settlement in Castra 99

was £637, and the average size was 232 acres, which was large compared to those in Castra and North Motton as my investigation of local closer settlement estates will show later in this chapter.

It is acknowledged that closer settlement generally, whether natural or contrived by Government, can also yield a positive result by increasing the population density of rural areas, as well as greater diversity of crops and extension of new farming areas. We have seen that additional people helped to encourage growth of new village communities and infrastructure. Pike wrote that denser farming populations encouraged services and facilities in nearby country towns (1962, 30). In 1900, about half of Australia's population lived in the country. The majority of those were yeoman landowners he called 'smallholder farmers'. The term derived from Britain where Lord Salisbury publicly supported 'a small proprietory' on up to 50 acres, backing Jessie Collings' push for parliamentary change that resulted in *The Small Holdings Act* 1892 (Orwin and Whetham 1964, 330–33). That political ideology was matched in Australia and attests to the durability of the yeoman ideal in the UK. Pike argued smallholders helped to create an Australian tradition in complete contrast to the mythological 'typical Australian' represented by roving pastoral workers, espoused by Ward in 'The Australian Legend' (1992).

The smallholder epitomised Pike's preferred 'typical' image. This figure was a family man, civilised by the company of wife and children, sharing responsibility for the minutiae of daily life, 'curbing his uncouth language, manners and dress', and developing his skills and ingenuity in coping with the wide variety of tasks upon which his family's survival depended. Even when things went wrong, or crops failed, and he had to leave to get paying work, he maintained his inherent independence and the belief that his property would pay dividends and justify his pride in it and his family. Pike went on to argue that mateship had a practical reality in the settled farming life, and obligations to help out sick or needy neighbours outranked those to any formal institution. He had also discovered that there was much less class consciousness in the smallholder's world compared to patterns well-established in pastoral societies; 'no Joneses had to be kept up with, and any traveller could yarn and eat with the family in the smallholder's kitchen' (Pike 1962, 32).

This assessment describes very succinctly the family farmers established in Preston and Castra, and is developed in more detail later. It also matches the conclusion drawn by Donald Denoon after his research into settlers across the southern hemisphere. He found that workers, by becoming smallholders, became part of a 'coalition of landowners and merchants' that 'abolished' class differences, assisted by the willingness of the state to redistribute land and facilitate the asset-accumulation of smallholdings by encouraging purchase (1983, 226). Whether workers came from the 'distressed artisans' Roberts mentioned or those leaving Britain displaced by industrialisation that Haines discussed, Denoon's argument that small rural settlements were dominated by 'a single class . . . in a calm and industrious milieu . . . and the state functioning as Good Shepherd of the whole social flock' fitted well in the forested settlement areas of Tasmania at the turn of the twentieth century.

Castra closer settlement

The number of farmers across the Castra parish rose from 40 in 1900 to 136 in 1914, with very few other resident categories listed in the post office directories. This expansion of settlement by family farmers must have been close to a boom in population and drove a consequent demand for community assets. But did it justify closer settlement investment?

By 1915, at three local sites, the CSB had bought the Werona Estate of 597 acres in Gunns Plains, the Isandula Estate of 784 acres just to the north of central Castra and 315 acres at Upper Castra on the edge of the village. The Minister of Lands, James Belton, Labour MHA for Darwin, decided in January 1915 to suspend any further purchases of land for closer settlement, due to 'financial stringency', although the Government would continue to complete those under negotiation. Purchases that year had been a record, costing £63,000, bringing the aggregate amount to slightly more than £250,000, for over 72,700 acres (News 1915g). It is interesting that the question of whether closer settlement was needed did not arise, despite financial stringency.

The 1915 Board Report made the point that activities in north-western areas had been favourable, but the Midlands had been badly impacted by drought, and those settlers would be allowed to defer rent until next harvest. The system operated in Tasmania based on the Board looking to maximise the State's advantage but still prepared to act with understanding when negative local conditions such as drought or disease impacted on lessees.

The Leven District valuation rolls of 1905 to 1908 provide evidence that, from late 1907, unimproved and unoccupied Crown Land was being made available in small acreage lots on 14-year settlement periods. Even while tenancies were being promoted under closer settlement, the Government was still engaged in regular sales of unalienated Crown Lands that were advertised and reported on in local newspapers, not just in Leven but Penguin and North Motton Municipalities. Crown Lands in and near the Leven Municipality registered in 1917 reappear in Chapter 5 (AB125-1-1, 22). Roberts called this 'the evil of having auctions of good lands in operation concurrently with selection', a situation that demonstrates the political conflict between strategies for revenue raising and those for settlement (337).

Werona Estate, Gunns Plains

The Werona Estate land had been farmed by William Henry since 1897 and consisted of 601 acres of high-quality agricultural and grazing land. He and brother John migrated from Scotland in 1854, arriving in Tasmania about 1872, and bought a major trading company at Don; William and another brother Frederick concentrated on farming. Werona was formed from the Anglo-Indian lots of Fulton, Wilson, Shaw and Crockett. In 1915, when the opportunity for purchase came about due to William's poor health, it was almost cleared of trees and stumps. The CSB divided it into six farms in areas from 88 to 156 acres to be let to tenants, five of

Closer settlement in Castra   101

whom lived in Gunns Plains and already knew the quality of the land. The Crown bought the property for an understood price of £25 10 shillings average per acre for the whole (News 1915a).

Research was conducted by Gunns Plains local descendant Raymond Hyland (2017) into the long-term outcome of each lot, which I cite here (without names) as an example of the Government's long commitment to lessees (54–55). Lot 1 was leased from 1915 to various occupiers and various durations until it was purchased in 1969, 54 years later. Lot 2 was leased to one occupier from 1915 until he purchased it in 1953, a period of 38 years. Lot 3 was leased in 1915, taken over by a returned soldier, John Coots Colhoun, until it was cancelled in 1925 and a new lessee took over in 1926. Then in 1938, a portion was split off and sold for a house block to a member of the lessee's family. Lot 4 was the largest block, 156 acres, and it included the homestead built for William Henry in 1898. It was leased until 1924 when it was leased by another occupier from whom it passed to his son and grandson until it was sold in 2008. Part of it was annexed off as a lease in 1947 and bought in 1958. Lot 5 was leased in 1915, renewed in 1935 and purchased in 1953. Lot 6 was leased in 1915, extended by another occupier in 1935 and purchased in 1953, both of these leases lasting 38 years.

In 1916, William Henry sold a further 261 acres of the adjoining Werona Estate to the CSB. The newspaper reporter opined that only if land was of 'first quality' would small acreages with 'the right class of men as tenants' make 'success' possible, and the confidence that the CSB had in this land was evident (News 1916h). Lot 7 was taken up in 1916 until 1923 when it was purchased and subsequently sold in 1947. This lot included Frederick Henry's house, that still exists, built in 1907; Frederick Henry had owned Lots 7 and 8 until 1916 when they were bought by the CSB. Lot 8 was leased from 1916 until 1924, when the lease was transferred to an occupier, who passed it to his son. It was then transferred in 1937 to another occupier together with Lot 1, but the end date of that arrangement and/ or purchase from the Board is uncertain. The final lease may have ended on 22 June 1939, according to data recorded on the CSB plan (AF396-1-710). Although there were difficult years from time to time, sometimes caused by floods, Werona tenants managed to survive well with dairying, which led to cheese-making and pigs producing bacon, and crops of potatoes, oats, barley and peas, all providing their mainstay incomes, such that saving to purchase was certainly possible, as shown from data earlier in this chapter.

Dealings at Werona were somewhat different than the procedure set down in the 1906 *Act* in respect of valuing properties. The *Act* specified valuing the land separately from any improvements like house and buildings, but at Werona one valuation was made for each lot that included buildings, 'the idea being apparently that lessees would not be under an obligation to repay the cost of the buildings and would therefore be in a better position to establish themselves' (Memorandum, AB17-1-97). So the capital value (or 'option price') of the land included the buildings, and the rent charged was 5 per cent of the option price. This unusual arrangement may have been a judgement based on the quality and number of buildings, or the high quality of the land, either or both of which conditions would have made

102   *Closer settlement in Castra*

the option price high, but this could be better handled by rent payments rather than a high initial outlay of capital. This offers us another example of the adaptability of the CSB and its officers in making pragmatic, locally appropriate decisions. However, the downside was the cost of insurance on existing infrastructure to protect the CSB's investment, but increased the lessee's rent debt. Lessees at Werona were asked in the 1940s to advise the Board if old buildings were demolished and new ones erected, and to keep the insured values of their buildings up-to-date, since any loss to fire, which was not all that unusual, might mean they would receive less than needed to replace buildings lost; this was important as building costs were 'steadily increasing' (e.g. Letter, CSB to lessee, AB17-1-689).

When the lessee decided that he wanted to purchase his farm's freehold, the amount he owed the Crown through the Department of Land Settlement (DLS) at the Agricultural Bank was assessed and, once the purchase was completed, the director notified the local council clerk of the matter. The consideration (amount) was advised as was the fact that the price did not reflect the value of any improvements the farmer had made at his own expense (Letter, Director, DLS to Ulverstone Council, 6 May 1953 in Hyland, 69). This would enable the council to assess the rateable value at the time.

Isandula Estate

The Government purchase in 1909 of the Isandula Estate for closer settlement was reported (News 1910a). This land extended from the southern area of North Motton parish into Castra parish, but 'hopes were dashed to the ground, the estate being afterwards cut up into such small and inconvenient holdings that no one would look at them and the place is still unsettled' (News 1910a). From the start, this project proved to be unsuccessful and that did not change. It was divided into 14 lots varying from 35 to 101 acres (nine were less than 51 acres), but the sticking point was the topography of the land. It was surveyed by District Surveyor, Arthur Caplan Hall, Richard Hall's son, in 1909 (AF396-1-704). That year, five lots had applicants and, although price was not mentioned, the figure of up to £40 per acre for adjacent land was quoted (News 1909d). A Select Committee looked in depth at the workings of the *Act* and physically visited certain closer settlement estates between July and November 1909 (Report 1909, Vol. LX, No. 18). Isandula received a very negative overview, which justifies its reproduction in full:

> ISANDULA. This property is on the North-West Coast, and in the municipal district of Ulverstone. It is about nine miles from the township. The area is 794 acres, and it has been subdivided into 15 selections, having an area of from 35 to 101 acres. In the opinion of your Committee, a very grave mistake has been made in purchasing this property for closer settlement, as a large portion of it is green scrub, and heavily timbered with green trees, and every witness examined, including members of the Board, gave evidence that this class of land could not be settled upon under the conditions imposed by the existing Acts. In the opinion of your Committee, a further error was made by

Closer settlement in Castra   103

the Minister of Lands, in conjunction with the Chairman of the Closer Settlement Board, over-ruling the recommendation made by Messrs. Rudge and Von Bibra to purchase other property adjoining Isandula. The additional land would have made residence on the estate possible. At present the larger portion of the estate is unlet, and, under present conditions, it will be very difficult to find tenants. The Board made a further error in dividing the estate into such small sections, it being practically impossible for a man to maintain a home on the proceeds of 35 acres of land at a distance from a township. Much of the land is of good quality, and under proper conditions it would be taken up readily. The Committee have evidence that 50 or 60 people inspected this with a view to selection, but only five blocks were applied for, and some of these are likely to be forfeited (ii).

The Report went on to stress the Board's grave error in purchasing Isandula and other estates in terms of their suitability, the high acreage cost and unviable size, while being satisfied with others (iii). The Minister was found to have overridden the Board's majority decision in some cases; at Isandula, this meant failure to add adjoining land, and a discrepancy of accuracy in reporting the price asked. He had also failed to put in promised roads on which tenants were paying the interest on money set aside (iv). The Committee recommended that 'several important amendments be made' in the *Act* before any further purchases, to see if the amendments were working satisfactorily (vii). A list of estates offered to the CSB was tendered by Chairman Edward Counsel, and it is noteworthy that Hubert Nichols offered various lands as vendor's agent (4–5, 86–89).

The Committee's comments about Isandula are put into context by the evidence retold here:

Nichols offered the CSB Stockley's [Anglo-Indian] block and Clarke's block, both in Castra, and land in Nietta district, as well as Isandula, which was purchased. He also proposed 500 acres at Gunns Plains and 470 acres at Wilmot that had not been inspected. He gave evidence to the Committee. He was agent for Isandula, and thought it more suited to 9 lots (rather than 15) and assessed that it would take 2–3 years for a man to build on it, and 10–12 years to make a living. An adjoining lot of 164 acres owned by Ellis would have been a better block at about £4 per acre. There was also William Lewis's homestead of 240 acres adjoining, offered at about £8 per acre. It was inspected but refused – Nichols did not know the reason. Clarke's 322 acres were also adjoining to the south. If this had been bought, he had told Clarke he would not ask for commission because he believed it was the best value and suited to the CSB's purpose because it was suitable for immediate occupation and better than most for dairying. Rudge and Von Bibra recommended but the Board did not. Colonel Stockley was offered £10 per acre for his 369 acres by cable to Britain which he accepted, well priced and also adjoining, but then the Board refused. Nichols said it would have fetched between £11 and £12 for the CSB and had frontage to a main road.

104 *Closer settlement in Castra*

The estate was the subject of much frequent review in the state's newspapers. The lack of sales or development at Isandula Estate was again commented upon in 1913, when only two sales were made to neighbouring farmers who wished to extend (News 1913c). One instance was Lot 5 of 35 acres added to Honorah Roden's 18 ¾ acre freehold next door, but her lease was cancelled in the *Tasmanian Government Gazette* of 12 September 1916 before being re-leased on 1 October 1916 to Mark Bakes, lessee of the adjacent Lot 1 at the time. Close inspection of the Plan reveals words like 'forfeited', 'surrendered', and 'cancelled' with *Gazette* dates appended that apply to most of the Lots and are clear evidence of the difficulty the CSB had in finding durable lessees. The 1917 CSB annual report was less than positive and stated only 120 acres 'in aggregate' were cultivated (News 1917d).

Criticism was that the money paid was too high for the 'average' quality of the land, the lack of metalled road and the eight-mile distance from markets in Ulverstone. Apparently, it cost the Board £7 10 shillings an acre, but most of it was being used by 'bush vermin', so the suggestion was to cut the rent, making it tempting for settlers 'starting from scratch' to rid the 'whole district' of the 'eyesore' (News 1913c). In contrast to the favourable CSB 1927 report on Werona, the same on Isandula emphasised the bad season, peas a failure, potatoes only one ton per acre, and oats very light; vacant lots were covered in blackberry and rabbit infestation and farmers would never do well on the light soil in dry seasons. Only 104 acres of new season's crops were planted and livestock levels were low compared to Gunns Plains (News 1927e). After a few fresh attempts by the CSB in the 1930s and arrangements of one-year leases, eventually most of it was gazetted in 1944 as 'Withdrawn from the provision of the *Closer Settlement Act* and proclaimed a State Forest Reserve' (AF396-1-704). It was planted out to radiata pines, and continues as such, having been harvested in 2019-2020 and being replanted.

Upper Castra land

This land at Upper Castra (AF396/1/709) was split into four Lots of 50, 85, 79 and 92 acres. It included the original Anglo-Indian purchases by Bernard and Heathcote, but by 1915 these were becoming available, having been bought in the meantime by settlers already mentioned who had made good improvements and conducted dairying enterprises. The Plan again tells the history of lessees who had varying duration of tenure. Lots 1 and 2 were both leased in 1915, then combined into one Lot and leased from 1927 to 1932. Crops in the 1926/1927 season had been limited to potatoes and hay. The Board President W. Hurst reported that year that Lot 2 with its original homestead was the only lot that could grow enough to keep a settler and family, and the others were only useful as runs for stock (News 1927e). It became vacant in 1927, but had been relet until the end of financial year 1932. At this point, Robert Henry Crawford leased it from 1932 until 1964 when he eventually purchased it. This land fronted the Nietta Road, was next to a Hall and opposite the recreation ground, the shop and near the two churches in Upper Castra village.

Across the road, Crawford also acquired the lease of Lot 3, 92 acres, in 1936. Perhaps his motivation was running stock supported by the local Board Inspectors. He purchased Lot 3 from the CSB in 1948. There is evidence on the plan that rent for Lots 1 and 2 combined was £20 per annum for the first two years, rising to £30 for the next three. Where buildings on Lot 2 were valued at £250 in the 1920s, additional annual rent was charged that was calculated to pay them off with interest in 21 years. In common with the Isandula land, Lot 4's 79 acres were reserved for forestry purposes in 1947. Other land as it became available was offered for soldier settlement, discussed in the next chapter.

Was the closer settlement scheme a success in Castra? On the balance of the evidence, Werona was, but it started from a much higher standard of usage and was on superior quality soils and level topography. There was also the intangible benefit of familiarity by those who took on the leases, having already farmed for the Henrys, and a lease meant they could direct their funds to seed and livestock, as predicted by the special arrangement there. Although the land was subjected to periodic flooding of the Leven River across the plains, this is recognised as contributing to fertility of the land.

At Isandula, in-depth analysis would probably reveal it was not financially beneficial to the State Government where no village evolved to help hold people together. Subsequent forestry may have been better but, even today, the steep hills are a challenge for log trucks when they need to haul timber out. As to Upper Castra, we saw some change from lease to ownership, no doubt helped by village assets of churches and school and earlier development of the Anglo-Indian farmlands.

When Meikle (2014, 472) weighed up lessons that should have been learnt by Government and community from the *Waste Land Acts*, she highlighted problems that came with establishing small farming where high transport costs and limited local markets existed – problems that continued with closer settlement. We have already discussed the additional difficulties caused by inadequate quality roads. Whatever the potential for other areas of Tasmania, closer settlement was disadvantaged in the settled forest areas of North-West Tasmania for a deeper reason than the variable qualities of land, the difficulty with water in dry years or poor road access, or even the quality of the prospective lessees. I argue that the concept of *renting* land went against the grain of the aspirations of the yeoman-inspired settlers of the previous 50 odd years. Agricultural immigrants who were attracted to come to Tasmania, especially the North-West, were motivated by the desire to *own* their own land. The conditions of immigration for decades encouraged that prospect by Governments setting prices low, offering extended periods of purchase price repayment or even giving land away under certain conditions.

From Colonel Crawford onward, rural settlement was always about owning land to sustain the livelihood for a good life and to hand on to one's sons, with the family benefitting from what they built for themselves. From that perspective, becoming a tenant on leases of 99 years would have been most unappealing to the many small farmers who sought settlement with independence. Their elder generations who had come from Britain from the 1850s onwards could remember

106 *Closer settlement in Castra*

its 'high farming' system of tenants and landless peasants. They would have been hard pressed to recommend to their younger generations that any landlord, particularly a Government one administered by potentially inexperienced public servants, was a good idea.

We have seen that rentals were often in default and interest charged on loans was often below the cost of the money lent to the Government (News 1927e; Keneley 2002, 375). While default on rent may have been due to flexibility on the part of local Inspectors, it may also have characterised what Pike referred to – that formal institutional obligations took second place to local imperatives. Given the variable take-up of initial leases, and frequency of early surrender as well as rent defaults, it is surprising that the scheme continued, but perhaps vested interests supported its continuance due to the positive promise of a better year next year, as suggested in CSB annual reports (e.g. Perry in News 1917d).

While closer settlement has had critics in hindsight for a variety of reasons already covered, it is also true that land dealings in Tasmania were never straightforward and accepted without contemporary criticism, even from the time of earliest colonial settlement (Bigge 1823). I think this is related to the entrenched ideology of landholding in the English aristocracy and gentry from the seventeenth century, called the 'aristocratic ethic' by Clark (1985). He argued that British traditional society had two ideals, the ideal of a Christian and the ideal of a gentleman. The first was underwritten by the second in a society whose 'families, landowners, Anglicans, masters, kings partly echoed both'. The aristocratic ethic, with its exemplars of the aristocracy and gentry, gave credibility and continuance to 'a lofty social hierarchy . . . . The vitality and power of the aristocratic ideal' was immensely important in both eighteenth century England and France (1985, 93–95). This was brought to Van Diemen's Land by the earliest settlers, who were imbued with the same ideas but without being of the aristocratic class. This colony presented a clean slate to the early pastoralists, who saw their position as the new 'aristocracy' or gentry of the island colony. They discovered that land bestowed power and influence, which they used to their own ends and, in so doing, entrenched the 'land is power' ideology into the leadership structures of the colony and then the State (Reynolds 2012, 165–68, 1969a, 61–72). From their large estates, they were less concerned with settlement of the forested areas, especially after profiteering from pre-emptive rights was quashed in the 1850s. This left the field open for agricultural immigrants, the yeoman farmers, both actual and aspiring, who accepted they were responsible for doing the hard work of creating farms for themselves, as their own masters, the same independence we saw that was characteristic of yeomanry across centuries and global locations.

Even as some disadvantages of the closer settlement scheme were pointed out by people in the know to politicians, there seemed little enthusiasm for questioning the rightness of continuing the scheme, only in creating further amendments (News 1905c). Because closer settlement was the business of State Governments, this allowed them to continue to implement it to suit their political and economic priorities without any interference from the Commonwealth Government, which was in a position to have an overview of the state of affairs across the whole

Closer settlement in Castra 107

nation. It was this overview advantage that benefited the Dominion Government in Canada and the national Government of New Zealand, so they were each able to tailor their policies to the needs of their particular national circumstances and support the ideals and aims of yeoman farmers in their national interests.

Social demands merged with politics again as soldiers who had served in the Great War began to return home to pick up the threads of their lives, and this is our next topic.

5 Soldier settlement in Tasmania and Castra

We have seen in early settlement decades that strong ties bound the farming families of the Castra communities. Was that spirit of solidarity carried through in supporting the next generation of young men who wanted to settle down to farming after their return from years of war? Despite scholarly opinions reviewed in this chapter, the yeoman ideal was not outdated in North-West Tasmania. My argument is that families who had cleaved farmlands out of forest epitomised yeoman ideals. For them, the ideal was best supported by backing their returning sons, 'self-reliant, hardened by the rigours of war', into farming if that was their choice, even if it meant taking on a government lease (Rost 2008, 39). In contrast to the closer settlement lease, there was such public support for repaying 'the boys' for their efforts that parents would have seen it as a stepping stone to ownership, which was, after all, the aim of Australian Governments at every level. Coming home to settle into their wider supportive community and embracing the idea of living a peace-filled life on the land was intended to persuade, and succeeded in urging, country Tasmanians to endorse the scheme.

Through an in-depth analysis of cases where soldier settlers were approved to lease Castra farmlands, I consider how their links to this locality and its residents contributed to their longevity and eventual evolution from 'Occupier' to 'Proprietor' in the yeoman farmer tradition. But first, I review the soldier settlement historiography, considering arguments about failure, and set the scene for Tasmania's soldier settlement scheme.

Much has been written about what happened to soldiers when they returned to their homelands after the Great War, and this has included processes of repatriation, rehabilitation and settlement in Australia, Britain, Canada and New Zealand (Scott 1936, 698–850; Fedorowich 1997, 47–80; Powell 1981, 64–87; Fedorowich 2002; Roche 2002, 23–32). Because land settlement was one of the major strategies of the Australian repatriation process, it has been studied with various emphases (Fry 1985, 29–43; Lake 1987; Powell 1985, 225–29; Garton 1996; Scates and Oppenheimer 2016; Macintyre 1986, 198–221; Rost 2008, 38–56; Johnson 2005, 496–512). Fedorowich observed that Australia has a particularly rich selection of works about post-Great War soldier settlers, often undertaken by graduates, that sheds light at regional and local levels, containing useful material not readily accessed (Milton 1968; Parker 1982; Reynolds 1982).

DOI: 10.4324/9781003229841-6

Soldier settlement in Tasmania and Castra 109

In Tasmania, this local relevance is found in several recent studies, each having a specific focus (Beresford 1983, 90–100; Martin 1992; Richardson 2005; Gerrard 2015, 23–39; Dingo 2010). Beresford argued there was political collusion to avoid public knowledge of the 'human tragedy' unfolding in the settlement scheme (98). Richardson's close focus on political decision-making across the gamut of returned soldier repatriation activities led him to agree that the settlement scheme had been 'a disaster by any standard' (394). Gerrard's study included three Aboriginal soldiers who took up leases in the North Motton area (29). Martin looked at the scheme in the Huon where orchard plots averaging eight acres were too small to withstand the 'vagaries of weather and export markets', and orchardists lacked government help in marketing. By 1935, of the 158 soldier settlers, fewer than a third remained. The more successful men there had gone onto family-owned land that added to their previous orcharding expertise and provided capital for development from sale to the Closer Settlement Board (CSB) (209–10). That strategy was active in Castra and is discussed in the next section.

Settlement for returned soldiers

There was a history of land grants in Australia to ex-marines in the earliest years of European settlement when Governor Phillip was instructed to offer them 'every reasonable encouragement' to 'settle in the country' to grow food crops to supplement state farm crops (Davidson 1981, 46–47). From that early imperative to produce food for the fledgling settlement, ex-soldiers were granted 30-40 acres of land conditional on residence and improvements with major concessions like tools, seed and one year's rations; a common practice was a rent-free grant for ten years, in lieu of being obliged to employ, feed and clothe convict labourers; fulfilling this arrangement could lead to land being rent-free forever (Reeves 1902, 197). They were later preferenced over private settlers (Grenville to Governor Phillip, 19 June 1789, "Governor's Dispatches." HRA Series I 1914–15, 124–28). In early nineteenth-century Tasmania, we have seen how ex-military settlers received land grants and other benefits, often after their service in India. Rather differently in the 1860s, the government support integral to Colonel Crawford's plan for ex-servicemen was only legal, rather than moral or financial – certainly, no convict servants, no rations or livestock, no improvement conditions and not even a road.

Persuasive arguments by British race patriots were made to the British Government that settlement of its veterans onto lands overseas would not only strengthen imperial bonds but would also be a reward for their service. These arguments built on the long-held ideology of the yeoman farmer and so-called 'backward-looking' agrarianism that Fedorowich argued was 'another facet of dominion settlement policy' (Fedorowich 1997, 2). These arguments were a push to subsidise British soldier migrants, but evolved to support the use of British loans to fund Australia's scheme, which would also include British veterans. Potential post-war mass unemployment in Britain was seen as a breeding ground for radicalism as early as 1915, but similar fears, amplified by sectarian unrest after the conscription debate, were held in Australia too (Powell 1988, 96; Lake 1987, 26–36; Macintyre 1986, 187–89).

110   *Soldier settlement in Tasmania and Castra*

Garton argued that the Australian strategy to settle returned Australian Imperial Force (AIF) soldiers was the 'third great government effort since 1860 to establish a self-sufficient yeoman class of agriculturalists', referring to selection and closer settlement. Since the highly variable results of both these schemes on settlers and cultivated acreages were well known, his argument went that planners should have been well aware of potential obstacles to success (Garton 1996, 119). But the lure of the idea that country life could restore and renew by working the land was powerful when counterpoised with the vision of newly developing city streets thronging with returned soldiers without work but with potential to be politically radicalised by experiences of war. Newspapers across Australia were already carrying reports of riotous soldiers and looting in Sydney (News 1916b, 1916c, 1916d, 1916e). The promise of rural settlement had already formed part of mid-war recruitment propaganda for volunteers (Lake 1987, 25). Settlement on the land was again linked to the yeoman ideal as a potentially stabilising conservative factor in rural populations, with one Australian newspaper applauding the scheme for Australian men whose previous lives 'had been twisted out of shape' by their wartime experiences with many needing a new start, while noting the doubts already expressed by British authorities about settlement on the land for British soldiers (News 1916f). So, public support in Australia for the idea of a peaceful country life with 'homes for heroes' and 'a debt repaid' blended with the need for national economic progress (Beresford 1983, 90). These ideas comprised a complex mixture of public endorsement, political expediency and policy advantages backgrounded by the need for speed.

The potential for difficulties between levels of government in Australia could well have been foreseen, but enthusiasm and good intentions masked the problems ahead when national plans were made. Australian state administrative structures for closer settlement were already in place and could be adapted for the new challenge (Powell 1988, 8). But the States were not prepared to surrender their longstanding authority over land resources to a federally supervised scheme. When all the Premiers met Commonwealth representatives from 17 to 19 February 1916, they decided to agree to Commonwealth funding providing it was under state management. The newspapers closely followed each day's deliberations (News 1916g). New Zealand's Premier Massey was the first to authorise purchasing land for soldiers, but his advice that all but experienced men should have training was generally ignored in Australia (Scott 1936, 842).

Powell noted that all soldier settlement schemes shared similar features, most having potentially negative impacts:

> The need for quick decisions at every level to cope with the flood of exservicemen; the effect on these decisions of local patriotism and general sympathy and feeling of responsibility for 'the returned men'; the heavy pressure from special interest groups representing veterans; and liberal finance granted – too often against little security.

> (1971, 144)

Soldier settlement in Tasmania and Castra 111

Almost without exception, scholarly accounts of soldier settlement schemes have argued they were a costly failure, not just in financial terms but also because of the hardship caused to so many families – costly to them in human and social terms. Powell qualified judgment of overall so-called 'failure' as not correctly descriptive for every situation, except where soldier settlers themselves were often 'disappointed and distressed' at shortcomings in the political and administrative systems (1981, 72). What has been lacking is any discussion about soldier settlers with family farm connections or their own resources who did not apply for settler leases and therefore do not appear in archival sources for historians to study. Family connections proved to be important in Castra as we shall see.

Lake's 1987 book, *The Limits of Hope*, had a major impact as an early work focussed on Victoria, and she stressed the scheme's failure. She argued the 'yeoman-ideal' was out of step with market-oriented and capital-intensive farming beginning to prevail before 1914. Control structures with local inspectors were established generally, but, in Victoria, many inspectors had little agricultural expertise, and this control system set up adversarial circumstances, leaving settlers in invidious situations when they were forced to plead for assistance. Men's dependency on their family's labour, causing hardships to wives and children, flew in the face of the 'breadwinner' ideology because they were unable to 'fulfil their family responsibilities', often through no fault of their own; problems beyond their control were drought, rabbits, poor temporary dwellings and bureaucratic delay (174). By the end of the 1930s, 'the decision to jettison the yeoman model of land settlement' was an acceptance that the settlers' failure was not their fault (233–39). The inspectors' growing attitude about business management imperatives on farms would be echoed by the blatantly capitalistic basis of the Rural Reconstruction Commissioners in the mid-1940s who believed 'farmers had to be efficient to obtain reasonable returns, [while] earning and paying good wages' (Canberra 1944). By then, lessons from the past meant an emphasis on appropriate farm size and farm advisory services driven by economic rather than emotional factors. Australia lagged behind the United States in adoption of rural production technology, due to its prevalence of small farms (Connors 1970, 77, 80).

I disagree with Lake's opinion about the yeoman ideal, an opinion that Victorian historian Templeton also argued eloquently against (Templeton 1988, 42–50). By concentrating on soldier settlers as 'victims', Lake missed the 'unprecedented, unshakeable optimism' of the era, when science was playing an even stronger part in agricultural advancement as well as increased mechanisation – both ways that made thousands more yeoman farming families have the potential to achieve the ideal (43). Templeton made a number of relevant points, including that individual government files might contain ten or 20 years of misfortunes, because they tended to catalogue problems – agricultural, financial or personal – but not the successful times (49).

It is important to consider how soldiers' experiences mirrored those of other settlers and how communities handled common challenges. Fahey wrote that Lake's study was 'marred by an inadequate sample size' and her 'regrettable failure' to

112   *Soldier settlement in Tasmania and Castra*

consider the full range of available files (Fahey 1988). He agreed with Templeton that Lake also under-rated various government concessions that enabled many to persist, either until prices rose, disease was mastered by science, or just simply, more experience and improved expertise was carefully adopted while overcoming the 'long pioneering period' (47). When Lake did mention success, Templeton saw her devaluing it, being due to 'good fortune' rather than valorising the hard work settlers and family members had achieved to earn it (48). The recognition of hard work done collectively was borne out decades later in the Murray river-lands soldier settlement after the Second World War (George 1999). In light of these critiques, Lake's story of Victorian soldier settlement was unbalanced by failure accounts that ignored the continuing importance of small farmers in agricultural and horticultural production, and call into question her claim about out-of-step yeoman farming.

Scates and Oppenheimer disagreed with Lake's argument about the over-bearing power of the inspectors because of their scarcity in mainland 'back-blocks' where settlers were obliged to negotiate with city bureaucrats (2016, chapter 1). New South Wales's archival records evidenced families who battled against bureaucratic obstacles, believing they were being let down on their just 'entitlements' – their moral rights as returned soldiers (Scates and Oppenheimer 2014, 229–53). They highlighted the importance of wives and organisations like the CWA to help with social contact and community spirit. Even so, probably because they also focussed on records of the 'failures' who had left their land by 1939, they too judged the whole scheme to have been a failure (2016, 204–17). When 'failure' dictates the archival or historical narrative focus, different measures of success are often under-assessed. This ignores the beneficial effects of social collaboration in developing community assets like postal services and schools, together with the ability to pass farms on to successors. Roche suggested academics should look beyond a 'book-keeping interpretation of failure and success', and that micro-scale studies offered more interpretive value (2002, 28). He also pointed out that telling the failure stories first and successes second created the implication that failures predominated (47). This is an interestingly nuanced perspective in such a well-researched arena.

It is important to remember that, nationally, 50 per cent of soldier settlers stayed on their farms achieving the yeoman ideal, surviving and eventually thriving and that 'state-provided welfare [was] substantially more generous than that offered to other Australian citizens and to veterans in comparable nations' (Holbrook 2018, 228–30). Scates and Oppenheimer acknowledged that survivors who lasted to 1939 and their descendants had 'voices that must be heard', citing data showing that in June 1939, 43 per cent remained on their land in South Australia, 33 per cent in Western Australia and 63 per cent in Tasmania (1514 out of 2380 settled) (2016, 236, 240). These Tasmanian figures are much higher compared to the 1928 figures collected by Mr Justice Pike (777 remained out of 1976) (Pike 1929). Garton also argued soldier settlement was not the great failure portrayed by critics, because 20,000 families were assisted across Australia (Garton, 141). In 1929, Mr Justice Pike, as Royal Commissioner for the Commonwealth, estimated

Soldier settlement in Tasmania and Castra 113

a national settler retention rate of 71 per cent (see Powell 1988, Table 14, 105). Among the problems, he found many farms across the nation were too small for the settler to meet his commitments and provide 'reasonable comfort' for himself and his family while coping with quirks of weather and markets, and he made particular mention of this problem in Tasmania. Mr Justice Pike wrote 'The definition of a "Home Maintenance Area" means such an area as, when worked by an industrious settler, will, under average seasons and circumstance, return him sufficient to meet his commitments to the State and to maintain himself and family in reasonable comfort' (19) The basic wage then was £4 per week (Wadham 1967, 46). Pike's definition supported Mr Justice Higgins' determination in the Harvester Case relating to adequate income for the 'normal needs [of an Australian worker] living in a civilised community' (Crowley 1974, 284; Williams 1975, 98). The link between the 'Basic Wage' and the 'Living Area concept' was formally acknowledged when mainland marginal wheat farms were reorganised in the 1940s.

Tasmania's situation and administrative arrangements

In Tasmania, the potential of settling returned soldiers on the land was a very acceptable strategy to the predominantly rural population (Richardson 2005, 279). It also appealed to the Department of Lands and Surveys which understood difficulties caused by the loss of workers in farming communities where young men had enlisted (JPPP 1916–17,Vol. LXXV, No. 23). Tasmania's major problem was a shortage of good quality agricultural land, much of which was already either owned or leased under closer settlement. By 1918, 31 per cent of prime land in Tasmania was in private hands (Powell 1988, 103).

Briefly, the *Returned Soldiers' Settlement Act* 1916 (hereafter *RSS Act*) set out to 'make provision for the Settlement of Returned Soldiers on Crown and Settlement Lands' by amending the *Closer Settlement Act* 1913. It contained 'compulsory purchase powers, to use monies for administration, buying land, surveys, subdivision, clearing, draining, fencing, of improving of such land, the making of roads, erection of buildings (none to cost more than £250 per allotment), and making [financial] advances to soldier settlers'. It laid down that 'Allotments may be sold or leased to the settler, but may not, without consent, be transferred within ten years'. No deposit was required and no rates or taxes levied for four years. The settler may be assisted by advances to generally improve his allotment and to purchase implements, stock and seed, plants and trees (News 1916g). It was the duty of the Closer Settlement Board (CSB) '[a]s far as is practicable to assist applicants in acquiring allotments suitable to their experience, capital and physical fitness' (S.9 (8)). Aspirations of Members of Parliament that, 'in every possible way, the [*Act*] guards the soldier settler from hardship, and holds out a helping hand wherever it is needed' were reflected in the newspaper report of proceedings (News 1916g). Despite national discussions, the *Act* made no mention of provision of agricultural training, although 'vocational training' was provided for by the State War Council. Julian Green pointed out that provisions in this *Act* followed those in the

114 *Soldier settlement in Tasmania and Castra*

Crown Lands Act 1911 to avoid speculation by, for instance, limiting the area relative to the class of land (2018, 385). The conditions applying to settlers appeared to be firmly settled, but evidence discussed further in this chapter suggests that flexibility could be applied case-by-case.

The administration of the *RSS Act* utilised what was already in place with the appointment of Phillip Perry as President to supervise the CSB. His 1917 Annual Report advised that future vendors should supply suitable, eligible applicants for subdivisions, thus easing the departmental burden to inspect. In effect 'rounding off' the business of civilian closer settlement, he said this was its tenth year, so those lessees of 1906 could now purchase their blocks in fee simple. Under the *RSS Act* 1916, the Board would concentrate exclusively on estates suitable for settling returned soldiers (News 1917d, 1917e). This opened the way for land agents to become even more involved in recruiting land and settlers.

The Board focus on previously farmed land is significant because there had been discussion in Parliament in 1916 about using unalienated Crown Lands for soldier settlers, which had aroused a negative response from Hubert Nichols, MLC for Mersey, who had personal experience of virgin land clearance at Nietta. He told members that it took three lifetimes to clear the bush, and would be quite unsuitable for soldiers who were expected to earn money to repay debts and to live (News 1916i). George Godfrey Becker, MHA for Bass wanted any reference to settling soldiers on Crown Land struck out, to which Joshua T.H. Whitsitt, MHA for Darwin responded that, 'if the VDL Company could clear land, build a house and then dispose of the area, surely the Government could do the same', but experienced men should do the clearing, not expect returnees to clear land. James Belton, also MHA for Darwin and then current Minister for Lands and Works, had past experience as a timber-worker, farmer, butter factory owner and Councillor in the North-West. He too understood the immense amount of work to bring bushland into productivity and thought soldiers should generally have cleared land unless they themselves chose to settle on Crown Land. He urged that the Government 'should never induce' returned soldiers onto unproductive land without providing three to four years financial support (News 1916j). It is hard to find evidence of these concerns having any effect in practice especially in the largely undeveloped forest land around Nietta in the southern reaches of Castra, where some men left within a couple of years, which I discuss later in this chapter. The alignment of soldier settlement with earlier closer settlement would seem to indicate the inevitability of any vacant lots being directed to returned soldiers, without consideration that current vacancy might argue against its suitability.

Each year, the Minister for Lands presented a statement of land settlement activity to the House of Assembly. 1919 was a major year of rapid demobilisation and Minister Alexander Hean, MHA for Franklin was appointed as an additional minister to help with the increased volume of work and the Department of Lands and Works became two separate departments. He spoke of the new department and, because of demand in the North-Western districts, Burnie resident G.G. Noyes was appointed to the Board. Hean added that each soldier's wishes cannot be overlooked, as his own selection suits him best, often being near relations for

Soldier settlement in Tasmania and Castra 115

guidance. During the financial year, 30 per cent of settlers were doing well, the same were making fair progress and the balance 'from little to no progress'. But over 3,600 acres were being cropped where only half had been cropped before (News 1919c). This report demonstrates important Departmental issues that become relevant further in this chapter.

By October 1921, Minister Hean reported that land purchases had slowed, and all applicants had been allocated property by the end of June. Reduced hay and potato prices had started to bite into remunerations, although dairying operations were yielding returns. Already some settlers were abandoning or cancelling their leases after their free period ran out, and these were re-offered to other interested soldiers without difficulty. Applicants preferred 'single ready-made farms', encouraged probably by the presence of houses. Forty to 50 men were still waiting and after those were settled, 'the task begun in 1916 of settling our returned men should be complete'. He referred to the 1921 amendment that excluded ex-British soldiers from the benefits of Tasmania's scheme, making them a Federal Government responsibility, which shows political understanding that Tasmania could not support the national strategy in this way. The Minister concluded by stating that individual soldier settlers' problems were so varied, they needed addressing one-by-one. Hopefully, members would continue their 'sympathetic and cooperative attitude towards the department' in its 'gigantic work restoring our returned soldiers' (News 1921b). This hope is a distinct echo of government and popular support for the scheme.

To assist with local-level administration, local Advisory Committees were formed, which meant three members of the Leven Council were chosen to give advice on offers of properties and 'ensure these men secured property, which would enable them to succeed in life'. Concern was raised consistently throughout 1919 spurred by the Closer Settlement Board (CSB) overturning a local decision and deeming rejected land suitable. Local dissatisfaction continued as their expert knowledge was ignored, because the Government Valuator was making decisions to accept land prior to obtaining their advice. Councillors emphasised the importance of local knowledge of Committee members in advising the CSB re properties on offer; their knowledge of local conditions, situation, and soil character and value was important to protect the soldier. Council was concerned that land agents frequently accompanied the Government Valuator to properties where they had a financial interest, but Hobart advised that the owner or his agent could be present (News 1919a). Councillors unanimously objected to agents interested in selling the property being at the inspection (News 1920a).

Dissatisfaction may have led to a Select Committee appointment in 1921 to report on soldier settlement administration, potential for expansion of leasehold Crown Lands to provide 'bush runs on small areas' and improvements made to currently held lands (JPPP 1921–1922, Vol.LXXXV, No.61). After extensive state-wide research, the Committee found land prices and advances were too high – 'practically impossible for many to meet their liabilities' – and on forested land, repayments were due before there was any crop to sell, bearing out the warnings of Belton and Nichols. It found much variation in local Advisory Boards,

116 *Soldier settlement in Tasmania and Castra*

with occasions when they and Valuators had either over-valued land or disagreed about suitability. They heard evidence that supervision had largely been inadequate, that half-yearly visits were of little use to the inexperienced settler, and improvement was necessary. It was their opinion that about 15 per cent of settlers were unsuitable due to inexperience or physical disabilities, about 5 per cent were 'non-triers' and many others wanted more expert supervision. Based on written off or outstanding amounts, the Committee recommended a fixed interest rate of 4 per cent for five years from January 1922, that arrears be capitalised, and that building advances be regarded as part of the reappraised capital value of the property. Perhaps most importantly, they recommended permanent supervisors should be appointed who had power to visit as often as necessary to provide essential advice to settlers and to keep the Minister informed of any default in the lease conditions. At that time, 2,395 soldiers were settled, 197 leases had forfeited, 29 were empty holdings and 674 soldiers were settled since June 1920 (Select Committee Report 1921–2). The value of quality inspection and supervision in Castra is discussed next.

The recommended administrative 'improvement' came about after another Select Committee in early March 1923 recommended formation of six District Advisory Boards to hear appeals for remissions and revaluations from soldier settlers that could be forwarded to the Minister for decision. Each board would include members of the Returned Sailors and Soldiers Imperial League of Australia (RSSILA) who could argue the soldier's case (JPPP, Vol. LXXXVI, 1922–23, No. 60).

Appointment of a Royal Commission into soldier settlement in mid-1926 was instigated by Premier Joseph Lyons because of his growing concern about Tasmania's ability to cope with losses accrued (News 1926c). This news provided additional stimulus for meetings of unhappy soldiers, one of which was on King Island. Soldiers there worried they would not be represented at the Commission, so Inspector Cooper sent a record of their problems to McGough, secretary of the CSB, who forwarded it to Chief Justice Nicholls, Commission chairman (14 August 1926). Not only were its contents taken as evidence, the 'very sensible letter' was quoted verbatim in the Report, because it encapsulated problems the Commission had found to be widespread. The reliability and competency of local inspectors and the soldiers' dependence upon them was noted, and the point made that the Board was responsible for them to deal in a 'conscientious, candid and impersonal' way with settlers.

The Report was handed down in September 1926. The most prevalent fault discovered related to bureaucratic failure to select adequately knowledgeable and experienced settlers who knew how to work hard but also how to manage a farm. High prices were a consequence of 'commission agents' who affected prices and 'induced unfit men to go on the land'. They found 'it was taken for granted that every man who wanted a farm got a farm whether he was fit or not' regardless of having private capital. Comment was made about lack of systematic training for the unskilled although lack of time had precluded anything of value being managed and many settlers drifted away to the cities when they realised their inability to make a success of their farms. The Commission agreed with applicants' case for revaluation, already in train, and this must be done to retain existing settlers on the basis 'of what each settler has got from the State, not of what he has to show today'. As to purchase of buildings, the Commission found it strange to expect men to buy buildings on land they did not own, and better explanation was necessary. Deserted farms should be sold by tender at prices reasonably reflecting value, preferably in fee simple, as a way of avoiding lessees combining to 'enforce their demands by political action'. The Commission summed up by expecting the State would make more losses because this scheme could not be run as a private business, and that any Minister attempting to do so would not have survived the party system. If administrators tasked with daily decision-making were given 'responsibility without undue interference' and considered the question, 'Can this man carry on with a reasonable hope of success?', then remaining settlers would be treated reasonably according to their personal situation (Royal Commission 1926).

Minister Belton addressed various matters of dissatisfaction in his recommendation of a Commission. In his 20-page response, he agreed his Inspectors had advised revaluations were necessary for continuing farmers. While acknowledging 'the great importance of the scheme' to soldiers and taxpayers, it was impossible for the Minister to be involved in daily minutiae and he welcomed 'a thorough investigation' to clarify reasons for rising arrears and write-offs (Belton, 20 included in the 1926 Royal Commission Report).

Throughout Australia, the parlous financial state of the scheme became more evident following various State Enquiries and Royal Commissions, so in 1927, the Commonwealth Parliament appointed their own Royal Commission under Mr Justice George Herbert Pike to investigate the financial aspects of soldier settlement, because the funding came from the Commonwealth. This Commission's findings were published in 1929 (CPP 1929, pp. 1901–59). His final remarks actually provided an endorsement of yeoman family farming: 'there is no question that in very many cases, particularly in the grazing and mixed farming propositions where the settlers have been given sufficient area, the settlers are doing well and making quite a good living' and that, 'taken as a body, the soldier settler holders of Australia will compare more than favourably with any other body of settlers in the different States'. As he shrewdly observed, remission of debts would not turn the soldier on land that was too small to meet annual expenses into a successful farmer (pp. 1924–5).

Local political activity

The RSSILA aimed to sustain the common bond of wartime friendships and forge cooperation to promote 'the strongest alliance in the country' through its official access to ministers and representation to every government level, as well as raising funds to help distressed returnees and widows (Macintyre, 189; Lake, 123). It actively encouraged soldier settlers to air their grievances about matters to do with their farms. 'Big picture' matters affecting soldier settlers across Australia related to the 'plummeting commodity prices' during the 1920–1922 seasons that

118   *Soldier settlement in Tasmania and Castra*

created a cost-price squeeze, making the prospect of financial survival seem unattainable with potential long-term indebtedness. Lack of cohesion in matching small farm commodities to available or potential markets and deficiencies in the States' agricultural research and education services both affected sound business and scientific decision-making. Then there were local problems in dealing with administrators about their individual situations. By 1922, Ulverstone had its own sub-branch of the RSSILA that held annual reunions and regular meetings to build on the sense of unity forged during the war for Leven's returned soldiers. Prior to the State annual conference, farmers in the Leven area were encouraged to relate their grievances to two Ulverstone delegates who would attend it in Burnie on 16 June 1922 (News 1922a).

Ongoing concerns about introduction of revaluation recommended by the Select Committee of 1921 and other problem issues continued to be aired in the local newspaper (News 1919a, 1922a). The worries that were part of North-West Tasmanian soldier settlers' lives were attracting much public attention. On 5 May 1926, over 50 Upper Castra farmers attended a meeting pursuing similar arguments. Cr. Hubert Nichols chaired and John Chamberlain spoke about the need for revaluation, referring to the difficult seasons experienced since 1923, paying tribute to Inspector George Edwards' conscientious work and supporting Minister Belton's recent view that revaluations should be made, even though the CSB had subsequently refused (News 1926a). By August 1926, a meeting of soldiers was held in Preston about the same problems (News 1926c). Another large meeting of soldier settlers met at Riana, the next farming area west of Gunns Plains, again seeking revaluations immediately to avoid 'heavy losses to soldiers and taxpayers' (News 1926d).

A soldier's wife wrote to the *Advocate's* editor decrying the conditions for settlers who 'don't want charity' and 'only want to hold their own with the men for whom they risked their lives', but instead, 'they are burdened with debt, struggling to make ends meet' when half their small cream cheques are taken by the Board – 'all were holding great hopes for the revaluation scheme' (News 1927b).

Meetings continued as politics interfered and problems were slow to be solved. In 1927, a well-reported Ulverstone meeting was attended by returned men from Wynyard, Burnie, Forth, Upper Castra, Preston and elsewhere (News 1927c). Warden L.R. Parsons, obviously aware of the Commission, defended the Government for doing its best but, knowing what the men were experiencing, he advocated drastic action. George Wing, then a successful Preston farmer and father of two who enlisted, one of whom died in Egypt, expressed his opinion that soldiers' land he knew was valued too high for its quality, that none was worth 20/-[£1] an acre and, with rates and taxes added, he believed that amounted to about 30/-[£1 10/-] an acre, a level impossible for a farmer more than two miles from the port to be able to pay with crop expenses, and get a living. He supported his argument with figures showing the hopelessness of the situation for the soldiers.

Captain Roger Jones, president of the (now-renamed) Ulverstone Returned and Services' League (RSL), agreed. Soldiers were weighed down by high interest on land, improvements and houses, annual repayments for 25-year loans on

Soldier settlement in Tasmania and Castra   119

buildings, the cost of seed, stock or implements over 11 years, with failure to pay adding overdue interest charges, which he claimed was morally wrong. On top of all this, the soldier still had to care for his wife and children and pay for all labour, seed or stock needed. He asked, 'Is this what we expect after a man has given up his best years for his country?' (News 1927c).

Jones spoke of recent Royal Commission disclosures that, of 2,000 men settled originally, only 800 remained and were still reducing. He believed more than 75 per cent were in arrears, and when they did pay money, it went off the overdue amounts first, not the principal interest owing. Justice Pike would later refer to storekeepers who gave credit accounts to the soldier settlers. When the government took all their income from crops to pay debt, storekeepers would eventually close soldiers' accounts, making their circumstances even more hopeless. Many men used their war gratuity to pay arrears, but 'soldiers were fighting an unequal chance' especially when vacated farms were put up for tender at half the original rent, and recent revaluation had not placed the settler on a 'very much better footing'. He put forward some resolutions; the first was to amend compulsion on the settler to purchase the buildings over 25 years on a lease-hold property; the second was that farms should be leased on a fair rental basis, not the capital value as currently; and third, that charge of overdue interest on arrears should be 'cut out'. These were seconded by John Chamberlain (News 1927c).

From the floor, Chamberlain asserted that soldier settlers 'did not put forward a lot of hard luck tales'. The re-letting of properties at greatly reduced prices should convince the public of the soldier settlers' just cause for complaint, especially as an anomaly allowed big landholders and already well-established farmers to take them over. Chamberlain argued this was 'totally opposed to closer settlement principles and was not in the State's best interests'. Civilian renters were not obliged to live on the property, so they could rent out the house, work the land with their own farm and hand it back at the end of the lease 'cropped out' and worth even less rent, but leaving the bill for renovating fences and buildings to the taxpayer (News 1927b). Speaking of building repayments, it was a most unjust clause, condemned by the Royal Commission but ignored by Cabinet, who saw it as security against depreciation. Soldier settlers were compelled to carry out annual improvements so were disadvantaged compared to civilians. The recent government attitude about revaluations, touted as a 'concession' to the soldier settlers, was rejected by Chamberlain, who emphatically stated that 'we have a much stronger claim than a legal claim. Our claim is a moral claim and I feel sure that Mr Lyons is not a man to shelve a moral claim or responsibility when he realises that it is such'. He pointed out that soldier settlers prepared to take on the heavy task of clearing bushland should be given every support, since their efforts would lead to more cleared, productive land – good for both soldier and State. He suggested a deputation should go to State Cabinet (News 1927c).

Other speakers supported claims of unfairness of treatment. The Chairman claimed land values had reduced by 50 per cent since 1919, and he questioned the inducement for a man to pay for buildings when faced with being forced to

120   *Soldier settlement in Tasmania and Castra*

leave his property. He said the men should get a fresh start. Government wanted returned men to be given preference for employment, so 'when a property was put up for tender, the soldier-occupier should be given the opportunity to retain the property at the lowest tendered price'. He felt the 'public would not squeal if the Government put its hand in its pocket to help the soldiers' (News 1927b). It was suggested that other local sub-branches of the RSL could appoint delegates to join the deputation to the State Cabinet (News 1927c). These resolutions were agreed at subsequent meetings at Wynyard and Burnie and some of their members joined the deputation (News 1927d).

The opinions aired here are interesting because the reference to 'a moral claim' and unfairness about issues like capital-value assessment and civilian buyers' lower prices indicated issues similar to the mainland States. This 'sense of moral economy' fuelled New South Wales soldier settlers' assertion of entitlement to 'the promised "land fit for heroes" when dealing with similar circumstances and a hostile bureaucracy' (Scates and Oppenheimer 2014, 229–53). The Tasmanian Royal Commission had considered complaints about bureaucratic administration and the role of the Minister. Minister Belton's address to the Commission was fully reported in the *Advocate* 5 August 1926, 7. The complaints voiced so clearly at this local meeting would be echoed in Pike's Report in 1929.

Soldier settlement – Castra district

This section focusses upon all local soldiers appearing on the Honour Rolls of Preston and Gunns Plains who took up settlement leases in Preston, Gunns Plains and Upper Castra. Most soldier settlers listed were sons of local Castra families, who benefitted from honour and respect earned through their war efforts, which extended in some cases to giving help and support in their new lives. Some were successful and eventually able to purchase their land, some left the locality for other work, and some were very short-term failures. Following the Roche model, we discuss the successes first.

Of these 25 men listed here, it can be seen that nine remained in Castra from three to ten years, eight remained between 11 and 29 years, and eight remained between 30 and 44 years, about one third in each cohort. The first group averaged seven years, the second 21 years and the third 35 years. Where possible, reasons for the shorter durations are stated or deduced from available sources. But the big question is why such a high proportion stayed on their farms for more or less the rest of their working lives in this district, compared to anecdotal stories of failure told in the historiographic sources. My explanation lies with three elements that reinforce the characteristics of the yeoman farmer; first, the connection these men already had to farming that meant they understood the potential of soils and climate in this particular locality; second, their connection to the social relationships and institutions established locally, or their readiness to work at creating their own place within it (as John Chamberlain did, for instance); the third is their willingness to 'plan their work, and work their plan', committed to hard work that attracted positive notice from Inspectors.

Soldier settlement in Tasmania and Castra 121

	Start	Finish	Number Years Resident
Last. Clarence	1920	1928	8
Chamberlain. John Hartley	1919	1953 (death)	34
Smith. Bernard Horace	1920	1946	26
Smith. William Joseph	1919	1939	20
Smith. Harry Andrew H.	1919	1922	3
Wing. Roy William Diaper	1920	1954	34
Cameron. Peter Talmage	1920	1928	8
Smith. Mervyn John	1928	1972	44
Johns. George R.	1920	1954	34
Johns. Sydney	1920	1948 (death)	28
Johns. Robert R.	1923	1953 (about)	30
Kirkland. Robert W.	1921	1954	33
Ewington. Henry K.	1921	1929	8
Ewington. George S.	1921	1930 (about)	9
Cullen. Allan Lindsay	1920	1949	29
Cullen. Ira Stanley C.	1922	1929 (about)	7
Dunham. John Jnr.	1920	1937	17
Dunham. Thomas	1920	1931 (death 1933)	11
Johnson. Henry (Harry)	1920	1925 (about)	5
Gillam. Stanley Roy	1920	1960 (after)	40
McPherson. Burns T.	1920	1954 (after)	34
Wright. Ernest	1917	1924 (about)	7
Marshall. William S.J.	1919	1940 (about)	21
Chilcott. Leonard D.	1920	1930 (about)	10
Wing. Raymond Alfred	1919	1937	18

Main Sources: Applications to Lease TA. *Tasmanian Towns Index*. Electoral Rolls for Leven. *Advocate*.

Names are listed according to their order in the discussion and highlighted in bold.

Generally, good farm management appears to have been the key to survival. Soldiers who gave up lacked this skill, which became increasingly clear to Inspectors and eventually at State and Commonwealth levels. In Castra, applicants had absorbed management skills growing up pre-war and their relationships with family and neighbours were of critical importance, aided by the connections with local organisations already mentioned. With benefit of hindsight, the ability to be connected to and in the community must have been even more important through the tough inter-war years than it was after World War II when its importance was better acknowledged (George 1999, 12–15, 367–68). Winter thought soldier settlers' isolation on their land meant it was harder to cope with challenges, because they lacked the solidarity enjoyed by factory or mine workers (Winter "Foreword" in Scates and Oppenheimer 2016). This ignored the fact that soldier settlers, often on quite small properties, were near their neighbours, were often married to local women or may have been born locally, a situation perhaps more common in North-West Tasmania than elsewhere in Australia or in the United States. In a sense, Woodley was imagining the solidarity of a farming community facing common difficulties with his premise that problems like low prices, rabbits and crop diseases 'did not discriminate . . . according to whether a farmer was a soldier settler or not'.

122 *Soldier settlement in Tasmania and Castra*

He suggested more attention should be paid to social and economic exchanges and relationships between settlers and neighbours (Woodley 2017, 97–99).

When the Tasmanian Royal Commission identified the problem of highly priced land, it emphasised commission agents' role in aiding inflation, but actually they were fulfilling the *Act* by finding vendors and purchasers for the CSB. Colonel Crawford's son Alexander was a Valuer, Land, Estate and Commission Agent in Ulverstone. Having spent most of his youth in central Castra, helping to clear forest, cropping and working with his father, then later, working his own farm and years of operating his agency business, he was very well qualified to assess land for quality and value. He proposed larger acreages to the CSB that could be sub-divided (Wright's land in Central Castra and Rockliff's land in Preston were examples) as well as small farms like the 82-acre property on the outskirts of Ulverstone, that he thought might suit **Clarence Last** (born 1893), a returnee from Gunns Plains. Another instance occurred in 1919 as agent for James Marshall of Upper Castra. Crawford attached a hand-drawn plan of the land to his letter to the CSB indicating its suitability for five soldier settlement lots, with 'first class quality soil and water in every block'. He wrote that, if the land met with approval, he would be able to find applicants for it, noting that 'rabbits may be a trouble' (Marshall AB3/1/107, file no. 1947, 1–8). Applications required past work experiences and were signed by a JP; both William Delaney of Preston and Hubert Nichols, local magistrate and MLC for Mersey, frequently occur.

Because of the many steps needed from soldiers' applications to occupation, and perhaps too, due to the heavy administrative demand on the Board, it could often take a long time to find out about their future. This meant the returned men, many with wives and sometimes children, depended on family connections to provide temporary accommodation. This could be a benefit, as in the case of **Clarence Last**, who went home with his wife, able to help out with summer farm work and recover somewhat from his wartime experiences. Brothers William and Oscar Last were closer settlers at Werona and another died at the Somme. More importantly, Clarence found out about another farm that was nearer to his family networks and would suit him better, so his application was amended to 149 acres with an extensive boundary to the Leven River at the southern end of Gunns Plains. The land was valued at £1,760, buildings at £250, approved 14 May 1920 (LSD190/1/667). Here was an example of the Minister's advocacy for land the soldier desired near to relatives for guidance.

In 1928, Last was still farming at Gunns Plains, but the next information about him was in 1936; he and his wife Dorothy lived in South Burnie and he worked as a motor driver; from 1954–1958, he was a milk vendor and he died in 1966 in South Burnie. This information is insufficient to suggest that he failed as a farmer – he and Dorothy may have had many reasons for moving to town for work, which clearly suited them.

There are difficulties associated with discovering soldier settlers' stories after settlement approval. Archival records of applications are readily available, but when attempting to answer, 'what happened then?' the search is made awkward because Tasmanian records follow the pre-CSB-purchase landowner rather than settler.

Soldier settlement in Tasmania and Castra 123

One has to fall back on valuation rolls (imprecise for rural addresses) and electoral rolls (not completely reliable, but indicating occupation and residential ward). State archives often have wills, and post office directories can be useful as well as obituaries – a veritable jigsaw of sources. And there seems to have never been any historical or official attempt to follow the futures of soldiers who did not apply for official help but still went farming, unless they rose to prominence in political roles, such as **John Hartley Chamberlain**, whose settlement story is now addressed.

While Chamberlain's political involvement became a matter of public record and is considered in a later chapter, here I focus on his farming life. When Chamberlain (born 1884) returned at the end of the war in June 1919, he immediately applied for land in Preston, part of Ritherdon's Lot 5467. He stated 15 years general farming experience, married to Ada Sarah with children aged eight and ten years, some personal assets and deferred pay, and needed financial assistance for seed, stock and implements (LSD190/1/286). He applied for 96 acres, owned by Ellen, Peter Jupp's widow, beside the Ulverstone-Nietta railway with boundaries onto South Preston Road, Rifle Range Road and Henry Johnson's home-farm. His father was Baptist Minister in Latrobe who had baptised both Henry and Sarah in 1892, which may have been a pertinent encouragement. The land was valued at £1,310 and buildings at £400. He was approved on 24 September 1919 for cash of £1,700 and crops at valuation. The plan was recorded in Leven Ledger, AB19/1/423, page 20. Chamberlain was described as 'brimful of energy with a strong desire to succeed' (News 1919b).

In 1928, he sent his lease to the CSB for revaluation; in October 1931, his land was then valued at £1,000. Two months later, he applied to surrender his present lease for a 'balance lease' on the revaluation of £1,000 for land and £350 for buildings, leaving 87 years of the original 99-year lease from 1 September 1931. He entered State Parliament in 1934 and in September 1943, he wrote to the Agricultural Bank Manager about his lease being transferred to his only son Philip Lionel, because his duties as MHA precluded him from working the farm, and his son had already been working and improving it with 'hard work and good methods' (Chamberlain to Manager, AB19/1/423 file 1302). Transfer to civilian Philip meant his interest rate would be 4.5 per cent, he was not entitled to soldier settler privileges, stamp duty and transfer fee had to be paid by his father, and he had to agree by witnessed statement (done on 3 December 1942). This went to the CSB Chairman, then Premier, then Minister of Agriculture to be approved. The transfer was effective from 1 September 1943. In 1935, application had been made to take off one acre on the Main Road, so Philip could build himself a house (Leven Ledger, AB40/1/26, 86). By 1945, the lease value needed to be reassessed because Philip wanted to buy the farm; the equity the Lands Minister had in the property was £797 10/-; building improvements done at the lessee's cost were not included. In April 1945, Philip owned the farm and was granted the deed. True to the yeoman ideal, Chamberlain was able to use the conditions of soldier settlement to pass his farm onto his son, who was eventually able to purchase it.

The Rockliff 'Estate' in Figure 5.1 was 321 acres in Preston previously bought by William Rockliff in about 1898, sold by his widow, Matilda Rockliff of Sassafras to the CSB for £12 10/- acre. Alex Crawford was agent with Cameron and

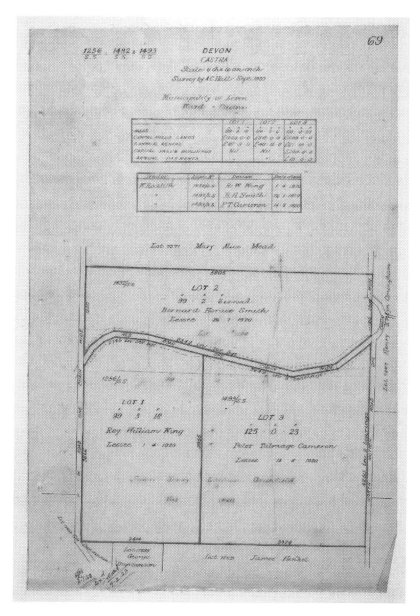

Figure 5.1 Division of Rockliff Estate, Castra Ward, September 1920 for Soldier Settlement.

Source: Plans of Land Settled – Leven Municipality, AB40/1/26 p69. Tasmanian Archives.

This plan is a good example of the typical information gathered for the CSB. The main road north-south is right, deviating because of a hillock; the original Anglo-Indian grantees are shown (Greenfield, Coningham belonging to Wm. Delaney, Mead belonging to E. McCulloch, and Henkel); the creek is shown in blue with direction arrows. The bottom left corner shows the administrative entries dated 1923, indicating the work back-log.

Soldier settlement in Tasmania and Castra   125

Smith as ready buyers (AB19/1/1025 File 2748) It was taken up by three soldiers, one of whom was **Bernard Horace Smith**.

Before the war, **William Joseph Smith** and his two sons, Bernard and **Harry Andrew Harford Smith**, a blacksmith, farmed in West Ulverstone. Bernard enlisted in early 1916 at 16 years (claiming to be 18), gave three years' service and was awarded the Military Medal. His father also enlisted in mid-1917; they were together in France hoping to meet Harry who had been wounded, which shows their close family ties (see *Weekly Courier*, August 30, 1917, 5). Bernard's application for 99 acres north of the dissecting Waringa Road was approved in July 1920 for land worth £815 (£8 4/- acre) without buildings (LSD190/1/1419). It had plenty of water from the permanent Preston Creek running through near where he built his house. In 1937 it was revalued, and he was recommended to cancel the long lease (99 years) and take a short lease with option to purchase for £481, with £1,358 to be written off and charged to revaluation. By 1942, the inspector advised the farm was unoccupied for weeks, because Bernard was in the Hobart Eye Hospital for a serious condition. Bernard advised the CSB that his brother-in-law was caretaking the farm (occupation was a condition of soldier settler leases). Perhaps his sister and brother-in-law were living on her father William's property next door.

Obviously, Bernard's health was a factor in proposing to transfer his lease in February 1946 to Vernon John Smith of Exton for £1,200. Vernon Smith was described as a 'member of a well-known family in Exton' and the transfer was approved from 1 March 1946. When Vernon came from Deloraine and took over from Bernard (no relation), it included a house and usual farm outbuildings and labourer's hut. Bernard Smith worked hard to make buildings and manage a good farm over 20 years until health issues made things hard for him. He and his wife, Lillian Annie, moved to Ulverstone to live and in 1958 he had no occupation (possibly early retirement due to invalidity). Vernon applied to purchase the farm in 1957, and this was completed in September for £873 plus fees (AB19/1/1025 file 2748). The farm has remained with Vernon's descendants, his eldest son Ernest, and then *his* son Peter, the present farmer, who remembers Bernard was nearly blind when old (Peter Smith, pers. comm. 2019).

A few months after Bernard's approval, in October 1919, **William and Harry Smith** (LSD190/1/340 (Joint)) applied and were granted a lease on 216 acres (£8 13/- per acre), fronting the original Preston-Gunns Plains road, land £1,865, buildings £585, to the west of Bernard's land with a common road between (Leven Ledger, AB40/1/26, page 23). This was four McCulloch lots amalgamated that were settled in the early 1900s. The start of the common road is left on Figure 5.1 running north. William continued to farm as lessee until after 1939 but by 1943, he had retired to Spreyton, near Devonport. Harry stayed only until about 1922, when he decided to go mining in Queenstown, but had moved to Melbourne by 1925, working for many years as a tramway employee (Electoral Rolls (ER), Melbourne Ports, 1925 and 1936). As neighbours, it seems reasonable to believe William, Harry and Bernard collaborated in building and farming in the yeoman tradition, perhaps helped by their sister and her husband some of the time.

As can be seen in Figure 5.1, the remaining Rockliff land made two further lots over the road, 99 acres taken up by **Roy William Diaper Wing** (George Wing's

126 *Soldier settlement in Tasmania and Castra*

son), in April 1920 (LSD190/1/1184, £1,253, no buildings, £12 13/- per acre); and 125 acres with side frontage to the main road by **Peter Talmage Cameron**, in August 1920 (LSD190/1/1420, £1,239, £240 for buildings, £10 5/- per acre). Roy was approved for a house in 1923 (AB15/1/214, no 7132). His was another case where health made an impact on his ability to farm. In 1928 he applied to the CSB with a Medical Board doctor's certificate to leave to a warmer climate, and install a 'conscientious man' at Preston. McGough of the Advisory Board provided a reference to Victoria's CSB in 1929 because Wing was enquiring about land there and he was 'a capable farmer, regarded by the Department as one of its most successful settlers'. Letters in AB19/1/1025 file 2748 show Wing's willingness to sell but not to lose the intrinsic goodwill, because 'of outsiders just waiting for the downfall to step in and reap the benefit of our slavery', a certain indication of the fear of speculatory exploitation, another aspect of the history that has received little attention in the literature.

Eventually Wing returned to Tasmania and applied to buy the farm in early 1935 for £677 and was granted the deed in October. Roy and his wife Ruby retired to Ulverstone by 1954 and Ruby's death in early 1983 was mourned by old friends in Preston's Ladies Fellowship for her service as Secretary and long-time membership (Minutes 1977–1986). Their farm was inherited by their son, Donald George Wing, born 1938, who was MLC Launceston (sometime Paterson) from 1982 to 2011 and Past President of the Legislative Council (Roy W. D. Wing Will no.41979 of 1961 AD960/1/92). It is worked for him by neighbour Peter Smith because he lives in Launceston. Roy's health had obviously benefitted from warmer weather because he and his wife were appreciated as part of the Preston community for about 30 years.

Cameron was recorded as a Preston farmer in 1922, but by 1928, he was farming near Table Cape (ER 1922, 1928). His application LSD190/1/1420 showed initial interest in land at Preolenna, nearer Table Cape, so conceivably location was his reason to leave, rather than disinterest in farming. His leaving created the opportunity for Henry Smith of Smiths Road, South Preston, to take over the 99-year lease in May 1930, which was then transferred to his soldier son, **Mervyn John Smith** in December that year (photograph in *Weekly Courier*, November 15, 1917, 24, No. 13). Inspector Edwards reported that Mervyn had cleared 20 acres in two years and done fencing and that he was a 'hard working honest soldier settler' (Edwards, July 22, 1931-report in file 2748). Months later, Mervyn applied for revaluation and, because 'the house was unfit to live in', he wanted help with a better house. Edwards again reported that he was 'one of the best settlers in the district' and that he had a wife and children; that Mervyn was prepared to supply timber and foundation stone, but needed inside linings supplied. Mervyn enlisted John Chamberlain to take up his case and by early 1932, agreement was reached with the CSB to approve his purchase of the land for £1,214 plus £150 for a new house to be built; the lease was surrendered in March 1932 (AB19/1/1025 file 2748).

The outcomes for these three farms were positive, for the soldiers and for the State. Inspector Edwards played a pivotal role at significant moments by making fair assessments of the men and their value as farmers. Despite difficulties,

Soldier settlement in Tasmania and Castra 127

revaluation had benefitted them and facilitated conversion from leases to purchases. There were two aspects of soldier settlement in Castra that I turn to now because they build the case that the ties that bound community and family networks were intrinsic to local success of yeoman family farming. The first relates to brotherhood and the other is father-son support.

Brotherhood was not a strange concept to rural communities like Castra, held together as they were by their membership of churches, extended families and associations like the RSL and the Lodge. Brotherhood is an ancient notion of group belonging based upon Christian ideology, and poet William Blake was inspired by the fraternity of the American and French Revolutions (Ferber 1978, 438–47). The camaraderie of years of war that the RSL sought to sustain was evident among brothers in several settlement decisions in this district, three of which I recount.

Of four Johns brothers, brought up in Gunns Plains, who enlisted, two survivors, **George Reginald Johns** (born 1893) and **Sydney Rupert Johns** (born 1897), applied for James Marshall's land at Upper Castra (Hyland 2014, 15, 17). They applied on the same day for Lot 1 of 74 acres for £1,361 (£18 8/-acre) and Lot 2 of 71 acres for £1,519 (£21 8/- acre), and were both approved on 26 June 1920 (LSD190/1/1453 and 1454). In April 1921 Sydney requested a modest house on his land; the contract for £358 11/- was signed March 1924 (AB15/1/80). Perhaps the three-year delay and living in temporary shelter made his health problems from gunshot wounds sustained in France worse. Despite the land being cleared and either cropped or grassed, the work may have been too much for Sydney, because, in August 1923, the third Johns brother, **Robert Roy Johns** (born 1895), was approved to take over Lot 2 from him for the same price and conditions (LSD190/1/1875). The decision to start together was supportive of the injured youngest brother and then, when necessary, the third one stepped in to maintain the advantage of their recent work on the land and promised dwelling. It was also an example of pragmatic flexibility by the CSB.

Robert had married a Preston girl, Alice Kirkland, in June 1923 (News 1923a). Her parents had land in Warringa Road, and her brother **Robert W. Kirkland** had already applied in January 1921 for a soldier settlement lease on 102 acres (£8 2/-acre) of Allan Lorenzo Tongs' land and buildings quite near them along Waringa Road, probably for sale because of Tong's rheumatism and decision to go to New South Wales; it was approved in July 1921 (LSD190/1/1845; AB19/1/1273 file 4291). At the age of 42, Tongs had enlisted in 1915 and was medically discharged in December 1917. In 1922, he applied for land on a soldier settlement at Finley, Riverina, where he lived out his life. He was great-uncle to the McCulloch boys in Preston, and in 1930 Edis went there to help with the wheat harvest (McCulloch 1998, 48).

Robert and Alice Johns had a son, Keith, and a daughter and remained on their farm until the early 1950s, and in 1968, they lived with Keith in Launceston (ER Bass 1968). George and wife Jessie Johns also remained on their farm until about 1943 when they had moved to Devonport and George retired (ER Devonport 1943). Sydney Johns later married, had ten children and farmed in Gunns Plains,

128 *Soldier settlement in Tasmania and Castra*

but his health may never have been good because he died at the age of 50 in 1948 (News 1948a). On his way to their farms at Upper Castra, Robert Johns took the first wagonload of hay over the new road from Gunns Plains to Preston, completed in March 1921 to cut the distance from the valley to the Preston railway station (LSD35/1/1573; News 1921a). This close family collaboration between Upper Castra and Gunns Plains served the brothers very well for many years, evidenced by their survival in both places; cooperation helped manage occasional floods in Gunns Plains, or when the grass died off at Upper Castra.

Thomas and Jane (nee Peebles) Ewington owned 45 acres in the centre of Preston village in 1920, which may have been the motivation for Thomas's two brothers to return from war to apply for soldier settlement land in South Preston, though their parents Joseph and Elizabeth farmed in North Motton. **Henry Keep Ewington** and **George Simmons Ewington** applied on 1 April 1921 for Lot 1(158 acres) (LSD190/1/1297) and Lot 2 (157 acres) (LSD190/1/1298) of the Barnes Estate, both £6 10/-acre. They clearly saw advantage in farming next to one another and close to family in their new lives. Their applications were approved within weeks on 9 May 1921. Neither lot had any buildings. Henry was 24 years and married with one child. George was 28 years and single. They appear on the Leven ERs as farmers in Preston as late as 1928 (*Wise's Town Directory* 1929, 152), but by 1936, Henry had taken up farmland at Lower Mount Hicks, south of Burnie, and by 1943, George was a farmer in Gawler, on the outskirts of Ulverstone. They did not appear in the valuation rolls prior to 1928 though, as mentioned earlier, these have been unreliable for soldier settlers. Denzil Harding (2018) told me that his grandfather, Harry Harding, bought George's land next to his farm. Perhaps these Ewington brothers had the prospect of better land elsewhere or family reasons for leaving Preston, but Thomas continued with his home-farm in Preston, and in 1928 purchased an extra 80 acres of Crawford's Deyrah in central Castra (VR, Castra Ward 1928).

The third case of brothers involves two of Thomas Cullen's sons. He settled in Preston between 1892 and 1896, established a store, mail coach and his farm and was well aware of potential of forested land further south. The CSB purchase of land at Nietta was used to support the Minister of Lands and MHA for Bass, John Blyth Hayes' defence against accusations from the Table Cape Council that land considered for soldiers was overpriced, fit only for rabbits and bought in secret (News 1917e). Cullen's son Stanley had already made a Crown Purchase of 99 acres in the same area in 1906 on a 14-year lease (VRs Castra Ward 1926–28). He may well have been the farmer referred to by Hayes. Understandably, his two returning brothers were keen to acquire land adjacent. **Allan Lindsay Cullen** (pictured in *Weekly Courier* 9 March 1916, 24, 19) was approved for 98 acres in Nietta (AB40/1/26 page 36). **Ira Stanley Charles Cullen** took on 100 acres next door to Allan, but his case was different; he applied under the 'Soldiers Free Selection' scheme and purchased his land outright (AB40/1/26 page 68). In 14 December 1922, across Tasmania this scheme had attracted 564 applications (LSD 166/1/496, page 1). In the months before he enlisted in 1916, Ira had married a Hobart girl, Millicent; they came to settle on

Soldier settlement in Tasmania and Castra   129

their land on what is still called Cullen's Road. They were living there to receive his medals in May 1923. But by 1930, Allan was listed as Occupier, and by 1935 Ira and Millicent had left the district to go to New Zealand where they lived until Ira died in 1946 (NZ ER Manawatu-Wanganui, 1935; NZ Death Index). By 1949, Allan was employed as the Ulverstone Agriculture Officer, living in Ulverstone (ER Leven 1949, 1954).

These different cases of brotherly decision-making were all examples that demonstrated the variety of outcomes and differing longevity of each, which lend credibility to Tasmanian Government members' understanding that every settler's situation was unique. None of them could justify being judged 'failures' – from this distance in time, with no access to the soldiers themselves, and without descendants' enlightenment, one can only speculate on reasons for individual or family actions, such as Ira's decision to go to New Zealand.

Reasons for durability may be easier to explain by examining the sense of unity exemplified by father-son support, which, in Castra, reflected circumstances identified elsewhere in Tasmania by both Martin (1992) and Gerrard (2015), that is, fathers selling part or all of their farms to the CSB so their sons could take over under soldier settlement lease arrangements.

John Dunham decided to do this. From 1907, he farmed Anderson's 160-acre Anglo-Indian lot south of James Peebles' land, where he ran a sawmill and built and lived in one of Preston's significant houses, Lonash. Two of his sons enlisted, **John Dunham junior** and **Thomas Dunham,** and on return, their father sold the home-farm for £9 10/-acre to the CSB (AB19/1/664 file 1787). The land could be sub-divided along the railway line, a diagonal N/S barrier across the middle of the land. They were approved in March 1920. John had Lot 1 (land £846 and buildings £280), fronting Preston Road, and Thomas had Lot 2 (£663), fronting Jacks Road (LSD190/1/788). Thomas surrendered his lease in 1931, and Clarence Geale, a civilian, successfully grew potatoes there. Thomas was shot in the abdomen during his four-year service, and must have been in poor health because he died two years later.

Meanwhile, by 1937 John wanted to surrender his lease, so three local civilian farmers tendered, including Geale who wanted the house, but Philip Chamberlain, then about 28 years old, took over John Dunham's 99-year lease on Lot 1 for five years, marking the end of the Dunhams in Preston. In 1944, Geale sold his Lot 2 to David Peebles, because it adjoined his farm (Rob Peebles 2018). Philip transferred his lease to Clifford George Johnson, another of Henry Johnson's grandsons, in 1956, who later purchased it for £756 plus fees in August 1963.

Years earlier, Clifford's grandfather had shared the same idea of helping one of his returned sons, **Henry (Harry) Johnson** (born 1888), wife Elsie and their three children, onto 41 acres of his farm (land £380 and £230 for buildings) in May 1920 (AB19/1/839 file 2290). The payment of £9 5/-acre from the government purchase may have provided capital for Henry Johnson Snr's land purchases elsewhere. His other soldier son, John, due to inherit the home-farm, is discussed elsewhere. Harry and Elsie only stayed a few years, perhaps to adjust from war or for health reasons, or the children to have access to their grandparents, and

130   Soldier settlement in Tasmania and Castra

family sources show they went to Victoria where he died (relatively young) in 1937 (Banks 1999). The land did not pass out of the Johnson family.

Stanley Roy Gillam was another case of leasing back his father William Edward's farm (land £1,030 buildings £520, £11/acre) and the lease started 1 April 1920 (AB19/1/959). Although he sustained a leg wound at the Somme where he earned a Military Medal (NAA/205348), his lease was his 102-acre home-farm fronting the eastern side of South Preston Road (AB40/1/26 page 30). The continued help from his father and mother would have been valuable and may have contributed to his successful application in spite of his physical health. Stanley continued to have 'a deal of trouble' from his persistently painful war wound, including hospitalisation in Ulverstone twice in the 1920s (News 1926e, 1928b).

Ulverstone was lucky to have a hospital, but it was obviously under pressure in the early post-war years, because Matron E.B. Watt wrote to the RSL asking if memorial funds could be used to add a new 'Memorial Ward' (News 1922c). An ex-soldier wrote supporting the idea because 'a men's ward is a crying need' and offered more community benefit than 'a stone pillar or cenotaph'. Even so, Ulverstone got its soldier cenotaph, and the hospital has gone, so perhaps the ward idea did not go beyond an idea, whereas Zeehan on the West Coast did get a maternity ward called the 'Peace Memorial Ward' and X-ray equipment with their funds (News 1922b, 1925). Stanley married Annie and had three children; his parents eventually retired to Ulverstone, and Stanley and Annie stayed there farming. Stanley was South Preston postmaster for years, providing additional income *(Towns Directory* 1948, 201). In 1960, they were able to purchase the farm. Eventually they sold up to another Johnson son and retired to Ulverstone. Stanley lived in Ulverstone until dying in 1987, a long life for a man who had sustained such severe and troublesome injuries in war, but testament to the effectiveness of his operation at Ulverstone Hospital.

An alternative twist on parental help was **Burns Thompson McPherson** who enlisted from Gunns Plains and was approved 1 December 1920 for his mother's 103-acre farm at Abbotsham (LSD190/1/1237). An interesting point here was that he was not charged for the buildings (the amount was listed but struck through), so perhaps they were not included in the sale to the CSB because her surviving son was lessee. Burn's older brother John had been in the first contingent to leave Tasmania, was wounded at Anzac Cove, then wounded again, and sent back to the field in France where he was killed in action in April 1917 (Hyland 2014, 2). Burns was also wounded and hospitalised during his four-year service, and had met and married his English wife Fanny in April 1919 before his return to Australia (Hyland 2014, 30). They seem to have settled successfully, farming there with their two sons, as Fanny McPherson was a group leader for Abbotsham Red Cross fundraising at the start of the Second World War in 1939 (News 1939c).

The Dunham, Gillam and McPherson cases are just a sample providing strong evidence of the value to soldiers fortunate to return home, not just to their neighbourhood, but to their home-farm. Here they found on-going support, and the expertise and assets their parents had accumulated added to their chances of successful survival. Their return was honoured, their wives and children were

Soldier settlement in Tasmania and Castra   131

absorbed into the community through church and school, and in times of illness, the community was kept informed, so friends could rally round. From Gillam's situation, it is evident that good facilities for medical operations were available in Ulverstone, and district concern for returnees attracted sympathy.

What of failure to survive settlement? One case stands out that might have been predicted if it had happened years later. **Ernest Wright**, who was an early returnee when he applied in June 1917 and was approved almost immediately for 70 acres (£350) of Nietta land only (LSD190/1/18). His service record shows he had spent three years in the 'Old Volunteers' near Launceston before going to possible work as dairyman at Colac, Victoria and was married (NAA/133313). Nietta's higher altitude means it is very cold and wet in winter. What is curious about his case is why he was drawn to Nietta. There, the lack of a dwelling (perhaps living in a tent?), the climatic demands on his health (rheumatism was surely a contra-indication?), probably heavily forested land, long distance from the coast, the small lot size and lack of obvious family connections to call on for assistance were all factors suggesting the inevitability of failure. His name did not appear on the list mentioned here, so he may have lasted into 1923. But by 1924, his medal request was to Elizabeth St, Hobart and, by 1931, he was back on the mainland (NAA/63559, 1–27). The incidence of respiratory disease, tuberculosis and rheumatism had all risen as outcomes of military service when national data was collected in 1924 (CPP Vol II, 1926–27–28, No.69). Ernest Wright clearly fell into that category of persistent ill health. I can find no further evidence of his later life.

If failure is judged by very short tenancy, then a few more early failures appear among records of soldier settler 'ex-lessees'. Treasurer Walter Henry Lee asked the Minister for Lands Ernest Blyth in November 1922 to supply a list of such cases as of December 1922 (AB47/1/1, 265–70). The only cases listed for Castra were:

C.A. Lucas 160 acres Nietta, no bldgs., vacated 30 October 1922; land not relet

A.E. Graham 132 acres, Nietta, farm, vacated 21 August 1922; relet 11 September 1922

C.T. Chilcott 103 aces, Preston, sheds, vacated 1 February 1922; not relet by 30 June 1922

Chilcott's Victory medal was sent to Tullah on the West Coast on 1 November 1923, indicating he may have gone to mining or infrastructure work there. He was a Driver during his European service, an asset for employment (NAA/118625). Two more cases nearby show some blocks could be relet quickly. The brothers, **H.V.** and **A.A. Stott**, leased adjoining 74-acre lots at Riana with buildings in March 1920, but surrendered them by 10 July 1922 and both lots were relet by 18 September 1922. **W.N. Hearps** leased 124 acres on very steep land from a deceased estate at North Motton on 1 April 1920 and vacated by 5 August 1922; 36 days later it was relet. Most of these men were single (no helping hand from

132 *Soldier settlement in Tasmania and Castra*

a wife), their past experience had been as farm labourers (lacking farm business skills), all needed advances to get started (potential stress over payments), some were far away from family (e.g. Devonport and Forth), and some had declared lingering health problems from the war. The burden of proof linking poor health to war service was explored by Richardson (2005, 113 especially f/n 41, 401). Perhaps settling was just too hard, and, like Charles Chilcott, getting a job seemed a more attractive option.

Nietta *was* a challenging environment, but two photographs in *Weekly Courier*, 24 June 1920, 22, 3 & 4, provide examples of people 'making a go' of life there. Superficially, the family sitting in front of a very basic timber hut appears to be in hardship until you see their smiles, they all have good boots and leather gaiters (snake protection) and there are four young men with sleeves rolled up to help their parents. The smartly dressed young man was Private H.W. Bryant, a Nietta settler and secretary of the Nietta Progress Association (32 members in 1920, 90 per cent of residents) and the Nietta branch of the Farmers' Union (News 1920b).

The wide variety of reasons why men *might* give up has attracted little case-by-case follow up in the literature, where much reliance for Australia has been on results of relevant State Royal Commissions and on Pike's overview for the Commonwealth Government. At these levels, failure was always expressed in numerical terms – numbers of men, money expended and written down. As my data have shown, information from publicly available sources provided hints as to reasons why they gave up and reasons why they stayed, survived and thrived. No doubt delving into family memoirs might reveal more qualitative stories to enrich the record. The gaps are tantalising, especially after settlers severed their connection with the CSB and files were closed. My results in the Castra district have demonstrated that temporal criteria can be reinforced by other data to enrich the story of individual experiences of the scheme. The longevity of the men I researched, especially those who were able to become 'proprietors', fulfilled the ideal of yeoman farmers, who treasured their land and were able to hand the value of their hard work on to their progeny.

These men and their families add value to the whole settlement story, as alluded to by Holbrook and Scates and Oppenheimer. Connections between soil quality, proper management for productive longevity, size of acreage and suitability for chosen uses, whether cropping or grazing, invites further research. One of the significant reasons men gave up everywhere was the small size of properties that were inadequate for the agricultural use chosen.

Cost of land for local soldier settlers

In Castra, pioneering families had benefitted from up to 40 years of establishment, familiarity with their markets, good seasons with potatoes, their main cash crop, and strong systems of kin or neighbourly cooperation. When prices dropped, it was hard for all farmers. Not surprising that they were concerned for local young men who, having lost years of their youth and often their health, were expected to make a success of their new challenge. When George Wing stood up for local

Soldier settlement in Tasmania and Castra 133

soldier settlers, he knew the prices the CSB paid and passed onto settlers. However, it was a well-meant exaggeration because Crown Land had been that price since 1870. Despite the early rhetoric of Ernest Blyth, MHA for Wilmot, who had said that 'as to Crown Lands, any Tasmanian who returned from the front should be given free a piece of the land he had been fighting for', this dictum was of little relevance to the settlers discussed here because the CSB consistently bought land from previous owners.

Reasonably, by 1918, prices *should* have reflected the farming improvements wrought since the 1880s. Valuators assessed present development and agricultural potential when recommending a price. This is not to ignore the inflationary effect of high demand by the Government buying small farms and livestock across Tasmania. As the Tasmanian Royal Commission reported, there was insufficient time for bargaining, and Government failure to satisfy the demand would not only have attracted public criticism but would have risked the scheme's survival. As to land prices, the Tasmanian Commission gained the opinion that prices paid to existing farmers reflected the value of their farm to them, but:

> Those farms were handed over to men who were not selected physically, mentally, by training or experience, by reason of owning capital, or in any other way. As soon as the scheme was set working its wreck was assured.
>
> (RC 1926, 15)

To investigate this, I have selected some land-only prices in Castra for comparison.

At Nietta, **Ernest Wright** paid £5 acre in 1917. For land not previously farmed, but cleared, near Preston, **Robert Kirkland** and **Bernard, William** and **Harry Smith** all paid over £8, while **John Chamberlain** paid nearly £14 a couple of miles away for an established farm. On Jacks Road, the eastern edge of Dooleys Plains, the CSB paid £10 per acre, but experienced trouble keeping soldiers there. In Upper Castra, lots ranged from £7 15/-acre to **William S. J. Marshall** to over £18 and £21 acre charged to the **Johns brothers** – an extraordinary contrast, especially in view of the known presence of rabbits. In Gunns Plains, **Leonard D. Chilcott** was approved for 131 acres at £11 5/- acre, consistent with £11 16/- that **Clarence Last** paid nearby. By contrast, **Raymond Alfred Wing** was approved for 49 acres of J.A.W. Wing's farm, at £6 7/- per acre, which may have been due to its small size beside the Leven River.

Preston's more northerly areas and Dooley's Plains, Gunns Plains and Upper Castra had each experienced agricultural development and a growing reputation for productivity, especially of potatoes. All three villages had churches and schools, representing attractiveness for settlers and probably reflected in land values. The new road connection from Gunns Plains to Preston Station gave better direct access. The Ulverstone-Castra road had been improved through Upper Castra to Nietta. The more southerly land in minimally settled parts of South Preston and Nietta was cheaper because it was less cleared. But there, nearness to the Nietta railway terminus (within two to five miles) for sending timber and potatoes to market provided advantage.

134   *Soldier settlement in Tasmania and Castra*

The quality and condition of the soil (i.e. extent of clearing, whether in crop, etc.) was obviously critical to the value. I found no evidence in the archives of prices being appealed by prospective lessees – perhaps they felt unempowered to argue? Or did local knowledge and family input for many of them influence their acceptance without qualms? Good crop prices during and just after the war may have been influential, but, when prices dropped in the 1921–1922 recession, just as some first crops were coming on stream, settlers were in a double bind that made them susceptible as interest on their loans accumulated. Hence the intolerance of bureaucratic practices over payments and the clamour for revaluation.

Board inspectors

The Inspectors' role was also considered by the Commission, especially aided by the King Island report, and in taking evidence about selection processes and reliance upon references (RC 1926, 8). It made positive comments, finding them reliable and competent (23). In Leven, long-time Upper Castra farmer and past Councillor and Advisory Board member Thomas Bingham served as Inspector for years after leaving Council. He was interviewed for the *Advocate* 15 November 1920 and expressed his previous early uncertainty about the scheme and his questioning of the possibility for farm labourer applicants to adapt to the responsibilities of being in 'sole control'. Then he went on:

> My experience has shown that the men have succeeded in this respect to a marked degree, and I have no hesitation in saying the position today gives promise of considerable success, and with freedom from blight and other drawbacks, with moderate prices ruling for produce, the majority of the men will be able to get into favourable financial circumstances. I found the men cheery and optimistic, and exhibiting the same characteristics as at Gallipoli and France, which made the name of Anzac known throughout the world. With one or two exceptions, they all express satisfaction with the manner the department has treated them, and a feature most gratifying to an inspector is the thorough and workmanlike manner in which they do their work; so far, no depreciation of the property secured for them by the Government is apparent. Out of 70 men in the district, there can only be said to be a very small percentage who might be considered disappointing.

By 1923 Inspector George Edwards had replaced Bingham, and, when Lot 3 Werona Estate of 91 acres at £25 15/-acre came available in 1926, he was point of contact for the CSB. His opinion about how to handle vacating lessees was positively referenced by the Tasmanian Royal Commission.

In Castra, Edwards' reports feature in other files, too. One example concerned a 60-acre farm in Jacks Road, which, by 1925, had already been through two transfers leading to a forfeiture, unique in Preston. The second transfer was to a British ex-RAF soldier, Donald Malcolm McLeod, a farm labourer/carpenter,

Soldier settlement in Tasmania and Castra 135

only in Tasmania one year (LSD190/1/1746). In June 1925, Edwards advised that McLeod had vacated and gone to Victoria. Edwards was involved at each stage of change. After two failures having no connection to local kin, he recommended preferencing the neighbouring civilian farmer, Ambrose Burgess, over two other tenderers, to which the CSB agreed. Burgess and, later, his son farmed the land from 1928 to 1938 in conjunction with their own farm, demonstrating this was a valuable recommendation. This very thick archive file is an excellent example of the range of problems found on some blocks of land, and the sheer volume of administrative work that went into finding solutions. The major problem here was the land's smallness and hilliness and a very poor house by the 1940s, and throughout the correspondence, one can see the almost desperate attempts of the Board to find a good resolution. As the CSB had discovered at Isandula Estate a few miles away, land vacant even for one season meant inundation by rabbits and blackberry, and made it unattractive for even nearby farmers to take it on.

This chapter started from the premise that community and connectedness enabled soldiers to regain their lives after war. Most of those whose histories are told here made strong efforts to do well on their land and their longevity is testament to their success. The number of farmers continued to increase to 164 in 1921 and even more, reaching a peak of 179, in 1931, aided by new farmers establishing in Nietta and towards Loongana and influenced by available Crown Lands (*Town Directories*).

All Tasmanian returned settlers were let down by the CSB's tardiness to respond to revaluation demands, coming not just from Minister Belton, but also from the public, who were aware of, through newspapers, the difficulties farmers were experiencing. Survival became particularly difficult when crop returns slumped. It seems as if the financial pressure on the CSB Secretary outweighed the pragmatic view about losses and abandonments expressed by the Tasmanian Royal Commission. It was in no doubt that the scheme was never a business and should have been expected to be costly from the very start. The best action to take was to make it possible for farmers, working hard and running their farms appropriately, to be assisted into staying, by revaluations and/or remissions as most appropriate.

On the whole, the cases explored here have shown that the ties of family relationships, whether through brotherhood or father-son, were significant in promoting successful farming for the long-term and a good life for their wives and children as well as the chance to pass on somewhere of value to the next generation. Even those who left Castra were able to get work, something quite difficult in the 1920s (Beresford 1983, 98). These men, their wives and their children that stayed all contributed to the human and social capital of their village communities and Castra as a whole. Characteristic of yeoman farming families world-wide, they created gardens and kept livestock for food in addition to cash crops, thus protecting themselves through the Depression years and emulating the self-sufficiency practices of families and neighbours. Agriculture Professor Samuel Wadham reflected in 1935 on impacts of the Depression in

136   *Soldier settlement in Tasmania and Castra*

terms of land development; causes of non-expanding overseas markets, lack of superior land for expansion of settlement (largely inferior quality) and the several years it took to improve pasture. Those yeomen smallholders operating with family labour and low level of farm purchases were the best equipped to survive during periods of depressed prices, because farming was their life, land was their 'sacred possession' binding the family with 'bonds of sentiment', and their 'actual standard of living may be relatively high as far as food and physical comfort are concerned' (67). In this way, family farming activities in the Castra community sustained the yeoman ideal and set the example for their next generation.

6 Succession and inheritance in Castra families, 1900–2000

Yeoman family farmers who settled in North-West Tasmania shared a commonality of interests and ambitions as they created productive agriculture and self-sufficient farms from heavy forest. As they and their family members all worked hard for every-day subsistence and engaged in cropping and dairying for distant markets, their long-term motivation was the hope of handing on benefits to succeeding generations. Family patriarchs knew it would take another one or two generations to complete the gradual clearing process and develop the land's productivity to its best advantage. Some, like James Peebles, George Wing Jnr. and the Brown brothers, had lived through that experience when their parents had already done the same thing elsewhere; they saw that new 'frontier' land offered opportunity for progress – even prosperity. Strong companionate, highly fertile marriages were not only important to provide crucial family labour but also potential heirs for their farm and wives for heirs of other farms. Tasmanian farming families were typically large, nearly half having more than eight children in the late decades of the nineteenth century (Moyle 2020, 128–29). So the sons were their father's apprentices and the daughters were their mother's. This chapter looks at the large families that prevailed in Castra, and how they compared with family size elsewhere in Australian twentieth-century society. Having looked at studies about inheritance overseas and in Australia, I move to tangible examples from Preston families to demonstrate their strategies for succession and inheritance. Inter-family marriages that brought daughters into the picture consolidated valuable close relationships among and within families as well as inheritance of land, which usually benefitted sons. The strategies used by Preston families contribute to our knowledge because they illustrate the flexibility possible in other settlement societies.

Large families in Castra

Typical of family size of the Victorian era, Colonel Crawford's surviving family of eight born in India and three born in Tasmania was the earliest large family that lived in Castra. Also, at central Castra, Thomas William Wright Senior and wife Sara had nine surviving children born between 1860 and 1874. Their fourth child, John Forsyth Wright (1864–1930) married Emma, one of George Lewis'

DOI: 10.4324/9781003229841-7

138   *Succession and inheritance*

daughters from Preston, in 1892 and they had ten children on the farm at central Castra. There were other families from the 1860s with many children:

- William and Elizabeth Brown had six children between 1865 and 1877.
- Peter and Elizabeth Jupp of North Motton had eight children from 1866 to 1889.
- Henry and Sarah Johnson had 16 children, from 1878 to 1908, of whom 12 grew to adulthood.
- Peter Jupp Junior and wife Ellen Brown had seven children from 1886 to 1895; four survivors and three premature infant deaths.
- Arthur William Brown and wife Ada had 12 children in 14 years from 1896 to 1913.
- John and Mary Ann Stevens of Upper Castra had 11 children from 1887 to 1901, and three of their daughters married Henry Johnson's boys.
- James and Margaret Peebles had 14 children starting in 1889 and ending in 1907.
- Harry Harding had nine children, five boys and four girls from 1890 to about 1905.
- Henry and Elizabeth Sarah Smith of Smiths Rd, South Preston had eight children, with the youngest born about 1906, of whom two daughters married people in this study.
- Henry and Sarah's son, Ambrose, and wife Alice Johnson had 14 children from 1908.
- Their daughter Phoebe and Ernest Marshall had six children between 1911 and 1923.
- Another daughter Sarah and Peter Marshall of Gunns Plains had 12 children from 1909 to about 1930.
- Henry's heir, John, and wife Jane Johnson had 12 children from 1918 to 1944, of whom 11 survived.
- George, his next brother, and Dulcie Johnson had eight children from 1922 to 1942.
- Albert, the next, and Florence had seven children between 1920 and 1932.
- Lance and Flora Eustace of Jacks Road, Preston had nine children from 1947 to 1958.
- Frederick Tongs, a prominent horse breeder and local councillor, and wife Rosena Brett of North Motton had 11 children from 1899. Two sons, Mervyn and Vernon, settled in Waringa near Preston, succeeded by two more generations.

What could explain this local prevalence and persistence of large families in Castra from the 1860s through into the 1950s? Moyle's study of Tasmania showed fertility falling slowly from the 1860s to 1890s much in line with other colonies. Women born between 1832 and 1876 had an average of nearly eight children to nearly six, and by the 1921 census, the averages had dropped to five, although Tasmanians were still higher than the overall Australian average (Moyle 2015, 201,

Succession and inheritance 139

Table A2.1). Later, she followed three cohorts of marriage date, 1860–1870, 1880 and 1890, and her most relevant analyses were those segmented by occupation (farmer) and religion (Anglican and Methodist). Farmers consistently had more children than any other group, and Methodists had higher fertility than other Protestant groups in 1890 – 14 per cent had ten or more children compared to 10 per cent of Anglicans with ten or more and, interestingly, 5 per cent of *all* families had more boys than girls, which resonates with Preston families (Moyle 2020, figs. 6.5 and 6.8). Using international studies and her Tasmanian data, she confirmed that farmers were the last occupational group to adopt fertility control measures; 64 per cent of all births were rural (2015, 193–96). She concluded that Tasmania's transformation to a more urbanised and industrialised population combined with feminism allowed women to take more control of their own fertility.

However, remembering that immigration impacted on family structures and severed previous kinship groups, and that Tasmania had a predominantly immigrant rural population, large families were a delayed functional outcome of a non-industrial society, especially during the nineteenth-century decades. The high birth rates in rural yeoman families compensated for lack of potential apprentices and live-in servants, previously common in the Old World. Large families in agricultural communities were a way of establishing kinship relationships to assist their household's long-term survival, in addition to their need for family-based workers. This is evident because Australian families generally were shown to be consistently larger than in the 'mother country' up to 1901 (Jones 1971, 324).

Working in the 1960s, Day provided evidence that Australian families *were* much larger than elsewhere. His survey extended further into the twentieth century than Moyle's. His sample included married women from 40 to over 80 years in 1954, which could have included many in my local list. The older the woman, the more children she was likely to have borne. Rural wives across all age groups continued to have large families; 60 per cent of those married between 1910 and 1914 had more than five children (Day 1965, 156–67).

In attempting to explain these larger, rural families, Day suggested some influential factors that have relevance in Castra. The 'different fertility norms' of immigrant groups influenced perceptions of 'normal' family size. Historical research of a Queensland German-immigrant farming community agreed that differences occurred in particular communities where social mores affected decisions about when and who to marry, how many children to have and high fertility reflected their past society's norms (Cole 1985; Jones 1971). Day proposed a cultural example when couples were influenced by seeing 'everyone' around them having babies, so their children grew up having playmates and parents shared their experiences (164). When eight Johnson cousins were all born in 1952, a year of post-war optimism and bumper potato crops, this was their family experience.

One reason some parents did not reduce child numbers has been called the 'unbounded-fertile-family ideal'. Pooley (2013, 100) argued this was 'notably potent' among fathers where labour was costly, and among Irish Catholic mothers, for whom high fertility was part of Irish family culture. Virility was valued highly and so was the expectation of fathering large families. She agreed

140   *Succession and inheritance*

with Day's cultural norm factor, arguing it could contribute to ideals of *either* unbounded families *or* controlled fertility with fewer children, especially when circulated orally through social milieux. Tasmanian rural women were less used to using informal sources to spread ideas and values about fertility limitation than urbanites (Moyle 2015). Whereas limiting fertility was seen as a male responsibility separated from women's child-rearing responsibilities, gradually parenting became more inter-connected and each parent became more involved in their children's societal well-being. Fertility-limiting practices worked better in more gender-equal companionate marriages, and with the approach of male sexual 'caring and sharing' that became more characteristic in the first half of the twentieth century (Pooley, 102–3; Szreter and Fisher 2010, 387–89). Considering family size examples given earlier, there seems little congruency with Castra district families over fertility limitation, although I argue consistently that companionate marriages were critical for the success of the yeoman ideal.

For farmers and small business owners, children had value because they could work in, then inherit and carry on the family enterprise, as well as provide proximity of care when parents grew old. In the Australian context of rural yeomanry, the choice to have large families during the early half of the twentieth century is more readily understood, as is the option that smaller families became more appropriate as farms mechanised and labour needs reduced after the Second World War, and the likelihood of death in infancy receded (Heer 1968, 452). By the 1970s and 1980s, Castra's smaller families matched social change towards an increased emotional investment in their fewer children, and reflected changing parental and adolescent aspirations.

Family farming and inheritance

Family farming in British colonial societies had ideological connections to yeomanry that went on to infuse concepts of closer settlement and returned soldier settlement. Inherently, family farming was an intertwining of business and household, and of production and consumption that evolved with the family life cycle. Yeoman family members provided most labour requirements where farming was their main income source. The relationship between the land and the family was crucial to success as well as being key to developing continuity of ownership in settlement communities (Greven 1970; Demos 1970; Gagan 1976). The few North American studies reviewed here include one considering farm transfer behaviour of American Corn Belt farmers between 1870 and 1950, researched by Friedberger (1983). He found that the stability of permanent families (as opposed to impermanent renters) who were able to pass on their land successfully limited outsiders' access to land. The widowed mother was most vulnerable, but the father's will could include terms under which suitable arrangements for her care and maintenance would be the inheriting son's responsibility that could include purchasing the farm, thus providing cash for distribution to other siblings (1–13).

Mays (1981, 185–211) studied family continuity within one rural Ontario township. He found that holding onto land acquired early in the settlement process was

Succession and inheritance 141

the critical key to build and sustain families' prosperity. It provided their children who had helped the family to accomplish their ambitions with patrimony, so when land was passed from one generation to another, this meant succeeding children had their 'place to stand'. Stable permanent families intermarried with their neighbours, and this in turn cemented ties to the community. Over his study period, land was mainly sourced from the family, either by direct sale, early inheritance or sub-dividing after death of the principal landholder. Conditions were placed on early (i.e. in the heir's thirties) inheritance that were reflected in below-market-prices, and included care for aging parents and financial backing for siblings to establish independently. This option was preferred because it left the farm viable and intact – the basis of family status and security. Because the family was the prime source of land and finance to set siblings up as small independent entrepreneurs, a high level of stability was promoted in the community going back to the first generation of settlers. Castra is a smaller community, but Mays' study is particularly resonant.

Salomon, an ethnologist, compared two Illinois communities settled in the mid-1800s from very different ethnic backgrounds to argue that the yeoman pattern had been neglected by economists assuming that all farmers shared the entrepreneurial pattern. The groups were German Catholic immigrants for 1899, 1930 and 1982 from Westphalia and Yankee pioneers from Kentucky, Indiana, Ohio and other Illinois areas, from 1902, 1930 and 1981 (1985, 323–40). The first group maintained the typical yeomanry approach to landownership, especially when it came to inheritance – 'keep it in the family forever'. Over generations, their intergenerational transfer of land was to one son, who generally bought the favourably priced farm, so money could be distributed to other siblings. Because the son was often the youngest, extended families were common in early marital years. The community's highest priority was continuity of family ownership of farms that were usually quite small and utilised mixed farming with more intensive livestock husbandry, usually pigs. Families had little debt, modest economic expectations and valued their community institutions and social events. The resulting tight land market meant that other sons, who wanted to stay close to home by the 1950s, went to new areas about 15 miles away to establish their own farms. This suggested that entrenched succession practices would encourage continued invasion of land, further from the early settled district. The genesis of the 1880s influx to Castra was just that, as we have seen.

By contrast, the Yankee group lacked social cohesiveness in the early settlement period, institutions were less important, agriculture was monoculture grain cash crop and land was regarded less sentimentally as a commodity that could be bought and sold for the best price, although some generational farms did survive. Salomon identified Yankees as entrepreneurial farmers who were 'profit-minded' and much less concerned with intergenerational succession; sons had to 'do for themselves' because their independence from family was valued. At the same time, entrepreneurial strategies carried more risk of failure (greater indebtedness), and higher land turnover led to more absentee owners, but less outward expansion. Not only did cultural norms (or lack of them) impact on social community

142   *Succession and inheritance*

structure, but the attitude to inheritance had very different lasting effects on land use. Salamon saw the yeoman strategy as more likely to assure survival in the long-term for small family farms and their communities, a significant conclusion in the early 1980s, well ahead of later concerns about family farm survival.

Ostergren (1981, 400–11) also found that cultural norms continued about land and inheritance in seven Swedish communities in Minnesota, where, during 1885–1915, the aging migrant generation was succeeded by its children. Ownership and inheritance were important, because, although land represented potential entrepreneurial profit, more importantly it was viewed as 'the giver of life' and a 'symbol of familial accomplishment and identity in the community', so the long-term goal was 'orderly inheritance' to maintain those qualities. As occurred in the Castra district, the coming of the railway branch line and consequent improved access to markets raised the value of land and 'control of landed wealth' became even more the basis of success for these yeoman farmers. The more conservative families planned carefully, arranging property transfer while the father was still active. When sons were able to start farming earlier on their own family's account, this was much better for the community than waiting to hand-over when the father was old or dead. Inherited farms were generally over 80 acres; two-thirds of those below that were liquidated. Ostergren concluded that the property transmission methods chosen could indicate either stability or mobility in settler communities.

Some Australian historians have looked at land transmission and inheritance in pre-Federation societies. Buxton (1967, 208) wrote that farmers' unions in 1891 were angered at the local Land Board's refusal of selection by a settler's daughter, arguing she was a dummy for her father; 'petitions were signed, uproar [was] created, all over the Riverina' at the perceived abuse of the 'sacred principle of family selection' and a father's right to endow his adult child (by supplying the money). The Board's decision seems to reflect the not unexpected opinion of the time that daughters were unable to farm. The speedy reaction caused a reversal of the decision. 'What shall we do with our sons?' was 'the old cry' let loose over other land matters in the *Wagga Advertiser* that year, which shows how entrenched patrimonial inheritance attitudes were among settlers (News 1891a).

Grimshaw and colleagues (1985) examined land transaction outcomes in Horsham, Victoria, and discovered that adolescent children who had worked without pay were rewarded by 'prospering parents'; rate rolls exposed that fathers frequently settled land on their wives, sons and daughters. The authors argued that hard work had its rewards for successful farm families, which included joining the landowning class and the 'security of property ownership', and, if selectors of the 1860s and 1870s survived the first few seasons, a 'more comfortable' income would continue to grow, and permit land expansion or monetary settlements. Evidenced from wills, farmers' widows were expected to pass land onto their children because patrilineal descent was their customary world-view – land was something to be held in trust for descendants.

Beer's interest was in Highlander Scots who emigrated to Victoria's Western District in the mid-1800s (1989). They tended to have small acreages, and often

Succession and inheritance 143

moved as their children attained adulthood. By moving northwards, they could acquire larger acreages and their children could be selectors too, in contiguous areas, so the family might continue the advantage of family labour. This strategy echoes the Riverina settlers of the 1890s. Even many of the less successful managed to have some of their own land and left wills about its disposal to their sons and cash legacies to their daughters. Beer found that all children received something even if the estate was liquidated, but nothing went to anyone outside the family. Wives were rarely left the entire estate without conditions about its disposal after their death. Some men were anxious to protect land left to daughters from predation by husbands, so 'hard-won real estate' would not leave the 'family fold'. Her conclusion about this group was that 'land emerges as the most valuable commodity to the Highlander', a finding that linked to the prolonged reality of landless peasantry in the Highlands (Matthias 1969, 61). Beer's conclusion certainly has congruency with Scottish migrants into North-West Tasmania and was pivotal to Highlander John McKenzie's belief in lands for the people in New Zealand (Brooking 1996).

There appears to be a gap in Australian historical literature about inheritance in the twentieth century, so more socially targeted work is briefly reviewed because it reveals consistency and durability of attitudes. Prevailing conditions in Australian agriculture towards the end of the twentieth century led some researchers to suggest the 'only possible way for children to enter into farming' was for two generations of the farm family to work together (Kaine, Crosby, and Stayner 1997). Because of its national predominance and salient consequence for rural policymakers, family farming came under the spotlight from a variety of researchers, including contributors to Jim Lees' 1997 edited book, *A Legacy under Threat?* Poor management of farm transfer between generations was found to cause conflict and further financial problems in farming families that had become more obvious by the late 1980s and 1990s (Kaine et al., 62).

Rural sociologists (Barclay, Foskey, and Reeve 2007) contributed Australian data in 2004 to the International Farm Transfers Study for comparisons between England, France, Canada, USA, Japan, North Germany and Poland, such was the importance given to this issue globally. Key Australian findings included: older retirement or adapting to semi-retirement later were more frequent than elsewhere; farm families more often discussed succession and inheritance; more than half identified their successors, most usually a son, because daughters were provided with good education instead; better qualifications for all were encouraged and could be part of a 'professional detour' (their term); small farm successors in Australia, Canada and England took the 'direct route' to control by working alongside the older generation; alternative options – more prevalent in Australia than other countries – involved taking operational responsibility for a separate enterprise within the farm business or a 'professional detour' either working off-farm, or on another farm, or other career, prior to succeeding to the home-farm. Common across all countries, it was financial decisions that were last to be handed on to the next generation (Barclay et al.).

144   *Succession and inheritance*

From these studies and that in 1970s Ireland (Commins and Kelleher 1973), it is clear historically that farm transition issues across the Western world have really changed very little over the decades. The intangible assets of family farms, like managerial skills and farm-specific knowledge were part of benefits we saw previously when soldiers were able to take over their family farm. Reasons for hanging onto the reins reflect yeomanry values – independence, financial control and purpose in life. The range of transitional approaches found since the 1970s are quite consistent with attitudes characterised by actions of Preston farm families up to a century earlier, and also reflect the current twenty-first century feelings of the Peebles brothers, and descendants of the Browns and the Johnsons expressed in interviews with them.

One modern (post-1980s) development in succession planning is concern about possible divorce triggering a 'subsequent loss of a lifestyle, livelihood and future in agriculture' for all members involved in a family farm partnership. Female dissatisfaction with the marital relationship was a higher 'predictor of farm sale than farm size or profitability' (Barr 2009, 80). Here is a modern alternative to the distant echo of the Highland father wanting to protect his daughters' inheritance from his sons-in-law, but exhibiting a similar attitude to values bound up with the land.

Farm transfer approaches

Farm ownership may be transferred in two ways; first, by selling to an outside party, which then breaks connection to the land. The second is by inheritance or sale within the family, thus maintaining continuity. In the latter situation, the process is differentiated by the timing of transfer, which may be either *prior* to the death or departure of the family/household head, or *after* death under conditions of a will or other legal alternative. Partible inheritance means provision is made for all the children (sometimes by splitting the land). In France, for example, the Napoleonic civil code introduced equal division of land between sons, and in Ireland, sub-division of small farms was usual in the early 1800s due to the productivity of the potato, but this was stopped legally after the 1840s famine disaster (Doveri 2000, 30; Commins and Kelleher 1973, 4). Impartible means the property may not be divided or partitioned. This was the trend among Preston farmers, with an active strategy of buying and selling in order to extend or consolidate the home-farm.

Because landed wealth symbolised family status, its independence and, in the case of first settlement, its past achievements in clearing and creating farming land, and all the sacrifices and hardships that had entailed, it was always reasonable for the patriarch and his wife to be concerned with the choice of transition strategy. Relatively recent Irish and Australian research has shown discussions with younger family members was unusual. But this was much less an issue in earlier times because patrilineal inheritance was assumed. In Australia this is rooted in legal structures and social mores inherited from British colonial ancestry. Because of the Tasmanian *Probate Duties Act* 1868, it made sense to arrange land transfers before death, especially when land value might exceed the £100

Succession and inheritance   145

above which duty was due until 1935 when it ceased (*Administration and Probate Act* (No. 2) 1935).

From this expectation that a son *should* inherit the family farm, Voyce (1994) argued the Australian legal system supported farmers' patriarchal land ownership ideology in several ways: ownership rights are justified by past exploitation and development of the land; the law endorses protection of private property rights, thus supporting the 'rural ethic that a farming son who has worked the land should inherit it'; and the owner is free to decide who inherits (called testamentary freedom), although in New Zealand and Australia around 1900, the potential injustice of this resulted in a social justice compromise that supported the family unit and the wife's contribution, called a 'discretionary approach'. Voyce argued that 'patriarchal legal discourse' endorses the 'patriarchal form of reproduction' on the farm in that it supports the notion of the son's work (that is, *male* activity) being rewarded by future ownership (80).

Voyce then discussed the law of trusts, which, under life tenancy, permits a widow's use of income, but not depletion of assets. He argued this is also patriarchal, because 'it relegates the woman to a conduit on behalf of her husband's children and grandchildren' (80). However, this option could be seen as fitting with an ideology of maintaining the widow's sustenance and supporting retention of access to her experiential wisdom about the farm as well as involvement with the grandchild generation. The future of a widowed father has not attracted much attention in the literature. One exception is Wall (2002) who looked at widowers' co-residence from 1891 to 1921. Even less occurs in succession and inheritance sources, yet, as Castra experience will show, sometimes they could outlive their wives.

Preston succession and inheritance strategies

There were always some farm families that could not achieve farm transmission; often this reflected the complexity of providing either a start on the 'agricultural ladder' or adequately for death or retirement. Sometimes the children were lured by the call of the city, a well-recognised feature of the twentieth century. In Castra, several circumstances meant liquidation. Sometimes the remaining widow was too old to continue, or heirs needed funds to share out, or some farmers remained single, without direct heirs. Sometimes original lots were too small to be sufficiently economic. Such occasions suited demand for 'starter' farms for sons. *Town Directories* quantify liquidation. From the 1931 high of 179 farmers across Castra, this had reduced to 140 by 1941, showing farmers' drive to add to existing farms to assist young men starting out.

Large families were associated with the ability to extend family land holdings, particularly as the children grew to adulthood and substantially contributed to the farm enterprise. Both Henry Johnson and David Peebles expanded their holdings to accommodate sons into the farm. Henry Johnson kept investing in nearby blocks of land to set up his boys, gradually selling to them as soon as they could afford to buy (Amby 'Tas' Johnson, grandson, 2017). The blocks were small,

146 *Succession and inheritance*

about 20 or 30 acres, but proximity to his original grant was their selling point to gain benefits from collaboration.

Based on information collected from and about Preston families from the 1880s to 2000, I found evidence of seven different strategies used for succession and/or inheritance, some of which were identified in the studies reviewed. I discuss each family in detail, highlighting the strategies chosen by each generation, endeavouring to blend information about the farmer's life course with the farm's life course and how its size was maintained or extended. It is notable that there were no instances where a daughter inherited the family farm under any circumstances. I drew upon archival materials, newspaper reports, military service records and valuation rolls in addition to my interviews with Preston family members. With their consent, I include interviewees' names and some nicknames for clarity.

The traditional strategy is patrilineal succession and inheritance of the home-farm. The next is where sons were established on new land with the patriarch's help, which might depend on critical events such as a son achieving late adolescence, or the legal age of majority (21 years), or when marriage occurred or was proposed. Liquidated properties assisted this process. The third strategy was the farmer selling his son the home-farm. When retiring parents moved to other accommodation, this strategy varied in the execution; while some left to go to Ulverstone, some parents maintained an interest in the farm, even continuing to provide seasonal labour when needed, and being involved with the upbringing and care of grandchildren. Some families were impacted by losing sons to war, although death in war was not their only loss. Due to the weakened health or physical capacity of their returning sons, fathers could lose their contribution of hard work and farm management responsibilities, or even their potential interest in farming. Other soldier sons returned to carry on, like George and John Johnson and George Peebles. Another strategy was when the farm was liquidated by the heir/s or owners. The final strategy was where son/s chose another career in alternative employment.

First, the **Johnson family**. Henry Johnson was the outstanding example of a father helping his sons onto their own farms. Sarah joined Henry at their new home-farm at Dooley's Plains around 1906. Then, six sons and two daughters were still living with them. Henry helped Harty John (1884–1956) onto land at central Castra, and Ambrose (1886–1954) and George (1896–1966) onto land both sides of Jacks Road (on one home-farm boundary) as they grew old enough.

Their eldest son William (1878–1971) and wife Rose had already bought a house and several small adjoining lots near his father's land at the southern end of Jacks Road, possibly based upon William's own collateral from working on farms in Sassafras before following the family to Dooley's Plains. His eldest sister, Ada, married Samuel Burgess and lived elsewhere. William Burgess and Ambrose Burgess jointly owned 93 acres at Dooley's Plains after Ambrose married Elizabeth Butler at Preston Methodist Church in 1905 (VRs 1905, 1907). By 1908, they had a 0.83-acre block in Preston where they may have had a blacksmith's shop, still appearing in the 1939 roll. William and Rose later moved to Devonport, and their

Succession and inheritance 147

land holdings were retained by the remaining Johnsons. The connection with the Burgess family was significant because Samuel, William and Ambrose Burgess were three siblings out of 15, all nephews of Henry Johnson's wife Sarah Ann Burgess, providing an early example of interwoven families (Banks 1999).

Another son John (known as Jack), born in 1894, was only about eight or nine when his family moved to Rifle Range Road, and along with his older brothers he would have learnt from actively helping to establish the home-farm – their father's apprentices. When war broke out, being just the right age, John enlisted in the army in October 1916, only briefly because he was medically discharged in March 1917 after appendicitis. He married Jane Elizabeth Stevens, who came from the Upper Castra farming family, in December 1918. Her two sisters married two more of Henry's sons, Ambrose to Alice in 1908 and George to Dulcie Fay in 1921 after he returned from war. This inter-marrying particularly served to reinforce the kinship ties among that generation of Johnsons and their children. As Tas Johnson, Henry's grandson, told me, they had plenty of cousins close at hand to play with as those couples had children.

I was not told why it was John, the fourth surviving son, who took over the family farm. But there is evidence to suggest that once the older brothers were settled on their own lands, much of which needed a huge labour investment in clearing, and started families, they would have been more inclined to stay put. Reticence to move indicated a growing attachment to their own farm, and being close to family and community helped reinforce their sense of belonging. For example, son Harty John remained the rest of his life farming at central Castra (News 1941b).

Ambrose was settled on his own Upper Castra farm, near his Stevens in-laws. He and Alice started their family of eleven boys and three girls with a son, Albert in 1908, who went to school at Upper Castra. When Albert grew up, he helped support his family on the farm because his father had poor health (Glennys Johnson, grand-daughter, 2017). Once he was able to marry Thelma Marshall in about 1940, he bought the Marshall family farm at Upper Castra from her eldest brother who had bought it when their parents retired to Devonport. Thelma was left a widow while their five children were still at school. She remained with all their help on the farm until they had all left home, then she decided to liquidate her farm because she could not drive. The story of the Marshall farm at Upper Castra was one of sale to an eldest son, then to a sister's spouse and finally liquidated by the elderly widow.

George Johnson enlisted in September 1916, but got sick and was sent home for three months' recuperation before he rejoined his unit in February 1917 (News 1917a). He returned in April 1917, married Dulcie Stevens and ran his farm sited down a lane near the Preston sports ground. They had two sons, Trevor and Clifford, and four or five daughters. George's farm passed to Trevor, then to *his* son, Darryl, owner in the late 1990s. Clifford bought the 89-acre farm with its high-quality Dunham family home from Phil Chamberlain (see Chapter 5) (Kevin Johnson, Henry's great-grandson 2018). In due time that was inherited by his son, Ned, then sold to his cousin Len Johnson, who sold it in about 2000 to Peter Smith, a third-generation Waringa Road farmer (Peter Smith, pers. comm. 2019).

148   *Succession and inheritance*

This was an example of the eldest son taking over the home-farm, and the second son farming on land next door, then handing it on to his son.

By the time John Johnson got married and their first son had arrived, he was a mature 22-year-old, and his father was in his early sixties. In 1919, Henry handed over the family farm (Tas Johnson). Henry and Sarah moved to Ulverstone until Sarah died in 1926 (he was about 70); then Henry returned to live with John and Jane until he died at 85 (News 1941b). Sometimes he caught the mail truck to ride down to Gunns Plains to stay with daughter Sarah and farmer husband Peter John Marshall and their many children (Georgie Johnson, Henry's grandson, 2018). The Johnson home-farm story was an example of the father agreeing to succession by patrilineal inheritance, and his later involvement with grandchildren back in the home he had built. This fitted with old traditions of absorbing the widowed grandparent into the family circle, and Wall's findings about co-resident widowers.

John and Jane had nine sons and two daughters. They also helped their sons onto farming land of their own, possibly helped by John's additional trucking business income. When land off Waringa Road, inherited by Fred Tongs from his grandfather Frank, came up for sale in 1950, John bought it with that idea in mind. Georgie told me:

> The land was 215 acres, three lots of fifty acres each and one with a house on it of 64 acres. As soon as it was my twenty-first birthday [1952], Dad took me to the lawyer in Ulverstone to put one into my name. I chose the one with the house, so I could live in it straight away. [Brothers] Sidney and [Gordon] Bill took over the other parts of the land on the western side of the road and worked it with Dad until he died in 1957.

Georgie married Iris in mid-1954, a few months before Tas married her older sister, Merle (Iris Johnson 2018).

Emulating his father's succession decision, when John and Jane wanted to hand over the management of the home-farm, they bought a house in the centre of Preston village. Their eldest, Sidney (born 1918) succeeded to the family farm probably soon after his last sibling, Jeanie, was born in 1944 (Marie Harrop, John's grand-daughter 2017). Brothers Keith, Denzil and Tas continued to live with Sidney when he was first married, because they were working the farm with him (Tas Johnson). Gordon 'Bill' (born 1921) eventually had a farm on South Preston Road, as well as the land at Waringa. Keith (born 1924) farmed land on Jacks Road, possibly the land his uncle William had occupied. Johnny (born 1926) had his farm on the western side of South Preston Road. Denzil (born 1928) farmed on land on Rifle Range Road (the old Castra Road) again possibly one of William's blocks. Tas farmed about 200 acres on South Preston Road before selling to his brother Bill, when he became farm manager at Sprent Farm School and they bought farmland near there.

John continued to help his sons in other ways. John and Sidney grew potatoes together on the Waringa block, after organising bullocks to clear the land owned

Succession and inheritance 149

by Sid and Bill. He would go to the livestock market regularly and buy cows for Georgie's and Iris' milking herd, 12 altogether over time, but the bill always turned up later for them to pay, Georgie told me good-humouredly. Jane died young at 56 in 1955, and John died at 63 two years later. By then some of his brothers were married, so his eldest sister, Alice and the sisters-in-law helped their father out at home with their young sister Jeanie, who went to live with Sidney and Jean after her father's death (Georgie Johnson). Again, patrilineal succession was the strategy here combined with off-farm retirement, but close enough to provide active help to farming sons. Since both John and Jane died relatively early, their timely decision meant most of their sons were already established on their own farms and the home-farm had transitioned to their first son.

Fitting the 1950s demographic trend, Sidney and Joan only had three children, Joan born in 1950, Marie in 1952 and Kevin in 1955. Sidney was still working the Waringa land bought by John, but in the 1950s, he bought two 50-acre blocks at Waringa to work with the home-farm. In 1965 Sidney had an opportunity to extend the home-farm by buying what had been John Chamberlain's farm later sold to the McPherson brothers, because it surrounded the home-farm on two boundaries, one being Jacks Road (Marie Harrop). He liquidated the Waringa 50-acre blocks and took that opportunity to extend. In about 1971, Kevin started working with his father at 16.

At the end of the 1990s, two farms north of the extended home-farm were for sale. Darryl Johnson wanted to sell his grandfather George's farm, and the other was the Chamberlain farm located on the Coningham Anglo-Indian lot between that farm and the home-farm. It was for sale because Phil Chamberlain (known locally as "Pa" – a lovely man according to local opinion) died of cancer and his wife decided not to keep the farm going (Kevin Johnson).

Plantation foresters were looking to buy in Preston and other North-West districts. Rather than let both these farms 'go to trees', Sidney decided to liquidate the rest of the Waringa land to the foresters and buy both properties. Sidney subdivided off the half-acre with Mrs Chamberlain's house on it beside the main road where she ran the Waringa Post Office, so she continued living there. Kevin said they did not want to be surrounded by plantation, already established on the southern side of Rifle Range Road. Sidney and Joan, with Kevin then about 18, moved to a newly built brick house on the larger of these new blocks for the rest of their lives. Later, Kevin built a new house on the original home-farm to start his married life in 1981, where he and his wife still live. They have two girls, but Kevin does not expect them to be interested in succeeding to the farm with careers and families inter-state. Kevin realises that sale after four generations is inevitable.

The Johnson home-farm life-course has been a straight case of patrilineal inheritance with a lot of help to most of the many sons in two generations. The future succession of several Johnson family farms is in doubt, with only one descendant, Bruce (Bill's son), having a son or son-in-law who may be interested in carrying on (Kevin Johnson). Liquidation seems the likely outcome. Georgie and Iris, both in their eighties when I interviewed them, held onto their farm rather than sell to foresters, but finally decided they could not manage anymore and sold their

150 *Succession and inheritance*

farm in 2019 to incomers who are continuing to farm. I asked whether they had considered handing on the farm to either of their daughters, especially Judy who had shown aptitude over handling the dairy cows. Georgie said that it may have been different if either of them had married farmers, but they both moved to town with husbands who had other work. They moved to Ulverstone near family and Georgie died in 2020.

Second, I discuss the **Peebles** family. James and Margaret Peebles had plenty of sons to help with the farm clearing and planting as they grew older and became strong young men. In a 1910 family photograph, at least seven boys look big enough to provide real help. There were still treed areas to clear for decades as well as farming. However, the Great War intervened, and the first son who decided to enlist was Alexander James Peebles, the sixth son, in July 1915 at 18 years and nine months old. He was wounded in early 1917 (News 1917a). He returned home on final leave on 8 March 1917 (News 1917b). Alexander became a bricklayer and with his wife, Eva May, and lived in Sydney where he worked laying bricks on the Sydney Harbour Bridge (June Peebles, pers. comm. 2019). They eventually retired to Launceston and he died without heirs there in 1965.

Then George, the seventh son, enlisted in February 1916 at nearly 19 years old. He was killed in France on 1 February 1917. The third son to enlist was Allan Peebles, the fifth son, who enlisted two weeks after George in March 1916 at 20 years and eight months old. He returned from war, married Marion Jessie Dick of Riana and had a shop in Preston. He died in 1922 intestate, described as a storekeeper with shop stock worth £100 amongst his other assets (Will, AD963/1/1–941). His widow returned to her father's home with her two children. When she died in 1936, five Peebles brothers-in-law were pallbearers.

The fourth son to enlist was Andrew Henderson Peebles, the third son, who enlisted in February 1917 at 24 years old and was killed in action in France on 28 March 1918 (News 1918c).

Did any of the remaining Peebles sons go farming in Preston? Henry, the second son, acquired the 80-acre farm north of the home-farm, with land sited on each side of the main road. It is likely that James saw advantage in helping Henry, especially as they shared a long boundary. An additional easterly block of 40 acres was added because it joined the home-farm at the corner, making it easy to move livestock between properties. Later Henry acquired another 100-acre adjoining block opening onto Jacks Road. Henry married Louie and had two sons, Gilbert and George Henry, and two daughters, Ella and Grace Amelia. Gilbert 'Snow' chose to work away from the farm. George was farming with his father after his service in the Second World War and may have been intended to inherit, but he died unusually young, possibly due to rheumatoid arthritis diagnosed in New Guinea (Army Records, B883, No.TX14416). This loss probably triggered Henry's sale in the 1960s two years later (Rob Peebles and Bub 2018).

Henry and James Robert ran their farms together and when James' youngest son David left school, he joined them and continued to live at home. James died in late 1929, when David was in his mid-twenties, and he continued to work the farm with Henry as before, living with his mother, and his widowed sister Ruby

Succession and inheritance 151

joined the household. James looked after all his children with substantial cash bequests, but David was also left the farm (AD960-1-54, Will No 17623). David married Alice Johnson, the eldest daughter of John Johnson, in 1942. They had four children, three boys followed by a girl, Margaret. The eldest son, Neville, worked at Ellis' Preston village shop as a young man out of school and then followed a life-time career as an auctioneer based in Ulverstone.

For some years, David Peebles' other two sons, Gordon (Bub) and Robert (Rob) farmed with him in a business called 'David Peebles & Sons'. When Rob returned from national service in 1969, the two brothers formed a partnership, working together as in the past. When they told their father that they were considering buying the McCulloch's old farm on Mead's Anglo-Indian lot that was nearly next door, Dad said to them, 'If you want to buy a farm, buy this one!' (Rob Peebles and Bub 2018) So they did. David and Alice stayed living on the farm, with Margaret, until she moved to town for work, and their sons until 1971 when Bub married June. Rob continued to live on the home-farm with his parents and when David died in 1992, he stayed with his mother until she needed more care and moved to a local nursing home. She died in 2008. Rob has not married. Rob and his brother operate both their farms under their partnership, 'Peebles Brothers' (June Peebles).

Bub and June Peebles bought their own previously rented farm on Waringa Road when they started their married life. This farm is worked in conjunction with the home-farm and the partnership, while remaining their own. They have a daughter and son, both of whom have careers, children and homes in Ulverstone. Bub, June and Rob gradually purchased other small farms from the 1980s onwards in Preston and Central Castra, one of which is Colonel Crawford's original farm, Deyrah, more in order to stay financially viable than as potential starter farms for the children (Bub and Rob Peebles). There are no succession plans (in 2021) because they all continue to work.

The Peebles' home-farm life course is a story of patrilineal inheritance from James to the youngest son David with years of working together alongside David's much older brother, Henry. The sale of the farm to his sons in partnership while the family continued to live there in the farmhouse demonstrates a different type of successful transmission strategy. Passing the farm by inheritance to the youngest son after years working together was a well-recognised succession strategy in yeoman farms as Salamon found in America.

Now the **Brown** family. Five generations of the Brown family have farmed in Preston, though not always on the same land. Their story is a valuable addition to the history of succession, inheritance and attachment to the land in Preston. Arthur William Brown took up 104 acres of land in 1901 on Dooley's Plains Road. His wife Ada's brother John Porter had already selected land near George Wing in the 1880s at Preston's northern end. This was passed to his own son, John Hogben Porter, eventually. Arthur's oldest sister, Ellen, married Peter Jupp, and they also bought a house and 100 acres of land in Preston by 1903 that featured in Chapter 5. Arthur and his brother William took advantage of the release of many small blocks of unalienated Crown Land in the later years of the first twentieth

152 *Succession and inheritance*

century decade, and, according to the Valuation Rolls, they soon owned a number still occupied by members of the Brown family well into the 1940s. When Albert Hedley (Joe, born in 1905) decided to marry Gladys Smith from the large Smith family in Smiths Road, they lived on one of these. They started their family with a daughter followed by their only son, Kenneth Albert Brown, born in 1938. Ken told the story that he started school at Nietta in about 1943 or 1944 and had to walk three miles along the railway line to get to school each day (retold by Bub and Rob Peebles).

In about 1946 or 1947, Joe and Gladys decided to buy the farm near Barren Hill belonging to his uncle John Hogben Porter (1875–1956). He was about 70 and his sons, in their forties, wanted to work for the Post-Master General's Dept, which was taking on a lot of men at the time, so he was ready to sell to go to town. The Browns took on the 95 acres and an old house (Ken Brown 2018).

When Ken finished school at 15 in 1953, he worked full time for his father, and after marrying Josephine (Josie) in 1960 or 1961, he bought a 58-acre farm on the opposite side of the road nearer to Barren Hill. They worked the farms together. He and Josie had three children, John, Paul and a sister all close in age. The family lived on that farm until the children were about six, seven and eight years old, respectively. Then they bought the farm on Chisholm's Rd opposite, which is Paul's now. They funded this by selling the first farm to Denzil Harding (see further in this chapter). They lived there for ten to 12 years until the tail end of the children's school years. Ken and Josie moved into his parents' house after the death of his father in 1981 because Gladys decided to move to Ulverstone. Under the terms of his father's will, Ken had to buy the farm for $12,000 to give his mother money to support her the rest of her life (Will no. 69331). This was the transmission strategy that catered to the needs of the patriarch's widow.

Son John always wanted to farm just as his father had, and in about 1987, he bought the house and land that had been the Lewis' home where the post office operated for so long, located opposite. He lived there four or five years before he married. In between the two Brown farms, George Wing Jnr's son, Stanley's property was for sale after his death in 1981 (News 1981). John and Ken went halves in it, which amalgamated their family farming interests on the same side of the road. John later sold the Lewis house on a small curtilage but retained the farmland. He has two sons, Joe, in his twenties (2018), and Travis, an apprentice mechanic, and a daughter. Joe was growing potatoes for Simplot Factory in Ulverstone in 2017–2018 on his grandfather's land but on his own account (Paul Brown, uncle, pers. comm. 2018). Starting from his great-great-grandfather William Brown, Joe is now the sixth generation of Tasmanian farmers from the original Norfolk farming immigrants of the 1850s.

Paul Brown provides one example of what was termed a 'professional detour', and his nephew Travis may well turn out to do the same with his very appropriate apprenticeship as a mechanic. Paul did a boilermaker/welder apprenticeship, working in Ulverstone for about 15 years. He bought another 49-acre block west of the farm in Chisholm's Road where he grew up and that is worked with other family land. He helps his father, now that Ken is in his eighties. Ken and

Succession and inheritance 153

Josie continue to live on his parents' home-farm in the brick home they built for themselves. Ken's sisters left Preston once they were old enough, and Ken's own daughter settled in Devonport. Meanwhile Joe looked for his own land and found some at Kindred, a farming settlement seven miles away, still near enough to contribute to the family farm enterprise. This outcome is reminiscent of Salamon's study where sons moved up to 15 miles to settle.

The Brown family present a strong example of collaborative farming across two and three generations together, coupled with an expectation of each generation buying their own land to get started on. From the decision to come from South Preston to Preston made by Albert Hedley, the following generations have been able to expand their holdings to advantage the farming collaboration. The pattern of patrilineal descent has been clear and appears to be set fair for the future.

Finally, the **Harding family.** This family's connection to Preston land was started by the two Harding brothers who bought one of two Ewington soldier settlement farms, 158 acres accessed at the top of Smith's Road, South Preston. Herbert H. Harding bought and farmed with his brother Harry. William Henry Harding, Harry's son, grew up there. He started as a young man by buying into a share farm with Mrs Lee down Smiths Road. He married Melvie Smith, Gladys Brown's sister from the Smith family also in Smiths Road. Perhaps by selling his share, he bought 37 acres adjoining the Harding farm accessed from Tongs Road (Denzil Harding 2018).

During the tough 1930s depression, William and Melvie left Tasmania with Wilma, born in 1930, and Denzil, born in 1931. William worked near Tully, Queensland, and at Kooweerup, Gippsland, for two years. Returning in 1940, he bought a farm near the Preston recreation ground, and they had another daughter, Beryl, in 1941. This farm was nearer the school and was part of William Delaney's farm, the rest being held by Frank, William's son. When Pearson's adjacent 103-acre block on Smith's Road on the original farm's south side became available, William bought it to consolidate the Harding home-farm.

Denzil finished school at 14 and worked on the family farm. While he was still a teenager, his father bought Les Porter's 50-acre block below them on the main road for £500, half down and half the next year, for Denzil. Here, Denzil grew potatoes and ran a few cows, continuing to labour on other farms until he was 20. He eventually sold this land to Ken Brown's uncle, Harold Brown, who had farmland down Browns Road. He married Margaret when he was 21 in 1952, and got a job working for Forestry planting trees at Isandula for eight years with a supplied house.

A big change occurred when Harry Smith, his grandfather, died in 1960, after being widowed in 1933 and continuing to farm and care for his unmarried children. William Harding bought the Smith family farm for £1,500, so two daughters and one son still at home could move to Ulverstone. This property, called Spion Kop, became home to Denzil and Margaret with their four boys and one girl. Denzil added three neighbouring properties liquidated when Mervyn Tongs died, which meant the farm was 330 acres. Meanwhile he also bought a 58-acre farm near Barren Hill from Ken Brown, initially to work it, rent out the house

154 *Succession and inheritance*

and offer it later to a son. The Harding sons worked on the farm until they were ready to go their own way. Denzil and Margaret continued to live there until 1996 when poor health was good reason to sell to the plantation owners and move to the smaller farm owned by his two sons in Kindred. Only in his sixties, he helped them with all the tractor work there until Margaret's death in 2004. He retired to Ulverstone near their son Selwyn. The youngest, Kelvin (born about 1966) and his wife lived in Devonport, had two sons, both now living inter-state, and ran a business until early retirement back to the Barren Hill 58-acres this century. In terms of farm transmission, the Harding story is interesting, because there is no direct line of patrilineal descent and yet, assistance when death occurred gave William the chance to provide Denzil and Margaret a generational farm of their own, which allowed later consolidation with other properties. The pattern of early help to get started was provided to William and then by him to Denzil, who later provided actual labour to help his other sons, and the investment farm to Kelvin.

Overall, these families' stories have provided evidence of consistent independent action and willingness to seize expansion opportunities from liquidation. This common thread aligns with histories reviewed earlier. Flexibility, adaptability and taking advantage of changing circumstances were typical yeomanry approaches to land ownership. Careful succession planning and enculturated independence in farming sons sustained durable connections to the land that contained decades of investment of previous hard toil, reinforced often by kinship and marital relationships.

This chapter has featured the underlying drive of its pioneers not only to create viable, sustainable family enterprises, but also to perpetuate generational permanence through astute inheritance strategies combined with advantageous consolidation. These histories have been chosen because the families are still farming in Preston. Other generational families, such as the Wings, the Lewis brothers, the Delaney brothers, the Stuarts, the Tongs, the McPhersons of Preston, the Marshalls of Upper Castra and the Wrights and Crawfords of central Castra, all had stories about early pioneering and generational transmission of land ownership, and their eventual liquidations have contributed to these families' stories, because they were all gone by 2000.

Historically, marriage was a critical event associated with prospective economic security (Hareven 1977, 64). This and the status of well-established family farms certainly featured in Castra marriages. The suitability of prospective in-law families and well-suitedness of the sons and daughters, most of whom came from farming families within easy reach, is exemplified by the frequency of intermarriages that played their part in keeping that sense of permanence through social and communal structures. As Mays found in Toronto Gore, children were surrounded by neighbours who were 'brothers, sisters, grandparents, uncles and in-laws of various degrees . . . in maturity, they would aspire to settle nearby and seek marriage partners among neighbours who were similarly inclined' (Mays, 208). Castra's very large families from the 1860s to the 1960s exceeded the Australian general fertility rates of farming families by extending

Succession and inheritance 155

longer into the twentieth century, but they proved functional for the survival and prosperity of yeoman farming.

It was realistic that farmers with their wives would consider carefully what would happen when they got old, and there was evidence of far-sighted transition planning among our Preston families. Death is possibly an even more critical event than birth and marriage that can impact quite profoundly upon other family members unless preparations have been put in train in a timely manner, as did Henry Johnson, John and Jane Johnson, James Robert Peebles and David Peebles.

The transmission of property ownership can also mean a change in power relations within the family as assets are redistributed. The person most vulnerable when death occurs was the widow. We saw ways this was managed, as with Thelma Marshall, who could stay on the farm while she had teenagers to help, or Gladys Brown who inherited the wherewithal to move to town, or Alice Peebles who kept a home going for her adult son while he ran the farm after her husband David's death. Widowers Henry Johnson and John Johnson both continued to contribute in valued and supportive ways till they died, while Harry Smith spent nearly 30 years as a widower keeping his farm going for and with his children.

By the 1980s, a feature of the farming landscape across Australia, not just in Preston, was the necessity for farmers to decide whether to expand to stay viable or to sell and leave because their farm was too small to yield a living income in the contemporary market climate. Small families were another feature. Corporatized food processing and contract farming had huge impact in an increasingly globalised world. As farmers aged, it was easier to run cattle grazing operations than cropping. By 2000, the last vegetable crop of broccoli was grown and harvested in Preston on Don Stuart's farm for freezer processing. The last seed potatoes were harvested in 2006, because the Peebles brothers were tired of needing to irrigate in drier spring seasons. Forestry plantations, advantaged by lucrative tax breaks for their non-farming shareholders, were starting to make inexorable changes to the hard-won agricultural landscape into the next millennium. Gradually, the survival of sustainable family farming was being seriously threatened.

7 Childhood and youth in Castra

This chapter is about rural farm children growing up and being incorporated as youth into their parents' yeoman world. From historical sources, I briefly examine attitudes about childhood, child labour, education and adolescence through the later 1800s and their impact on yeoman children's lives. During those decades, family 'modernisation' approaches gained strength, epitomised by middle-class social attitudes about children and adolescence. There is little evidence of this affecting Castra life from the 1920s to the 1970s. Drawing largely on personal interviews, I illustrate how established yeomanry social and behavioural characteristics were maintained in twentieth-century Castra children. Not until the 1980s can those modernising attitudes be found impacting upon parental and adolescent aspirations that appeared to threaten the yeoman ideal in family farming.

History of children and work

For centuries, young people had worked in England for larger yeoman farmers, boys with livestock or crops and girls in the dairy, where butter and cheese was made from the farm-produced milk, while smaller landholders used their own children's labour (Orme 2001, 310). Through the eighteenth century, although experience across Britain varied, subsistence farming was increasingly supported by part-time employment of women and children in a dual economy of domestic industry, particularly in the Midlands, Yorkshire and Lancashire (Hay and Rogers 1997, 115; Mathias 1969, 61–63). By 1780, rural village life had begun to change as cottage industries were taken over by factories. Spinning by agricultural wives and children was lost first, most markedly after 1800 and in southern counties particularly (Snell 1985, 65). Work in village trades like tanning, milling, saddlery, cobbling, brewing and cloth-weaving provided employment for small subsistence freeholders, but was gradually moving into the towns. Independent cottagers and small-holders with their women and children were forced to labour for larger farmers or face a move either to town or to emigrate in a process that impacted more in England by 1820–1830 than elsewhere in Europe. This disruption was a trigger for early migration to British colonies (Trevelyan 1926, 717–19). The world that rural immigrants knew as normal was characterised by all household

DOI: 10.4324/9781003229841-8

Childhood and youth in Castra   157

members including children working either at home or away in other households of large yeoman farmers (Snell, Ch. 2).

Throughout the nineteenth-century Anglo colonial world, families were the taken-for-granted element in the image of the yeoman ideal of self-sufficient farmers that was so politically acceptable. Wherever countries favoured yeoman settlers, population increase through many children was an additional desirable outcome, the long-term societal assets being their valuable labour as they grew up and short-term economic benefits from increased demand (Dingle 1984, 58–61).

The post-Napoleonic War years coincided with the settlement of the Swan River Colony in 1828 and South Australia in 1836, neither of which were designed to use convict labour in settlement (Hetherington 1992). The solution to the labour problem for Swan River 'capitalist settlers' was to finance the migration of servants and labourers with families, because every person arriving had relative value in extra acreage for the sponsoring capitalist, including women and children over three years. Ten-year-olds had the labour status of adults. Colonial Office regulations were obviously designed to encourage whole families to be funded because they allowed land in respect of 'Children of Labouring People' of between 40 and 120 acres for each child under ten and 200 acres for each woman and child over ten (37). Within ten years, Governor James Stirling advocated that the colony support smaller country establishments amongst large scale properties, to 'offer steady and constant employment to boys and women, and even children, and tend thereby to keep families together under parental supervision'. Boys and men were employed as servants doing cooking and other tasks, quite different from existing practices in England, a reflection of the reality that females often married, thereby annulling their work agreements (40–41).

In England, away from mid-nineteenth century industrial towns/villages, young agricultural children continued to pull weeds, glean and stone-pick; older children and women did potato setting, turnip singling, hoeing, weeding and crop gathering, often while their infants were tucked into the shelter of hedges (Orwin and Whetham, 207; see Kitteringham 1975). Heywood (2001) has reminded us that the majority of European and American children lived in rural farming areas, and smaller children 'helped out' with easy, time-consuming chores until they grew stronger.

Family labour was crucial to keep Lancashire yeoman farms viable from the 1800s to the 1940s, in spite of local factories (Winstanley 1996). They produced milk, eggs, poultry, butter and cheese for the expanding town markets using improved railway and transport links. Farmer-retailers supplied textile towns of Lancashire and West Yorkshire. Potatoes and other vegetables on coastal farms added to farmer-fishermen's income. Produce was sold on market stalls or door-to-door and catered to increased summer demand from holidaymakers that developed from 1870. As late as 1911, despite mandated schooling, 41 per cent of boys and 91 per cent of girls from ten to 14 years were in the agricultural workforce (183, Table 4). Work by family members from the young to the elderly on small farms was significant for agricultural production and for farm enterprise viability;

158 *Childhood and youth in Castra*

women's predominance managing dairy operations indicated plenty of work for adult daughters (194–95).

In America, yeoman farmers needed family labour to maintain economic independence and its importance was more inferred than explicit (Ford 1986; Wilkison 2008; Appleby 1982). Agrarian frontierswomen were expected to 'produce a labor supply in the form of many children' (Riley 1977, 195). Mid-West state censuses showed girls from five to 19 were 31–35 per cent of all females, implying a major work-force ((Hunter and Riney-Kehrberg 2002). West (1989) wrote about frontier sons' and daughters' lives – different from the eastern states – embracing adults' tasks like herding and hunting, and in ploughing and planting teams. Neth (1995) examined early twentieth-century mid-western family farms, and ways young people were incorporated into farming. In Ohio, each person did what their strength allowed. On wheat and mixed farms, the need for field work from women and girls reduced, but in tobacco-growing specialisation, their fieldwork was more essential (23). In New Zealand, a high demand for hand labour existed in dairying from 1870 to 1930 (Hunter and Riney-Kehrberg,137). In Castra, girls and boys were accustomed to helping with potato and vegetable harvesting well before similar dairy specialisation with its high labour demand before electric milking machines arrived.

The 'dearth of historical scholarship about rural girls and young women' identified by Hunter and Riney-Kehrberg (136) was picked up in recent work about American child labour by Grattan and Moen. They drew attention to the 'almost obsessive focus' scholars and reformers have addressed to the 'villains' of exploitation of children in industrial work. They suggested it seemed a 'curious silence' about the many more occupied in agricultural work (Grattan and Moen 2004). For example, in 1910 and 1920, over 60 per cent of child workers were employed in agriculture, and fathers in farming families 'believed in keeping children busy once they could perform simple tasks' (358). The perception that children working on parents' farms was beneficial fitted the Jeffersonian yeoman ideal, although children in Texan cotton fields and mid-western tobacco farms often worked for landlords, without parental protection (358).

In Australia, experiences of life for Victorian selectors' women and children recorded in diaries are particularly rich sources for picturing children's contribution, when 'play quickly became work as their physical capacities developed', like stick and root picking following the plough, fetching the cow for milking and other errands to help mother who was occupied with the newest baby, preserving food or making butter or jam to sell for cash or barter (Dingle 1984, 69–72). The essential hard work of their children enhanced women's child-bearing role and 'everyone worked across all classes of settlers' (Grimshaw and Willett 1981, 136–50). Across newly selected areas 'a large family of willing sons and daughters old enough to work' was almost better than capital, since men with young families had to pay for help or take smaller, more manageable lots of land (Dingle, 71). Gradually, universal education was spurred on by 'child-savers' in Australian states, drawing their inspiration from British and, especially, American philanthropic counterparts ((Wimshurst 1981,

Childhood and youth in Castra   159

338, n.3; Sanson and Wise 2001, 38–39). One Tasmanian response to such calls for progressive social reform forbade children under 12 years in factories, but excluded seasonal work in jam factories (*Women's and Children's Employment (Factories) Act* 1884). Schooling would impact on the time country children had for work, as we see next.

Children were 'the silent ones of history, the least observed, consulted, understood and the least revealing about themselves', which highlights the elusiveness of available sources from children themselves and its difficulty for historians (Phillips 1985, 25; Ward 1988, 10; Pascoe 2010, 1142). Scholarly studies of country children have often focussed on children's folklore and play-ways. In Britain, the classic study is by Opie and Opie (1970); in New Zealand, see Sutton-Smith (1981). Factor (1979) looked for 'Fragments of Children's Play in Nineteenth Century Australia', noting that children's lives were then a virtually ignored topic by historians. Failure to record children's activities was due to the demands and urgency of pioneering life where certainly 'a sense of freedom from responsibility to work was a rare commodity' for them (55). Cannon (1973) also pointed out that 'children were put to work from the earliest possible age'. He cited examples of boys and girls becoming 'shepherds as soon as they could walk and talk, watching flocks during the day' and sometimes even at night (54–55, 155).

There are few historical sources about or by twentieth-century farm children, especially in Tasmania where diaries are rare. This history is enriched by access to Clarence McCulloch's Preston autobiography from 1920 to 1940 (1998), and Ray Denney's youthful memories of Upper Castra from 1924 to 1937 (1993).

Farm work and school

From its inception, Castra yeoman farming families were large. We should not under-estimate the contribution their children made in the process of establishing successful farms. The age-old tradition of country children working had a long history of colonial acceptance, and, in Tasmania, it was taken-for-granted in rural small farms and businesses. Sprod (1984, 32) argued that Tasmania lagged much longer behind urban bourgeois ideas about child labour because children were incorporated into the family's economic needs in closely settled farming districts. In the major towns, voluntary societies motivated by fear of emerging criminality by orphan and pauper children had set up ragged schools following Government-sponsored institutions from Governor Arthur's time. When Governor Franklin was regulating for public schooling in Tasmania in 1839, he was considering children of the colony's 'respectable inhabitants' (Phillips, 26).

Child labour was legal and supported in the Tasmanian press (Sprod, 30). Referring to the 1867 Royal Commission into Education (HAJ, Vol. XV, 1867, No. 31), *Mercury* Editor James Allen pointed out, on 17 August 1868, that proposed measures to monitor attendance appeared heavy-handed; parents would be

160 *Childhood and youth in Castra*

summoned and fined for their child's non-attendance. Echoing locally accepted ideology, he stated that:

> industrious and labouring classes in this country must know that the labor of every healthy child, between 6 and 12 years of age, becomes an indispensable help to its parents, either in minding younger children or assisting them in lighter labor . . . rural and bush children from seven to ten or twelve years of age will always be found fully employed in assisting their parents.

He claimed that the Commissioners supplied sufficient material to 'protest against [compulsion] being pressed into the service of public education in Tasmania'. The Report showed that over 70 per cent of parents of students in existing schools in 1866 were from labouring and artisan classes, of which about 23 per cent were *rural* labourers and small- to medium-scale farmers (News 1868b). Eventually, demand that had been growing from 1852 for publicly funded schools was met when the *Act* was passed in 1868. The same year, Edward Swarbreck Hall, Chair of the Benevolent Society Executive Committee and also Hobart's health officer, presented a petition to both houses of Parliament in support of compulsory schooling, expressing Society concern that many parents did not send their children to school (HAJ Vol.XVI, No.67; LC, No.59). *The Public Schools Act* 1868 required that children aged seven to 12 years living within one mile had to attend school; the only annually granted allowable exemption was 'That the parents cannot do, in whole or in part, without the labour of such child' (S.15(4) and s.16). Tasmania was the first Empire colony to mandate free education for children aged seven to 12 years to an adequate minimum standard (Wood 1981, 3), a claim made hollow, according to Phillips, because it did not raise attendance or community interest (54–58).

Public schools were established in larger Tasmanian centres from 1869, so both Ulverstone and Castra (later Sprent) public schools opened that year. But developing rural districts were slower to be included and the *Act*'s compulsory attendance provisions did not apply in rural districts (Phillips, 54–58). There were still periods when farmers needed all available family labour to cope with seasonal demands (Aitken 2007). Expectation of seasonal absenteeism was tolerated by school inspectors as long as farm children attended for the yearly minimum period. Compulsion and exemption clauses of the *Act* were handled by Local School Boards of Advice, where community representatives, many of whom were farmers, held positions. Another role for Boards of Advice was monitoring regular attendance reports with explanations for unusually high absentee figures (Henderson 2016).

It was the same situation under the *South Australian Education* Act 1875 that stipulated 70 days/half-year (Wimshurst, 388–90). Local inspectors knew when child labour demands were highest. So, in Victoria's market gardens, children's help was most needed on Friday afternoons (Quiggin 1988). On Queensland's Darling Downs, the local economy depended on large families to work hard due to the 'precarious nature of commercial farming' (Waterson, 150–51). Chronic absenteeism was less prevalent in mixed farming families there, endorsing the political belief that yeoman mixed farming families could survive hard times better because they produced much of their own food (151–52).

Childhood and youth in Castra   161

Tasmania's 1873 *Amendment Act* increased leaving age from 12 to 14 years and mandated attendance for children living within two miles. Extending distance saved costs by reducing schools needed in small rural communities; but this had ramifications for Castra communities. They only gained a local school if they supplied the building; the Government supplied a teacher when there were more than ten pupils.

Access to school in Castra villages did not change the expectation that farm children should continue traditional work helping production on self-sufficient yeoman farms. From pioneering settlement in the 1880s to well beyond the Second World War, farm work continued to be an essential element of childhood. Large families like the Johnsons and Peebles catered for a lot of people, but that meant more children able to contribute as they grew older. Tasks were allocated according to age, not gender, and were a rehearsal for life as a yeoman farmer or his wife. Boys were responsible for attending to working bullocks and horses, their own horse when they were old enough to ride, and the working dogs (McCulloch 1998, 54). Most children routinely rose before sunrise to fetch their four, five or six cows that they milked before breakfast and school, and, where girls were available, they were often better milkers than boys. Skemp recalled an old bush settler saying, 'I like to see a few nippers about the place. When a child's five it ought to be earning its keep'. During the dairy season, children worked long hours added to their school days, but good and plentiful food was not spared (Skemp 1952, 128). Both parents and children accepted this routine as normal.

Local memories of daily life

In many Castra families, boys predominated. Dairy farm labourers' sons, like Murray King (born 1929, seventh out of 12) and his brothers, contributed to their father Robert's employment by each milking several of his employer William Last's cows before and after school (King, pers. comm. 2019). Typical of Castra experience, Tas Johnson (born 1933) milked several cows, then separated the milk and fed the calves. He walked cows to the day's paddock, then walked two miles to school with up to five brothers joining him across the paddocks. Milking happened again after school, but the Johnson boys 'collected wood and sticks for the fire and peeled a pot of spuds' too, in tasks very similar to those on American family farms (Georgie and Tas Johnson; Neth 1994). From northern Preston, only son Ken Brown (born 1938) recalled doing early milking too, as well as feeding calves and pigs, and setting rabbit traps before joining a group of about 15 to 20 other children walking another mile to school. Pat Smith (born 1943) daughter of Vernon Smith (see Chapter 5) had one younger and three older brothers. She affirmed the ungendered system and gave insight into seasonal variety:

> Chores were passed down along the children as they grew. My chores were chopping sticks for firewood, feeding the hens and collecting the eggs, milking and checking the lambs. In winter, there were often lambs to feed and keep warm.

> (Pat Smith 2015)

162   *Childhood and youth in Castra*

Glennys Johnson supported the same course with her male and female siblings. The pattern indicates that age was most important in assigning childhood tasks. It emulates the universal traditional expectation that children tackled what they had the size and strength to manage, age being more significant than gender. Neth found older daughters engaged in more diverse, less-sex-typed activities that matched their preference or negotiation, especially on farms exceeding 240 acres, and that their early practical skills influenced their wifely work choices (Neth 1994, 566). Early triumphs might encourage later specialities and consequent community standing, like Clarrie's mother – renowned for her cream cakes.

When Georgie Johnson left school at 14, he continued doing farm work, but, as his older brothers had already done, he spent his first two years working under mother's supervision helping with her pigs and poultry, milking, the wood pile and other jobs, while he built up his strength for heavy farm work. This was his father John's idea, which Georgie's wife called 'an apprenticeship in the house first, before they did proper farm work, and this meant they knew how to look after themselves and others' (Iris Johnson). This practice was certainly unusual in Castra, and did not appear in any other sources, but was very far-sighted because it eased lads into physical fieldwork and gave them insight into the domestic routine, developing their later understanding of their wife's responsibilities.

Opportunity to play was often limited to evenings or, once they started school, to the walk to and from school. In late nineteenth-century England, Flora Thompson suggested that, while the attempt to 'convert little savages' and civilise children was being made at school and home, the journey between these influential spheres allowed children freedom to 'revert to a state of nature' and even make a little mischief (Thompson 1939, 157). More recently, Pascoe called this the 'split worlds' of children's lives, with home more permissive, and school having a 'traditional approach to control and punishment' (2009, 217). Stories about the cane (as traditional control) abound in Preston school history prior to 1959 when headmaster Kevin Pearce ceased its use (Margaret Pearce, wife, 2015).

After the Second World War, across Tasmania, smaller country schools closed and their pupils joined more centrally located schools. So, when schools at South Nietta, Lowana at the southern end of Gunns Plains valley, Central Castra and Gunns Plains gradually closed, students attended Preston School. After the 1947 fire that burnt Preston School to the ground, the Education Department decided to rebuild a new larger building with potential for increased student numbers, which may have impacted on the survival of very small schools nearby. It was opened by Premier Robert Cosgrove, also Minister for Education, in February 1949, who promised a desk and comfortable seat for each pupil as soon as available (News 1949a). The new premises also hosted a major event celebrating 50 years of education in Preston, bringing together local leaders, 'old scholars' and former teachers (News 1950a).

Lowana children went to Gunns Plains when its school closed, though its building continued as a Hall and playgroup until 1959. South Nietta School (at Nietta Railway terminus) closed in about 1950. Nietta children bussed to Upper Castra from the 1940s. The Sprent Primary School operated until February 1950, when it

Childhood and youth in Castra 163

became an Area School, taking local primary children as well as grades 7–10 from 'back-country' schools, including Preston. Gunns Plains School closed in 1954. Travelling by bus, the chance to play was constrained, although there were practical jokes; for example, Peter Carter (born 1957) was 'thrown off the bus for pulling the girls' hair' and banned for two weeks, so he had to bicycle up-hill from Gunns Plains (Carter, pers. comm. 2015). The majority still walked or cycled home along quiet roads or across home paddocks, affording them a breathing space in nature.

June Peebles and her brother walked two miles from their farm near Wilmot to catch the school bus. They collected neighbours' mail and newspapers from the village shop to deliver while walking home. She told me, 'We didn't question it, it was just what you did'. They walked even during snow or rainy weather (June Peebles 2017). The underlying lesson was that neither farming nor helping others were fair-weather options.

Calf Clubs that combined farm learning and free-time were run for older children in Tasmanian rural schools from 1930 onwards as a strategy to engage future farmers and overcome traditional conservatism in parents (Haygarth and Jetson 2018, 5). Children had a calf to look after, groom and teach to be paraded. Clubs were instituted by the Department of Agriculture, and local advisors were judges. At Preston School's second year, 22 calves were exhibited 'to a high standard' in 1935 (News 1935c). The Smith children remembered loving to care for their calves in the 1950s (Pat Smith). At Preston's last Calf Club in 1954, winners included Neville Peebles (three prizes) and Bub Peebles (two prizes). Other prize-winners were Clarrie McCulloch's nephews, Malcolm winning three and Greg winning two (these were Edis and Sheila McCulloch's children who then lived at the home-farm); brothers T. and K. Harding gained three between them. George Wing Junior's son, Stanley, a dairy breeder, was the judge. There were eight categories for calves (dairy and beef, bulls and heifers), best leading calf, two lamb classes and 'unusual pet'. Tea proceeds added to the school improvement fund, well patronised by the crowd that came from Sprent, Gunns Plains, Castra and Motton. Press coverage was substantial because the *Advocate* agricultural writer 'The Tiller' had a whole page (News 1954). Preston head teachers took this activity seriously, supporting a show from 1934 each year until 1940, then from 1947 to 1954 as reported each year by the *Advocate*. From 1954, older children began attending Sprent Area School, which had its own Calf Club. It is hard to assess how often girls entered a calf, unless fully named as prize winners, like two in 1939 (News 1939d). But many children were encouraged to compete, which would not have happened unless it was seen as useful by parents and enjoyable by students.

Rural freedom and children's place

Recent research about rural childhoods has attracted geographers (Matthews et al. 2000, 141–53), who prompt historians to recognise that children have always lived 'in place'. Matthews thought country children were 'invisible within the rural landscape', echoing Phillips' point that they were the 'silent ones'. For

164 *Childhood and youth in Castra*

North-West Tasmanian farm children, bush and agricultural environments integrated nature and culture in their home 'space'. According to Riley, 'the farm space [was] not simply a space of work or play, but one imbued with emotion . . . that embodied their personal and family history' (2009, 256) in a form of chronological connectivity. He argued that children were 'knowledgeable, social actors – both within and beyond the farm' uniquely positioned to develop and display autonomy (245–60). Cresswell wrote that 'place is also a way of *seeing, knowing and understanding* the world' which connects to children growing in width and depth as they mature from infancy to adolescence (2004, 11, my emphasis). Their autonomy grew from familiarity in the whole-farm expanse, their cousins' farms too and fragments of remaining bush, reinforcing their sense of belonging to the land. Natural surroundings entrenched these emotional connections and 'an openness to ways in which certain spots at certain times were particularly significant' (Atkinson 1998, 16). Kiddle wrote movingly of the selectors' next generation in Victoria's Western District that would be echoed over 50 years later in Preston. Despite the hard life, they:

> took joy in the things beloved by all Australian children . . . in spring on open country, they watched for the first blue orchids, . . . they climbed trees, fished the creeks, hunted wallabies, trapped rabbits and tiger cats. These children made the country their own and were themselves a part of it. They were children of sunshine, self-reliant, venturesome, giving promise for the future.
>
> (1961, 428–29)

The attachment to place in Preston interviewees' sense of identity figures prominently in reflection on their lives, even among women who moved away for marriage. For one Preston son, happy childhood memories and love for Preston led to choosing 'Preston' as his son's second name (Hilda Johnson, his grandmother, pers. comm. 2018).

Hetherington argued that children developed ideological understanding of the world through their parents passing on 'natural' ideas and attitudes from their own youthful memories (1998, 2). Endorsing this, Edgar described families as 'cultural conveyor belts, the carriers of images, traditions, the meanings of life' prone to many interpretations of 'normal' (1991, v). Castra children, most of whose parents grew up on farms themselves, learnt ways of acceptable behaviour through parental behaviour models, family stories and community socialisation. Their relative freedom placed strong emphasis on resilience, learning when to take risks, how to make safety decisions, being trustworthy with animals and younger siblings, and being respectful to adults. Their school provided the learning space for developing reciprocity, loyalty and social trust, belief in people to fulfil expectations and take their responsibilities seriously (Halpern 2005, 163). School interactions developed understanding of boundaries.

Churches were so much part of community life for the post-1880 Castra settlers onwards that they played their part in forming identity. 'Methodism occupies a large place in Tasmanian life', wrote Reverend Charles Clifford Dugan marking

Childhood and youth in Castra 165

its Tasmanian centenary (1920, 8). The Mersey Circuit had started in the 1860s on the eastern edge of the North-West. It included Sassafras, where the Johnsons and the Peebles attended church, but Methodism had a strong revivalist tradition and early ministers made great efforts to serve new, small bush communities, despite the appalling trackless forests. At Barrington, for example, there were 'prayer and class-meetings twice on Sundays and once on week nights' even before the settlers had erected their own church in 1870. Local travelling preachers might hold three services each Sunday and 'tramp' from one church to the next (72–73). According to the Protestant ethic coined by Max Weber (Grabb 1990, 53) hard work and thrift connected one to God and eternal salvation, and, based upon John Wesley's dictum, time-wasting, laziness, idle gossip and excess sleep were seen as unproductive activities, hence the adage 'the devil finds work for idle hands'. In the strongly Methodist communities of Castra, when this ethic reinforced the ideals of yeoman farming life, it comes as no surprise that children's time tended to be controlled to avoid idleness, and even early child play was channelled towards usefulness. The ideology of responsibility, care for the land and all life on it was further reinforced by regular Sunday School attendance in all the Castra villages. Methodist 'Stewardship of the Whole of Life, physical environment, social relations and personal development' was emphasised (Stansall 1975, 10) and borne out consistently in autobiographies and interviews.

Across the ages, young girls and boys enjoyed roaming 'unsupervised in fields, on common land and roads' playing amongst themselves, mostly without misfortune but generally unseen and unrecorded (Factor, 57). Rural children improvised according to their surroundings and gender, girls often being creative and imaginative and boys keener to go exploring, tree-climbing, hunting and fishing (Heywood 2018, 160–63). Both girls and boys had pet animals, including cats, dogs, guinea pigs and ferrets (Sutton-Smith, 124–27) as well as pet lambs and poddy calves that they fed (Kiddle, 295). In 1908, young Tasmanian diarist Mildred Hood tried several times to keep wild birds as pets – a parrot, a pair of pigeons, even a baby rabbit in a cage (1908–11). Free time was always subject to completing their chores, which continued well into the 1970s for interviewees growing up in Preston and Upper Castra. As Sutton-Smith wrote of New Zealand bush children, 'rural play was admirably suited to the development of their natural interests, initiative and independence' (98–99).

Parents and grandparents formed a child's community. For farm infants, their child play experiences were usually limited to homestead environs where the poultry, dogs and horses were kept, providing their earliest appreciation of living near, and caring for, livestock (Parker 1976, 79). They also discovered joys of collecting warm eggs and feeding the 'chooks'. Because they were growing up in an adult world, role playing was a significant part of rural children's learning, including those in Castra. Where children worked under direction of either their father or mother, they were able to observe them in their individual realms. Learning by imitation under a protective eye was the age-old way for the apprentice/trainee in any field over the centuries. McEwen (1985, 191–92) argued that 'the bonds between father and son went beyond consanguinity and the family economy' in

166   *Childhood and youth in Castra*

settler families, strengthening their ties through mutual dependence. These bonds have resonance with succession decisions too.

Rural parents generally, and early bush settlers certainly, were well aware of potential injury from sharp tools, snares and guns, snakes, machinery and falling tree limbs, so cautionary advice would have been heeded and absorbed into children's activities. When accidents did happen, the resultant local papers' coverage drew community attention to them, as when William Johnson's accident with an axe needed stitches (News 1904f). Castra children understood the security of living where all families knew each other's children, and of group safety when near the Leven River. In Gunns Plains, two instances were recounted in 2015. Mitch Freeman (born 1956), Preston pupil for six years from 1961/1962 with three siblings, spoke of the group of about eight children who all had bikes and played together, because 'parents all knew each other in the Valley' and Peter Carter (born 1957), with brother born 1955 and sister born 1958, told me about swimming and fishing in the Leven and selling rabbits caught with their own ferrets for two shillings a pair. Only one catastrophic death of a child from snake bite occurred in an earlier Johnson generation (Jeanie Loughrey nee Johnson 2019).

In Western societies where children were expected to aspire to success, physical games prevailed (Child and Child 1973). Inglis (1974) wrote that the games people had watched and enjoyed back home were transported with them to the colonies. Lt.-Colonel Godfrey Charles Mundy observed outdoor games in 1846 ranging by season from marbles and knucklebones to cricket, improvising targets for the wicket and ingenious versions of balls (quoted in Factor, 56–57).

The yeoman farming society was no different, where activities like Calf Clubs were competitive, encouraging a winning ethos and were well supported by adults. Boys' games and sports, as they grew older, were predominantly physical, but girls were different; in youngest age groups, girls enjoyed creativity, orienting towards physical play up to 12 years old, after which it dominated their choices (Child and Child, 142–43). The recreation ground next to Preston Hall was formed in 1922 (News 1922h). Clarrie McCulloch recalled:

> At school, the pupils played team games in the school yard that was big enough for football and cricket. They paraded before class on the playground covered with sharp white gravel [from nearby Barren Hill]. Sports Day, at the Preston Recreation Ground about 15 minutes' walk up the road, was memorable with 70 or 80 excited kids all in different events.
>
> (35)

From 1930, Preston School participated in Leven combined-schools annual Anzac Day sports, winning in 1935. Between 1971 and 1976, Pam Dobson, mother of two girls, used to help at the school and recalled the gendered nature of school physical activities. Girls were allowed to play under the trees, on monkey bars, hopscotch or skipping but were not allowed to play 'footy', even though both boys and girls played softball (pers. comm. 2015). Once the netball/tennis court was created in the late 1960s, the girls' netball team was added to competitions

Childhood and youth in Castra 167

with eight other schools' sports days (News 1935b; Dobson, Carter 2015). In 1975, Peebles' paddock adjoining the school was used for the cross country races (*Preston School Newsletter 1975*).

For young girls, their creative urge was easily directed by mother or grandmother into activities like sewing, mending, cooking and making butter or jam, especially reinforced in the 1960s when sewing and cooking became a popular part of the curriculum, because the children took home what they made (Carter, Tongs, Dobson, all students then, pers. comms. 2015). Creativity was enhanced in the school by parents with hobbies or interests, which included craft, photography, cooking, music, history projects and sport coaching, regular assistance that added 'richness and variety of experiences' for the children (Prescott, parent and P & F member, pers. comm. 2016). Consistently, from the 1920s to the 1990s, concerts and stage productions (Aladdin, Snow White and perennial nativity plays) were organised by the school in the Hall, attended by parents and residents (e.g. News 1928b). Regular fundraisers on such occasions allowed purchase of a sewing machine (News 1927f). These experiences enabled learning of life-long social and practical skills respected by parents, so shows in front of parents and friends were about more than performance and helped to sustain the ties of Castra communities across all ages.

Devotion to football and cricket in Castra, discussed later in this chapter, appears to support the ideology of winning and competitiveness and also indicates their value to adolescent youth. The Methodist tradition meant that physical sport was to be more about healthy exercise than about entertainment (van Krieken 2000, 648).

Local testimonies confirm that little distinction was made between 'work' in school, 'work' at home or farm, and activities in the in-between time-spaces; each had potential for learning, pride in achievement, competitiveness, pleasure and, of course, for making mistakes and failing. For children, 'the distinction between work and leisure was not always clear', a truism that is supported in Castra (Smith, Parker, and Smith 1973, 127).

Clarrie McCulloch (born 1918) reminisced about his favourite after-school job riding his horse to collect mail at Waringa Post Office, and afterwards to the paddock to fetch the cows for milking. He and his brothers always had dogs trained to work but they were obviously great pals, going everywhere with them, judging by his book's photographs. His maternal grandfather Frank Tongs gave him a hunting dog when he was nine, and they had lots of adventures together; 'Rover was great at digging out rabbit holes' (41).

The regular occurrence of snow and heavy frosts in winter was the chance for sliding down snow-covered, steeply sloping paddocks. When asked for a stand-out event of his childhood, Rob Peebles said:

> The one thing I really remember was when we got really heavy frosts; you could slide down the hill here above the school. We don't get heavy frosts now like that. It was unbelievable, you'd get to the top of the hill and you would just slide – no tin tray, just on your boots. More snow more often,

168   *Childhood and youth in Castra*

I just remember about one or two foot of snow, that was the year it was bad in Ulverstone too, snow down there.

Tas Johnson remembered this year too; it was July 1951, when there was a huge amount of snow, from the mountains to the sea that stopped the Castra school bus for two weeks. Clarrie remembered the heavy frosts, often lasting two weeks in mid-winter, and puddles would freeze but not Preston Creek. Lengthy cold spells were hard, causing chilblained feet (55). Hand-knitted woollen socks would have been a boon, so it made sense for the boys to learn how to knit and darn their own (Tas Johnson).

There was never much money in farming communities, especially through the Depression years, and ingenuity was useful to earn pocket money. Clarrie combed the excess horsehair from their six or seven horses to sell for sutures. He also collected charcoal from the farm's big log heaps to sell to the Preston blacksmith for two shillings (42). His money was spent at the Show or buying auctioned donations at Harvest Thanksgiving (38).

The natural advantages of Preston countryside, creek and its waterfalls provided good boggy areas for waterfowl, land interspersed by watercourses and woodland trees for climbing. It was the setting for a most evocative account of imaginative and creative play in Tasmanian bush by Clarrie playing alone, because his older brothers were already working full-time on the farm (18). He discovered that finger-thickness dogwood 'made ideal fishing rods' and larger ones made a frame work for man-fern fronds, making 'the most marvellous hide-aways for games of "Bushrangers" with his visiting school mates'. He also loved finding fallen trees lying over the shallows where he could 'lie and watch the small creatures living out their lives on or in the water', of gentle, rippling cascades above the fall over the edge of a basalt cliff. He would see water striders and water boatmen rowing back and forth, sometimes a brown trout darting out from the bank, and once he saw two platypuses. Sometimes, he watched grey fantails build their nests suspended over the water; another time he discovered a nest of ring-tailed possums, learning from experience how to watch from an adjacent tree without disturbing them (18). Preston Creek used to be well populated with Tasmanian Giant Freshwater Lobster (*Astacopsis Gouldi*) as well as platypuses.

Growing up on an Upper Castra farm, Glennys Johnson (born 1949) and her four siblings had very little free time out-doors because of their father's early death when she was 11. Instead, she enjoyed children's radio programmes. The Devonport station, 7AD, had the 'Koala Club' for child listeners that reached Upper Castra (News 1953a). As well as the ABC, the second local commercial radio station 7BU from Burnie aired the 'Sun Polishers Club' before school and at 5 p.m. each day, followed by the popular long-running show, 'Dad and Dave'. The hook to keep listeners was calling out children's birthday wishes. As Glennys and her siblings grew up through the sixties, summer was too busy, but in winter, she played badminton at the Upper Castra Hall, and she joined other young people walking miles to and from the very popular dance in Wilmot, arriving back in time for milking (Glennys Johnson, pers. comm. 2019). She told me badminton was very popular in

Childhood and youth in Castra 169

the 1930s and 1940s and both her parents were top players in the local league that ran in the 'back country' villages (Glennys Johnson 2020).

Margaret 'Margy' Peebles (born 1952) had a special relationship with Preston school, just next door. At four years old, she visited to play with the teacher's children, because Rob was five years older, already at school. Significantly for Margy's childhood, seven of her mother's Johnson siblings had babies in 1952, which guaranteed plenty of cousins to play with at family and community functions (Margy King nee Peebles 2017). Bicycles were both passports to freedom and opportunities for parental errands. As Margy and her friends got bicycles, they cycled to each other's houses or to Ellis' village shop. Margy had her share of chores like helping with orphan lambs, feeding calves and collecting eggs and later, with harvesting potatoes and peas.

'Family visiting was huge', Margy told me, which meant there were frequently enough children for informal cricket. The custom of Sunday visiting had long been an established tradition in settlement communities, what Kiddle called the 'social game' in Victoria's Western District from the 1870s. Children sitting in their best clothes quietly watching elders gossiping was supposedly 'excellent training' for them (296–97). The similar practice, based on dominant British manners, existed in colonial New Zealand, where children were told to 'mind their place, not to show off or to act better than they should be', all designed to imitate upper-class models that proved less applicable in their New World (Sutton-Smith, xv).

Pat Smith (born 1943, fourth of five siblings) said that the Sunday routine for most Preston families was morning Sunday School for the children, then Church, home for 'dinner', followed by family visiting. This was 'a slow Sunday drive with children being seen and not heard, and a get-together including afternoon tea of beautiful cakes filled with fresh cream from the host's cows'. Arrangements by then had usually been made by telephone. That traditional idea of 'seen and not heard' had a life well into the 1950s. In the bigger families, as Margy recalled, numerous children were 'released' to the garden to play together – a sharp contrast to the formalised strictures of elite society in colonial Victoria and New Zealand.

Light evenings with daylight saving from October to March, reintroduced in Tasmania in 1968, extended everyone's outdoor time. In winter, activities were constrained by limited light from candles, Tilley lamps or kerosene lights until electricity came to Preston in about 1945 and to Gunns Plains in 1952. Lamplight did not stop the Johnson boys from learning how to darn their socks after tea, listening to the radio in front of the fire until bedtime (Tas Johnson). Georgie learnt to knit as well, still so proud of this skill in his eighties. Before electricity, radios worked off a battery that needed to be recharged. The Peebles had long had a radio, but when television arrived in about 1961, Margy said they 'were all glued to it'.

Marie (born 1952) and Kevin Johnson (born 1956) were great partners. They picked blackberries and cherries for their mother to bottle or jam. Sometimes they were allowed to go to the shop to buy a pennyworth of broken biscuits. In the orchard planted by their grandfather John was a tree swing. Marie loved kicking a ball around, and remembered that her dad used to kick the ball so far up the lane

170 *Childhood and youth in Castra*

to make her run for it (Marie Harrop nee Johnson 2017). Just because a girl could not play in the team did not stop this father playing 'footy' with his daughter.

In their youth, Bonfire Night was massive. They spent all year gathering house and farm rubbish to build a huge fire not far from the washhouse, almost as tall as the house. The best ingredient was feathers from all the year's poultry pluckings. At the appointed time, they lit it and up it went! One year, it was so hot and high, they became frightened of it burning down the washhouse and ran to get help from Dad. He said, 'You lit it, you put it out!' and so they had to cope with carrying water to make it safe. By making them take responsibility for their actions, Sidney was imparting a strong, unforgotten life lesson. There was a certain pragmatism in the Johnson family towards training children for life that perhaps reflected Grandfather Henry's attitudes about self-responsibility as well as doing what was best for the whole family, attitudes that served the family well for several generations. These values, so clearly recalled many decades later, are manifested in Marie's memories and Georgie's preparation for hard toil of farming.

Kevin remembered his limited free time was spent fishing local creeks for lobsters, but he 'played a bit of football' and went to Church for a 'good few years'. When fatherhood came in the late 1980s, he and his wife Gillian drove their two daughters to sport activities; one loved riding her horse, which she looked after and participated in Pony Club at North Motton; both girls went to Youth Group and played netball in Ulverstone. Once they had their licences, Kevin's mother bought each of the girls a car (Kevin Johnson 2018). This example shows the dramatic transition in one generation of after-school activities well beyond reach of walking or cycling, and their need of a car and driver to participate.

June Peebles' father taught her tractor driving because she was his 'right-hand-man' as a teenager. So, when her daughter Sharon asked, she taught her too, a skill that gained Sharon her first job. June said, 'You have got to be able to do those things'. While this is an example of a mother teaching her daughter something of lasting value beyond the domestic realm, it also demonstrated that the realities of yeoman farm life were not advantaged by gender stereotyping over such a useful skill.

For June and Bub, supporting their children's activities was important, which, in the 1980s, meant driving them. Although they still attended Preston School, Sharon went to Youth Group in Ulverstone, Mark attended Cubs at North Motton and played football at East Ulverstone. Both children enjoyed farm work while they were young, even though employment took them both to Ulverstone; June's view is that 'once you breed your children, [the land] is in their blood' – an attitude exemplifying the values of yeoman family farming. Now her grandchildren love visiting and absorbing attachment to the farm, just as their parents did.

Preston sports meetings and hall happenings 1899–1990

Historically, village sports and pastimes punctuated task-oriented rural life patterns dictated by seasons, milking and feeding demands. In the Riverina, for example, 'Old English Games and Sports' were celebrated on holidays from the 1860s,

Childhood and youth in Castra   171

and small towns often organised annual race meetings with sponsored prizes, and most had cricket teams (Buxton 1967, 95–96). The inauguration of the first annual sports in 1899 in Preston fitted that tradition. The Anglican Church benefited from its proceeds and from dinner prepared by the local 'ladies'. William Delaney ran the events with other local 'gentlemen' (News 1899e). A similar typical event at Upper Castra featured in a *Weekly Courier* photograph of 21 June 1902, 1, 3. In 1904, Delaney offered part of his own property for future annual sports to feature wood chopping, horse jumping, trotting and single-handed sawing (News 1904b). The next year, Preston had its own Athletic Association with members from Sprent, Kindred, Gunns Plains and North Motton as well from Preston, meeting in a 'speedily erected building adjoining the hall'. Members from Preston were Thomas Cullen, Frank Tongs, William Delaney, Henry Johnson, John Smith, Peter Jupp, G.E. Clarke and J.J. Gillard, most of whom had only come to the Preston area a few years previously. This indicated wide appreciation for country sports and already a commitment to local community endeavour. Delaney was Secretary and Treasurer, and Gillard was Chairman in 1907 ready to organise the 'programme for New Year's Day' 1908 (News 1907c).

Numbers and varieties of entries and attendees increased annually, as did 'liberal prize money' such that, by 1928, foot races and novelty events were added to customary chopping, sawing and horse events (News 1928a). Accumulated funds enabled the formal purchase of ground for a recreation oval from William's son Frank Delaney, who caretook the new Preston Hall and was regular dance MC. The Hall was just behind the Methodist Church, forming a convenient complex with the oval (News 1922h).

Before radio from the 1920s, recreational events were family affairs for everyone to enjoy. Preston Hall provided plentiful opportunity for these, with religious festivals and weddings easily accommodated next door in the church. The Methodist Church sponsored many activities like Church Fairs and the Wesleyan Badminton Club, and had a choir made up mostly of young people.

In what has been termed 'dynamic localism' where kinship was part of the extended neighbourhood, the regular dances held in all Castra village halls attracted locals and visitors from other districts (Reay 1996, 258). These evolved into cabarets at Preston after the Second World War, because, by then, Wilmot had become *the* place for a dance; it was where June Buxton met her future husband Bub Peebles (2018). Glennys remembers the dances well, especially the music provided by local bands or a piano; one man used to play the tin whistle to accompany the dances, and, if no musicians were available or failed to arrive, there were always accomplished whistlers, like her mother, who could render a tune. Always well-attended, the dances included traditional favourites like waltz, foxtrot, Pride of Erin or the progressive barn dance (Glennys Johnson, pers. comm. 2020).

Spring picnics and end-of-year school events were supported more by the mothers, because fathers were often too busy cutting hay or silage in the long evenings, and these might be arranged to coincide with events like the surf life-saving carnival at Ulverstone beach (News 1931a). Weddings, too, were usually arranged in winter to suit the milking cycle when the cows were dried off (Harrop).

172   *Childhood and youth in Castra*

Annual sports meetings were part of this selection of social gatherings that gave young adolescents the chance to mingle. Sports meetings as well as agricultural show competitions occurred throughout rural communities in Tasmania when skills in wood-chopping and sawing received strong support. The United Australian Axemen's Association was formed in Latrobe in 1891, led by Hubert A. Nichols (known as 'Chopper Nichols' probably in recognition of his axe-wielding skill) as Secretary, with a committee including members from central Castra, Upper Castra, North Motton, Sprent and Forth (Ramsay 1980, 188). James Skemp made the point that 'axemanship is the first requisite in a pioneering and timber-getting community', which was why they were the most popular competitive sport in such districts (Skemp 1952, 160).

Although Tasmania was suffering an economic depression in the 1930s like the rest of the world, there was still time for recreation and social contact, maintained by visiting neighbours in the evenings to play cards, sing and exchange gossip. Despite hard times, by 1930, the Preston Sports had grown even more, with cordial, fruit and sweet stalls, and 'luncheon' and afternoon tea run by farm wives. Local dignitaries, like Warden John Forsyth Wright, and prominent citizens took the opportunity to attend, often performing the formal opening. Events provided an outlet for young men to hone their skills and win prize money, as well as a family outing. Proceeds went to running the Hall and to keep adding improvements to the sports ground (News 1930b). Gender-separated activities, like the agricultural society and sporting clubs for the men, the Church Guild and CWA for the women, and Sunday School for the children, were all based around these facilities, which became the hub for local social capital, and supported occasions when surrounding villagers could participate at Preston too.

Despite religious exhortations about sport being focussed on health, as it surely was for the high level of fitness required for skilled events, the opportunity for fundraising was fitted into the Methodist ideology and alcohol was not served, respecting the temperance viewpoint. Temperance may well have supported the financial and mental well-being of the community as a whole, avoiding drunkenness that typically accompanied social gatherings, as for instance in the Riverina, where Roman Catholics from the numerous Irish population ran second to Anglicans, and Presbyterian and other Protestants that advocated temperance were fewer than 20 per cent (Buxton 1967, 92–93).

By the mid-1990s, in Preston and other Castra villages too, the potential for local social get-togethers was more limited than it had been since the first decade of the century; the shops and the railway and stations had gone, both churches had ceased and post offices, where newspapers had been collected and gossip exchanged, had shut. When Preston School closed in 1994 that ended its focus for community social life of special days and memorable functions unconnected to religious affiliations. Children and older students were bussed to primary and high schools in Ulverstone, and their after-school activities were centred on friends in Ulverstone, or even in Devonport for some sports. This served to deplete bonding and bridging social capital and community sustainability in the 'back country' villages. The school's closure impacted especially on the women for whom it had been a dependable, safe social space and a stimulus for social and cultural activities (Henderson 2016).

Long before this happened though, team sports were important to all: for the men and aspiring 'men', for the 'littlies' playing on the sidelines, and for the wives and mothers catching up with each other's news. The next section focusses on two team sports that were valuable opportunities to cement solidarity between farming families and their community networks, thus sustaining the yeoman ideology of mutuality and strong connectivity for the entire twentieth century with competitiveness to add spice.

Castra district football and cricket – sport for players and spectators

Sport had to fit between school and work. All Castra villages – Gunns Plains, Preston, Upper Castra and Nietta – had Australian Rules football teams. Preston and Upper Castra were competing against each other in 1922 (News 1922a). Upper Castra and Nietta teams formed in 1911, playing each other often in their first season (News 1911c). They soon joined other local teams in a league competition, and, in 1923, Upper Castra competed for the premiership against Preston (News 1923b). Winter football occupied young men, generally in their twenties, and most also played summer cricket. The local League comprised Preston, Upper Castra, Nietta, North Motton and Gunns Plains. Games were hard-fought and strongly supported both at home and away (McCulloch 1998, 68–69). The Harding family's connection with Preston football started with Harry Harding, Denzil's grandfather. He was a keen Umpire for decades, while three of his sons, Herbert, Thomas and William Henry, Denzil's father, were in the team (Denzil Harding 2018). Families already familiar were represented, most of whose boys were born in the early 1900s: Joe Brown (Ken's father) and Bal Brown (cousins), George Johnson (Henry's son), David Peebles (James' son), Athol McCulloch (Clarrie's 17-year-old brother), Albert Smith (cousin to the Brown and Harding boys), Lou Ewington (David Peebles' cousin) and L. Cullen (brother of the two Cullen soldier-settlers). They were local Premiers in 1929, with Harry Harding awarded 'Gold Umpire'. Four years later, in 1932, they were still the undefeated Premiers with most of the same members (Tas Johnson).

Tas Johnson (born 1933) 'felt very blessed in his football career because it lasted thirty-five years', starting when he was 14. After usual Saturday morning farm work, they would go to the Club. They were not paid but good performances earned prizes, and he once received the 'best on ground' prize of £10. By 1952, Preston did not have a team, but Tas was invited to play for North Motton, and then in 1967 Preston and North Motton amalgamated to form the Motton-Preston Club, 'The Demons'. Tas never sustained injury all those years. Amalgamation was forced by scarcity of players old enough in both districts. The combined Club won the Premiership again in 1967, with eight out of the 20 players under 20 years old, according to Rob Peebles, President of the Community Centre Committee for

174   *Childhood and youth in Castra*

25 years; in 2017 at the 50th Birthday Celebration, Rob Peebles, Ken Brown and Murray King, all long-time Life Members, were made 'Icons' of the Club.

William Harding played well into his fifties until injured while son Denzil was Team Captain. Denzil could have played for Ulverstone but for wife Margaret, who 'hated football and wouldn't go down to watch'. Son Selwyn (born 1958) was a boundary umpire at ten years old until he was 12, when he started playing; he loved the game and the camaraderie. Although he has lived most of his adult life in Ulverstone, he maintains his Club connection as sponsor (Selwyn Harding 2018).

According to the Peebles brothers (2018), their father David was very keen and played football for many years, prior to marrying at 36. This probably explains why the three brothers 'were sports crazy', playing both football and cricket. Both Neville and Rob were coaches as well as players; Neville was coach when they won the 1967 Premiership. Their sister Margy told me the family's social life revolved around it once the boys started playing football. All went to watch wherever the games were played. Players' sisters would amuse themselves at games. Tonts found that Australian Rules football had a particularly high degree of social connectivity (93 per cent agreed about 'keeping in touch with friends and neighbours') in Western Australia, because of its emphasis as a family outing for spectators as well as players (Tonts 2005, 143). Max Brown (born 1958) told me (2019) that 'Preston footballers had achieved an almost unbelievable record for a small village team' having four players in the Tasmanian Hall of Fame: Garth Smith (no. 148), Noel Carter (no. 176), Max Brown (no. 177) and Wayne Wing (no. 253). Once Margy reached high school, she played softball and hockey competitively in Ulverstone. A carload would be driven by either her father or Uncle Ned Johnson.

The first Preston Hall had a high ceiling that suited winter badminton for both men and women from the 1930s until the 1950s, when the Preston Wesleyan team won the local C-Grade Premiership (News 1933b, 1953b). This feature must have been similar in all the 'back-country' halls because badminton was popular in all of them (Glennys Johnson, pers. comm. 2020). At Upper Castra, the main sports were cricket, badminton and football (News 1922f).

Cricket was the summer sport in all the Castra villages and teams formed early, in Preston by 1904, Gunns Plains in 1905, Upper Castra similarly and the Nietta team soon after. By the 1920s, Preston Cricket Club was established at the recreation ground. John Dunham, a member of the Club, whose farm was next door, was 'an ardent follower of the game', and was the first Preston owner of a battery-powered wireless set. Clarrie McCulloch regularly joined a roomful of other enthusiasts to listen to the English Test series (43). He and his brothers used to practice cricket and football in the 'big yard' at home between two big tree stumps (62). Ray Denney also listened to the Tests with friends in Upper Castra (1993, 31). The Cricket Club office bearers were local men and the Ladies Guild reliably catered for home matches. The Preston Club keenly encouraged young players, so in 1972 to 1973, when the subscription was $2, schoolchildren only had to pay 20 cents each week towards the balls (Preston Cricket Club Minutes 1945–1975). David Peebles played cricket, passing on his enthusiasm to his sons. Bub Peebles

Childhood and youth in Castra   175

was the team coach in the 1980s for three years while his son Mark was playing. Upper Castra had two cricket teams and players all cycled to play at Preston, Sprent, Nietta and Abbotsham (Denney, 31).

High days and holidays

Unfortunately, Tasmania is poorly blessed with testimonies of ordinary farming folk's pursuits of the twentieth century. Charles Ramsay's account of pioneer days around the Mersey River mentions farmer's 'great occasions' being the Latrobe Agricultural Show, the Axeman's Carnival and the Mersey Regatta (1980, 278–79). However, beach, lake or river picnics were popular with a long history among settler communities. They might mark Boxing Day, New Year's Day or Easter. A picnic might be a church outing or an end-of-year school treat. In the 1850s, Louisa Meredith extolled 'the calm, bright, settled summer weather of this delightful island [Tasmania], far better adapted for [picnics] than the fickle climate of England' (Meredith 1852, ch. 6). For Myrtle Bank children in the early 1900s, a school picnic marked Empire Day celebration on 24 May each year, and then parents joined in picnic races on the last day of school (Skemp 1952, 159).

Tasmanian tennis parties with elaborate picnics were common before the Second World War. Tennis picnics offered more than gathering with friends, it was also the opportunity for the 'marriage market' to operate (Hodson 2002, 103–4). Tennis courts were a popular addition to country social facilities, including at Preston Hall from the early twentieth century.

Celebratory picnics experienced by families featured in this work strengthened the ties that bound the families together, even when living miles apart. For the extended McCulloch families of Upper Gawler, Abbotsham and Preston, Boxing Day and New Year's Day were special opportunities to picnic at Ulverstone beach, when the cousins would play together (McCulloch, 47–48).

In Glennys Johnson's family, there were always plenty of chores to do because, compared to others of her age, they had an 'old-fashioned sort of life' with open-fire cooking and water supply from a bucket down the well. Even so, if the hay was all in by Christmas, their father would drive them all down to Ulverstone beach for a day-out treat when they were little, very special because of its rarity (Glennys Johnson 2017).

For Preston farming families, Christmas Day was usually spent at home, which meant usual morning chores before any celebration. Marie and Kevin Johnson's presents were put under the tree, and they had to wait until Mum and Dad had finished the milking. One year, when they were little, they saw a snake around the tree, and ran out to tell their parents. Dad said it would have to wait until the milking was finished, but they needed to go back inside and watch the snake until he came in. Then he caught and killed it (Harrop).

A special, notable occasion at the Preston Hall occurred in 1941, about which a full report was written by women's page reporter 'La Donna'. The article ran to many column inches and is a 'who's who' of the locality (News 1941a). It was a 'Juvenile Ballette' organised by the Preston C.W.A. who provided the supper, and

176 *Childhood and youth in Castra*

also put great effort into costume making, room decorations and rehearsal training of the children for the grand march, each member credited in the article as well as detailed descriptions of the costumes. One can imagine the anticipation before the event and the keen reading of the report in the paper afterwards, in which every child's costume was described, in a way that points to why the paper was so popular; I cite examples of one girl and one boy as illustration:

> Dark-eyed May Ewington was an attractive "Spanish Dancer" wearing a black lace skirt and red bolero. Gay beads and other gewgaws were worn and a tambourine was carried. A red flower was tucked into the Senorita's dark hair . . . . A wee boy, Donald Brown, aged two-and-a-bit, looked cuddlesome in pale blue Teddy Bear woollies, with a blue beret set jauntily on his head.

Each girl was partnered by one of the boys listed at the end of the descriptions. Such content was a relief from current war news. It may have been the model for annual fancy dress balls held in the Gunns Plains Hall in the 1970s and 1980s. For adults, there were annual dinner-dances that were always well patronised and were a great opportunity to catch up with friends (June Peebles, pers. comm. 2016).

Adolescence

In the late nineteenth century, as western societies became more urbanised, there was growing middle-class concern about young men, and, in 1904, Stanley Hall, an American psychologist and educator, popularised the term adolescence as the period from 14 to about 25 years (Hall 1904, vol. 1, xv). Heywood saw this concern and Hall's ideas as reflective of the contemporary social and cultural environment and pressures on the young, mixed with 'widespread anxiety over the future' in the major nations. The British were particularly humiliated by the Boer War outcome (Heywood 2001, 28–29). In urban Australia, there was concern that processions and large sports meetings encouraged a 'criminal larrikin sub-culture' (Buxton 1974, 197, 214). Rather less concern focussed upon rural life, probably because country youth were kept occupied in farmwork and team sports, and were much less visible for prejudicial stereotyping as 'larrikins', a somewhat derogatory term in late-1800s Australia (Kociumbas 1997, 127–29, 43).

One strategy was the establishment of secondary schools across Australia between 1905 and 1915, but there was quandary over the approach to study – academic or technical. Besant articulated this period as focussing on male preparation for paid employment contrasted with girls being prepared not for work, but for raising a family and running a home for a bread-winner husband. This was the 'modernising' ideology of the middle-classes, quite incompatible with the reality of working-class life, and certainly out of kilter with life for daughters on family farms, where so many of the so-called 'pre-industrial' productive activities were still undertaken every-day (Besant 1987, 25–26).

Childhood and youth in Castra 177

Exemplifying this ideology, those traditional productive and highly valued household and farm tasks performed by young girls from New Zealand, the American mid-west and Australia were perceived as unbecoming by the 1920s (Hunter and Riney-Kehrberg 2002, 136–42). Girls were urged to develop more 'desirable domestic accomplishments' and be less involved in outdoor farm-work. New ideas of prosperous, leisured womanhood, undeniably supported by working-class servant girls, was of little relevance to the females of yeoman farming families, who were already learning preparation for farming motherhood, especially in the busy years of that decade and Depression in the next (Besant 1987, 25–26). It was not until the 1980s that these modernising ideas began to have persuasive force in Castra society.

The amalgamation of ideas for young men being acceptably occupied and readied for defence led to changes in cadets' training. After the *Defence Act 1909* passed, Australia's first universal training scheme started in 1911, requiring Australian males from 18 to 60 years old to perform militia service within Australia and its territories, which meant male youths' participation was compulsory and, by 1913, over 8,000 schools were training junior cadets (Lundie and McCann 2015). Alexander Crawford was captain of the No.1 West Devon Company of Volunteers in 1900 (*Cyclopaedia of Tasmania* Vol. 2 1900, 282). Both Athol and Edis McCulloch were members of the 'militia' in 1920s Ulverstone (McCulloch, 27). Rifle clubs were encouraged prior to the Great War, supported by the Commonwealth Government that issued rifles and ammunition for each member. A Rifle Corps or Association was already established in Tasmania in 1887, one of the state's oldest sporting bodies, and it ran annual championships from that year on, except for the 1914–1918 war years. Clubs were formed in many other centres. Preston had its own Rifle Range and Club which started on land that had been set aside for Castra village reserve. Grant to the Commonwealth for this purpose gave rise to the road's new name. In 1918, Hubert A. Nichols, MLC for Mersey, donated the Nichols Shield for team rifle shooting, and clubs in Ulverstone, Burnie, Devonport, Latrobe, Penguin and Preston supplied teams to compete, some members of which were under 20 years old. Nichols' aim was to encourage young lads to learn to shoot (News 1918a). By 1926, the Club was well supported under Frank Tongs' chairmanship and L. Burgess, Phil Chamberlain, P. Chisholm and three returned soldiers, Robert Kirkland, Tom and John Dunham as committee members (News 1926d). Shooting would remain a useful skill for country boys, not just for the next war, but for hunting wallabies and rabbits for the table.

Ray Denney (born 1919) wrote vividly about his return as a 14-year-old to the Denney family farm at Upper Castra, to work half the farm with his uncle and aunt on the other half (1993, 22–32). Ray had plenty of relations locally to go hunting and fishing with as well as going to Bible Class and Christian Endeavour meetings at the Methodist Church, built largely by his family. He remembered Christian Endeavour rallies at Ulverstone, Penguin, Burnie and Castra, where he sang boy-soprano solos. He and his cousin Ted Bott would cycle to most occasions (34). A highlight was Christmas 1935 when he, his elder sister and father drove to Hobart for the Kingston Convention, an all-denominations religious gathering.

178   *Childhood and youth in Castra*

He wrote of meeting author Marie Bjelke-Peterson, who held an afternoon tea at her home.

A rural approach to adolescence was the development of Young Farmers Clubs (YFCs). Agricultural education had started in Tasmania in the early 1900s to educate rural farmers who were averse to changing their conservative farming practices (Haygarth and Jetson 2018, 2). Gradually, it was believed that involving young adults would persuade their fathers. About 1928, Tasmania's Department of Agriculture set up district education centres, one of which was located at Burnie, to provide practical scientific knowledge, finance and marketing advice (CPP 8/1928, 4). By 1939, YFCs existed at Preston, Nietta, South Riana and Riana, Upper Castra and Abbotsham (AD9/1/2115 5/22). Despite war year difficulties, agricultural clubs continued, even supplying judges for local Agricultural Shows at Burnie, Wynyard and Stanley. Fourteen was the entry age, providing young people five more years to learn concepts of farming as 'seniors', thus bridging the gap between school and adult life (Haygarth, 25). Bennett, a member of the North-West Department of Agriculture, thought members benefitted by citizenship training as well as skills as future farmers or farmers' wives (Bennett 1947). At meetings, boys learnt farming methods, girls learnt bottling and jam-making (even though many had been working on farm for years!), and they all received debating and citizenship training (Haygarth, 258). Bennett's ideas were enshrined in the Club objectives as described in a 1962 call-out for new clubs with at least 15 eligible boys and girls. These were to 'train for responsibilities of citizenship and leadership, to encourage and develop technical skills, and to provide an organization of National and International magnitude' that enabled social meetings with each other (*Tas. J. of Agriculture* Vol. XXXIII, No. 1, 1962, 346).

Tasmania's North-West remained the movement's heartland well into the mid-1970s; 'from 1954 to 1974, the . . . north-west coast from the Blythe River near Burnie to Sassafras contained the greatest concentration of Rural Youth clubs in Australia' (Haygarth, 258). Occasional visits by senior agricultural officers to potential farm districts helped to emphasise the value of keen participation by junior farmers and adult community members, and encourage new clubs to form or even to re-establish like Preston (News 1953c). The North-Western Annual Regional Ball in the 1960s, held in Ulverstone, 'was one of the biggest of its kind in Tasmania attracting between 400 and 600 people'. (Haygarth, 254). From the 1950s onwards, education in tractor maintenance, poultry raising, bee-keeping, and growing fruit and vegetables was offered. The leaders had to balance the organisational aims of 'serious' education or instruction with enjoyment (Haygarth, 45). For many, membership was the way they met their future marital partners, another lasting value of clubs to young people.

Pat Smith was a member of the Young Farmers' Club which then was at North Motton, about six miles away, probably driven there by one of her brothers. She told me in 2017:

> I joined the Junior Farmers' Club when I was fifteen or sixteen after I left school. This was the main social activity for young people in rural areas once

Childhood and youth in Castra 179

they could drive. Our group always put on a huge pavilion display for the Ulverstone Show, it was a very big event in those days. I had a trip with the Club to a farm in Gippsland one time and that whet my appetite to get away and see what was beyond Preston. I did not want to be a farmer.

Prior to the Second World War, horses and bicycles were the general mode of transport before gradual accessibility of motorbikes and cars, especially for work like Ernest McCulloch's as a Government Herd Tester (McCulloch 1998, 26–27). But for the 1940s-born lads, a car was seen as essential to get to dances and socials and to find a wife. So it was for Bub Peebles; when asked how he went courting, he laughingly replied, 'we had cars when you were about seventeen and you could get a licence; the car might not have been worth much, but [life] was no good without a car' (Bub Peebles 2018). A common rural story was that young people, used to driving various vehicles on or between farms, had no trouble getting a licence at the legal age (Brooks, born 1940, 2014). As the adult Peebles and Johnsons found in the 1980s, they had to supply transport until their children could get cars, because activities were further away.

In conclusion, for twentieth century Castra children and youth, seasonal changes brought variety in work and school activities, regular high days and holidays, and free time in nature. Their work routine and ways they learnt from parents and nearby kinfolk established a melding of work, school, church and play in tune with traditions of yeoman farming, reinforcing the ties that bound the community and inter-related families together and readying them for a future farming life. Such traditions resonated with earlier patterns set by yeoman settlers in America and New Zealand. Work chores were taken for granted and food was plentiful, even during the Depression, due to vegetable patches, orchards and home-reared meat and milk. Memories cited here contain evidence of physical, collaborative and imaginative activities from the 1930s to the late 1970s.

Access to cars and technologies of radio, then television, expanded children's horizons. The turn of the century 'economically worthless, but priceless child' ideology and associated ambitions began at last to seem relevant in this rural society by the 1980s (Zelizer 1985, 3). Parents willingly provided 'taxis' for their fewer children, who gradually spent more time in town through education and after-school activities. Adolescents strived for a car to go independently to their activities, and Castra farmers were able to finance their aspirations for adult life away from the farm. This chapter has given an insight into preparation of generations of yeoman farmers and potential farmwives, and the changes wrought as horizons widened and modernity affected both parental and young peoples' aspirations. The next chapter features women – partners in farm, family and social life in Castra.

8 Women play their part – tradition and change

Sustainable family farming is my persistent theme because it characterized the yeoman ideal as recognised in Australia and manifested in North-West Tasmanian society. This chapter focusses on farm women, whose attitudes and behaviours were crucial to enable family farming to survive. They did this with several strategies. Primarily, they produced and socialised their many children, who provided valuable labour while growing up. Equally important, farm women worked hard, a continuing feature of rural settlement in pioneering societies of the Anglophone world, arguably because yeomen and their 'yeowomen' wives, coming from 'similar social backgrounds, shared the same capacity for hard, physical work' (Brooking 2019, 142). Keeping family members fit and well enough for hard work was also essential, often rising in the dark to make both family members and hired labour a hot breakfast. They were often the people collecting supplies and mail, acting as the 'conduit with the outside world', as Sarah Lewis did for years, riding her horse to North Motton (Broome et al. 2020, 142). In addition, they collaborated with decisions for succession and inheritance planning, and they supported plans assisting their sons to establish their own farms. They made and sustained ties that bound family and kinship networks together, which played a role in encouraging suitable matches for their adolescents, and they extended this connective process within community organisations and institutions.

Building upon previous material about Castra women, this chapter demonstrates how they exercised their significant influence in this latter context of kinship and socially connective activities. They collaborated with adaptation to 'modernising' trends and improving technology in the twentieth century. I explore how women accessed useful help, and what happened when death occurred. We look at how traditional work benefitted the family farm until the structural transition of 1970s-1980s Australian agriculture combined with the 1970s demographic change in family size. Reappraisal of farm practices evidenced the impact on women's productive work and changed the earlier distinctiveness of yeoman family farming.

When histories of rural women have been written, the term often used has been 'invisible', and emphasis has been placed on the dominating or exploitative aspect of patriarchy, power and gendered labour divisions in farm structures (Sachs1983; see Haney and Knowles 1987, 797–800; Hunter 2001, 180). Spender (1985, 64,

DOI: 10.4324/9781003229841-9

Women play their part – tradition & change 181

68) led the argument that all women were invisible through language. Murphy (2010, 46) pointed out that 1890s Australian census officials excluded agricultural women, because of stigma applied to fieldwork.

Questioning this, some Australian scholars have highlighted how farm women often had personal power through teamwork stemming from their essential productive contribution to the farm's activities (Alford 1984, 188–89; Alston 1995, 25; Saunders and Evans 1992, xix). A detailed study of American 'female yeomanry' concluded that they were significant in local society, their work and cash contributions were important economically, they were responsible for the family's 'moral tone' and gained prominence in religious institutions (Bryant 1980, 73–88). The 1980s yielded a rich variety of American historians' work about agricultural women's lives, attitudes and work, many capitalising on oral histories (Jones and Osterud 1989, 551–64). Further, although women's selection of husbands could be based upon 'romantic love, social mobility or upward status', the competition for wives meant marriages became more equal and companionate, especially when the only cash for the subsistence farm household came from their efforts, an attitude leaving no scope for repeating 'European-style patriarchy' (Bryant, 77, 83; in Tasmania, see Gothard 1989, 387, 402). The urge for 'rough equality' was a similarly significant notion among yeoman farmwives in New Zealand from the settlement era of the 1880s. They produced large families for 'cheap and willing labour', just as they did in Castra (Brooking, 71).

In Australia, Grimshaw and Willett (1981) found much the same development of companionate marriages by 1900, with little coercive control over choice of marital partner. Families seemed bound together by both instrumental and affective ties. Women were highly valued and in short supply, aiding introductory sexual egalitarianism. Supporting their argument that patriarchal exploitation was neither characteristic nor useful, it was the typical family's self-sufficiency and reliance on all its members' contributions that encouraged this 'modern' way (152–53). Their analysis fits with those of American historians using the terms mutuality and reciprocity (Neth 1988, 1994; Osterud 1988, 73–87), and Osterud's recent work on mutuality between farm-owning husbands and wives (2015). Daniels found 'a much more sanguine picture' of women in assessment of the 'typical family' and therefore the 'typical woman' (1982, 43–46). This perspective also gives full value to the families of the yeoman farmers and small tradespeople and business owners that constituted Australian yeoman society, of which Castra is an example.

Rural women were co-opted into the political push for closer settlement in Australia. From 1903 onwards, official rhetoric idealised rural womanhood and the 'naturalness' of country life to encourage rural settlement and fecundity, contrasting it with the debilitating health, morality and 'oppressive working conditions' of 'cramped' city life (Murphy 2005, 2.1–2.15). Stratford (2019) highlighted Anglophone governments that co-opted feminine embodiment to achieve ambitions for a healthy population. By the 1920s, the image of the 'maternal, womanly woman' as the model of the 'best woman' fed the concept that 'national greatness' vested in the conservative yeoman farming family (Murphy, 2.7–8).

182 *Women play their part – tradition & change*

Addressing the gap in women's history about never-married farm women, Hunter's research found numerous written sources of their satisfaction in land ownership and 'pride in their prowess' in the context of yeoman farming (2004, 189–91). Her conclusions were relevant to rural wives and mothers too.

Using Castra women's oral histories, this chapter explores their experience to a degree that archival sources alone do not enable, informed by the work of American agricultural historians, notably Jones and Osterud (1989). Identifying interconnections between farm, enterprise, home and family, they have challenged ideas of male and female separateness, and stressed that women shared the same intergenerational goals of land for their children. Others have also traced women's historic contributions to family livelihood and how they changed with capitalist rationalisation (Fink 1986; Jensen 1988; Neth 1988).

Community connections

One key to sustainable yeoman farming was how countrywomen connected with one another and their wider society. The yeoman dream of successful farmownership was not achieved in isolation; rather the reverse, as we saw in earlier chapters dealing with the importance of establishing social and religious institutions. Participation by everyone in their community meant establishing the ties that bonded kinship relations and reinforced other spheres of life, and here women were of critical importance in the integration of family and community, that is, 'women spun and wove the social fabric' (Haney and Knowles 1988, 7).

Castra farm women controlled their daily lives within constraints of livestock and child needs, because all the wives were 'in the same boat', as it were, especially from the early development years through to the end of the Depression. Tonnies' classic concept (1887) of *Gemeinschaft* is an apt description of the social system in small agricultural communities like Castra's villages, where society was held together by a combination of personal and traditional relationships and customary obligations; all behaviour operated in known and accepted ways by members of the community. People ignored social inequalities because of the value in sustaining these important ties. In the dominant family pattern, all members worked their farm or family-owned business. Despite 'wide differences in the socio-economic and educational background of settlers' (Grimshaw and Willett 1981), family structures were similar even if living standards varied. Differences might become visible in stocking the farm, the quality of the house, or financial capacity to buy a truck or a tractor, but commonalities across all families were stronger. Poiner endorsed this arguing that 'to invest social difference with discord is a denial of the understanding of what they perceive community to be' (1990, 97). When wage labourers eventually formed part of the yeoman scenery, they were very often inter-related with the landowners, though unreflected in statistical counts; grown-up sons without 'farmer' status were categorised as 'labourers'.

This lack of distinction dramatically contrasted with areas of Tasmania founded on convict labour and owned by self-perceived 'gentry'. Lack of snobbishness comes through in women's community interactions and togetherness.

Women play their part – tradition & change   183

Arnold's argument that small farm associations gained by banding together, 'under-girded by a sense of community', provides parallels in Preston (128). While men shared common interests in working bees for community projects or reciprocal farm-work, so did the wives with the complex and diverse tasks of caring for children, elders or kinfolk and supporting their husbands and farm (Murphy, 45; Sachs, 132).

Women always made time for life's social aspects. As chief social organisers, they connected the whole community, men and children as well as themselves, to culturally meaningful traditions that enhanced cohesiveness and loyalties. Hunter wrote of ways women accomplished this, by 'maintaining the machinery of community' through visiting and building reciprocal relationships, including those that often smoothed introductions leading to marriage (ch. 2). In Preston, this was done through kinship, friendship and neighbourhood networks, not just with other women, but in activities open to all community members, for example, by organising and catering for weddings, church fairs, sports days or welcome home parties for sons returning after war. Wives were the arrangers for holiday visits by distant relations and evening visits to play cards with neighbouring friends, such as Georgie and Iris Johnson's card-playing evenings with his younger brother Aubrey and wife Lily who would come over from their Abbotsham farm. Sometimes, Iris's aunt and uncle would come from the coast for the weekend in the 1960s; Joan Johnson, Marie's mother, arranged for Devonport relations to come each Boxing Day.

Spreading information about community and social happenings was what made newspapers an important organ of social contact for the needs of rural women. Lack of space allows only a brief mention here of their value in connecting women to the wider world of social news, fashion, decorating hints, relevant advertisements and of course, readers' letters. The *Advocate* ran a 'Women's Forum' consistently from the 1920s, subtitled – Social and Domestic – Political – Fashions – Educational. By 1935, it also included a serialised story, and the 'Social Gossip' included comings and goings under the heading 'News from Town and Country' (News 1935d). They were pivotal in publicising charitable efforts as we shall see next.

In Castra, sociability in the early decades was limited by greater 'tyranny of distance', so women's local friendships were important, as Fink argued was the case among women in early twentieth-century Iowa (Fink 1986, 100). Farm women relished their connections, and their socialising fitted the imperturbable rhythms of season, associated work and common responsibilities. Having been settled by yeoman pioneers, Iowa was a similar social environment to yeoman farming districts across North-West Tasmania. As in Castra, churches were generally central to farm lives, and, through the creation and continuation of church clubs, women had 'material control over church priorities' often through their vital donations. For Preston women, social interaction with other district clubs extended potential for new friends. Through shared work and visiting, women supported common goals in their own social spaces (Warner-Smith and Brown 2002, 40). Even though activities of various clubs often centred on family themes, there were still

184 *Women play their part – tradition & change*

opportunities for women to assume local leadership roles. The Methodist Church and Hall in Preston was a natural centre for a number of women's organisations.

Long-standing practices of sharing and charitable contributions are clear from records of the Preston Methodist Ladies Guild that started in 1936, later becoming the Ladies' Fellowship Group, meeting monthly in the Hall (NS499/1/3222, 3213, 3214, 2644, 3233, 2643, 2641). The first Treasurer of the Ladies Guild from 1936 until 1950 was Louie Peebles, married to the Peebles' eldest son Henry. Her much younger sister-in-law Alice Peebles was a long-time member of the Church and Guild Treasurer from 1961 to 1986. Other prominent women in Preston took leadership roles, many tied by family interconnections; two generations of McCullochs, Ewingtons, Tongs, Cullens, Smiths, Parsons and Iris Johnson. By 1982, June Peebles was Under Secretary, effectively making a third generation holding office. Following inclusive tradition, Elsie McCulloch encouraged her new daughter-in-law, Sheila, to get involved too when Edis and she took over the home-farm in 1939. They would stay until the 1980s.

Margaret Pearce, the headmaster's wife, was Secretary from 1960 to 1962. Her appointment showed acceptability of short-term residents, especially if they contributed to community affairs. The women became familiar with each other's strengths as their relationships deepened. Young female teachers who came to teach at Preston School over decades boarded with local families, and were merged into women's networks and encouraged to join in social activities, as Margaret Pearce did (Pearce 2015). This led to marriage in at least one case to a young local farmer; Don Stuart married Ruth Bucis, who lodged with Max Brown's grandmother Irene's family at Dooley's Plains (Max Brown, pers. comm. 2019).

Examination of the Guild/Fellowship Minutes evidenced several overarching themes that showed attachment to the female community as well as a willingness to be global in outlook by interest in overseas charities (these included Indian Relief, a Nepal school, Fiji Appeal and Reverend Flynn's Australian Frontier Mission). First was fundraising and deciding which charities to support; second was fellowship with each other and interaction with other local branches' members; and third was local community support, like welcoming new residents, or visiting and helping ailing members, usually done on 'sick visitor' afternoons, or working together on frequent community functions, raising funds or catering for working bees.

Typical meetings included guest speakers, visiting another group, or trips to Launceston, with members from Sprent and North Motton making up numbers. Annual participation in the Amalgamated Church Fairs where each branch had its own stall enabled fund-raising; Preston hosted the Fair in 1979. This gave the opportunity to display Preston 'pioneer' photographs that I wish were traceable now.

By the late 1970s, there were only 14 or 15 members, and aging stalwarts were retiring to town, including Sheila McCulloch, who cleaned the church for years. That building was a 1930s replacement and by the 1980s it needed repairs on top of running costs. Fellowship members were asked to fund them, indicating that they were taken for granted as fundraisers by Launceston-based church

Women play their part – tradition & change 185

administrators, who appeared unwilling to provide financial help. Various sugges-
tions were made about the Church's future, including the proposal that a youth
group might justify its continuance. Dwindling regular churchgoers and few Fellowship Ladies remaining, despite a membership drive in 1981, led to the final
meeting and dispersal of funds and assets in 1986. After being President for two
years (1970–1972), Iris Johnson was Secretary from 1975 to the end. Iris had also
contributed 15 years on the football catering committee, and many years in the
Mothers' Club at Preston School (Georgie and Iris Johnson 2018). Her record of
hard work for farm and family, and unfailing contribution is an inspiring example
of a yeowoman and her 'yeo-topia' (the blended word used by Brooking (91) 'to
capture the important role played by women and children in the attempt to revital-
ize the yeoman ideal in a new land').

In Tasmania's early post-Federation period, organised associations connected
to philanthropy and church work became more common. The Girls' Friendly
Society (G.F.S.) and Mothers' Union were two Anglican church organisations
formed across the North-West following a visiting mission from Britain in 1908.
An attempt to start either group was made in North Motton in 1913, but without
success, and no other Castra villages had either group (News 1913a). This was
probably because of the strong affiliations to associations centred on Methodist
churches, like those at Preston.

The Great War and Castra women

As Neth discovered in America, women were the core of grassroots organisations
benefitting social and whole community needs – 'raising funds, organising locals,
creating social cohesion and group loyalty, and educating family and neighbourhood' about important issues (342). There was no more important issue than when
many young sons left Castra to enlist in the Great War effort. From a population
of 307 in Preston, 19 enlisted; from 543 people in Castra, 11 enlisted; from 83
in Gunns Plains, six enlisted; from 22 in Nietta, three enlisted (data based on
enlistment address). Out of all these, Castra parish lost eight men (Broinowski
1921, 215). Understandably, it did not take long for Castra women to mobilise
their support in spite of their distance from Ulverstone. Preston became a major
centre of activity because of its importance as a major farming centre and its many
enlistments.

The Tasmanian Red Cross first formed in 1914 (Kremzer 2005, 302–3). Ulverstone, Devonport and Burnie all opened League branches that year. Eventually
190 branches formed to knit and sew items. Ulverstone 'Leven' branch's first
president was Mrs William Henry, wife of the previous large Gunns Plains farmer.
Nietta had a sub-branch until 1964 (Anon. 1989). Early fund-raising efforts supported the Belgian Relief Fund and Red Cross hospitals in Egypt, Malta and the
Dardanelles for sick and wounded soldiers (News 1915d). Communal charitable giving fitted in well with the strong Methodist following across North-West
rural communities, since charitable ideals came from the Methodist idea that
wealth should glorify God. Ulverstone and Preston both had branches of the

186   *Women play their part – tradition & change*

On Active Service (O.A.S.) Fund (Broinowski, 189). On just one occasion in November 1917, a huge collection of tinned food, tobacco, cigarettes, socks and money was sent from Preston to Ulverstone for dispatch. The local newspaper even acknowledged pocket-money contributions – threepence each from Clarrie McCulloch's brothers (News 1917f). Throughout the Great War years, Preston women were continually organising donations to provide 'comforts' and money, all attracting public notice. Adult daughters like Misses Chisholm and Dunham took charge of collecting, and the tiny, precious amounts given by children were noted in one report that is a useful and infrequent record of female family members and children (News 1918d). Mothers also contributed small gifts via their children in local schools, boys donating cigarettes, girls donating soap and tinned foods (News 1917c). In what was probably typical across the nation, the 1915 Empire Day celebrations at Preston school included parents and visitors as well as the 70 pupils; the children did flag raising and a marching display, Ashmead Bartlett's newspaper account of the Australian landing at Gallipoli was read out by headmaster Mr Priestley and their monthly contributions of over 17 shillings were collected for the Belgian Fund. 'Generous refreshments were provided' by the parents (News 1915d).

Gossip is 'a significant feature of human language', the social worth of which has often been disparagingly dismissed (Tebbutt 1995, 1; Spender, 107). But, for Castra women during the twentieth century, their gossip was a social skill that contributed to personal resilience and social solidarity, confirming 'they were all the same' (Tebbutt, 167–68). In the Castra community, it might well have been even more important for mothers or wives whose men had enlisted in the Great War and bad news might arrive at any time. In this way, gossip could be a force for inclusion, reinforcing bonds of community and kinship by matriarchs.

Once the war was over, and surviving soldiers had returned to settle and find wives, the women's social and community life encompassed their men and boys' sporting interests in addition to their own groups. Even women who did not relish watching husbands and sons playing football, like Margaret Harding, were still happy to join the women's fun in the clubhouse, catching up on gossip while preparing and serving food (Denzil Harding). Gossip spread through the local grapevine from at least two travelling traders selling fabrics and sewing notions to farm women through the thirties and forties, and deliverymen acted as social glue. They shared news among women who were more tied to the farm, especially before the early 1950s when they were able to converse by telephone. Later, in the 1960s, Neville Peebles in his early twenties delivered 'all round the farms' in Gunns Plains, Waringa and South Preston for Ellis' Preston store three days a week (Rob and Bub Peebles).

World War II and the CWA

In 1936, the first Tasmanian branch of the Country Women's Association (CWA) opened in Launceston, followed by Burnie and Ulverstone (Cosgrove 2005, 88; News 1936b). During the Second World War, work for the war effort was

Women play their part – tradition & change 187

obviously stimulus for new country branches. Women also used it as an organ to publicise war shortages like yeast to make bread and candles in 'outback areas' that had no 'electric light' (News 1947). The Empire Day school sports at Upper Castra contributed funds for the Red Cross and the Comforts Fund through the Parents and Friends (News 1940b). In 1941, the Preston CWA branch ran a major fundraising function already discussed in the previous chapter, when Mrs William Stuart was President and Mrs Thomas Ewington was Secretary, (News 1941a). CWA ideals and projects were reinforced in its own magazine, the *Tasmanian Countrywoman*, posted to subscribers for 3/- per annum (News 1940a). Every small settlement across the North-West had a branch. In the 1944 annual report, North-West had 31 branches and 916 members, and 'although numerically weakest [compared to North and South], North-West leads in funds raised, £3,748' in the previous year. Sheepskin vests and camouflage netting work was appreciated. Baby clinics, restrooms and CWA Girl's Club plus aid for prisoners of war, bush fire relief, Chinese relief and hospital visiting were all activities that benefitted. The Nietta 'Younger Set' was specially mentioned (News 1949b). The value of contributions for both bushfire relief and vests from Preston, Central Castra, Gunns Plains, Upper Castra, North Motton, Sprent and Nietta were included in the North-West list in 1944 (News 1944b). As many as 13 branches' meetings were reported in 1948, always backed up with the magazine advertisement (News 1948b). Meetings were usually a talk, handicrafts and afternoon tea, though Acton (1987) claimed the CWA was *More Than Tea and Talk*. In 1939 or 1940, central Castra and Preston started CWA groups. Gunns Plains had a branch by 1945. In Preston's first six months, it doubled its membership, 120 skeins of wool were knitted up for the Comforts Fund and donations went to the Red Cross, the Hospital and the CWA Restroom in Ulverstone (News 1940c). North-West branches contributed 882 camouflage nets to Ulverstone CWA in 1942.

The women of Preston CWA bought trees for an official planting ceremony at the Recreation Ground in recognition of the 'boys who offered their all'. Among other dignitaries present, John Chamberlain MHA led the speeches as Recreation Committee chairman (News 1942). La Donna was still the *Advocate*'s correspondent for 'The World of Women' section in 1953, reporting on 20 NW groups' meetings. Preston started its own Red Cross branch that accepted women's sewing and knitting in 1940 with Councillor Stanley Wing as President and Robert Kirkland as Secretary. It is clear to see that there was a huge call upon any possible spare time the women of Castra had to make goods to send away or to sell for funds. Not surprising that Patti Cosgrove described members raising funds, providing food parcels, making socks, vests and camouflage nets around Tasmania during the war as 'outstanding work' (88).

Osterud explored in Canada how 'cooperative labour' extended the concept of reciprocity to encompass activities performed together – such as sharing wedding sewing, children's school shows or putting together knitted squares to make rugs, and caring for one another. Membership of these community organisations, which generally had an altruistic ethos, offered a way of 'sharing and caring' for people or a cause, coupled with social benefits outlined earlier. In Castra,

188 *Women play their part – tradition & change*

women were well aware of the inherent value of the exchange economy, but saw their efforts as reciprocal mutual aid without monetary value, where needs were met and each contributed according to their skills (Osterud 1993, 23–24). For instance, Alice Peebles frequently helped out at her brother Ned Johnson's house where seven children arrived within nine and a half years. She often had extra children to stay when mothers were due to give birth, because of her many Johnson family connections (she was the elder sister). She was following the tradition set by her mother-in-law Margaret, whose table often included 'extras' to her family of 14.

Caring and coping with health concerns and death

Books gradually became more affordable, and books of advice were particularly useful if they related to health and treatment of illness. From the early years of the twentieth century, they endorsed the idea of scientific motherhood. Apple (1995) identified the 'tension-laden contradiction' of an ideology that made them responsible for the health and welfare of their families, yet denied them control over child-rearing by advertised importance of professional advice ('Ask your Doctor') and processed baby foods. Advertisements also implied that mother's and grandmother's advice was inadequate for 'healthful child-rearing' (164).

For the second generation of Preston women, this dominant set of notions seemed like 'senseless urban middle-class norms' that were irrelevant to hard-working countrywomen (Osterud 2015, 426–43). More important to them was their ability to access the experience and common-sense methods of their mothers or mothers-in-law, whose advice they were unlikely to ignore, especially if it was accompanied by additional help on farm or at home to ease the burden of caring. Mothers taught their daughters nursing skills and how to care for most family illnesses (Durdin 1991, 56). Because women in the Castra district, in the era before cars, were hours away from professional help, the usefulness of a book with simple diagnosis and treatment methods was invaluable and there were a range of available choices: Black's *Everybody's Medical Advisor* c. 1880s; Black also wrote *The Doctor at Home and Nurse's Guide* (1927); *The Home Physician and Guide to Health Book* 1935 was American available through the Tract Society, Brisbane; or *The Ladies Handbook of Home Treatment* (Richards 1939); and for child-care, Dr B. Spock's *The Common Sense Book of Baby and Child Care* (1945) that counselled readers 'You know more than you think you do . . . . Bringing up your child won't be a complicated job, if you take it easy, trust your instincts, and follow the directions that your doctor gives you' (3).

Iris Johnson showed me her big medical tome that she had referred to her whole married life. Although published in Detroit in 1887, *Dr. Chase's Complete Receipt Book and Household Physician* was also printed in Sydney, so available in Australia. I was able to see the prized and handed-down 'Memorial Edition' of Dr Chase's book that had been used by a local family for generations.

In America and other Anglo societies, in earlier centuries, most people healed themselves at home and relied on books or pamphlets to know what to do when

Women play their part – tradition & change   189

injury or illness occurred. Increasingly, new ways were found to provide health advice, 'a very marketable commodity', through newspaper columns and advertisements as well as specialised almanacs (Rosenberg 2003, ch. 1). As early as the colonial period, Carolyn Chisholm had urged the writing of a medical text for intending settlers to Australia, in the belief that they would need to be self-reliant about their health; one was Jebez Hogg's *The Domestic Medical and Surgical Guide* (1853), another was Eneas Mackenzie's *Australian Emigrant's Guide* (1852) and later, Revd. John Flynn's *Bushman's Companion* 1910 (Pearn 2012, 167). Ellen Viveash's *Letters* support Chisholm's convictions with her quite graphic description of various encounters with doctors and acting as her husband's nurse when living at country Baskerville in mid-1830s Van Diemen's Land (Slatham 1992, chapter 13).

An early Australian medical text suited to lay-persons' needs was written by Hobart Health Officer Edward Swarbreck Hall in 1880 and was pertinent to the incidence of diphtheria and typhoid, both serious Tasmanian public health problems. Health information from annual reports was published in newspapers. In 1911, the State's main identified health risks were: tubercular disease or consumption; enteric or typhoid fever (gradually being controlled in the towns through fly control and a double pan service for sewage disposal); diphtheria that continued to increase in Leven and Devonport; scarlet fever, also very infectious and increasing; and whooping cough that was 'exceptionally severe and widespread' (News 1911f). Unfortunately, three Upper Castra children died from direct cross-infection carried by the woman who was laying out the first victim, before the local authority could be advised to supply the available diphtheria anti-toxin. This incident helped establish where the germs were harboured (News 1913b).

Traditional home remedies were also handed on through families, one instance being when Iris Johnson and her sister Merle had whooping cough as children; their auntie made up hot poultices of garlic and vinegar for their chests, a memory so strong that in her eighties she still cannot handle the smell of garlic. The limited numbers of infant deaths in early twentieth century Preston families were testament to expectant mothers' access to good quality food of known pedigree, plenty of fresh air, sunshine and exercise, and clean water either from deep wells, springs or rainwater tanks. Kevin Johnson (2018) told me that Preston farm folk 'all fed well and their houses were clean'. There was awareness of simple rules of hygiene because the women practiced them in the dairy. Conventions about outside toilets, the 'old dumpty', were observed carefully, according to Clarrie McCulloch's description of the 'long drop' system with an adult-sized and a child-sized hole and heavy lids in a five-foot long seat, ashes to shovel in after use, and a long bit of fencing wire threaded with squares of newspaper to serve as toilet paper (24).

Advertisements were appearing in Tasmanian papers for patent medicines to treat diarrhoea from 1903. One was Chamberlain's *Colic, Cholera, and Diarrhoea Remedy*, which advocated it was a 'good thing to keep in the house . . . it might save a life'. Diarrhoea was a frequent summer complaint (News 1909a), borne out by an article lauding the *Remedy*'s success 'during nine epidemics of dysentery' and listing local suppliers (News 1910e). As well as advertisements,

190   *Women play their part – tradition & change*

articles directed towards women kept them abreast of ongoing disease prevention improvements.

Mothers would certainly have had an opinion about the problems of over-crowding at the relatively new (built in 1913) Preston school in 1920. Councillor Frank Tongs of Preston told Leven Council that 95 pupils in one room, 32 feet by 22 feet, was a health risk to children, especially during the hot weather and, when Dr Moffat visited to assess conditions, he agreed that 12 inches for each child was completely inadequate (News 1920a). A second room was added, helped by Tongs' advocacy.

Early death of an adult was a rare event in Preston history and when it happened it received attention in the newspaper. One tragic loss was that of Caroline Guest (aged 31 years) of South Preston, who died under treatment in Launceston, leaving behind a husband and four small children, who later left the district (News 1904e). Parental death, but particularly the death of the mother, can have very far-reaching effects in the lives of surviving children. Schafer (2009, 92–95) argued that:

> Childhood loss of a parent is a unique type of disadvantage in that (1) it is an emotionally devastating event, breaking up the family unit without anyone's consent; (2) it involves the loss of a contributor to household activities forcing survivors' roles to shift to compensate for it; and (3) it is an 'off-time' transition far afield from age-based norms.
>
> (81)

When Jane Elizabeth Ewington (nee Peebles) died during the birth of her eleventh baby in 1934, there would have been a lot of pressure on her husband Thomas trying to cope with domestic demands of his family while continuing to farm. In spite of the children's grandmother, Margaret Peebles living half a mile away, and her sister-in-law, Louie, living opposite, there was a limit to what consistent help these and other women could do while keeping up their own family obligations. Within a few years, Thomas married Effie Cullen, the daughter of Thomas Cullen of South Preston. She was already a member of the Preston social and Methodist community, and took over care of the children, as well as acting as the Secretary of the Guild from 1936 to 1951. But she also continued providing board and lodging during school terms to the young female teachers that came to work at Preston School. It may have been a happy experience and a financial benefit for the Ewington family since it went on for many years. Margaret Pearce remembers a succession of them even into the mid-1960s when she and her husband would give them a lift to Ulverstone on Fridays.

In another case, Iris, her sister Merle and their other two siblings lost their mother to appendicitis in Wynyard hospital in 1944, when they were all under 15 years old. At the time they lived on a farm further west, but their father could not manage alone, so he sold his farm and they moved to another almost adjacent to his parents in Gawler, so that his mother and sisters could help care for the children (Iris Johnson 2018). In a farm context, it is easy to imagine the magnitude of

Women play their part – tradition & change   191

the loss of the important contribution to both home and farm of all these women, each in different ways.

In addition to the immediate impact of loss, Schafer also found that early stand-in responsibilities meant children felt older than their peers as they grew to adulthood, an enduring sense of feeling old for one's age (93). When Iris received her proposal of marriage in 1954 from Georgie Johnson because he already had his own farm, Iris told me she was only 16 or 17 years old, very young to get married, 'almost too young, but farmers couldn't wait for their women for one or two years [to grow older], they needed a wife to help them on their farm', so when her father gave permission, they went ahead. Her preparedness to embark on life as a farmer's wife (on challenging land, much of which still needed to be cleared) appears to bear out that feeling of maturity Schafer described. The evidence is that the effect of loss went further and explains the value Iris assigned to her book of medical advice, to avoid ever leaving illness undiagnosed too long motivated by loss of her mother.

Much historiography about women's roles includes them acting as midwives and nurses in pioneer settlements (Durdin 1991). I have no evidence of that in Castra, though there probably were women 'invisible' in the record who had those skills. But in Ulverstone, a Benevolent Society Hospital was established in 1906, and taken over by the State in 1910 to provide hospital and medical services. It merged with the Levenbank Private Hospital in 1949, under a District Board of management and continued to offer midwifery and maternity services, so many interviewees, mostly born before the 1950s, were born at Levenbank (CSD22/99/187; CSD22/144/157; LSD35/1/5294).

Traditional work – inside or outside

In the past, women's economic contribution to family farms has either been under-counted by economic historians, devalued as 'pin money' or ignored by statisticians. This has been countered by Americans Fink (1986), Schwieder (1980, 1986), Jensen (1988) and McMurry (1994). In Britain, there has been research by Valenze (1991) and Bouquet (1982) and a comparative history with America from McMurry (1992) and, in Australia, by Alford (1984) and Ford (2011). All these scholars have explored the farm women's productive role from pioneer times onwards, notably in the dairy, in milk, cream and butter production; the fowl-yard, and eggs and poultry production; and orchard, vegetable and fruit gardens. Each domain contributed to self-sufficiency and a good family diet, and could earn cash income, or credit to acquire goods they could not produce. The mixed regimen of crops and animals protected the soils and took advantage of interdependencies between crops and livestock. This was even more important before increased access to chemical fertilisers. Castra women made use of milk by-products (whey) to fatten pigs, and free-ranging techniques circulated natural fertiliser from animal manures. The later hazards of dairying mono-culture were highlighted as causing widespread pollution of water sources in NZ by the 1990s (Brooking 2019, 83 onwards).

192 *Women play their part – tradition & change*

Adams (1988, 454) described the pre-Second World War yeoman farm economy in 'idealised agrarian' farms as being either self-sufficient or able to use mutual exchange with similar farms, what she called a system of 'mixed capitalist-quasi-peasant agriculture'. Production was regulated by 'use-values' and accommodated the dynamism of the family life cycle as children grew up. Use-value described cash from produce sales converted into something useable in the home (Fink, 37). Historically, it seemed exceptional for farmwives to not bring some cash into the home or, at least, reduce the cash outflow by bartering for necessaries as well as men's farm-work (Riley 1977, 189–202; Schwieder). As seen from 1880 to about 1910, Castra families concentrated on producing for themselves as they cleared the land, and self-sufficiency was effective in Castra. It was not long before potatoes would provide an enduring cash crop, with seed for the next year and some for family consumption, especially as most families had many mouths to feed. From the start, Castra women had poultry of various kinds, cows for daily milk, pigs for ham and bacon, and small numbers of sheep kept mostly for family meat, since the climate was less suited to wool-growing than the Midlands. This variety formed part of George Wing Jr.'s family farm as described by the *North West Post* correspondent in 1899, when he also mentioned Wing's marriage nine years previously and 'sundry young Wings arising'.

Much later, in the 1980s, when the bottom dropped out of the beef market, the Peebles brothers did run sheep and invested in a shearing machine because wool offered a better price for a few years (June Peebles 2018). Sheep, especially fat lambs, continued to be part of the livestock mix especially on hillier farms with limited water supply.

Wives had particular interests that influenced the livestock balance. For example, while Margaret Peebles had small numbers of milking cows and chickens for family consumption from 1903, daughter-in-law Alice was really keen on poultry and always had chickens, ducks and turkeys; poultry was the regular Sunday dinner. In the 1940s, she and husband David had a herd of up to 70 cows to milk, and Alice did the milking and looked after the dairy until 1971, when June came to help after her first baby was born.

For Joan Johnson, Marie's and Kevin's mother, poultry was her special interest. She kept sufficient laying hens to supply eggs to Ellis's shop in Preston and to preserve enough for year-round use. She kept about 100 meat chickens as well as geese, of which they ate about 30 each year, and ducks, all of which were processed at home before sale. Joan also kept pigs for sale and home consumption, freely ranging in the orchard after fruit-picking (Marie Harrop).

In Castra, some women gained a reputation for certain specialities. Mary Ann 'Granny' Stevens, mother of the Stevens daughters who married three of Henry and Sarah Johnson's sons, lived at Upper Castra most of her life. She had a reputation for wonderful dressmaking and sewing; she used to come across to Preston for holidays with Dulcie and George Johnson to teach her six granddaughters how to make their own dresses. Along with most local women of her generation, she loved her flower garden, a place of pleasure and solace, and source of flowers for church and gifts (Iris Johnson). Love of the farm's open spaces that MacKellar's

Women play their part – tradition & change   193

grandmother's generation experienced, albeit in the hard toil times of early settlement, meant an hour's evening walk was 'an escape from the confines of the
house and a chance to walk in open spaces' (MacKellar 2004, 11, 20).

Creating a garden that produced flowers as well as vegetables was an important source of pride and sense of belonging, enjoyed by most of the farm women
I interviewed. June Peebles' garden always has colour and interest year-round,
and Josie Brown, Ken's wife, now well into her eighties, loves her special hybrid
shrub selection and works year-round in her garden, both in 2020 still maintaining lovely flower gardens (Ford 2011, 110; Holmes, Martin, and Mirmohamadi
2008, 5–6).

Women's work was linked to harvesting because workers had to have hearty
regular food in work-breaks. When neighbours, extended family members and
paid labourers came to take their turns hay harvesting or potato picking, June
Peebles said it was typically a full day's work for wives like her – morning and
afternoon tea with 'eats', a substantial lunch and then a hot supper meal at about
10:30 p.m. or when work finished. In the 1940s, Denzil Harding remembered a
dozen men scything his father's peas for the Ulverstone factory, and his mother
Melvie having to cook for them as well as her usual work; he said it was very
hard for women in those times, but in the 1960s too, for his wife Margaret, with
farm work and five children. They stopped dairying in the 1970s when the herd
size had to be 200 to justify the milk-truck. Margaret reared piglets from their
four or five sows, and vealers reared on mother's milk did well. Denzil recalled
that they made good money out of the pigs, when each sow produced seven or
eight piglets each. Margy King recalled the work in the 1960s involved with her
father David Peebles' annual pea crop. When the pea vines were cut, she helped
the boys rake the peas into rows ready for the harvesting machine, which gathered
up and trucked the crop away to the pea vinery at Gawler. The pea harvesters went
to Johnson's farm too for several years in the 1960s, and Marie told me that meant a
lot of extra cooking for the gang, but this was the genesis of her life-long interest in
cooking that was her employment for many married years.

Farmer's wives and older daughters always had occasions when their work was
indoors. The most important room in the farmhouse was the kitchen, with its large
central wooden table, the place for supervising toddlers, sharing food preparation
or sewing bees, playing games with children or friends in the evenings, or for
companionable gossiping over a 'cuppa'.

Long before Illich identified 'tools of conviviality' in 1973 (11–13), settler farm-
women always understood the power of 'autonomous and creative intercourse
between persons' and that between persons and their environment. He argued that
'individual freedom realized in personal interdependence' and 'its intrinsic ethi-
cal value' was the essence of conviviality. While this was just as true for the men
and the children, it was the women who sat around kitchen tables together that
enjoyed their place in the yeoman life.

Women's visits to each other maintained close ties, enabling shared wisdom
about child-rearing, illness or farm lore about their poultry or the dairy. Gollan
drew attention to the loss of the central table when, from the 1950s, kitchens

194 *Women play their part – tradition & change*

transformed to a table-less place. Women lost the tangible relational connection between those who used to sit around the table, and have been standing in their domestic workspace ever since. Narrow, one-sided benches made the possibility of transferring knowledge to their next generation extremely difficult (Gollan 1978, 139).

Clarrie McCulloch remembered his mother always on the go, probably typical of all yeoman farm wives between 1900 and the coming of electricity around the mid-1940s. Elsie 'turned out an endless supply of cakes, scones, and biscuits' and meals on the Peters oven (common in the 1910s), until Ernest bought a new solid fuel range with hot water boiler in 1930. Her skill regularly won prizes at the highly competitive Church Fair. She made cordials from blackcurrants, raspberries and lemons, and old-fashioned ginger beer, and grew fresh vegetables year-round in 'Mum's domain'.

Gift-giving and exchange were vital elements of community survival. Sahlins identified a typology of reciprocity, differentiating on strength of value (1974, 188–209). Osterud's work on togetherness and mutuality emphasised the gendered interpretation (1988, 73–87). Moreover, mutuality formed by farm women in this way was an empowerment strategy that strengthened bonds of womanhood and kinship (Osterud 1991, 275–88). It made sense to 'share the bounty' with one's neighbours and friends and worked particularly effectively in yeoman farming, based upon semi-subsistence and family teamwork (Arnold 1994, 129). In all yeoman farming communities, women's exchange and sharing of surpluses spread the benefits of personal specialisations in their highly valued work (Osterud 2015, 85–86). But with the move from cream to whole milk and then low prices, their farm-work changed greatly, causing many in Castra to leave dairying. We turn our attention now to that transition, using two parts of the Johnson family as contrasting examples.

Transition and change from the 1970s

For about a century, Castra farming women had played an essential part in the progress of their families, their farms and their community and, in so doing, had maintained the yeoman ideal alongside local capitalist commodity production, mainly from potatoes and milk products (see the next chapter) well into the 1970s. Then, major changes in agriculture started to affect the role of women as income producers. Somewhat ironically, 1975 marked a partial change in the counting of women's on-farm work in the ABS Agricultural and Pastoral Census. Before 1975 that Census excluded the work of farming women unless they were full-time *paid* workers on the farm; farm wives usually self-described as 'housewives' (Williams 1992, 22–23; Barr 2009, 76). In the ABS Census of Population, Housing and Labour Force, only a person's main job is counted, so when a farm woman had several jobs, off-farm work that was paid was chosen for declaration, but this meant that any other unpaid on-farm work went uncounted.

Rural population reduction occurred, not only because of fewer children but also losses of whole families through sales of small farms to amalgamate with

Women play their part – tradition & change   195

others. Fewer people inevitably led to social institutions contracting as happened over the Methodist Church and Hall, and would impact on the closure of Ellis' shop, loss of two post offices and, by 1994, closure of the school.

Adams traced the way American family farms integrated into the capitalist economy as 'petty [or simple] commodity producers' over the twentieth century (453–54). She argued this process 'decoupled' the farm household from agricultural production. Her evidence from the post-Second World War decades aligns with other scholars, demonstrating the separation of farm women from farm production, their reduced reproductive and household work, and their large uptake of off-farm work. She wrote, 'production is converted to cash and consumption is purchased with cash', a process that turned self-sufficient farm families into consumers who either needed to make high profits, expand or have external income to survive, which many did not, a result made more severe due to the subsidised structure of large American agricultural businesses and no subsidy for small self-supporters. Mechanisation in America fitted the 'modern farmer' and 'domestic wife' ideology even though wives still continued farm organisational tasks (Adams, 456; Garkovich and Bokemeier 1988, 223). In Australia, increasing numbers of farm wives in off-farm employment has meant that farm financial support still comes from wives who have become a different type of 'breadwinner', just not from on-farm productivity. Barr went further suggesting that 'more women in the workforce was changing the food-supply chain' and contributed to growth of supermarkets (Barr, 77, 3–4).

The dilemmas facing American family farms attracted attention of environmentalist-farmer Wendell Berry, who wrote feelingly:

> The family farm is failing because of the universal adoption . . . of industrial values . . . . The great breakthrough of industrial agriculture occurred when most farmers became convinced that it would be better to own a neighbour's farm than to have a neighbour. We have given up the understanding . . . that we and our country create one another, depend on one another, are literally part of one another . . . all who are living as neighbours here, human, plant and animal, are part of one another.
>
> (1987, 351, 356)

Both Adams' and Berry's studies mirrored the transitional process identified by Lawrence (1987) that occurred somewhat later in Australia, from the 1980s but with similar effect (See also *Report of the Survey of Women* 1988, 27–28). Adam's research helps us understand the process experienced by Castra farmers and Berry, amongst others, highlights the disadvantages of losing family-operated farms for the environment, echoing Brooking's New Zealand findings about industrialised agriculture despoiling natural water resources.

Fink's study of the effect on farm women in this situation is also helpful. Prior to the Second World War, women controlled their income and its expenditure, though this led to it being categorised as 'pin-money' because their labour was perceived as free. High demand, for eggs in her example, during and after the war

196 *Women play their part – tradition & change*

led to highly mechanised capitalist production by men, putting many women out of business (1986, 229–31, 153–59). Similarly, in the dairy industry, when milking and butter-making was done by hand, it was seen as women's work (albeit with the help of children), but the introduction of machines and factories transformed it into men's work. Jensen (1988, 825) marked this happening in the 1880s in the American butter industry. Facing similar changes to those charted by Adams and Fink, it was hardly surprising that the older women of Preston, like Alice Peebles and Joan Johnson, decided to move away from their poultry business. If more profit came by using the land for their husband's livestock, it made up for the loss and freed wives up to be emergency stand-ins or to do important tasks that otherwise might have been neglected.

Pressure had been building since the 1960s over financial viability of small farms, and gradually the better funded farmers bought out nearby small acreages to consolidate, hoping that getting bigger would be better financially, in what Barr (3) called 'the relentless escalation in farm size required to remain viable' that had started in 1950s Victoria. This was true of the Peebles brothers' partnership and of Sidney Johnson. Other farm sale evidence comes from property histories discussed in Chapter 6.

Sidney Johnson's family provides one example of transition caused by the 1967 change in the dairying industry that directly affected the farm wife's work. In their early years together after marrying in 1948, Sidney and Joan had a busy, productive yeoman farm enterprise – he had dairy cattle, sheep and potatoes working cooperatively with his six local farmer brothers; she had her poultry and pig businesses in the traditional style, with her money used to support the household bills and his to meet farm costs. In the mid-1960s, his changing land transactions, including an inherited pea contract extended three additional years, delayed his expanding the milking herd to take advantage of whole milk collection from higher minimum herds. But that expansion meant Sidney needed additional labour, supplied by daughter Marie for seven years until son Kevin finished school at 16 and started farm-work (Marie Harrop). Marie's labour was not quite 'free' in the yeoman tradition of family labour, but the cost of her wage plus living at home was less than paying a labourer that would have been financially difficult for the enterprise at the time. The extra effort of milking a bigger herd by both husband, wife and then daughter appears to have become the principal source of income, and Joan's ancillary activities were superseded in that 'decoupling' process described by Adams.

Georgie and Iris Johnson responded differently to the transition, because, from 1954, cream then milk, was always their joint 'simple commodity production', based on their relationship of a companionate marriage. Iris was the one who walked the cows into the shed and started the milking until Georgie joined her. In the 1960s, when cream was the product, they had pigs like everyone else to use the whey milk, until the start of whole milk and need for a herd of 200–300. For them, 1997 was the year of change, after 42 years of dairying and both in their mid-sixties, because their 70-strong herd was insufficient to justify the milk-truck. With no access to more land and no desire to expand, Georgie gradually bred out the Friesian strain using three Angus bulls of different genetics and transitioned to

Women play their part – tradition & change   197

rearing and selling weaner beef calves, which they were still doing at the time of interview and which proved to have been more profitable business than predicted (Iris Johnson pers.com. 2021). Because their lives had revolved around the milking cycle, Iris had time for her involvement in community activities already described.

After the 1950s post-war prosperity, most farm families had cars, making it easier to drive to Ulverstone for farm business, sociability in other organisations (especially as local ones folded, as shown earlier), shopping, or off-farm work that fitted with child care if grandmothers were not available. Julie Lee (pers. comm. 2019) was an example of a Preston farmer's daughter and wife, who had her three children relatively early and, once the youngest started kindergarten in 1988, worked part-time as school-bus driver, which ideally accommodated her children's needs and school holidays, until closure in 1994.

Feminists like Alston argued 'free' time actually furthered male domination, because women became more at their husband's 'beck and call' as gofer, as book-keeper and the one dealing with regulations (1995, 149). Another scholar highlighted the 'masculinisation' of farming following agricultural restructuring, which made the women's role subservient after the Second World War, especially with the move by women to off-farm work (Saugeres 2002a, 641–50). Curiously, manufacturers advertised farm machinery using symbolism that was addressed to farm wives into the 1950s because its purchase often involved obtaining credit (Garkovich and Bokemeier 1988, 222). A contrasting view is offered by more recent ideas of tractors as 'a symbol of masculine power' that create a barrier between men's and women's farm work (Saugeres 2002b, 144).

Findings related to power and gender were countered by historians who argued that Australian women have always confounded 'passive victim' stereotypes, by constructing their own 'spheres of autonomy', by networking and bonding with other women, and often engaging in 'informal paid work' that was invisible in official statistics. Matthews identified many types of paid work by married women that fitted with yeoman farming wives and daughters; for example, home-produced commodities like eggs, jam, fruit, craft products and foodstuffs, cleaning or laundry, seamstress and music-teaching (Matthews 1984). Saunders and Evans (1992, xix) highlighted the 'permeability of boundaries' between 'so-called' separate spheres, an argument that fits well with Castra farm women's experiences. I would add that the role of post-mistress/sometime telephonist was done by women in Preston until the last post office closed in the 1990s. Evidence supporting this counter argument comes from June Peebles, who said that, in the 1980s, her daily life still involved farm work of several months' potato harvesting each year, feeding out cattle in winter, and in between, 'you went to town to get the shopping and do things with and for the children', as well as all the accounts and paperwork.

In conclusion, for all Castra residents, the importance and value of all activities organised and executed by women that combined sociability, inter-connectedness and collaboration cannot be under-stated. For most of the twentieth century, they helped both local and distant worlds, especially during war years. As researchers had discovered among family farm women in America (Henderson and Rannells

198   *Women play their part – tradition & change*

1988) and in another Tasmanian rural community (Wood 1997), Castra women experienced meaning in their skills of integrating family, work and community activities. These skills gave them control over their lives, lasting friendships and multiple chances of contributing to success in a fruitful garden, a charitable project or a cohesive society. I showed how women's roles adapted as farming changed over the twentieth century. Even with less direct participation in production, they were still busy, catering to demands from harvesting, feeding livestock and keeping up with 'the books', and some engaged in off-farm work, melding it with domestic responsibilities. What did *not* change was their sense of partnership with husbands and commitment to their farms. My final chapter looks at the farming men – how they used their influence and kin collaborations towards the best life for their families and farms in the best yeoman tradition.

9 Men and their land – doing what was best
1880–1980

This history so far has shown how ties that bound Castra farmers and families together were linked to yeoman virtues of independence, thrift, hard work, fecundity, kinship, active Christianity and freehold ownership of land. I have made comparisons with qualities and characteristics held by yeoman farming families widely across the Anglo-phone world. Earlier chapters focussed on social and relational ties that connected and motivated men, women and children through daily life and through inheritance after death. In this chapter, the public face of Castra communities is illustrated through political ties that bound the men together, which they believed were important to support their farming and family interests. I use the potato and dairying industries as examples to show how they participated in politics from 1880 to the 1950s. Extending into the 1980s and drawing from oral testimonies, I show ways that kinship ties reinforced collaboration, and how men supported their farms with off-farm income. All elements were important in supporting survival of the yeoman ideal of sustainable family farming in Castra to the century's end or beyond. This was long after other Australian historians had written it off as 'economically implausible' by 1914, and where the 'yeoman dream' of farming in Victoria as a way of life was argued as anachronistic after the 1960s (Lake 1987; Waterhouse 2004, 451, 454). The 1980s' agricultural transition and resultant changes in Castra were addressed in Chapter 8, so that theme is not revisited.

The public sphere, newspapers and political participation

In the early twentieth century, leaders of North-West farming communities well understood the reality and value of the public sphere. Because newspapers turned private news of public interest into a saleable commodity, they played a fundamental role between zones of state authority and private business as literacy levels rose and readership increased. Criticism and comment about government activity were encouraged by publishers (Goode 2005, 5–6, 12–13). Provincial newspapers historically had long proved their importance in cultivating public opinion and enabling outsiders to join political debate (Lopatin 1998, 339). As the public sphere was the realm between society and state, the press provided the public arena (Koller 2010, 264). The community had its say because perceptions

DOI: 10.4324/9781003229841-10

200　*Men and their land – doing what was best*

of public and private could evolve and overlap. Whereas private life was the 'arena for intimacy, loyalty and similarity', public life was a realm of 'difference, accountability, respect and recognition, negotiation and bargaining, and public work' (Calhoun 1992, 351). The leaders featured in this chapter exemplified these public qualities.

Democracy was linked to the increasingly accessible public sphere, because it progressed when issue-oriented public meetings occurred and, when speeches of protest or deliberation on contentious issues were publicised in print, they were more likely to engage parliamentary institutions and representatives directly (Clemens 2010, 374–75).

For people of the North-West to exercise critical judgement on public interest matters, newspapers encouraged them to think of themselves as members of a wider community, not just as private individuals. Their political voice was enabled through the wide range available from the 1870s. In North-West Tasmania, these were *Devon Herald* (Latrobe, 1878–1887), *Wellington Times and Agricultural and Mining Gazette* (1890–1897), *North West Post* (Formby, 1887–1916), *North Western Advocate and the Emu Bay Times* (1899–1919) becoming *Advocate* from 1918 to the present, *North Western Chronicle* (Latrobe, 1887–1888), *Coastal News and North Western Advertiser* (Ulverstone, 1890–1893), *Leven Lever* (Ulverstone, 1919–1920), *Northern Standard* (Ulverstone, 1921–1923) and *North Coast Standard* (Latrobe, 1890–1894). According to *Wellington Times* editor Charles James Harris expressing editorial policy in its first edition, 1 October 1890, 2.:

> No large section of people can long afford to be without a newspaper. It is the one thing above all others by which to make known the various needs of the community and without it no district has much chance of securing proper consideration of its various claims . . . . We intend in every legitimate way to advance the material progress of the district . . . . Our news columns will be free to the community without partiality, equal publicity will be given to all public bodies.

Newspapers served as a 'signpost of official authority and a primary source of community cohesion', but they could only survive by catering to their readership's needs. The importance of advertising revenue is evident from front pages carrying only advertising. Kiddle wrote that, in 1870s and 1880s Victoria, newspapers fulfilled various functions: 'a retailer of local and general news'; a place to air grievances; to give agricultural help; and, by descriptions of events, they reflected all community life; plus, their offices provided the place for posting public notices (456–9). In the same way, in the North-West, readers trusted that content would be interesting and relevant, report on current government issues and provide regular market updates as well as social content about local notables, especially in the women's pages. One significant example of the former were regular reports from named or anonymous 'correspondents' of journeys through hinterland readership districts, like Hilder, whose work I have often cited.

Men and their land – doing what was best   201

From 1878, Tasmanians could access *Castner's Monthly and Rural Australian*, published in Sydney (1878–January 1887) available at six shillings annually with content addressed to rural families. But Tasmanian information was so much more relevant and, after the Council of Agriculture's establishment under *Council of Agriculture Act* 1891, it started publishing its regular *Journal* from August 1892 about diverse research on dairy, agriculture, poultry and fruit-growing. Major concerns are obvious from the first-year index: sparrows, noxious weeds, blackberry pest, codlin moth and *fusicladium* (black spot). Newspapers also reported Council activities regularly – an outstanding example was the six-foolscap-page equivalent for the annual report in the *Daily Telegraph* 20 August 1900, 2.

Thomas Wright, chairman of the Ulverstone Farmer's Club, formed an Ulverstone Board of Agriculture in 1892 and gradually, local Boards formed across the state (*Journal*, Vol. 1, No. 2 1892, 20). The Council publicised significant issues, often reporting what was happening in New Zealand, which had its own agricultural journal, *New Zealand Country Journal* from 1877 to 1898 (Wood and Pawson 2008, 337–65). The *Journal* served as an organ for proposals among Boards, like Frankford proposing a 3d/acre unimproved land tax, that Ulverstone discussed and endorsed (*Journal* 1887). Increasing fertiliser use drew attention to potential dishonesty through manure adulteration, which was its main topic in June 1893, and again in 1897 (*Journal* 1893, 1897). When the *Manures Adulteration Act* went to the Legislative Council in 1906, Hubert Nichols, already concerned for years over this, urged a strengthening of analysis conditions, though Attorney-General William Propsting, MLC for Hobart, stated that fertilisers imported into Tasmania already needed to have a certificate of analysis (News 1906d). Easteal showed that the problem continued until the *Fertilisers Act* 1912 tightened up conditions laid down in earlier *Manure Adulteration Acts* of 1893 and 1898 (Easteal 1971, 268).

In 1896, the *Journal* changed its name to *The Agricultural Gazette* but effectively continued the same role; a full run of issues held in the Tasmanian Archives are worthy of detailed research, but lack of space here means just a few examples are cited. The Ulverstone Board regularly sent meeting reports for publication, thus circulating news of their activities around the state. For Castra farmers to journey to Ulverstone over poor roads for meetings indicates their belief that the Council was useful in promoting farmers' interests. Familiar names – Thomas Wright, George Lewis and Thomas Shaw – were among the membership in 1893; in 1898 and 1899, they were George Wing Jnr, Hubert Nichols, John Bingham and John Robertson (*Journal* 1893, *Gazette* 1898, 1899). In 1902, William Delaney and Ed Delaney Jnr joined. Between July 1901 and June 1902, the Ulverstone Board submitted reports every month. That this was remarked upon indicates it unusualness, and shows the continuing enthusiasm of members' perceived best interests (*Gazette* 1902).

By 1902, growing disquiet about the Council's effectiveness, relating to conflicts of governance with the Department, spread across Tasmania's Branches at sufficiently high level for a Joint Select Committee to be called (JPPP Vol. XLVII, 1902, No.49). Hubert Nichols (MLC) and Dr McCall (MHA) were both

202   *Men and their land – doing what was best*

North-West Committee Members. In recognition of the large membership of the Ulverstone Branch, William Delaney was a witness. Delaney told the Committee that all Ulverstone members were dissatisfied with Council processes. Ulverstone branch was expanding, already one of the largest. When asked if the branch work had a good effect or was 'simply a meeting of farmers to have a chat', he replied that farming was the topic and the branch could do better 'if the Council was worked properly'. Asked how farmers felt about Departmental Secretary Tabart's administration of the Department, Delaney stated they felt it was unsatisfactory (Delaney, 8–9). Thomas Tarbert was also Chief Officer of Stock and his perceived conflict of interest was the root of the witnesses' evidential complaints. Recommendations were that Council should continue, with a controlling Committee, power over its budget, appoint its own Secretary and agricultural experts should be under its control; quarantine and stock issues should remain with the Minister, and that any future appointee to Chief Inspector of Stock should be a qualified Veterinary Surgeon.

There was sufficient interest by 1911 to form a Preston Board; citing just one meeting in August as an example of the topics, the agenda included distribution of seed parcels from the Department; responding to its request about land prices for immigration advice; a motion against prohibition of butter-colouring; support for a public meeting about railway communication via Preston with Nietta and telephone service to South Preston; and an invitation to Hubert Nichols to attend future meetings in gratitude for his service over railway advocacy (News 1911a).

Reynolds acknowledged that regionalism was inherent in Tasmania, so it was important that Parliament and public meeting reports were covered in sufficient detail to connect readers to state happenings whether they lived in the Huon, the North-West or North-East (Reynolds 1969b, 14–28). The 'hatches, matches and dispatches' entries were closely followed, enhancing local connections and providing a historian's treasure trove. Rootes went further, arguing that localism was a critical aspect of the public sphere, and 'local communities of interest' drove decisions in North-West communities (2004, 81–82). Through 'Letters to the Editor', newspapers encouraged active participation in public affairs, often airing protest issues that writers knew would reach a large audience. One excellent instance was the newspaper 'battle' fought over the siting of Preston School in 1912 (Henderson 2016).

Tasmanian newspapers catered to their large farming audience for decades with relevant government and organisational annual reports. From as early as 1875, Tasmanian newspapers had included reports from dairymen's associations from New York, Wisconsin, Illinois, Vermont, Canada and Ontario, all areas where scientific dairying research was occurring and senior researchers were presenting their results (News 1890c). Comparison of New Zealand butter being better than Tasmanian or Victorian product led to calls for a Dairymen's Association to help farmers improve quality (News 1891b). The *Examiner* selected article reprints from the *Ontario Farmers' Advocate* in 1900, 1916, 1923 and 1924, and its Depression viewpoint (News 1931c). It printed research from the US on ways to conserve moisture where 'practice and science go hand in hand' (News 1924a).

Men and their land – doing what was best   203

These inclusions kept readers informed of international farming conditions and advances. The *Advocate* ran a weekly farmers' page with useful articles, interstate and overseas market prices, and advertisements for clearing sales, farms to let and farming product businesses, in particular the Farmers' Cooperative Auctioneers Ltd. (News 1923c). The replacement for the Council's *Journal* was the glossy-covered *Tasmanian Journal of Agriculture*, published quarterly from 1929 to 1981. Each contained horticultural, domestic and Q&A pages as well as agricultural matters. Contents pages demonstrate general usefulness for farmers and their wives engaging in yeoman-style mixed farming, and junior farmers from 1963. They were ideal for reference and passing round to family and friends.

The North-West hinterland farmers actively participated in the public sphere by following, and contributing to, newspapers and public meetings on important issues. Commonality of concerns and neighbourhood ties provided the numerical strength essential to promote their best interests to a State government habitually dominated by members predisposed to protect their own estates' best interests elsewhere in Tasmania. Some Castra men mentioned in this chapter used local government to contribute in the public sphere.

The importance of a political voice for Castra was obvious as early as 1870 with Crawford's inability to persuade the Tasmanian Government to keep their promise over the road/tramway from the coast into Castra lands. Lack of roads into so-called 'back-country districts' was regularly on the agenda, although many small settlements managed on tracks that they developed themselves, as through Barren Hill, or by lobbying the local Road Trust, as the Henry brothers did for road-building from Gunns Plains to North Motton. In consequence, meetings of the Leven Road Trust were compelling reading for tenderers as well as those hoping their road would attract funding. Preston was well and consistently represented on the Trust by its own trustee; in 1906, this was Alfred Tongs, and Thomas Cullen, storekeeper, was standing for election (News 1906a).

William Delaney, no stranger to this history, was a firm political activist for local affairs. As member of the Leven Road Trust in 1900, he had already proposed a transfer of the Lowana area into Leven because Lowana farmers on the western side of the Leven River were technically in the Penguin Road District but without a road out of the valley to reach Penguin. Bridges over the river allowed residents to travel through the valley on Leven Road Trust roads to North Motton and on to Ulverstone. George Wing Jnr. was Trust Secretary at the same time (News 1900e). It was not until 1943 that one was constructed (JPPP Vol.CXXIX, No.4, 1–2).

It is significant that many rock-crushing contracts for road building purposes were often let to local farmers, providing better road surfaces and extra income from the rocks they picked up from their fields. Tas Johnson remembers the crushing machine coming to crush paddock-rocks to lay on Jacks Road when he was about seven or eight (1940–1941). The use of rocks gathered from the land and often piled near the roads indicated the stoney nature of some of the land, but there was another tradition of using them to create rock walls, which have proved to be extremely long-lasting around Preston farms because of their high-quality

204   *Men and their land – doing what was best*

construction. Rock walls were an inherited cultural aspect of northern English and Scottish landscapes. Blackberries along the roadsides caused complaint and George Lewis of Preston did so at the September 1900 meeting after his brother James had cleared his roadside fence lines. Another perennial issue was collision danger from stock feeding along the roadside (News 1899d, 1900e). Just this one meeting demonstrates that Preston farmers were not reticent to defend their interests by committee participation or by complaint to local authority.

In 1906, municipal councils were established, and the Leven Municipality was divided into Wards with three men from each led by an elected Warden. Perusal of *Walch's Almanac* for 1911 (383–84), as an example, reveals the same names often standing out as political leaders; the Castra Ward was represented by the Hon. Hubert Alan Nichols of Upper Castra, who was also MLC for Mersey, Angus McPherson of Preston and Thomas Bingham of central Castra; the North Motton Ward was represented by William E. Lewis, of Preston (just within the southern boundary of North Motton) and Alfred W. Tongs. The Leven Medical Officer was Dr Lachlan Gollan, who was *accoucheur* at the Hospital and birthed many Preston children; some were given his name. Gollan practiced in Ulverstone from 1910 to 1946, first as partner to Dr John McCall (later to become Premier) (Large 2004, 54–56). Nichols was one of two Coroners. As was noted in soldier settlement applications, local leaders were often Justices of the Peace, and ten of the 24 in 1911 had some connection to Castra, including both Nichols and Delaney. John Bingham, Thomas Shaw (General Shaw's son and mill-owner in Castra Road) and Delaney were on the Licensing Bench, which is not surprising because Delaney was Methodist, a faith embracing temperance. Delaney was also Secretary of the Preston Hall. Post offices were well distributed in Castra, and operated by prominent families; Gunns Plains, Preston (Sarah Lewis), South Preston (Ada Cullen nee Tongs), central Castra (Thomas Bingham) and Upper Castra (Rachel Rebecca Wright). Nichols was on the Leven Harbour Trust, the United Agricultural Society, the West Devon Agricultural Society, the Australasian Axemen's Association and the Ulverstone Racing Club, and consequently was able to exert his influence widely.

Land agency business has been mentioned in connection with closer and soldier settlement. After Nichols sustained a bad accident in his twenties, he took up business premises in King Edward Street, Ulverstone. From his letterhead, he was a land valuer, land salesman, a stock and finance agent ('loans at short notice'), agent for stations, farms and town properties and seller of 'posts, pailings [sic], rails and firewood' from his or neighbouring farms at Castra and Nietta. Already a young entrepreneur, about 1886 Nichols had acted as a contractor clearing newly opened land in the Nietta area, beyond his Blackwood Park home, for early settler T. Oswin Button; anything under two feet across came down for 30/- per acre, myrtles above that size 1/- extra; the daily payment was 16/- per day of which 7s 6d was labourers' pay (News 1897; Fenton 1891, 174–75). He continued to buy land, evidenced in the 1920s valuation rolls, which supported saleable timber harvesting, renting to tenants or subdividing when it was profitable (VR 1923 and 1929). Another locally significant land agent was Alexander Crawford, who grew

Men and their land – doing what was best   205

to adulthood farming at Deyrah. This agency role is shown to be substantial as archival documents reinforce these men's intimate knowledge of people and land, and the power of their recommendations to the Closer Settlement Board (CSB) across a range of transactions significant to people in their hands.

The most important local farmer for over 30 years was John Hartley Chamberlain, who exerted influence in various political arenas on behalf of not only soldier settlers, of whom he was one, but also all small yeoman farmers. This influence involved membership of various farmers' organisations, especially at Preston, where he was President of the Preston Agricultural Bureau when local Bureaux replaced the Boards after Council was superseded in 1909 by the Department of Agriculture. Chamberlain had a 19-year political career, as MHA for Darwin in State Parliament and was Tasmanian Senator in Federal Parliament at his death in 1953. His notable public standing and longevity as a North-West political representative was no doubt due to his personal identification as a Preston returned soldier farmer and his intimate understanding of farmers' problems.

The Primary Producers' Association was another opportunity for farmers to make a political impression and was initially formed to attract electoral support for representation in Parliament. One candidate was central Castra farmer, John Forsyth Wright Jun. who, among others, addressed a large audience at Preston to launch the campaign in 1922. He told of his 'successful career on the land and in business' and his preparedness to devote his whole time to the 'business of the country'. The main issues were high cost of Agricultural Department inspectors, high railway freight costs, and better management for roads, railways and public works spending (News 1922b). This association did not last long under this name, but it was the starting point of a long political career for Wright, whose Council portrait hung in the Ulverstone History Museum shows his many years of contribution to the Leven Council; he was a significant member of the Tasmanian Producer's Organisation; Tasmanian Farmers' Federation; the Municipal Association; co-founder of the Agricultural Bureau; Potato Marketing Board; and Australian Potato Committee, eventually becoming MHA for Darwin in 1940. Known as Jack, he grew up on his parent's farm adjacent to Crawford's 'Deyrah' (Bennett and Bennett 1979, 229).

Potatoes

How did the *commercial* sale of potatoes and cream, and milk later on, fit with yeoman ideology? Although self-sufficiency was important in early settlement years, the yeoman ideal always allowed for farmers to make a living from farming beyond self-sufficiency. In America, 'self-sufficiency was adopted for a time until it would eventually be unnecessary', and, for Castra farmers too, poor market access was a major inhibitor to progress (Hofstadter 1956, 2). The yeomanry there were marketing their excess production in the early years of the American Republic (Appleby 1982, 833). Thomas Jefferson recognised that yeoman farmers were 'the most precious part of a state' (Hofstadter, 2). But clearly, self-sufficiency or 'modest abundance' alone would hardly advance the nation economically, which

206   Men and their land – doing what was best

was why he endorsed applying science to agriculture, advocated soil conservation, and enacted policies to encourage higher productivity and, importantly, commercial marketing of farm commodities (Appleby, 354). This open acknowledgement of yeomen as an entrepreneurial class was opposed by Hofstadter, who claimed the Jeffersonians created 'an agrarian myth with the yeoman farmer as the folk hero', a claim soundly rebuffed by Appleby. The conclusion from this and other 'agrarian' sources is that farm-grown products in commercial quantities fitted with the yeoman ideal. In fact, large squatting estates that were sub-divided into 2,560-acre grazing farms fitted the yeoman ideal in Victoria in 1864 and later in Queensland (Waterhouse 2004, 447). Moreover, Belich argued that yeoman farmers wanted 'independence from masters, not markets' (Belich 2990, 153). Additionally, it was acknowledged that farmers operating really mixed activities in North-West Tasmania were least dependent on seasonal and price fluctuations and more able to incorporate flexibility of rotational benefits and crop choices, so, when prices were low, cash crops could be fed to livestock (Easteal 1971, 274–77; Stokes 1969, 121). In 1895, an unnamed Castra farmer (perhaps Hubert Nichols) advocated a mixed farming plan for 50 acres: 25 acres best land for cultivation, of ten acres each for oats and potatoes and five for root crops like mangolds, carrots and greenstuff, leaving 25 acres for grazing, sufficient for ten or 12 cows, which could be fed all winter to extend their milk yield; oats would produce straw and some for sale (News 1895b). Leven farmers during the Depression years operated a regimen of grain crops, peas and hay in addition to the potato crop, whereas in the Penguin and Emu Bay municipalities a virtual monoculture in potatoes yielded 51-60 per cent of farm income (Kellaway 1989, 64–65). Combining two commercial products, potatoes and dairying (that complemented each other) meant better yeoman farming entrepreneurship.

From 1888, when George Wing sent his first cash-crop to the coast, potatoes were always the popular crop throughout the Castra district and were exported to Sydney through Devonport and Ulverstone wharves from the 1890s; one striking instance was 41 potato ships from Devonport sailed for Sydney in August 1890 (Taylor 2003, 13). Around Preston, eight or nine tons to the acre were reported in 1904; pasture had been enhanced by clover and cocksfoot grass; dairying was in evidence; all crops yielded above-average results; and prize-winning horses were being reared by the Tongs brothers, Fred, Alfred and Frank (News 1904d). In May 1907, G. and A. Ellis, at their Leven Store in Ulverstone, displayed a single potato root of 'all marketable tubers' grown by John Smith in Preston weighing over 14lbs (6.5 kgs), which, according to the reporter, 'gives proof of the productiveness of the soil in the Preston district'. The same report logged one day's deliveries of oats, peas, chaff, turnips, barley and straw as well as 3,530 bags of potatoes (News 1907b).

It is hardly surprising that potato diseases were the cause of a 'good deal of perturbation amongst potato-growers' in 1908. Concern had already been raised in early 1903 at a Preston meeting, convened by George Wing and chaired by Frank Tongs, about risks from imported potatoes and using second-hand bags, and a resolution was formed for the Minister of Agriculture through Dr John McCall,

Men and their land – doing what was best 207

MHA for West Devon, that 'prompt steps should be taken to prohibit both' practices (News 1903a).

Opinion by a North-West correspondent alluded to the lack of quality control by inspectors and that growers and dealers could not rely on local inspection certificates being satisfactory in the receiving markets. 'Indiscriminate export' of tubers of mixed quality was condemned because of the effect on its trade and reputation. Regulation should be perceived as a 'boon' to growers. The other issue was that 'bad seed will not produce good crops' and 'making light' of 'scab', 'gall-worm' or 'brown ring' in the past would no longer work. It was 'high time for a fresh start with clean, sound seed' (News 1908d).

Government entomologist Arthur Mills Lea had been researching causes, and growers were putting forward ideas such as 'scab' linked to excess potash in recently fire-cleared ground. Lea warned that planting diseased seed, unfit for consumption, into disease-carrying ground would compound the trouble in future (News 1908d). In May 1909, Lea and Chief Inspector Tarbart visited the Devonport wharf to examine 'brown rust'-infected potatoes. They commented on matters including storage in clamps, the similarity of 'brown rust' to English 'winter rot' caused by being stored before really dry, and the difference between potato scab (*Streptomyces scabies*) that did not affect potato's culinary use and the 'virulent Black Scab (*Oedomyces leproides*)' that was highly infectious. The local reporter ended his report by claiming that scientific research had done a lot for agriculture, and any farmer unwilling to listen to advice would be better 'hod-carrying instead of tilling the soil' (News 1909b).

As guest speaker at the Branch Boards of Agriculture Conference in Latrobe in July, Lea provided a comprehensive description of the various potato diseases and their treatment. Brown rust 'was not a calamity and would not wipe out the North-West coast' (News 1909c). Nichols was present and moved a motion that the Government send an expert to all Tasmanian potato-growing districts to allay concern, to inform on types of disease and methods of combating them. He alluded to his past experience, growing clean crops. Nichols supported growers' grievances with NSW inspectors when previously rejected cargos were resent, approved and then attracted top price. He asked for support of a resolution for negotiations at the forthcoming Melbourne conference of Agriculture Ministers to standardise intra-state efficiencies. Nichols also seconded a motion to pursue negotiations with the Federal Government if these failed (News 1909c). Clearly responding to concerns, the Government enacted the *Potato Diseases Act* 1909 that obliged growers to do whatever they could to eradicate and prevent disease spread (Part IV s.11; Part V, s.28).

The ongoing confusion and concern of growers generally became obvious by the much-reduced planting for the 1909–1910 season. Only about a third of the usual output was expected from Preston and half in Upper and central Castra (News 1909e). Yeoman farmers had trebled in the previous decade. There were 66 farmers in Preston and South Preston in 1911 (compared to only 11 in 1900) and about the same again in central Castra, Upper Castra, Nietta and Gunns Plains (*Town Directories* 1900, 212, and 1911, 236). This large number helps explain

208   *Men and their land – doing what was best*

why farmers' organisations were so well supported, local meetings had high attendances and why several men attained such high standing in this community that it carried them forward to higher office in municipal and parliamentary positions, where they knew they expressed their voters' voice.

Other repercussions from these *Acts* became clear at a large meeting of indignant farmers later in 1910 at Upper Castra, who felt the potato tax was a 'monstrous imposition'. (News 1910b). The Leven Council, represented by Cr. Thomas Bingham, had agreed to hold what the Council called 'indignation' meetings across the municipality about the tax of three shillings per acre on potato crops. Under the terms of the *Acts*, this amount appears to have been a violation. The Council may well have been privy to similar reactions across the North-West and presents a good example of the value when newspapers covered an issue of wide community interest. As a farmer, Bingham was clearly angry and stated that 'tax of 1s 3d per ton for inspections at the port was more than ample to cover everything' and that 'even members of Parliament had not expected the maximum tax to be imposed on down-trodden farmers'. It was particularly galling when they observed the behaviour of inspectors 'riding past on bikes and appearing to be interviewing kiddies' or relying on one farmer to report on his neighbour's acreage. Resolutions were forwarded to the Council, which Bingham hoped would yield 'sufficient indignation' to achieve reform, just as it had 30 years earlier when 'the cry went up for constitutional change, and they got it' (News 1910b).

As well as disagreeable taxes and inadequate inspectors, farmers contended with fluctuating potato prices, as in 1924, when 'ruinous' prices were the lowest since Federation. The *Land* editorial argued that all Tasmanian exports were ruled by mainland conditions, and the bumper season in northern NSW particularly had flooded the Sydney market, with the future of 'earlies' from Tasmania 'far from hopeful'. Farmers fortunate enough to have good volcanic soils in the North-West could adapt by increasing their dairying, bacon curing and early lamb production (News 1924b). Kellaway showed that, in the 1926/1927 season, 76.3 per cent of Tasmania's total potato acreage was situated between the Lower Mersey and Circular Head, which meant that potatoes were 'a central element of the farm economy' right across the North-West (63, fig.8).

Preston farmers' dissatisfaction with the NSW potato grading system in 1928 led to its Bureau resolving that the Potato Marketing Board take steps to rationalise standards used, and that Tasmania's Government pass only 'A grade' potatoes to manage supply fluctuations. Preston Bureau farmers also received on-farm advice from Government Veterinary Inspector Beardwood about cattle abortion (News 1928c). Such mixed agenda topics attest to Preston farmers continuing mixed farming, even though potatoes continued to be a most important economic contribution throughout Castra.

The Potato Marketing Board (PMB) was set up in 1927 to support the interests of producers with representatives to shippers and in prime (Sydney) markets, with a levy from growers, being pushed by the Agricultural Bureau as a marketing division within it (Kellaway, 71; News 1927a). It was clearly a nasty shock for farmers to find the PMB proposing the potentially damaging action

Men and their land – doing what was best   209

that would imperil the New Zealand potato embargo in 1933. Unsurprisingly, well-attended meetings in Preston and North Motton were organised in formal protest (News 1933a). The matter was so serious that Prime Minister Joseph Lyons (himself from the North-West) received a telegram from Frank Edwards, MLC for Russell: 'Please prevent contemplated lifting embargo New Zealand potatoes . . . . Consider embargo vital to farmers' rehabilitation and alternative means insolvency'. Nichols also sent telegrams and canvassed all State Ministers advising that Tasmania could supply potatoes without needing those from New Zealand. The 'rehabilitation' referred to soldier settlers who depended on this crop for their farm's survival.

Years later, Nichols wrote an opinion piece to the editor reminiscing about his past involvement in the potato industry. He included his exploits with W. Henry (Gunns Plains) and others in testing 100 varieties of potatoes under supervision of Council of Agriculture senior members. The resulting successful potato was the Brownell for early, middle and late cropping that was still 'the mainstay of the Tasmanian industry' in 1939 (News 1939a). It was not until the outbreak of war that demand came from NSW housewives' representative bodies and the Fishmongers' Association representing Sydney fish and chip sellers, who wanted access to the cheaper (subsidised) New Zealand potatoes. Despite Tasmanian growers' protests, the potato ban was eventually resolved at the highest level of both Governments (Mein Smith 2017, 48–49).

After initial experimental work at Myrtle Bank, the Brownell variety research was transferred to the Tewkesbury Potato Research Station (TPRS) south of Burnie in 1930, nearer to the main Brownell growers. By 1935, the first improved seed was available to registered growers, the first of which had to be 800 feet above sea level. From a low production average of two and a half tons per acre, the TPRS seed produced seven tons, but this reduced closer to the coast and after each subsequent year, as demonstrated at Lakin's Gawler farm field day. His TPRS seed yielded 6.3 tons/acre but when grown at the coast, only 4.9 tons/acre. The District Agriculture Officer Kjar warned growers not to buy seed unless it was tagged by the TPRS (News 1936b). All the potatoes sown in Castra's southern districts towards Loongana from the early thirties were destined for seed, indicating the start of a long-lasting trend (News 1932a). Higher altitude farms continued to be suitable for seed, and Preston was high enough for this, well past 1,000 feet; the Peebles grew seed until 1998.

Nichols was again at the forefront of public affairs, as Secretary of a committee proposing the first Tasmanian Potato and Roots Show to raise quality through competition and open to selected growers of two grades of 'elite seed' (News 1937). This led to local competitions and the Preston Farmers' and Stockowners' Association ran one for the 1938/1939 season, won by Robert Kirkland, Stan Wing and John Johnson (News 1939b). The wisdom about diversification was heeded, and by the end of the 1936/1937 Depression, the North-West region had 45 per cent more dairy cattle and 150 per cent more sheep (for fat lambs) than ten years earlier (Kellaway, 64–65). Nevertheless, potatoes remained a major income producer for North-West farmers. In 1946, as many as 8,000 sacks were railed

210   *Men and their land – doing what was best*

from Castra stations in July and August (News 1946). Then in 1950, 32,000 sacks of potatoes left in two ships from Burnie and Devonport in just one week, bound for Brisbane and Newcastle (News 1950a).

The Agricultural Bureaux

By 1908, the Council's Annual Report claimed agriculture was 'cursed by farming class apathy'. Small meetings and 'sluggishness to adopt improved methods' made this apparent (News 1908g). The first Dairy Class in Devonport that blended lectures with practical demonstrations attempted to address this, almost Council's last gasp (News 1909i). But, ultimately, the solution was thought to be local Agricultural Bureau branches, more accessible to primary producers, to develop experimental plots, expert field visits and discussion of advances. By 1930, other Bureaux were located at Nietta, Riana and South Riana, Sprent and North Motton (AD9/1/203).

The South Leven branch with John Chamberlain as President provided a monthly opportunity for visiting lecturers and agricultural reports as well as a forum for commonly shared concerns. Preston was the hub of Castra farming, and Stan Wing continued as Secretary following the AGM; there were 31 members and many more attending meetings. Warden of Leven, Hubert Nichols, MLC, stated in an interview that the Legislative Council was anxious for the farming community to benefit from the Department's subsidy of the South Leven Agricultural Bureau, which that year was about £6,000 out of State expenditure of £51,000 (News 1930c).

Often hosting visiting speakers who attracted farmers from Nietta to North Motton, Preston was very active from 1928 until 1935. The members were not slow to take issue with interstate and Tasmanian Government actions. One instance was Preston's 1930 Annual Meeting, when the issue was referred to the Executive about inspection tax on pork *into* NSW, but no inspection required *from* NSW to Tasmania. But members also carried a motion of disgust with the Nationalist Party for failure to reduce the number of Parliamentary members as promised (News 1930d). This drew publicised censure from ALP MHA Franklin, Albert George Ogilvie on grounds that political discussion was against Bureau rules, which Preston farmers resented, arguing only *party* politics were disallowed (News 1930d).

District Conferences were full-day opportunities for local branch delegates to meet instead of Tasmania-wide events. The Devonport Conference in 1930 was chaired by Alexander Lillico, MLC for Mersey. Branches from North and South Leven, North Motton, Nietta and Sprent attended from the Ulverstone hinterland. Stan Wing attended for S. Leven, John Wright for N. Leven, and John Chisholm for North Motton. Issues included herd testing – Stan Wing was dissatisfied with service and charges for small herds; rabbits – concern over poison prices; Bismark potato seed from Midlands – should be inspected for all diseases, not just 'corky scab'; lecturers should be available for every second branch meeting – letter to Director sent; more contact with farmers through field visits to stock sales – letter sent; and a letter of appreciation for annual *district* conferences that

Men and their land – doing what was best   211

were more accessible rather than *state* conferences; all conveyed to the Director of Agriculture(AD9/1/246).

However, in 1931, general discontent, expressed by Agricultural Bureau branches across the North-West, had high-level repercussions (covered in AD9/1/20, 3). It was brought to the attention of Agriculture Director F.E. Ward by letter from Chief Executive Officer Robert W. Winspear of the Launceston Agriculture Bureau office following his visits to several branches, pointing out that 'the position of farmers on the North West Coast generally is rather disturbing and in their present mood they are inclined to be very critical. I feel sure that it would be to your advantage to meet the farmers of the South Leven Branch to hear what they have to say' (Winspear to Ward 4 June 1931). Ward responded, agreeing to meet a delegation of two men from each branch when he came to the North-West the next week (Ward to Winspear 8 July 1931). After the 1931 State Council meeting, Winspear wrote to the Minister (3 August 1931) to confirm its support, despite branch criticism. By the end of that year, MLC for South Esk Alan Lindsay Wardlaw, an executive of the Agricultural Bureau, requested Ward to provide an overview of Bureau activities. Ward's responding Memorandum (18 November 1931) noted that the original 1927 recommendation of the Commonwealth Development and Migration Commission was that the Bureau and Agriculture Department be integrated (see 1928–9 AD9/1/21253). Ward wrote that in 1928, the Commission reversed this, recommending independence and a suggested estimated budget from the Government, run by a Bureau Executive. 'Entire independen[ce] from Government' was seen as crucial to 'effective action' of the Bureau. This had not happened. Since poor prices, the agricultural down-turn, and envisioned cooperative marketing had not occurred, Government assistance had been needed longer than hoped. In its defence, Ward wrote that the Department's Extension Service continually worked with 'liberal cooperation' alongside the Bureau. 'Increasing demands on officers' and 'reduced finance' 'will make it necessary in future for the Bureau to reduce its reliance on the Department' (Ward Memorandum, dated'18/11/31'). Lack of a marketing scheme for potatoes was a major drawback (Skemp 1952, 234). The failure to support growers during the Depression aggravated their discontent and lost the movement support.

South Leven members were outspoken about both Bureau and Departmental expenses, agreeing with Devonport branch members, particularly singling out the cost of the CEO's car and high living away allowances for officers, in light of possible Government grant reduction (obviously public knowledge in April 1931) (News 1931b). These actions demonstrate how branch concerns filtered through to the top organisational level, and clearly reflected the tightening economic situation in agriculture.

Another occasion, when the Agricultural Bank amalgamation with the CSB was mooted, over 50 farmers came to the Preston Hall to hear how this would affect them (News 1932d). During this period of low primary product prices, there was a further attempt to assist Tasmanian farmers through the Farmers Relief Bill 1935 that focussed on debt adjustments, developed by a joint committee of members and presented to both Houses. Of local significance, at the Committee's

212   *Men and their land – doing what was best*

Devonport meeting on 18 August 1935, George Ellis, owner of general goods stores in Ulverstone, Sprent and Preston and creditor for many farming families, gave evidence, as did John Forsyth Wright, central Castra farmer, and Hubert Nichols, having been MLC for Mersey and Meander, was examined as an Upper Castra farmer and land agent (Joint C'tee, JPPP Vol.CXIII, 1935, No. 15 and 20). This resulted in the *Farmers' Debt Adjustment Act* 1935. But already in February 1935, general discontent in Preston motivated a vote proposed by Captain Sidney Cannon of Gunns Plains and seconded by Thomas Ewington to disband its Bureau in preference to starting a branch of the Farmers', Stockowners' and Orchardists' Association (hereafter FSOA) instead. Robert Kirkland was delegated to obtain details (News 1935a). Cannon became President and later presided over a large protest meeting at Preston.

Reading the many meeting reports provides an understanding of Castra's farmers' no-nonsense approach – not afraid to air complaints, follow up with motions or requests for action, unconcerned by their opinions being aired in the press and not slow to follow more useful alternatives. Overall, these attitudes exemplify yeoman characteristics of independence, uncowed by authority, especially political, and appreciative of reciprocal assistance such as provided consistently by Hubert Nichols.

Local meetings, as outlined earlier, shared one characteristic during the first half of the century, that is, they were consistently well-attended, particularly true when held in Preston or Upper Castra. This suggests these meetings were about much more than the business being discussed. They were also an important means of maintaining the ties that bound the men together and provided them with harmonious collaboration over common concerns. For many farmers, their working days were solitary except when sharing work. Dates of meetings show that winter was consistently popular and provided the chance to meet and share gossip and opinions with friends and neighbours in a male environment. Murray King (born 1929) remembers his father regularly attending evening agricultural meetings (pers. comm. 2019).

The gradual diminution of local farming associations may have indicated social and demographic change and, perhaps, more accessible transport to travel further to centralised meetings at the coast. Another proposition put forward was that, by the 1950s, even though they had vehicles, farmers in the country were unlikely to travel to Ulverstone for evening meetings because the dominance of town representatives overwhelmed those of rural residents, whose interests were often disregarded (pers.com. 2019). This contemporary memory has added credence because of Rootes' data showing rapid growth of population after 1945 to 1961. The adult rural population was already slowing as farms consolidated and labourers became too expensive, so towns received the extra population gains (Rootes 2009, 155). The ABS noted an annual increase in Tasmanian population from 1945–1980 of 1.5 per cent, but growth rate during the 1980s slowed to half that, data that fit with the population changes in Preston (ABS 2002, 1384.6). The development of this feeling indicates early evidence of the 'rural-urban divide' that has been a catchphrase in defence of rural communities ever since.

Dairying

Keeping a few cows for family supplies of milk, cream and butter was a normal part of yeoman farming, usually falling under women's management. But when potato disease reduced farm incomes, other choices had to be made, and cow numbers and quality were increasing as pasture was improved. In 1901, one third (13,000) of Tasmania's dairy cows were in the North-West, and by 1913, another 12,000 had been added. 1901 marked the start of separators, enabling cream to be separated on-farm. The Babcock Tester in 1896 encouraged improvement, often achieved by culling to develop 'high class dairy stock' (Easteal, 227–30).

In 1900 the Government employed a dairy expert, Augustus Conlon. He addressed a large meeting in Ulverstone in 1909 to extol the virtues of dairying and to assist farmers to cooperate and takeover Murdoch Brothers' butter factory in Ulverstone, an idea sanctioned by the Minister (Cassidy 1995, 17; Stokes 1969, 153). Conlon spoke of the benefits Western Victorian and New Zealand farmers had gained from such schemes. A cooperative venture where all farmers were shareholders could ensure returns in direct proportion to the amount of butterfat delivered in contrast to volume, which might be adulterated with water. Based on his 'full inquiries' about local dairymen's feelings, Conlon believed the time was ripe for a successful venture (News 1909e). He held meetings at Preston, North Motton, Upper Castra and Sprent the next few days. Technical assistance and quality improvements would come, particularly through the Tasmanian Dairymen's Association, just formed in July 1908. In recognition of the symbiotic relationship between milking cows and pig rearing, pig breeders were accepted for full membership of the association (News 1909f). At the 1909 Launceston annual meeting, its progress on concerns was reported. The Ulverstone Butter Factory started in 1910, operating as a cooperative, and in 1911 production reached seven tons per week (News 1911e).

All this positive activity, combined with more farmers adding dairying to their potato operations, had been the catalyst for extending herds, but already there was public unrest from North-West farmers about Tasmanian Government restrictions on importing 'good dairy cows' from Commonwealth States while abhorring their embargo on sound Tasmanian potatoes. A feasible solution would be quarantine and a veterinary certificate of health, according to other North-West farmers at Irish Town (News 1909g). June Peebles told me most farms milked right through to the 1970s when she recalled that the churns originally used for milk were later used for cream for the butter factory; everyone had small herds, at least 30 or so milkers, to supply cream for butter and whey for pigs.

Thomas Bingham eventually moved from director of the Tasmanian Dairymen's Association to become President (News 1908g, 1910c). He was well qualified for this role, having established his 'very valuable, rich agricultural' farm Freelands at central Castra from its original state and then specialising in dairying. The farm was photographed for the *Weekly Courier*, shown in Figure 9.1. He had up-to-date cheese-making and butter-making appliances using his own

Figure 9.1 Top: Freelands, the Bingham house at central Castra; Middle: Bingham's Bush Dairy: students watch a demonstration by dairy expert, Conlon; Bottom: Portion of Bingham's herd, with Conlon.

Source: *Weekly Courier*, 23 December 1905, Insert 4, images 1–3. Tasmanian Archives.

Men and their land – doing what was best 215

handmade churns, and selling his well-famed products to the northern markets. His son Owen was a farmer too, who enlisted for the Great War.

From these photographs, the clearly high-quality house has an iron roof, the milking shed is rooved with shingles and its 'chimney' there indicates steam-powered equipment. The remains of ring-barked trees form the usual 'settler' landscape. Amongst the students are five women observing, Conlon is the man in the white hat and apron, and Bingham may be next to the boy at the wheel. These photographs give a clue to the strong relationship between Bingham and Conlon based on their common enthusiasm for dairying. Conlon would remain in the Instructor's role until he retired at 70 in 1928 (Cassidy 1995, 17). Unsurprisingly, Bingham assisted at a week-long Dairy School run by Conlon in Burnie. Eventually annual dairy schools were run by Conlon at Pardoe, east Devonport from 1909. Conlon supplied the *Weekly Courier* his photographs published on 14 December 1901, insert 2 of the factory, the modern equipment there and a large group of visitors attending a demonstration; the majority were females which clearly reflects that women still prevailed as dairy maids at the turn of the century (Cassidy, 18). Bingham commented that some students were a bit young at 14 to appreciate the value, and he was disappointed more farmers had not taken advantage of lectures and practical demonstrations that combined theory and practice to great effect (News 1911b). Bingham's view was prescient of what would become growing acceptability of educational lectures through the Agricultural Bureau and the later development of Junior Farmers Clubs and government Farm Schools, such as at Sprent.

In 1918, the North Western Butter Factories Association formed to advance industry-wide interests of all local factories, who provided delegates to the quarterly meetings (Cassidy, 35; News 1919d). By 1922, the Emu Bay Butter Factory Company Chairman was advocating rationalisation and amalgamation to benefit both the dairymen and the shareholders (News 1922g). Many small butter factories previously competed for cream supply against each other, but, after the rationalisation, an agreed standard price meant cream went to the nearest factory; this was more efficient and made substantial savings, but left the running of the factories in local hands from Duck River to Devonport (Cassidy, 35).

Dairying continued to grow strongly up to the 1930s when it was 'a safe haven during those difficult years' of the Depression (Henzell 2007, 133–34). Directors of the Ulverstone factory in 1926 included Frank Tongs and Captain Sidney Cannon of Levengrove, Gunns Plains. Most of its production went to Britain but margins were so small that takeover and closure recommended by the Association in 1928 was inevitable (Godfrey and Neilson 1992, 106; Cassidy 1995, 35). Butter-making generally peaked in the 1930s, and more regulation of the industry was deemed necessary, with major *Acts* passing to regulate dairy produce (*Dairy Produce Act* 1932) and products (*Dairy Products Acts* 1933 and 1934), the former relating to quality and the latter relating to manufacturers' quotas. A new Ulverstone factory was built, opening in October 1933 and operating until 1965 as Coastal Dairy Co. P/L (News 1932e). Tas Johnson recalled that the cream for butter, collected in 90lb. churns in the 1940s, went to the River Don Co. store in Ulverstone en route to the factory. Murray King drove a cream truck from 1956

216 *Men and their land – doing what was best*

(after the railway closed) round all the farms of central Castra and Sprent for years, picking up from raised road-side concrete stands built the right height for the ten-gallon churns to be rolled onto the truck tray; he delivered them to Coastal Dairy. He also trucked potatoes to town on the off-season.

Other local leaders

Another example of early political participation by men of Castra concerns one of the Tongs brothers. The family had been early settlers in North Motton. By 1911, two sons, Allan Lorenzo and Frank Allan Tongs, were farming at Preston, and their older brothers, Frederick and Alfred, were North Motton farmers, with a butchery and a butter factory from 1900. Frank (born 1870) was known for his prize-winning horse breeding and his post-Great War interest in fine Jersey dairy cattle (News 1906c). He was elected to the Leven Council in 1917, was Warden for three terms, finishing in 1929. He was a keen supporter of agricultural shows across Tasmania.

In 1925, when there was a huge gathering for the opening of the extended Preston Hall, Frank Tongs was invited to officially open it. Walter Stuart's speech acknowledged the contribution that he and Mrs Minnie Tongs had consistently made to Preston, prior to their move to Ulverstone, through his keen promotion of Preston's interest and long-term roles as Hall secretary/caretaker and chairman of both the Sports and the Recreation Ground Committees (News 1925b). He was so well-respected, with kinship links to two Preston families, that even at his funeral in 1940, ten Preston organisations gave tributes and wreaths (News 1940d).

Amongst the men, there was one woman leader. Mrs Joan Cannon and husband Captain Cannon bought into Gunns Plains in 1923. He was a Jersey breeder specialist and she was the first female cattle judge in Tasmania. She also regularly judged the Calf Club entries at Preston School and was President of Gunns Plains CWA, hosting meetings at her home (News 1935e, 1950b).

My final Preston contributor to public, political and community service is Stanley Wing. Born in 1896, he was the youngest son of George Wing Jnr and had already established his own 'Moola' Ayrshire cattle stud in 1913 on the family farm with his first two cattle. He became a member of the Ayrshire Cattle Society, was president twice, and frequently served on the Federal Society Council over 40 years; his cattle established the nucleus of Ayrshire herds in India and South Africa in the 1950s. He sold his herd in 1965, having been successful at every show for 50 years. Still interested in Ayrshires, even still commenting on their quality and observing the Ulverstone Show judging of them in early 1981, he was photographed for the *Advocate* just months before he died (News 1981).

He helped re-form the Ulverstone Agricultural and Pastoral Society in 1933 and was made a Life Member. He was a member of the South Leven (Preston) Agriculture Bureau and involved in herd testing. He was Councillor of the Leven Municipality in 1939–1947 and 1955–1959. In the early 1940s, he was chairman of the Light Company that was involved in getting electricity to Preston, and would have been responsible for inviting Agriculture Minister John

Men and their land – doing what was best 217

Lewis Madden and Mines Minister Henry Thomas Lane as well as other dignitaries to attend the official 'switching-on' in the Preston Hall (News 1944c). Later, he was appointed one of five members when the Potato Marketing Board was incorporated in 1952, representing Division 3 (Penguin, Ulverstone and Kentish) at the headquarters in Burnie (Select Committee, JPPP 1952, Vol.138, No.62.) Wing resigned in 1971, when chairman, after 27 years as a member (News 1981).

As mentioned, in 1936 Preston started its own South Leven branch of the FSOA of which Wing was the long-time President, and in 1937 he was elected to the Board of the Tasmanian Farmers, Stockowners and Orchardist Society; in total he gave 32 years of continuous service to this state organisation. In the years before the Second World War, the fierce annual potato growing competitions were judged by the District Agricultural Officer, N. Kjar. Quality was judged more important than quantity; in 1936, 20 Preston farmers took part – all winners were familiar names, but the best yield, thought to be due to its regular rotation of crops and pasture, came off Wing farmland 52 years after Stan's father had cleared it (News 1936b, 1936d).

Typical issues discussed at FSOA meetings over the years were labour costs, contract rates, fertilising regimes, rotation and potato seed quality, weather responses and their problems, as when their potatoes were dropped in the mud at the wharf (a wet sack cost them ten shillings at the Sydney market). They also heard about opportunity for fat lamb and sheep breeding to supply cheap meat to British industrial workers, as another alternative to potatoes and dairying (News 1936a, 1937).

During the Second World War, Preston farmers were feeling very harassed by Government over 'too many regulations' that they claimed were hindering the war effort. One major problem was demurrage charged on their produce when delivered to the Control Board depots but then not unloaded, meaning that any costly delay was beyond their control (News 1943).

The Ulverstone dehydration factory, run for the Government during the war, paid the Preston potato growers less than the contracted price per ton, a cause of 'perturbation' when they received their cheques. On members' behalf, Stanley Wing took up the matter with the manager and the correct amount was paid for future deliveries (News 1944a).

Wing was always actively interested in the quality of his milking herd and attended a lecture given by a 'world-famed Dutch geneticist, Dr Arend Hagedoorn'. On behalf of other breeders there, Wing questioned him on the best guide and incentive to higher quality. The response came down to keeping only the best types of cows in the herd, and adequate feeding and shelter, which was provided best by planting shelter belts of *Pinus radiata* against rain and *Cupressus macrocarpa* against wind. Questioned about the issue of Friesians for whole milk supply compared to Jerseys, Hagedoorn advised that the farmer needed to consider each case before making changes (News 1949c). The conversion to whole milk was clearly on farmers' minds and Preston farmers would eventually experience the effects too.

218 *Men and their land – doing what was best*

Field Days were another post-war opportunity for farmers to up-date themselves on agricultural advances, and Wing supported such events, as at Cressy's Government Research Farm in 1950. The Department of Agriculture's Superintendent of Extension and Technical Services Francis William Hicks was guest speaker, bringing his knowledge as President of the Australian Institute of Agricultural Science based in Canberra. Stan Wing spoke, emphasising the value of field days to 'practical farmers to avail themselves fully of the advice of scientists' in their efforts to "feed the world" ' (News 1951). He was airing wider recognition that population growth after the war meant more people to feed, which would stimulate more innovative scientific developments from Australia and abroad (Henzell, 143).

The increasing recognition that science and research were important in agricultural activities was one of two significant ideas originating in this period. From 1961 onwards. the CSIRO began publishing the *Australian Journal of Experimental Agriculture* as a vehicle to publicise research efforts across the nation. Research papers sourced from North-West Tasmania were chosen randomly from 1970–1990 journals. For instance, B.A. Rowe, 'Effects of limestone on Pasture Yields and the pH of Two Kraznozems in North-Western Tasmania', *AJEA* (1982); J.E. Duffus and G.R. Johnstone, 'The Probable Long Association of Beet Western Yellows Virus with the Potato Leaf Roll Syndrome in Tasmania', *AJEA* (1982); W.J. Fulkerson, R.C. Dobos and P.J. Michell, 'Relationship Between Predicted Energy Requirements and Measured Energy Intake of Dairy Cattle at Pasture', *AJEA* (1986). The CSIRO was pivotal too in research into cheese-making, casein and milk production, and showing how by-products of milk could be converted for human consumption, when 'in the old days' they went to feed pigs, often inefficiently (Henzell, 142–44).

The second idea was Hagedoorn's advocacy for shelter belts in the Tasmanian climate where cattle lived outdoors year-round, in contrast to Northern Europe where they are kept shedded for seven months of the year. Any visitor to the North-West can still see remaining *macrocarpa* shelterbelts planted in that era along ridges to break the wind. *Radiata* became the favoured tree for government forestry plantations, a Castra example being at Isandula, where Georgie Johnson worked pruning in 1958 to 1959, earning off-farm income to grow his dairy herd. M*acrocarpas* are distinctive components of the agrarian landscape that are gradually being removed in part because they are breaking down due to age, and often to make way for pivot irrigators that also cause loss of hedges and stone walls along paddock fence lines, but the timber is durable for all building uses, providing an excellent recycling resource.

Political input and leadership in establishing and sustaining the railway

David Peebles told his sons that the railway had opened up the Preston district in a unique way and contributed to the success of local yeoman farmers. Importance of a railway to Castra farmers is shown by pressure exerted very

Men and their land – doing what was best   219

early in the twentieth century to sort out which route it would take of three choices, and political lobbying, both locally and in Parliament, by deputations and local members of both Houses. The earliest efforts started almost as Preston's first cash crops were ready to market with a major push from Colonel Crawford and Dr McCall, MHA Devon, in the late 1880s. At one public meeting in early June 1889, chaired by Colonel Crawford at the Albert Hall, Castra, it was argued that 'railways were the cheapest and best means of transit to get produce to market, while the present narrow roads were totally inadequate to bear the immensely heavy traffic that was continually passing over them'. Newly selected land near Nietta had no road, and was too far from the markets and too far to get the expanding supplies of timber out (News 1889b). Following failure of the VDL Bank and the ensuing depression of the early 1890s, the Government supported 'agricultural railways of betterment' and better understood that 'it is not so much a 15-inch rainfall and good land which are the essentials . . . as it is the provision of cheap railway transport' (Roberts 1924, 402–3). This proved to be the case for the Ulverstone to Nietta Railway.

In 1905, Nichols, as MLC for Mersey and owner of Blackwood Park at Upper Castra, took up the baton on its behalf with Leven Stores' half-owner Arthur Ellis in forming the Ulverstone-Nietta Railway League. Though never seeking office, Ellis used his political influence nominating local men, mostly successfully, for Council, Alfred Tongs being one (News 1915e).

The Public Works Commission came from Hobart to meetings arranged by the Leven Council in Gunns Plains, Preston and Kindred in 1908 (News 1908c). The Ulverstone Board of Agriculture endorsed Nichols, its chairman, Tom Bingham and Upper Castra farmer William Dent to attend on its behalf to speak of the benefits for timber exports and dairying expansion that would come from the proposed line (News 1908b). Commissioners personally traced each of the three possible routes between 17 and 19 March, sometimes walking, seeing the problems of the huge descent from Preston to Gunns Plains. Local leaders accompanied them; they were Nichols, Dr McCall, Leven Council Warden George Barnard and Gunns Plains farmer William Henry. Evidence from sworn witnesses, all listed, was heard from acknowledged leaders among district farmers. Those from Preston were Theodore Wing, William Lewis, Kennedy Guest Sen., William Delaney and Walter Gillam. Tom Bingham, Alex Crawford and Arthur Hall (surveyor) were other witnesses we are familiar with. Because Nichols was so committed to the project, evidenced by his letter to the *North West Post* Editor, 15 July 1909, 4, it is reasonable that he was prepared with Johnstone from North Motton to supply local numerical data – comparative figures: 1891: produce grown 2,206 tons; annual value £17,000; but in 1907: 40,800 tons worth £36,116; estimated area under crop in 1908: 110,000 acres.

This evidence formed the body of the Commission's Report to Parliament (JPPP Vol. LIX, 1908, No. 18), and was aired in full in all the major newspapers (News 1908d). They took evidence from civil engineers Arthur Chaplin and James Barker about the route along the Leven River to Gunns Plains. A full

220   *Men and their land – doing what was best*

descriptive assessment of each can be found in the *Examiner* 6 June 1908, 9. The Commissioners favoured Route C via Gunns Plains, subject to survey. Route C was impractical in reality, because major obstacles were crossing the Leven River twice, rising 1,000 feet from the valley floor to the top of the hills before going down to Dooleys, and the extension to Nietta, Loongana and Moina had not been in the calculations of benefit and were barely alienated. This augured well for the eventual choice through North Motton and on to Preston and Nietta, which would have become apparent following survey, since Barren Hill was a comparatively short obstacle (3–5 miles) to circumvent.

No local men were Railway Commissioners during the critical years. Thomas Collett was an Ulverstone JP, so there was local representation on the Public Works Commission that investigated and reported on the possible routes in 'the most important and extensive district of West Devon' (News 1908b). The railway route was eventually surveyed in 1913 and work started; images in Field's 2016 book include the huge cuttings made through Barren Hill and work camps.

Eleven Preston farmers were so anxious to get 1,600 tons of potatoes to Ulverstone, they called a meeting at the hall in mid-1915 to make a deputation to the Railway Department to use the line on the down trip while the line was still under construction on the up-line towards Nietta (News 1915c) but agreement was unlikely, because by early December that year, the first test run with a loaded train was done by the Railway Commission, before the hand-over from Public Works (News 1915c). The line opened on 20 December 1915 with a formal ceremony at Preston Station In March 1916, 250 children and teachers from rural schools from Nietta, Preston and both Motton schools had their free day out to travel the railway (Field, 33–34).

The needs of self-sufficient farming families could generally be supplied by Ellis's Preston and Sprent stores, but for farmers, it was traffic both ways, confirmed by freight annual reports. Farmers used the railway for important deliveries of super-phosphate, seed, grain, potato sacks and lime. An enormous quantity of potatoes was transported out of the district as well as swedes, carrots and peas. Sheep, cattle and pigs were carried to and from the fortnightly sales in Ulverstone (Ken Brown). For a few years in the 1920s, there was even a passenger service for a half-day in Ulverstone to attend events like agricultural shows. Occasional excursions were organised for special sporting events in the mid-1930s, including the chopping carnival at Nietta (Field, 86–97). This railway was a significant milestone for Castra's yeoman farmers.

The railway, with five stops in the Castra district, created a number of additional jobs over its 40-year life. A new road for a shorter journey for Gunns Plains farmers to the Preston station opened in 1921 (JPPP Vol.LXXXLX, 1918, No.8; News 1918b; LSD35/1/1573; News 1921a). The Nietta terminus was the collection point for many small sawmills operating in virgin bush country south into Loongana, and in the Depression, Ulverstone timber merchant Edward Hobbs, Leven Councillor, MHA Darwin 1916–1934 and Gunns Plains farmer, used the rail to move timber from his Nietta sawmill and timber leases where five men

Men and their land – doing what was best   221

were kept employed. Unsurprisingly, he was a firm advocate of the railway. Sleepers, firewood, palings and sawn timber formed the timber mix. From 1938, pulpwood for Burnie's Australian Pulp and Paper Mill also contributed to freight out of Nietta (Field, 63).

Field (9–10) argued the railway would not have lasted out the Depression years of the 1920s and early 1930s had it not been for Nichols' firm commitment to the potato farmers served by the line. The main closure threat came after the poor planting year for potatoes in the 1930–1931 season and the timber industry being in a depression, when Nichols was Warden of Leven and MLC. Preston's Thomas Ewington was Councillor too. From Council's perspective any additional use by heavily laden trucks over Castra roads would result in additional maintenance costs at its expense, providing further impetus for Nichols' argument defending the line's continuation.

In early August 1931, Railway Commissioner F.P. St. Hill accompanied by L.C. Goss, the department's Devonport-based commercial agent, came to an Ulverstone conference to discuss the line's future with a representative group of electorate leaders. These were Legislative Council members A. Lillico, F.B. Edwards, H.A. Nichols and J. McDonald; the MHAs were T. D'Alton, Edward Hobbs, Phil Kelly and T.J. Butler. St. Hill was also chairman of the Transport Committee.

The conference was chaired by Alexander Lillico, who argued that services to 'back country' districts should be seriously considered as should methods of railway business management before any line closure was contemplated. St. Hill claimed no interest in closing the line, since he had been its surveyor and now regretted the enforced curve tightness that limited length going up-line. He was quoted as saying, 'The introduction of three-chain-curves had not had a good effect. It took three trains with empty trucks up to Nietta to provide for one train coming down. If they could take 40 trucks up in one load, it would be very different' (News 1931d). But, he said, the key to survival was patronage and figures showed that road transport from Gunns Plains and North Motton was affecting the freight volumes even though 'motor lorry' charges were often below viability.

Influential local men, all long-standing politicians, John Chamberlain, Stanley Wing, John Forsyth Wright and Thomas Ewington were all present and contributed their perspective. As he had been in the past, Nichols was well-versed in facts about each area in the Castra district that demonstrated the rate of progress since Crawford's 50,000-acre arrangement in 1865 (66 years previously); Loongana, 12 miles south of Nietta station, had 7,000 acres selected and much already cleared in the previous 25 years plus supplies of valuable timber; Gunns Plains had about 6,000 acres of the richest agricultural land in Tasmania; Lowana had about 5,000 acres of good potato ground; Preston comprised 'some thousands of acres of well-improved highest quality land and still more to clear'; Nietta had two sawmills and about 15,000 acres of alienated land and about the same area of well-timbered Crown Land; and the central Castra area also had many excellent farms. Nichols also provided freight-traffic comparisons and revenues from 1923. Nichols, with other locals, agreed with St. Hill's promise of a house-to-house canvas of users, and pointed out that extra road traffic would cause much more expense than the

222 *Men and their land – doing what was best*

short-term railway losses. St. Hill promised sympathetic consideration depending upon users' loyalty.

Goss conducted a less-than-thorough canvas of Castra farmers and woodsmen to identify freight demands and his Report to the Railway Commissioner was tabled by Nichols in the Legislative Council on 29 October 1931. After pointing out the Report's faults, he argued the line was 'vital to him and hundreds of settlers' and its closure would destroy a large portion of his life's work (News 1931e). The fight continued for Nichols well into 1932, as 'distinct' promises were broken, but the 1932 season had been good and heavy freights had been promised to Parliament as well the previous December's promises of support for the line by producers (News 1932b). Nichols' success in stalling the closure is even more laudable because two other North-West lines closed in those years (Stokes 1971, 22). Nichols died on 21 August 1940, fortunate not to see this portion of his 'life's work' closed forever (News 1940e).

Freight increased somewhat during the Second World War, partly because of petrol rationing, but expensive bridges to rebuild, unsuitable replacement rolling stock and flagging freight volumes created conditions where closure was inevitable (Stokes 1971, 27). Motor vehicles, especially cars, became a fact of life in the 1950s and, as the Peebles told me, having their own trucks gave farmers more flexibility to deliver and collect heavy goods and stock from Ulverstone, especially on the busiest day, Thursday market days. Furner's Hotel's Back Room offered a two-shilling all-you-can-eat meal in the 1930s that included farmers' horses getting a 'feed and rub down' in the hostelry's rear (Large 2004, 220). This was father David Peebles' regular day out.

The rail line closed on 7 December 1955, after 40 years serving its lumber and agricultural community (Field, 63). When the rails were removed by mid-1957, farmers were able to buy the land where the railway intersected their farms at the 'going rate' then fences could be removed. Kevin Johnson told me some parts of his land still has a government-owned easement where the previous owner did not take up the option, which he called 'a double-edged saw', because those acres would not be on the title if the farm was sold. One purchase example was on Johnson land in 1993 (AB567/1/6596).

The history of involvement in political affairs I have considered here gives plentiful evidence of the sustained influence exerted by and on behalf of the farmers in Castra. This may not have been unique in North-West agricultural communities, but the leaders operating from the close network of Castra farms did exert considerable influence despite their small numbers. They were passionate and energetic, easily proved from the recorded work of William Delaney, Hubert Nichols, Tom Bingham, John Chamberlain and Stanley Wing. Efforts made by them and others I have mentioned consistently supported their locality and its people, in ways that enhanced everyone's agricultural endeavours, Ulverstone's growth and their political capital. Castra men always supported the yeoman ideal through the exercise of benevolent patriarchy and leadership. The next section considers further enhancement through collaboration and acquisition of off-farm income.

Kinship collaboration and modes of additional income

As outlined in earlier chapters, oral testimonies provide insights into different aspects of yeoman farming experiences less likely to be covered by newspapers and parliamentary inquiries. Drawing on my interviews with farmers of over 50 years, this section examines extra economic benefits they enjoyed through mutual collaboration with family kin and neighbours, and through finding income-generating activities that assisted their farm cash-flow and helped their independence as yeoman farmers. At first glance, the former appears to offer nebulous gains in monetary terms. However, their gains came through the exchange value of labour or shared use of machinery. We met this mutuality and collaboration previously when discussing women's activities. It was crucially important to the men, who were able to achieve so much more with two or three working together than one man alone, and was particularly valuable in early settlement when there was little spare money to pay labourers year-round. But the shared use of harvesters, for instance, or use of a bullock team for specific jobs made economic sense. The practice helped maintain a 'level of comfort' in the farming families, as Kevin Johnson said:

> Nobody had money, everybody was poor. You had your gardens, you never went hungry, always had clean clothes, and your house was clean. And that was true of nearly all the farms in the district.

Perhaps the oldest man engaged in off-farm work was William Harding, Denzil's father, who still ran his farm but also worked as gardener at Sprent School (Selwyn Harding, grandson, 2018).

Denzil himself remembered the value of working with Ray Tongs next door and Ron Brown just below him. They went to school together and farmed together, especially at baling time. He needed a dozen helpers to harvest the peas with scythes in the 1970s before carting them to the pea vinery in Gawler, because the contractors would not go much farther than Barren Hill. Their reciprocation was economically essential.

Peas had come to prominence as a major crop during the Second World War, as shown by the Select Committee into the Rural Industries Bill in 1943. Ulverstone witnesses included George Arthur Ellis, representing the Ulverstone Industries Committee, Richard Parsons, an Ulverstone farmer, and E.H. Bentham, Ulverstone's District Agricultural Officer. The committee heard the North-West was very suited to growing peas for canning, and farmers were wholeheartedly growing the right variety for the proposed canning factory, though they were looking for government guarantees to cover their risk. Chamberlain (MHA) of Preston was a member of the Committee. A Rural Industries Board was created with powers related to primary industries, premises or factories to process, manufacture and market primary food products (Select Committee 1943, JPPP Vol.CXXIX, No.3). A processing factory began in February 1944 at Quoiba, near Devonport.

224 *Men and their land – doing what was best*

Working bullocks often involved the young lads. Georgie Johnson remembered his father John had two or three bullocks that wintered on the home-farm doing the heavy work. In summer, local bullock owners walked their beasts further south to Smith's Plains (beyond Nietta) for common grazing, but, in dry years, the boys would take them extra hay. Eight bullocks were owned by Tom Reid, whose farm was along Waringa Road. He hired them out to farmers to clear trees, and, when Georgie's older brothers Sidney and Gordon (Bill) wanted to clear their Waringa blocks, Reid's bullocks did the work in just a few days.

When a steer was killed for home consumption, the Johnson men would organise slaughtering and butchering, and cuts would be shared among the other Johnson households nearby. Much of the beef was corned to keep it well. Home-killed sheep were used up almost every week in big families. Sides of pork were salted and smoked for daily bacon rashers in a smokehouse; Ernest McCulloch had one to smoke bacon sides for home consumption (McCulloch, 15). A slaughterhouse was another essential small building on yeoman farming properties, and the Peebles' was still standing in the 1980s aerial photograph of the home-farm (Rob Peebles, pers. comm. 2021). Typical Victorian family farm households around 1911 needed 32 sheep, over 50 mixed poultry and made over 230lbs of butter from three cows for home consumption (Fahey 2011b, 245).

Georgie's next younger brother Tas also remembered that John had six farm horses as well as bullocks, before he moved into tractors. By the mid-late 1930s, John had invested in a truck and ran a carrying business with it, eventually having two or three trucks which he drove to farms all round Preston and central Castra, to take loads to one of the three railway stations – Preston, Dooley's Flats (on Rifle Range Road) or South Preston. Potatoes were his main rail freight. Not only did extra cash help the farm budget, but the trucks provided work for his sons as they grew older, or value for reciprocal bartering when he needed extra labour on his farm.

Georgie (born 1931) and his brother Edis (called Ned) Johnson (born 1930) were both employed at Preston station, loading potatoes and unloading freight from 1946 to 1955, and the limited timetable meant they were able to work in with the milking routine. 1952 was a bumper year for potatoes, over 2,100 tons (at 15 bags to the ton), a lot of man-handling confirmed by railway records (Field, 53–54). These two young fellows were happy to have wages, especially Georgie, who was living at home until 1952, when he got his farm for his 21st birthday. Ned married his wife Ruth in 1952, another reason he might remember it as a bumper year. Off-farm employment was always a factor for Ned, whose first small farm was opposite George Lewis' first grant, before he later bought land where the Preston station had stood, opposite Ellis' store. In addition to his own dairy herd, he was also Manager of Ellis' until it closed about 1971. After that, he obtained employment as a dairy inspector while keeping the farm going for his son Ian and wife Hilda to eventually take over.

Tas was about 20 when he first started farming on the main road south. After four years' experience on the home-farm for Sidney, at 18 he did national service at Brighton Army Camp. After marrying at 21, he and Merle continued mixed

Men and their land – doing what was best 225

farming until, at 34, he obtained a post as Sprent School Farm Manager. After selling to his brother Bill, they bought a 146-acre farm at Sprent and rented another block with good soil. They grew potatoes and milked cows, and he kept it until 1987 while he was employed by the Education Department. He grew 90 baconers (pigs) for the Sprent School farm once, and used to take up to 40 dozen eggs a week to the Ulverstone High School for cookery classes. Tas enjoyed sharing his farming knowledge with children, many of whom came from Preston and later had their own farms, until the 1992 closure of the farm. Tas helped another brother, Aubrey, on his Abbotsham cauliflower farm until formal retirement to Ulverstone.

After Ken Brown married Josie and bought their own farm opposite his father Joe's, they worked together with the typical yeoman mix of potatoes, oats and hay, about 20 milking cows, up to 30 pigs and sheep. But in the 1960s and 1970s, their main commercial crop without irrigation was peas, planted under contract to Edgells who also had bought the factory in Ulverstone. Joe and Ken would plant about ten to 12 acres when told by the company that also monitored the crop. The company sent machine mowers and rakes, then trucks to collect the crop to Gawler for threshing at the pea vinery, and from there, pods went to the Ulverstone factory.

It took 12 workers to do the harvesting and the farmer was responsible for finding the labour. All the young people locally got work during December and January, with a 4 a.m. start. The peas went for canning, but eventually the factory started freezing; the big brand name was Bird's Eye. This is an early example of contract farming, and the Browns were able to continue with peas longer than elsewhere because their farm was close to North Motton (Ken Brown 2018). The Peebles brothers tried peas too, but made nothing out of them, because 'the Edgells people wouldn't come far from Barren Hill to harvest', and, trialling poppies, they found them very demanding of the soil.

Pat Smith's eldest brother, Ernest (born 1930), would eventually take over their father's 100-acre farm, but he was always interested in tractors, even though his father still used draught horses. So, when he could, Ernest bought one and contracted out to neighbours, while working for his father. Pat thinks he may have owned the first tractor in Preston. Later he bought a second one. When he married, he built a house for himself and Betty at the opposite end of the farm, where they stayed farming until retirement in Ulverstone. Since it was understood that Ernest would take over the farm, their next brother, Edward (Ted) bought a truck and made his living with it around Preston until he left home to get married. From the huge volume of potatoes grown within ten miles, he was kept very busy from April to November just carting those. He was still operating his own trucking business in Ulverstone until 2016 when he was 85 years old. This is one instance of employment choices made by the non-inheriting farm sons. Pat's youngest brother, Alan, one of the first three children to complete Grade 10 at Sprent, was another, taking clerical work at a bank and eventually opening his own Ulverstone travel agency. Both are examples of business enterprise, running strongly in the Smith sons, consistent with the entrepreneurial characteristic of yeomen.

226 *Men and their land – doing what was best*

Figure 9.2 Henry Johnson's Preston Descendants, 1996.
Back row, left to right: Gollan (Georgie), John (Johnny), Keith (Kate), Amby (Tas), Jeanie.
Front, l. to r.: Aubrey (Aub), Denzil (Denny), Gordon (Bill), Alice (Darkie) Peebles, Sidney (Sid), Edis (Ned)
Source: Courtesy of Georgie and Iris Johnson, author's 2018 photograph from original.

The photograph in Figure 9.2 was taken in March 1996 when the 11 children of John and Jane Johnson were sitting next to the house their grandfather Henry built with his own labour in 1902 and where they had all grown up. That Johnson house has since been demolished.

The eldest, Sidney, was 78 years old and the youngest, Jeanie was 52 years old, giving us an example of the huge age difference in these typically large yeoman families. Marie Harrop (born 1952) remembers that in her childhood her father, Sidney, had seven brothers all farming in the Preston neighbourhood, giving them plenty of opportunity to collaborate. Because of this, she told me, her dad was often away working on one or other of their farms. With obvious reciprocity, her Uncle Johnny and Uncle Bill, each farming at South Preston, used to come to help Sidney with his potato harvesting.

In the Peebles family, there was collaboration across the generations. Henry (born 1890, second oldest) and David (born 1910, second youngest children of James Peebles) worked their neighbouring farms together. Bub and Rob (both born in the 1940s) told me:

> Henry and his wife Louie lived along Preston Road opposite the last post office. It had acreage and it included the paddock across the road that your

Men and their land – doing what was best   227

son farms now. There was land behind the house and another 40-acre block near the home-farm that came into the family's ownership. Henry had children, "Honest John" Gilbert (or Snow, as we used to call him) and George (who was farming, but didn't live a long life; he went to the Second World War but not out of Australia) and there was Helen and Amelia. Henry was so much older than Dad that Gilbert was nearly Dad's age. He and Dad used to get on really well; he used to work on the wharf at Burnie, and when he used to have holidays, it was nothing for him to come up here for a week. That was when we were growing up.

They went on to say that there was no money for wages in the period they were speaking of, so everyone had to work in together, because times were tough. When I asked how their father handled hard agricultural times, they said:

Dad managed alright. More ground was gradually cleared and you could grow more potatoes. Dad always reckoned it was the railway coming that made the difference – it opened Preston right up. Otherwise you couldn't get anything out.

I mentioned I had read that Preston was the busiest of the small lines in Tasmania. They replied:

That would be right, because Dad said, in those days, in every other paddock there were potatoes growing. And they would ship them off to Sydney from the station.

Rob continued:

You either struck it right or you struck it bad. The early 50s opened Preston up, there was more money about, so everyone had trucks, which meant the railway closed down. And tractors, too, the machinery gave farmers more flexibility.

That bumper crop in 1952 may have helped farmers to invest in trucks and facilitate consolidation of farms.

By the 1950s, the third generation of the 1900s settlers whose story we have been following were coming to adulthood and reaping the benefits of the hard work clearing land and the frugal, temperate, self-sufficient lives of their parents and grandparents, who followed Methodist tradition against idleness, following Wesley's dictum: 'Follow your labours with constant diligence. Redeem the time by saving all the time you can for the best purposes' (quoted by Thompson 1967, 88). Farmers and their wives and children certainly did this, tending to start early and finish late, with a 5 a.m. start usual for the first milking (Marie Harrop). Another example was 3:30 a.m. breakfast in readiness for the pea harvesting crew coming at 4 a.m., after family members had raked the peas into rows the evening

228 *Men and their land – doing what was best*

before (Margy King). At Smith's farm, Ernest raked on one tractor, working with his neighbour cutting on another in the same field, seen in a 1950s photograph in his wife Betty Hazel Smith's 'Preston Memories' book made for their son, Peter (2019). Farmers cut hay after dark by tractor light if rain threatened. Collaboration made this sort of timetable work better. So, too, the leaders made best use of their time in public affairs at various levels and still managed to run profitable enterprises on their lands. Working together, as Phil Chamberlain did with his father John, supported his father's activities in the public sphere.

Wadham wrote *Australian Farming 1788–1965* in 1967 and was able to reflect on twentieth-century agricultural progress in his lifetime. His observation (admittedly based on the mainland) was that the freedom farmers had had in choosing cropping and stocking regimens and varying methods guided or not by sound extension advice had resulted in steady yield improvements and cropping expansions. The move by farmers with little debt to enlarge farms and buy larger machinery using benefits from 1960s high prices had pushed land prices up beyond the reach of young men without capital seeking independence. His verdict was that:

> The period between 1950–1965 will go down in history as one of remarkable development in Australian farming in which the majority of rural districts attained standards of material prosperity for which their forefathers had struggled but never achieved.

(146–47)

What he could not foresee was that deregulation and removal of subsidies and protection exposed the farming environment, its agriculture and rural communities to global forces and consequent restructuring that Lawrence began noting in *Capitalism and the Countryside: The Rural Crisis in Australia* 1987. Vanclay characterized this as economic rationalism that would almost inevitably not go to plan, especially as 'farmers are not homogenous' and their world view influences their adoption of new ideas within their local operating environment (Vanclay 2016, 87). Their 'socio-cultural understanding' of the intrinsic qualities and values tied up in their land may, according to Vanclay, be the land's saving grace, because farmers will be less motivated to farm in ways that harm their land. The ideology of profit maximisation by often globally owned corporations at the cost of the land, seen in highly polluting Australian feedlots, or intensive dairying as found in New Zealand, contrasts sharply with the style of family farming featured throughout this work.

What of the next generation? Children born in the 1970s and 1980s spent early school years at Preston Primary School, then their secondary years in Ulverstone exposed to a wider world. Farming as a career seemed less attractive. During that agricultural transitionary period with low crop prices, farmers tried diversifying to improve income, sometimes with poor financial results (like the Peebles with poppies), or raising money to get bigger, all factors adding to the strain of farming, none of which would not have been lost on the growing children of that generation. Hardly surprising that off-farm careers looked tempting, and most boys

Men and their land – doing what was best   229

made different choices and yet, they were still imbued with family tradition of self-employed enterprise that derived directly from the yeoman ideal. For example, Mark Peebles trained as a plumber and gasfitter and went into partnership in Ulverstone with two other plumbers. Paul Brown did an apprenticeship as a boilermaker/welder and worked in Ulverstone for 15 years, before returning to help his father.

The Harding brothers, born a decade earlier, had already set the pattern – Selwyn gained varied farm-work experience when young and started his own business when he was 30 years old. Desmond became a contract bricklayer, and Kelvin had his own Devonport business while keeping his Preston farm until retirement. Despite the challenges of agricultural transition, the prevalence of family-owned, family-operated yeoman farms in Preston and the other Castra villages remained unchanged in 2000.

I have shown how public sphere political actions and local economic activities combined in progressing the wider community of hinterland and town. What motivated the outstanding leaders? I believe the comparative few built their robust enthusiasm and contribution on the shoulders of the many that attended meetings, supported motions, argued for, and encouraged, delegations and Members to push their interests in State Parliament. Through newspapers, they exploited deliberative protest that created influence to improve their farming interests. From the 1890s through to the 1950s, leaders evolved from Castra, and their efforts have been shown to have contributed greatly to the North-Western and other Tasmanian communities that engaged in self-sufficient mixed farming of the yeoman ideal.

Over generations, we saw men using collaboration, mutuality and reciprocal work in ways consistent with yeoman ideal traditions; the Crawfords started in the 1880s and those ways still exist with the Peebles brothers and three Brown father, son and grandson generations well into the twenty-first century. The farms, family descendants and, above all, the land their ancestors transformed survive because of the persistence of yeoman characteristics.

Conclusion

At the opening of this study, I asserted that family farming was intimately connected to the yeoman ideal from Australia's earliest beginnings. I set out to investigate how long that intimate connection endured and how it supported sustainable family farming. The setting for this rural social history was the family farming community that established in the parish of Castra from 1870. For a study extending over 140 years, it was appropriate to break my investigation down into themes. My starting point was the first selection of unalienated Crown Land by Anglo-Indian immigrant settlers that ensued from Colonel Crawford's vision. Contrary to widely held views about this project having failed, in Chapter 1 I showed that its outcome was more locally enduring and, because it spurred many others to migrate to the colony after long foreign service in India, their talents contributed beneficially to Tasmania.

The valuable work of surveyors was the theme of Chapter 2 and decisions made in Castra were shown to be of lasting value. The outcome of the Tasmanian Government's land and immigration policies from the 1850s, designed to encourage family farmers onto small farms, led to the new wave of agricultural settlers arriving there from the 1880s to 1910, discussed in Chapter 3. They brought inherited knowledge, agricultural expertise and enthusiasm to clear heavily forested land and create farms for their children and future generations. As first-generation Tasmanians, they exemplified the traditional characteristics of yeomanry so highly regarded by colonial governments. Before long they set up churches, schools, clubs and businesses that strengthened social and community ties between families. Government endorsement of closer settlement estates was shown in Chapter 4 to have been of limited success in this social environment founded upon land ownership. Soldier settlement was an historical arena that has attracted conclusions of failure across the Anglo-phone world, but, in Chapter 5, my investigation into over 30 local soldier settlers demonstrated that a localised in-depth approach of following their histories beyond the archival resources could tell a different story. The bonds of family and brotherhood were significant contributors to outcomes of overall success as many converted government leases into eventual ownership.

A major characteristic of the yeoman ideal relates to succession and inheritance of family farmland, and in Chapter 6 we followed the seven strategies of

DOI: 10.4324/9781003229841-11

Conclusion 231

inheritance employed by Castra families. Large families prevailed in Castra in line with trends of yeoman farming families elsewhere in Australia, but continued for longer into the twentieth century after the fertility transition had commenced in more urbanised areas. Tasmanian rural families were the last occupational group to limit fertility, and Castra fitted that finding. This meant there were many children growing up together, valuing their place in the evolving farming landscape. In Chapter 7, we saw that connection to land as children learnt from parental role-modelling and their own work contributions in preparation for adulthood as farmers or farmwives. During their adolescence, team sports were important opportunities to reinforce wider community and kinship bonds and explore the marriage market.

The women of Castra were indispensable in developing and maintaining the social and kinship bonds that 'glued' its society together, supporting their menfolk in companionate marriages and contributing income through their productive activities. In Chapter 8, we saw the active part they played in charitable and altruistic work during two world wars in the OAS, Red Cross and CWA, in addition to sustaining their churches' activities. The yeoman ideal associated with mixed farming and self-sufficiency was put under strain in the 1970s and 1980s as families became smaller and agricultural restructuring changed women's social and productive opportunities. Two different examples for managing that transitional period were examined. One demonstrated the need to expand farmland area for viability and focus all family labour on specialised large-scale dairying that effectively ended the wife's poultry enterprise. The other showed dairying continuing on existing land until the constraints of the milk processor's collection policy from small herds led to conversion to rearing beef calves.

Finally, Chapter 9 followed the theme of public sphere political input by the men, with particular focus on their capitalist commodity production in dairying and potato entrepreneurship. I argued that the yeoman ideal of independent self-sufficiency adapted to capitalist agriculture in Castra, as descriptions of Thomas Jefferson's idealism in America had previously showed. Overall, the evidence demonstrated that Castra produced a significant number of leaders for the size of the district, who took active grassroots farmer support as the catalyst to achieve gains for all Tasmanian small farmers. But the longevity and prosperity of Castra farms was linked to the willingness to engage in 'by-employment' entrepreneurship as well as strong collaboration with kin and neighbourhood labour, using reciprocity to mutual advantage.

I alluded to assertions of failure in both Anglo-Indian settlement and soldier settlement. My study has contributed evidence to refute them both. In the former, simplistic focus on Crawford and his family alone obscured evidence of other measures of success that had not received previous attention. No analogous settlement of Imperial officers to other colonies was discovered, although there were immigration pushes from other parts of the British Empire to attract such migrants. The Castra Association may have been unique, but otherwise, that history offers a comparative study opportunity.

232 *Conclusion*

In regard to soldier settlement, I demonstrated the value of extending research about individual soldiers' lives as long as possible, beyond the limit of archives that could reasonably be expected to focus on problems and demands while remaining silent on progress and success. There is scope for much more research at this 'micro-level' in any other community where returnees from the Great War settled. Due to lack of land, Tasmania soon decided to exclude British immigrant soldiers, so that offers additional research scope in mainland Australia or further afield. However, my study demonstrated the value of deep research into well-worn historical themes in a discrete focussed location to reframe over-generalised histories of the past.

Reflecting upon this history, I realised that each chapter could well be the subject of its own book, such was the potential to extend to additional topics. Just like the patchwork quilt of the North-West seen from the air, so the Castra Parish story provides us with a patchwork of social history over one and a half centuries. There is much scope for supplementary focussed research. Writing a longitudinal history entails exercising judgment over the areas or themes upon which to focus. Identification of yeoman characteristics in the Introduction set the selection model. The key was land ownership and yearning to retain and pass land onto succeeding generations. The yeoman farmers' land became inextricably entwined with their identity as being 'from' Preston or Gunns Plains or other Castra localities. Independence connected to self-reliance was another valued characteristic that did not preclude close kinship reciprocity. Commonality of circumstances mitigated against class consciousness and bonded the community together in ways that withstood change.

My study fills a gap in long-duration rural histories, and, across its breadth, I have shown that the persistence of the yeoman ideal was the underlying constant in Castra right into the twenty-first century. It was maintained through careful attention to affirmative inheritance strategies, collaborative family and kinship ties, and strong brotherhood. This evidence refutes assertions of the ideal's anachronism at Federation, and highlights that Tasmania cannot always be included appropriately in so-called 'Australian' histories when their research focus is on individual mainland states.

The yeoman ideal as manifested right across North-West Tasmania satisfied broad political aspirations common to all Australian jurisdictions for permanent, stable, politically conservative, large families on small family farms. This was found to be true of the Highlander Scots that Beer researched in Victoria's Western District, the Western Australian government enthusiasm for yeoman farmers that Tonts wrote about, Higman's small sugar farmers of northern New South Wales and Dingle's Victorian settlers following the lure of ownership to the Goulburn Valley, forested Gippsland and some Victorian Mallee districts. In New Zealand, Brooking told of yeoman farming surviving to the end of the twentieth century only to face the outcomes of water pollution from widespread intensification of 'industrialised' dairying as the new century arose.

The challenge for the Castra district was different. The dawning of the new century brought highly priced inducements for aging farmers to sell to plantation

Conclusion 233

forest operators, and varying-sized pockets of hard-won agricultural land with some of the best soils in the world were soon occupied by a 20-year monoculture crop and an unfortunate under-storey of blackberry. Remaining farmers had to come to terms with that change to their familiar surroundings. Their visiting retired aunts, uncles and sisters have expressed their sadness to me, seeing visible remnants of yeoman settler architecture in familiar homestead buildings demolished or gradually becoming derelict. The landscape, too, has changed dramatically, eroding strong connections to its beauty and diminishing each person's powerful feeling about place, their 'Preston-ness' assaulted.

Just as Brooking saw a glimmer of hope in New Zealand, so there is a glimmer in Castra, too. New people from the mainland and overseas have slowly taken up chances to buy small farms for their 'tree-change' and bring new skills and ideas for niche crops and livestock – garlic, mixed fresh vegetables, raspberries, peonies, buffaloes and Dexter cattle – or pick up the yeoman mixed farming ideal of a few beef cattle, sheep, heritage pigs and poultry for home-killed self-sufficiency. In America, responding to the 2008–2009 global financial crisis, Longman wrote extolling possibilities for 'neo-yeomen' to overcome work-life balance tensions, perhaps to work more from home, combining home and work to be less harried parents, with families getting a financial boost from home production. After widespread downsizing and higher unemployment, US government statistics showed that small-scale farms and farmers were increasing. Social movements are creating the drive to buy locally grown and locally produced food, evidenced by the immense growth in farmers' markets that offer scope to small producers to form relationships with their consumers. Other glimmers of hope for sustainable farming survival are even more widely spread. I suggest the yeoman ideal of independence remains alive still.

Acknowledgements

This book, and the doctoral thesis that preceded it, is my tribute to the valiant pioneers who were inspired to make a future among the Castra forests and cleave farmlands in the rich red soil they found. The families who made this a strong community provide us a rich story of resilience that has been a joy to recount, one that would have been much poorer without the interest and patience of the people of Preston/Castra who were happy to share memories of their past, a generous source of indispensable local knowledge. I am so grateful for their help.

The enthusiasm and support of other historians has been most important. Thank you to Stefan Petrow, Paul Turnbull, Philippa Mein Smith, Alan Mayne, Tom Brooking and Charles Faye, the last few for their encouraging remarks made about my work that were persuasive to the publishers. This work, in true regional history fashion, relied on geographic and cultural interpretation, and I thank Andrew Harwood for his perceptive comments.

On-going support from the School of Humanities at the University of Tasmania has been welcomed. The wonderful resources of Tasmanian Archives, both digital sources and personal help, make me realise how lucky Tasmanians are to have such commitment.

The editorial staff at Routledge could not have been more helpful in guiding this novice author through the publishing process and I thank them for doing such a good job.

The arrival of my first newborn grandson to Preston was the catalyst for my journey into the history of his home in the old Preston school and then later the whole district of Castra. Soon there were three, William, Pippin and Torren. I want them to know about their roots as second generation Tasmanians, but also about yeoman farming, their cultural inheritance from nineteenth-century Lincolnshire, now perpetuated by their farming parents. This book is dedicated to the boys.

The last thank you is to my husband whose great idea was to buy the school in the first place, and later the headmaster's house where we live next door to the family.

Abbreviations

ADB	*Australian Dictionary of Biography*
AJEA	*Australian Journal of Experimental Agriculture*
DPIPWE	Dept. Primary Industries, Parks, Water and Environment
HAJ	Journals of the House of Assembly
HTG	Hobart Town Gazette
HRA	*Historic Records of Australia*
JPPP	Journals and Printed Papers of Parliament
LCJ	Journals of the Legislative Council
LSD	Lands and Surveys Department, TA
LEx	*Launceston Examiner*
NLA	National Library of Australia
NWP	*North West Post*
NWAEBT	*North Western Advocate and Emu Bay Times*
PWD	Public Works Department
RSC	Royal Society Collection
TA	Tasmanian Archives, Hobart
THS	*Tasmanian Historical Studies*
THRA/THRAPP	*Tasmanian Historical Research Association/Papers and Proceedings*
UHM	Ulverstone History Museum
UPHG	Ulverstone Pictorial History Group
UTA	University of Tasmania Archives
UTas	University of Tasmania

Bibliography

Accounts and Papers, Parliament of Australia. 1916. "Report of the Conference of Representatives of the Commonwealth and State Governments and of the Federal Parliamentary War Committee in Respect of the Settlement of Returned Soldiers on the Land: Melbourne, 17–19 February 1916."

Acton, Amy. 1987. *More Than Tea and Talk: The Story of the CWA in Taroona, 1942–1946*. Taroona: CWA in Tasmania.

Adams, Jane H. 1988. "The Decoupling of Farm and Household: Differential Consequences of Capitalist Development in Southern Illinois and Third World Family Farms." *Comparative Studies in Society and History* 30 (3): 453–83.

Agriculture Council TA977. Council of Agriculture Reports 1891–1911. TA.

Agriculture Dept. TA370:

AD9-1-203 List All Bureaux in Tasmania, August 1930, and Memorandum: Ward to Wardlaw.

AD9-1-227 Riana Bureau.

AD9-1-228 Burnie Bureau.

AD9-1-246 6/44 Conference of Bureau Branches at Devonport 1929–31.

AD9-1-266 6/64 Re: North Western Conference – General Correspondence.

AD9-1-1032 6/3 List Bureaux Chairmen and Secretaries 1932–34.

AD9-1-1049 6/20 Conference of Bureau Branches at Burnie 1929–31.

AD9-1-2115 5/22 Dairying – Calf Clubs and Junior Farmers' Clubs.

AD9-1-21253 General Corres. Development & Migration Commission, 1928–9.

AD9-1-7868 20/9A Agricultural Organisations and Shows – Bureau of Agricultural Economics.

Quarterly Reports, Vol. 1–49. 1929–1978.

Agricultural Gazette: Journal of the Council of Agriculture. RSC, UTA. Issues of *Journal* and *Gazette* cited from Vol. I–IX from 1887–1902.

Aitken, Leanne. 2007. *A History of Stowport, Natone, Camena & Upper Natone, Tasmania*. Stowport, Tasmania: Author.

Alexander, Alison. 2003. *The Eastern Shore: A History of Clarence*. Rosny Park: Clarence City Council.

Alexander, Alison, ed. 2005. *Companion to Tasmanian History: Tasmanian Historical Studies*. Hobart: University of Tasmania.

Alexander, Alison. 2006. *Brighton and Surrounds: A History of Bagdad, Bridgewater, Brighton, Broadmarsh, Dromedary, Elderslie, Mangalore, Old Beach, Pontville and Tea Tree*. Gagebrook, Tasmania: Brighton Council.

Bibliography 237

Alexander. Alison. 2012. *The Southern Midlands: A History*. Longford: South Midlands Council.

Alexander. Alison. 2018. *'Duck and Green Peas! For Ever!' Finding Utopia in Tasmania*. Hobart: Fullers Publishing.

Alford. Katrina. 1984. *Production or Reproduction? An Economic History of Women in Australia, 1788–1850*. Melbourne: Oxford University Press.

Alston. Margaret. 1995. *Women on the Land: The Hidden Heart of Australia*. Kensington. NSW: University of New South Wales Press.

Alston. Margaret. 1998. "Farm Women and Their Work: Why Is Not Recognised?" *Journal of Sociology* 34 (1): 23–34.

Anon. c. 1875. *Colonel Crawford's Settlement in Tasmania*. Royal Society. Newspaper Cuttings to and from India. Collection Reference RS 2448.A260 later RS62. UTas Special and Rare Collections.

Anon. Preston School Newsletter 1975. June Peebles Collection.

Anon. 1989. *75 Years in Australia in the Service of Humanity, 1914–1989*. Launceston: Australian Red Cross Society. Tasmanian Division.

Anon. 1996. *Ulverstone Show Society Centenary Brochure 1896–1996*. Ulverstone: Libraries Tasmania. reprint 2018.

Anon. "Piguenit. William Charles (1836–1914)." *Australian Dictionary of Biography*. Accessed February 8. 2020.

Apex Club of Ulverstone. 1952. "Back to Ulverstone April 12–19. 1952." Centenary Celebrations 1852–1952 Official Publication and Programme.

Apple. Rima D. 1995. "Constructing Mothers: Scientific Motherhood in the Nineteenth and Twentieth Centuries." *Social History of Medicine* 8 (2): 161–78.

Appleby. Joyce. 1982. "Commercial Farming and the 'Agrarian Myth' in the Early Republic." *The Journal of American History* 68 (4): 833–49.

Archer. Daniel J.L. 2015. *Touring Tasmania in the 1880s: The Newspaper Articles of Theophilus Jones*. Youngtown: Self-Published.

Arnold. Rollo. 1981. *The Farthest Promised Land: English Villagers. New Zealand Immigrants of the 1870s*. Wellington: Victoria University Press.

Arnold. Rollo. 1994. *New Zealand's Burning: The Settlers' World in the Mid 1880's*. Wellington: Victoria University Press.

Atack. Jeremy. 1988. "Tenants and Yeomen in the Nineteenth Century." *Agricultural History* 62 (3): 6–32.

Atkinson. Alan. 1998. *History and the Love of Places*. Armidale. NSW: University of New England. Public Lecture. Armidale. November 17.

Atkinson. James. 1826. *An Account of the State of Agriculture*. Sydney.

Australian Bureau of Statistics. 1384. *Statistics – Tasmania 2002 and 2005*.

"Australian Cadet Corps." Accessed March 14. 2019. www.diggerhistory.info/pages-army-today/military_cadets.htm.

Australian Cemetery Index. 1808–2007. Wivenhoe. reprint 1966.

Australian Colonies Government Act. 1850 (UK). Royal Assent. August 5: 13 and 14 Vic.59.

Australian Electoral Rolls. 1903–1980.

Australian Journal of Experimental Agriculture. 1961-current. Clayton: CSIRO Publishing.

Australian Soldiers' Repatriation Act: Report of the Repatriation Commission for 1924–25. *Commonwealth Parliamentary Papers*. Vol. II. Paper No. 69. 1926–27–28.

Banks. Annette. 1999. *The Family of George Burgess and Ann Haines*. Austins Ferry: Author.

238 *Bibliography*

Barclay, Elaine, Roslyn Foskey, and Ian Reeve. 2007. *Farm Succession and Inheritance: Comparing Australian and International Trends*. Barton, ACT: Rural Industries Research and Development Corporation.

Bardenhagen, Marita E. 1993. *Lilydale – Conflict or Unity, 1914–1918: An Examination of a Tasmanian Rural District During the Great War*. Newnham: Author.

Barr, Neil. 2009. *The House on the Hil: The Transformation of Australia's Farming Communities*. Canberra: Land & Water Australia.

Bate, Weston. 1970. "The Urban Sprinkle: Country Towns and Australian Regional History." *Australian Economic History Review* 10 (2): 106–19.

Bayly, Christopher. 2012. "India and Australia: Distant Connections." In *Australian Historical Association Conference*. Unpublished Keynote Address, Adelaide, July.

Beckett, J.V. 1977. "English Landownership in the Later Seventeenth and Eighteenth Centuries: The Debate and the Problems." *Economic History Review* 30 (4): 567–81.

Beckett, J.V. 1982. "The Decline of the Small Landowner in Eighteenth- and Nineteenth-Century England: Some Regional Considerations." *The Agricultural History Review* 30 (2): 97–111.

Beer, Jane M. 1989. *Colonial Frontiers and Family Fortunes: Two Studies of Rural and Urban Victoria*. Parkville: University of Melbourne.

Belich, James. 2009. *Replenishing the Earth: The Settler Revolution and the Rise of the Anglo-World, 1783–1939*. Oxford: Oxford University Press.

Bennett, Don. 1947. "Junior Farmers' Clubs." *Tasmanian Education* 2 (6) (December): 22–23.

Bennett, Scott. "McCall, Sir John (1860–1919)." *ADB* 10. Accessed June 28, 2020.

Bennett, Scott, and Barbara Jean Bennett. 1979. *Biographical Register of the Tasmanian Parliament, 1851–1960*. Canberra: Australian National University Press.

Beresford, Quentin. 1983. "The World War One Soldier Settlement Scheme in Tasmania." *THRAPP* 30 (3): 90–100.

Berry, Wendell. 1987. "A Defence of the Family Farm." In *Is There a Moral Obligation to Save the Family Farm?*, edited by Garry Comstock, 348–60. Ames, Iowa: Iowa State University Press.

Besant, Bob. 1987. "Children and Youth in Australia 1860s–1930s." In *Mother State and Her Little Ones: Children and Youth in Australia, 1860s–1930s*, edited by Bob Besant and David Maunders, 1–19. Melbourne: Centre for Youth and Community Studies.

Betts, Captain T. 1832. *An Account of the Colony of Van Diemen's Land: Principally Intended for the Use of Persons Residing in India*. Calcutta.

Bigge, John Thomas. 1823. *Report of the Commissioner of Inquiry, on the State of Agriculture and Trade in the Colony of New South Wales and Van Diemen's Land*. London: Government Printer.

Binks, C.J. 1980. *Explorers of Western Tasmania*. Launceston: Mary Fisher Bookshop.

Black, George, ed. 1881. *Household Medicine*. London: N.Pub.

Black, George. 1927. *The Doctor at Home and Nurse's Guide*. London: Ward Lock & Co.

Blainey, Geoffrey. 1954. "Population Movements in Tasmania 1870–1901." *THRAPP* 3 (4): 62–70.

Blainey, Geoffrey. 1966. *The Tyranny of Distance*. South Melbourne: Sun Books.

Bolton, G.C. 1963. *A Thousand Miles Away: A History of North Queensland to 1920*. Canberra: Jacaranda Press.

Bonyhady, Tim. 2000. *The Colonial Earth*. Melbourne: Cambridge University Press.

Bouquet, Mary. 1982. "Production and Reproduction of Family Farms in South-West England." *Sociologia Ruralis* 22 (3–4): 227–44.

Bibliography   239

Boyce, James. 2020. *Imperial Mud: The Fight for the Fens*. London: Icon Books.

Braddon, Sir Edward, and Bennett, Scott, eds. 1980. *A Home in the Colonies: Edward Braddon's Letters to India from North-West Tasmania, 1878*. Hobart: Tasmanian Historical Research Association.

Breen, Shayne. 1990. "Land and Power in the District of Deloraine: 1825–75." *THRAPP* 37 (1): 23–33.

Breen, Shayne. 2001. *Contested Places: Tasmania's Northern Districts from Ancient Times to 1900*. Hobart: Centre THS, UTas.

Broeze, Frank J. A. 1982. "Private Enterprise and the Peopling of Australasia, 1831–1850." *Economic History Review*, 35 (2): 235–53.

Broinowski, L., ed. 1921. *Tasmania's War Record 1914–1918*. Hobart: Government of Tasmania.

Brooking, Tom. 1992. "'Busting Up' the Greatest Estate of All: Liberal Maori Land Policy, 1891–1911." *New Zealand Journal of History* 26 (1): 78–98.

Brooking, Tom. 1996. *Lands for the People? The Highland Clearances and the Colonisation of New Zealand*. Dunedin, NZ: Otago University Press.

Brooking, Tom. 2019. "'Yeo-Topia' Found . . . But? The Yeoman Ideal That Underpinned New Zealand Agricultural Practice into the Early Twenty-First Century, with American and Australian Comparisons." *Agricultural History* 93 (1): 68–101.

Brooks, Doug. September 11, 2014. Interview.

Broome, Richard, Charles Fahey, Andrea Gaynor, Katie Holmes. 2020. *Mallee Country: Land, People, History*. Melbourne: Monash Publishing.

Brown, A.G. 1980. *Law Relating to Land Boundaries and Surveying*. Queensland: Association of Consulting Surveyors.

Brown, Kenneth 'Ken'. June 9, 2018. Interview.

Brown, P.L. 1941. *Clyde Company Papers: Prologue: 1821–1835*. London: Oxford University Press, reprint 1956.

Bryant, Keith L. 1980. "The Role and Status of the Female Yeomanry in the Antebellum South: 'The Literary View'." *Southern Quarterly* 18 (2): 73–88.

Burroughs, Peter. 1967. *Britain and Australia 1831–1855: A Study in Imperial Relations and Crown Lands Administration*. Oxford: Clarendon Press.

Buxton, Gordon L. 1967. *The Riverina 1861–1891: An Australian Regional Study*. Melbourne: Cambridge University Press.

Buxton, Gordon L. 1974. "1870–1890." In *A New History of Australia*, edited by Frank Crowley, 165–215. Melbourne: Heinemann.

Cadell, Julie. 2003. "Introduction." In *Imperial Co-Histories: National Identities and the British and Colonial Press*, edited by J.F. Cadell and W.S. Haney, 3–17. Teaneck, NJ: Farleigh Dickinson University Press.

Calder, J.E. 1867. "Notes of a Journey: Through Parts of the Counties of Devon and Wellington, Tasmania, Undertaken in 1865." *Tasmanian Times*, May 18.

Calvert, Samuel. 1879. "The Dial Ranges and the Mouth of the Leven, Tasmania, Etching." *Illustrated Australian News*, August 2: 124.

Calhoun, Craig, ed. 1992. *Habermas and the Public Sphere*. New York: MIT Press.

Cameron, David. 2005. "Closer Settlement in Queensland: The Rise and Decline of the Agrarian Dream -1860s to the 1960s." In *Struggle Country: The Rural Ideal in Twentieth Century Australia*, edited by Graeme Davison and Marc Brodie, 6.1–6.21. Melbourne: Monash University ePress.

Cannon, Michael. 1973. *Life in the Country*. Melbourne: Nelson.

Carmichael, Henry. 1839. *Useful Hints to Emigrants*. London.

240 *Bibliography*

Cassidy, Jill. 1995. *The Dairy Heritage of Northern Tasmania.* Launceston: Queen Victoria Musuem and Art Gallery.

Castra & Co., Bombay, Meeting of Members, May 10, 1869, facsimile.

Castner, John L. 1878–1887. *Monthly and Rural Australian.* Sydney: Castner.

Cathcart, Michael. 1995. *Manning Clark's History of Australia.* Abridged 1962 publn. Ringwood: Penguin.

Chase, Dr. A.W. 1889. *Dr. Chase's Complete Receipt Book and Household Physician.* 3rd Memorial Ed. Detroit: F.P. Dickerson & Co.

Child, Elizabeth, and John Child. 1973. "Children and Leisure." In *Leisure and Society in Britain*, edited by Michael A. Smith, Stanley R. Parker, and Cyril S. Smith, 135–47. London: Allen Lane.

Claeys, Gregory. 2011. *Searching for Utopia: The History of an Idea.* London: Thames & Hudson Ltd.

Clark, J. C. D. 1985. English Society 1688–1832. Cambridge: Cambridge University Press.

Clarke, F.G. 1977. *The Land of Contrarieties: British Attitudes to the Australian Colonies 1828–1855.* Melbourne: Cambridge University Press.

Claydon, Anna. 2019. "Reading, Writing, Arithmetic: The Public School Curriculum 150 Years Ago." *Tasmanian Archive and Heritage Blog*, June 14. https://archivesandheritageblog.libraries.tas.gov.au/reading-writing-arithmetic-the-public-school-curriculum-150-years-ago/.

Clemens, Elisabeth S. 2010. "Democratization and Discourse: The Public Sphere and Comparative Historical Research." *Social Science History* 34 (3): 373–81.

Closer Settlement Board and Returned Soldiers – TA372:

AB3-1-75 image 8, Offer to sell, Hutton, Castra Road.

AB3/1/107, 1947/O, Offer of Jas Marshall's 296 acres, Upper Castra, Leven – A. W. Crawford, Ulverstone – images 1–8.

AB15/1/25 L. D Chilcott, Gunns Plains – House Plan Image 1.

AB15/1/214 R. W. Wing, Preston – House Plan Images 1–2.

AB17-1-97 840/22 – Werona Settlement, Gunns Plains J. V. Griffin.

AB17-1-306 44/26 Royal Commission on Soldiers' Settlement, Correspondence.

AB17-1-689 2/35 – Lot 5 Werona Estate, Gunns Plains – V. T. Bonney Lessee.

AB19/1/423 File 1302 E. Jupp, Preston.

AB19/1/664 File 1787 J. Dunham, Preston.

AB19/1/839 File 2290 H. Johnson, Dooleys Plains.

AB19/1/959, File 2575 W. E. Gillam, South Preston.

AB19/1/1025 file 2748 William Rockliff, Preston.

AB19/1/1261 File 4264 A. Smith, Preston.

AB19/1/1273 File 4291 A.L. Tongs, Preston.

AB40/1/26 Plans of Land Settled, Leven Municipality, pp. 9, 26, 30, 36, 43, 48, 58, 63.

AB125-1-1, 022. Register of Lots by Municipality. Leven and Penguin. 1917.

AB567-1-6596 010011 Grant Lot 35372 1.030ha. Nietta Railway Line Castra, Clifford G. Johnson, March 10, 1993.

Cole, G.D.H., and Raymond Postgate. 1961 (1938). *The Common People, 1746–1946.* London: Methuen University Paperbacks No. 22.

Cole, John. 1985. "Quantitative Reconstruction of the Family Ethos: Fertility in a Frontier Queensland Community." In *Families in Colonial Australia*, edited by Patricia Grimshaw et al., 57–63. Sydney: Allen & Unwin.

Colonial Secretary's Department, Tasmania:

Bibliography 241

Crawford. A. Letter to Colonial Secretary T. Chapman. August 1. 1874. (CSD10/32.494) now in NS1383/1/1.

Dry. Richard. Colonial Secretary. Tasmania. Letter to E.C. Bayley Esq. Secretary to Government of India. November 25. 1867. TL.PE 325.946 TAS.

Commins. P.. and Carmel Kelleher. 1973. *Farm Inheritance and Succession.* Dublin: Irish Farm Centre.

Commonwealth Year Book. No.5. 1912. *1901–1912.* 297. S. 6: Land Tenure and Settlement.

Commonwealth Year Book. No. 6. 1913. *1901–1913.* 233–34. S. 6: Land Tenure and Settlement.

Commonwealth Year Book. 1907–1913. 253. Tasmania Closer Settlement.

Condliffe. J.B. 1959. *New Zealand in the Making: A Study of Economic and Social Development.* 2nd Ed. London: George Allen & Unwin.

Connors. Tom. 1970. "Closer Settlement Schemes." *The Australian Quarterly* 42 (1): 72–85.

Cornish. Henry. 1880. *Under the Southern Cross.* Madras: Higginbotham & Co.: Melbourne: Penguin Books (facsimile version 1975).

Cosgrove. Patti. 2005. "The Country Women's Association in Tasmania (Inc)." *Companion to Tasmanian History* 88.

Crawford. Alexander M. 1900. *The Cyclopaedia of Tasmania.* Vol. 2. 282. Hobart: University of Tasmania.

Crawford. Colonel Andrew. 1865. "Letter to the Officers of H. M. Indian Services. Civil and Military." *National Library of Australia.* https://trove.nla.gov.au/work/237365020?keyword=%22Letter%20to%20the%20Officers%20of%20H.M.%20Indian%20Services%22.

Crawford. Memorandum to Purchasers of Castra Association. September 4. 1870.

Cresswell. Tim. 2004. *Place: A Short Introduction.* Malden. MA: Blackwell.

Crowley. F.K. 1954. "Immigration into Tasmania from the United Kingdom. 1860–1919." *Tasmanian Historical Research Association P.P.* 3 (6): 103–8.

Crowley. F.K. 1974. "1901–1914." In *A New History of Australia.* edited by F.K. Crowley. 260–311. Melbourne: William Heinemann Australia.

Cubit. Simon. 2001. "Tournaments of Value: Horses. Wilderness. and the Tasmanian Central Plateau." *Environmental History* 3: 395–411.

Cubit. Simon. and Nic Haygarth. 2016. *Mountain Stories: Echoes from the Tasmanian High Country.* Hobart: Forty South Publishing.

Curr. Edward. 1824. *An Account of the Colony of Van Diemen's Land Principally Designed for the Use of Emigrants.* London: George Cowie & Co.

The Cyclopedia of Tasmania (illustrated): An Historical and Commercial Review: Descriptive and Biographical, Facts, Figures and Illustrations: An Epitome of Progress: Business Men and Commercial Interests. Vol. 2. 1900. Hobart: Maitland & Krone. Digitised Version. Tasmanian Archives.

Dallas. Kenneth Mackenzie. 1968. *Horse Power.* Hobart: Fullers Bookshop.

Dallas. Kenneth Mackenzie. 1970. *Water Power: Past and Future.* Hobart: Fullers Bookshop.

Danbom. David B. 1991. "Romantic Agrarianism in Twentieth-Century America." *Agricultural History* 65 (4): 1–12.

Daniels. Kay. 1982. "Women's History." In *New History: Studying Australia Today.* edited by G. Osborne and W.F. Mandle. 32–50. Sydney: George Allen & Unwin.

Darian-Smith. Kate. 2002. "Up the Country: Histories and Communities." *Australian Historical Studies* 33 (118): 90–99.

242 Bibliography

Darian-Smith, Kate, and June Factor. 2005. *Child's Play: Dorothy Howard and the Folklore of Australian Children*. Melbourne: Museum Victoria.

Davidson, Bruce R. 1981. *European Farming in Australia: An Economic History of Australian Farming*. Amsterdam: Elsevier Scientific.

Davidson, Bruce R. 1997. "An Historical Perspective of Agricultural Land Ownership in Australia." In *A Legacy Under Threat? Family Farming in Australia*, edited by Jim Lees, 15–58. Armidale, NSW: University of New England.

Davison, Graeme. 2005. "Country Life: The Rise and Decline of an Australian Ideal." In *Struggle Country*, edited by Davison and Brodie, 1.1–1.15. Melbourne: Monash University ePress.

Davison, Graeme, and Marc Brodie, eds. 2005. *Struggle Country: The Rural Ideal in Twentieth Century Australia*. Melbourne: Monash University ePress.

Dawson, Carl Addington, and Eva R. Younge. 1940. *Pioneering in the Prairie Provinces: The Social Side of the Settlement Process*. Toronto: Palgrave Macmillan.

Day, Lincoln H. 1965. "Family Size and Fertility." In *Australian Society*, edited by A.F. Davies and Solomon Encel, 156–67. Melbourne: F.W. Cheshire.

Demos, John. 1970. *A Little Commonwealth: Family Life in Plymouth Colony*. New York: Oxford University Press.

Dempsey, Kenneth C. 1990. *Smalltown: A Study of Social Inequality, Cohesion and Belonging*. Melbourne: Oxford University Press.

Dempsey, Kenneth C. 1992. *A Man's Town: Inequality Between Women and Men in Rural Australia*. Melbourne: Oxford University Press.

Denholm, Bernard. 1980. *The Irrepressible Mr Dooley: The Biography of J.M. Dooley, Government Surveyor, Explorer, and Pre-Federation Politician in Tasmania 1855–1891*. Hobart: Author.

Denney, Ray. 1993. *The Long Way Home*. Scotsdale, TAS: Author.

Denoon, Donald. 1983. *Settler Capitalism: The Dynamics of Dependent Development in the Southern Hemisphere*. Oxford: Clarendon Press.

Development and Migration Commission: Interim Report 1927–8. 1928. *Commonwealth Parliamentary Papers*, vol. 8. Canberra: Govt. Printer.

Dingle, Tony. 1984. *The Victorians: Settling*. Vol. 2. Melbourne: Fairfax, Syme and Weldon.

Dingo, Sally. 2010. *Unsung Ordinary Men: A Generation Like No Other*. Sydney: Hachette Australia.

"Discovering Anzacs." National Archives of Australia. Various Records.

Doveri, Andrea. 2000. "Land, Fertility, and Family: A Selected Review of the Literature in Historical Demography." *Genus* 56 (3–4): 19–59.

Duffus, J. E. and G. R. Johnstone. 1982. "The Probable Long Association of Beet Western Yellows Virus with the Potato Leaf Roll Syndrome in Tasmania." *AJEA 22* (117): 353–6.

Dugan, C.C. 1920. *A Century of Tasmanian Methodism, 1820–1920*. Hobart: Tasmania Methodist Assembly.

Dumbleton, Major A. 1869. Letter to *Times of India* via Lt. Col. J Fulton, and Castra & Co. TC.P 325.946 DUM. TA.

Durdin, Joan. 1991. *They Became Nurses: A History of Nursing in South Australia, 1836–1980*. Sydney: Allen & Unwin.

Easteal, B. V. 1971. "Farming in Tasmania 1840–1914." Master of Arts, University of Tasmania.

Edgar, Don. 1991. "Foreword." In *Images of Australian Families: Approaches and Perceptions*, edited by Kathleen Funder. Melbourne: Longman Cheshire.

Eldershaw. P.R. 1962. "Introduction." In *Journals of the Land Commissioners for Van Diemen's Land 1826–28*, edited by Anne McKay. i–xxv. Hobart: UTas & THRA.

Electoral Rolls. Leven 1949, 1954.

Education, Dept. TA63-TA1297: Preston Primary School:
ED9-1-913 File 915/1911 Establishment of a Central School at Preston 1/11/1911-30/9/1914.

Evans. S. et al. 1923. *The Home Physician and Guide to Health Book*. Warburton: Signs Publishing Co., first published by Mountain View Pacific Press.

Factor, June. 1979. "Fragments of Children's Play in Nineteenth Century Australia." Royal Historical Society of Victoria: 8th Biennial Conference, Melbourne, UTas Special Collections.

Fahey, Charles. 1988. "Rv: Marilyn Lake's *Limits of Hope*." *Australian Historical Studies* 23 (90): 140–41.

Fahey, Charles. 2011a. "'A Splendid Place for a Home': A Long History of an Australian Family Farm 1830–2000." In *Outside Country: Histories of Inland Australia*, 231–66. Kent Town: Wakefield Press.

Fahey, Charles. 2011b. "The Free Selector's Landscape: Moulding the Victorian Farming Districts, 1870–1915." *Studies in the History of Gardens and Designed Landscapes* 31 (2): 97–108.

Fairburn, Miles. 1989. *The Ideal Society and its Enemies: The Foundations of Modern New Zealand Society, 1850–1900*. Auckland, NZ: Auckland University Press.

Fairfax, William. 1859. *Handbook to Australasia Being a Brief Historical and Descriptive Account of Victoria, Tasmania, South Australia, New South Wales, Western Australia, and New Zealand*. Melbourne: Wm. Fairfax & Co. (Tasmanian pp. 97–129).

Fawcett, John. 1818. "Blest Be the Tie That Binds." Accessed June 7, 2020. https://hymnary.org/person/Fawcett_John1740.

Fedorowich, Kent. 1997. *Unfit for Heroes: Reconstruction and Soldier Settlement in the Empire Between the Wars*. New York: Manchester University Press.

Fedorowich, Kent. 2002. "Ex-Servicemen and the Politics of Soldier Settlement in Canada and Australia, 1915–1925." *War & Society* 20 (1): 47–80.

Fennell, Rosemary. 1981. "Farm Succession in the European Community." *Sociologia Ruralis* 21 (1): 19–43.

Fenton, James. 1891. *Bush Life in Tasmania: Fifty Years Ago*. Launceston: Mary Fisher Bookshop, reprint 1964.

Fenton, James, and James Backhouse Walker. 1884. *A History of Tasmania: From Its Discovery in 1642 to the Present Time*. Hobart: Melanie Publications, reprint 1978.

Ferber, Michael. 1978. "Blake's Idea of Brotherhood." *PMLA* 93 (3): 438–47.

Field, Bill. 2017. *Methanga to Nietta: A History of the Ulverstone to Nietta Railway*. Melbourne: Author.

Fields, Barbara J. 1985. "Rv: Steven Hahn: The Roots of Southern Populism: Yeoman Farmers and the Transformation of the Georgia Upcountry, 1850–1890." *International Labor and Working-Class History* 28 (Fall): 135–39.

Fink, Deborah. 1986. *Open Country, Iowa: Rural Women, Tradition and Change*. Albany, NY: State University of New York Press.

Flynn, Revd. John. 1910. *The Bushman's Companion*. Melbourne: Presbyterian Church of Victoria.

Ford, Lacy K. 1986. "Yeoman Farmers in South Carolina Upcountry: Changing Production Patterns." *Agricultural History* 60 (4): 17–37.

244   Bibliography

Ford, Ruth. 2011. "'I Shut My Eyes and Picture our Place': Gardens, Farm Landscapes and Working-Class Dreams in 1930s-1940s South-Eastern Australia." *Studies in the History of Gardens and Designed Landscapes* 31 (2): 109–20.

Friedberger, Mark. 1983. "The Farm Family and the Inheritance Process: Evidence from the Corn Belt, 1870–1950." *Agricultural History* 57 (1): 1–13.

Friends, Sassafras Parents. 1988. *Sassafras: A History of Its Settlement and People*. Devonport: Sassafras School P&F Association.

Frost, Lionel. 1983. "Victorian Agriculture and the Role of Government, 1880–1914" (PhD, Monash University).

Frost, Warwick. 1997. "Farmers, Government, and the Environment: The Settlement of Australia's 'Wet Frontier', 1870–1920." *Australian Economic History Review* 37 (1): 19–38.

Fry, Ken. 1985. "Soldier Settlement and the Australian Agrarian Myth After the First World War." *Labour History* 48: 29–43.

Fulkerson, W. J., R. C. Dobos and P. J. Michell. 1986. "Relationship Between Predicted Energy Requirements and Measured Energy Intake of Dairy Cattle at Pasture", *AJEA* 26 (5): 523–6.

Fulton, James Robert Jnr. Copies of Diaries 1898–99. NS394/1/1. TA.

Gagan, David P. 1976. "The Indivisibility of Land: A Microanalysis of the System of Inheritance in Nineteenth-Century Ontario." *Journal of Economic History* 36 (1): 126–41.

Gammage, Bill. *Narrandera Shire*. Narrandera, NSW: Narrandera Shire Council, 1986.

Gardam, Faye. 2000. "Doctor Casey and the Forth Irish Farmers." *THRAPP* 47 (2): 79–82.

Garkovich, Lorraine, and Janet Bokemeier. 1988. "Agricultural Mechanization and American Farm Women's Economic Roles." In *Women and Farming*, edited by Wava G. Haney and Jane B. Knowles, 211–28. Boulder: Westview.

Garton, Stephen. 1996. *The Cost of War: Australians Return*. Melbourne: Melbourne University Press.

Gasson, Ruth, and A.J. Errington. 1993. *The Farm Family Business*. Wallingford, Oxon: CAB International.

George, Karen. 1999. *A Place of Their Own: The Men and Women of War Service Land Settlement at Loxton After the Second World War*. Kent Town: Wakefield Press.

Gerrard, Andrea. 2015. "Open to All Who Served or Was It? Soldier Settlement for Tasmanian Aboriginal Soldiers." *Tasmanian Historical Studies*, 20: 23–39.

Gillespie, William M., and Cady Staley. 1855. *A Treatise on Surveying*. New York: D. Appleton, reprint 1887.

Godfrey, Margery, and Ron Neilson. 1992. *Born of Necessity: Dairy Cooperatives of Tasmania 1892–1992*. Burnie: United Milk Tasmania Ltd.

Goldthorpe, J.E. 1987. *Family Life in Western Societies: A Historical Sociology of Family Relationships in Britain and North America*. Cambridge: Cambridge University Press.

Gollan, Anne. 1978. *The Tradition of Australian Cooking*. Canberra: Australian National University Press.

Goode, Luke. 2005. *Jurgen Habermas: Democracy and the Public Sphere*. London: Pluto Press.

Goodrich, Colin, and Kaylene Sampson. 2008. "A Place for Community." In *Making Sense of Place*, edited by Frank Vanclay, Matthew Higgins, and Adam Blackshaw, 257–67. Canberra: National Library of Australia Press.

Goody, J., Joan Thirsk, and E.P. Thompson, eds. 1976. *Family and Inheritance: Rural Society in Western Europe*. Cambridge: Cambridge University Press.

Bibliography 245

Goold, J. T. (researcher). "Brett Family Tree." https://www.wikitree.com/genealogy/BRETT.

Gothard, Janice. 1989. "'Radically Unsound and Mischievous': Female Migration to Tasmania, 1853–1863." *Australian Historical Studies* 23 (93): 386–404.

"Governors' Dispatches." 1914–15. *Historical Records of Australia*. ed. Library Committee. Series I. Vol. 1. Sydney: Commonwealth Parliament.

Grabb, Ernest G. 1990. *Theories of Social Inequality: Classical and Contemporary Perspectives*. 2nd Ed. Canada: Holt, Rhinehart and Winston.

Grant, Duncan. n.d. "Churches of Tasmania." Accessed March 10, 2020. www.churchesoftasmania.com/.

Grattan, Brian, and Jon Moen. 2004. "Immigration, Culture, and Child Labor in the United States, 1880–1920." *Journal of Interdisciplinary History* 34 (3): 355–91.

Gray, H.L. 1910. "Yeoman Farming in Oxfordshire from the Sixteenth Century to the Nineteenth." *The Quarterly Journal of Economics* 24 (2): 293–326.

Green, Frank C. 1956. *A Century of Responsible Government, 1856–1956*. Hobart: Shea, Government Printer.

Green, Julian. 2018. *A Legal History of Tasmania: An Historic Perspective on the Development of the Tasmanian Constitution and Law*. South Arm, Tasmania: Author.

Green, Kevin. 1990/91. "Immigration as an Alternative to Transportation: Van Diemen's Land 1852–55." *Centre for THS* 3 (1): 150–65.

Greven, Philip. 1970. *Four Generations: Population, Land and Family in Colonial Andover, Massachusetts*. Ithaca: Cornell University Press.

Griffiths, Tom. 1987. *Beechworth: An Australian Country Town and Its Past*. Melbourne: Greenhouse.

Grimshaw, Patricia, Charles Fahey, Susan Janson, and Tom Griffiths. 1985. "Families and Selection in Colonial Horsham." In *Families in Colonial Australia*, edited by C. McConville, P. Grimshaw, and E. McEwen. 118–37. Sydney: Allen & Unwin.

Grimshaw, Patricia, and Graham Willett. 1981. "Women's History and Family History: An Exploration of Colonial Family Structure." In *Australian Women: Feminist Perspectives*, edited by Norma Grieve and Patricia Grimshaw. 134–55. Melbourne: Oxford University Press.

Haines, Robin. 1994. "Indigent Misfits or Shrewd Operators? Government-assisted Emigrants from the United Kingdom to Australia, 1831–1860." *Population Studies* 48 (2): 223–47.

Haines, Robin. 1997. *Emigration and the Labouring Poor: Australian Recruitment in Britain and Ireland, 1831–60*. Houndmills: Palgrave Macmillan.

Hall, Edward S. 1880. *Information for the Early Detection and Care of Cases of Typhoid Fever and Diphtheria: Especially for Residents in Districts Where Medical Attendance Is Not Immediately Available*. Hobart.

Hall, G. Stanley. 1904. *Adolescence: Its Psychology and its Relations to Physiology, Anthropology, Sociology, Sex, Crime, Religion and Education*. Vol. 2. New York: Appleton.

Halpern, David. 2005. *Social Capital*. Cambridge: Polity Press.

Hancock, W.K. 1972. *Discovering Monaro: A Study of Man's Impact on His Environment*. Cambridge: Cambridge University Press.

Haney, Wava G., and Jane B. Knowles. 1987. "Women and Farming." *Signs* 12 (4): 797–800.

Haney, Wava G., and Jane B. Knowles. 1988. *Women and Farming: Changing Roles, Changing Structures*. Boulder: Westview Press.

Hareven, Tamara K. 1977. "Family Time and Historical Time." *Daedalus* 106 (2): 57–70.

246 *Bibliography*

Harding, Denzil. July 26, 2018. Interview.

Harper, Norman D. 1954. "Rv: J. R. Skemp, *Memories of Myrtle Bank*." *Pacific Historical Review* 23 (2): 185–86.

Harrop, Marie nee Johnson. December 12, 2017. Interview.

Harwood, Andrew Geoffrey. 2011. "The Political Constitution of Islandness: The 'Tasmanian Problem' and Ten Days on the Island." PhD, UTas.

Hay, Douglas, and Nicholas Rogers. 1997. *Eighteenth-Century English Society: Shuttles and Swords*. Oxford: Oxford University Press.

Haygarth, Nic. 2011. "Theophilus Jones: Tasmania Through Anglo-Indian Eyes in the 1880s and 1890s." *Launceston Historical Society P & P* 23: 51–74.

Haygarth, Nic, and Tim Jetson. 2018. *From Calf Clubs to Field Days: A History of Junior Farmers and Rural Youth in Tasmania*. Launceston: Rural Youth Organisation of Tasmania Inc.

Heathcote Papers. Ulverstone History Museum.

Heer, David M. 1968. "Economic Development and the Fertility Transition." *Daedalus* 97 (2): 447–62.

Henderson, John. 1832. *Observations on the Colonies of New South Wales and Van Diemen's Land*. Calcutta.

Henderson, Karla A., and Jean S. Rannells. 1988. "Farm Women and the Meaning of Work and Leisure: An Oral History Perspective." *Leisure Sciences* 10 (1): 41–50.

Henderson, Rena 2016. "Life and Death of a Rural School: The Case of Preston Primary School, Tasmania." Master of Arts (History), University of New England.

Henslowe, Dorothea. 1978. *Our Heritage of Anglican Churches in Tasmania*. Moonah: Author.

Hensley, Gerald. 1990. "Godley, John Robert." *Dictionary of New Zealand Biography*. Accessed September 26, 2021, https://teara.govt.nz/en/biographies/1g12/godley-john-robert.

Henzell, Ted. 2007. *Australian Agriculture: Its History and Challenges*. Collingwood: CSIRO Publishing.

Hetherington, Penelope. 1992. "Child Labour in Swan River Colony, 1829–1850." *Australian Historical Studies* 25 (98): 34–52.

Hetherington, Penelope. 1998. "The Sound of One Hand Smacking: History, Feminism and Childhood." *Journal of Australian Studies* 22 (59): 2–7.

Heywood, Colin. 2001. *A History of Childhood: Children and Childhood in the West from Medieval to Modern Times*. Cambridge: Polity Press.

Heywood, Colin. 2018. *A History of Childhood*. 2nd ed. Cambridge: Polity Press.

Higman, B. W. 1968. "Sugar Plantations and Yeoman Farming in New South Wales." *Annals of the Association of American Geographers* 58 (4): 697–719.

Hirst, John Bradley. 1973. *Adelaide and the Country, 1870–1917: Their Social and Political Relationship*. Carlton: Melbourne University Press.

Hobart Town Gazette.

Hodson, Elizabeth. 2002. "Tennis and Picnics." *THRAPP* 49 (2): 102–6.

Hofstadter, Richard. 1956. "The Myth of the Happy Yeoman." *American Heritage* 7 (3): 1–6.

Hogg, Jabez. 1853. *The Domestic Medical and Surgical Guide for the Nursery, the Cottage and the Bush*. London: Ingram, Cooke & Co.

Holbrook, Carolyn. 2018. "Rv: The Last Battle: Soldier Settlement in Australia, 1916–1939." *Labour History* 114: 228–30.

Holmes, Katie, Susan Martin, and Kylie Mirmohamadi. 2008. *Reading the Garden: The Settlement of Australia*. Melbourne: University Publishing.

Bibliography 247

Holmes, Michael. 2014. *Vanishing Towns: Tasmania's Ghost Towns and Settlements*. Hobart: Forty South Publishing.

Hood, Mildred. 1908–1911. Diary (Typescript Copy). NS568/1. TA.

Hudson, J.C. 1969. "A Location Theory for Rural Settlement." *Annals of the Association of American Geographers* 59 (2).

Hunter, Kathryn M. 2001. "The Drover's Wife and the Drover's Daughter: Histories of Single Farming Women and Debates in Australian Historiography." *Rural History* 12 (2): 179–94.

Hunter, Kathryn M. 2004. *Father's Right-Hand Man: Women on Australia's Family Farms in the Age of Federation, 1880s–1920s*. Melbourne: Australian Scholarly Pub.

Hunter, Kathryn M., and Pamela Riney-Kehrberg. 2002. "Rural Daughters in Australia, New Zealand and the United States: An Historical Perspective." *Journal of Rural Studies* 18 (2): 135–43.

Hurst, W.N. 1938. *A Short History of Land Settlement in Tasmania*. Hobart: Tasmanian Government.

Hyland, Raymond. 2014. *Gunns Plains Honour Roll: World War 1 Centenary, 1914–2014*. Ulverstone: Author.

Hyland, Raymond. 2017. *The History of Gunns Plains Through the Newspapers*. Cooee, Tasmania: Author.

Illich, Ivan. 1973. *Tools for Conviviality*. New York: Harper & Row.

Immigration Agents Department TA211:

CB7-12-1-4 Book 12, Passengers on the *Whirlwind*. 1855.

CB7-12-1-5 Book 18, pp. 16–17, Richard and Harriet Hall.

CB7-12-1-6, pp. 150–51, James Monahan and Alice Dooley and Children.

CB7-12-1-9, pp. 282–83, Jane Mong.

CB7-12-1-12, p. 16, James and Robert Peebles.

CB7-12-1-12-00155, William and Elizabeth Brett and Extended Family.

Inglis, K.S. 1974. *The Australian Colonists: An Exploration of Social History, 1788–1870*. Melbourne: Oxford University Press.

Jackson, H.R. 1987. *Churches and People in Australia and New Zealand, 1860–1930*. Wellington, NZ: Allen & Unwin.

Jeans, D.N. 1975. "The Impress of Central Authority Upon the Landscape: South-Eastern Australia 1788–1850." In *Australian Space, Australian Time: Geographical Perspectives*, edited by J.M. Powell and M. Williams, 1–17. Oxford: Oxford University Press.

Jensen, Joan M. 1988. "Butter Making and Economic Development in Mid-Atlantic America from 1750 to 1850." *Signs* 13 (4): 813–29.

Johnson, Amby 'Tas'. May 1, 2017, December 19, 2017. Interviews.

Johnson, Georgie, and Iris. April 22, 2018. Interview.

Johnson, Glennys. July 5, 2017, August 8, 2017, November 7, 2018. Interviews.

Johnson, Kevin. October 10, 2018. Interview.

Johnson, Murray. 2005. "'Promises and Pineapples': Post-First World War Soldier Settlement at Beerburrum, Queensland, 1916–1929." *Australian Journal of Politics and History* 51 (4): 496–512.

Johnston, J.G. 1839. *The Truth: Letters Just Received from Emigrants to the Australian Colonies*. Edinburgh.

Jones, Alan. 1989. *Backsight: A History of Surveying in Colonial Tasmania*. Hobart: The Institution of Surveyors, Australia Inc., Tasmanian Division.

Jones, Elise F. 1971. "Fertility Decline in Australia and New Zealand 1861–1936." *Population Index* 37 (4): 301–38.

248 Bibliography

Jones, Lu Ann, and Nancy Grey Osterud. 1989. "Breaking New Ground: Oral History and Agricultural History." *Journal of American History* 76 (2): 551–64.

Jones, O. 1997. "Little Figures, Big Shadows: Country Childhood Stories." In *Contested Countryside Cultures*, edited by P. Cloke and J. Little, 158–79. London: Routledge.

Jones, Rebecca. 2017. *Slow Catastrophes: Living with Drought in Australia.* Clayton: Monash University Publishing.

Joyce, Alfred. 1942. *A Homestead History: Being the Reminiscences and Letters of Alfred Joyce of Plaistow and Norwood, Port Phillip, 1843 to 1864.* Melbourne: Melbourne University Press.

Just, Thomas C. 1892. *The Official Handbook of Tasmania.* 5th Ed. London: Government of Tasmania.

Kaine, G.W., E.M. Crosby, and R.A. Stayner. 1997. *Succession and Inheritance on Australian Family Farms.* Armidale, NSW: Rural Development Centre.

Kee, Robert. 1972. *The Green Flag: A History of Irish Nationalism.* Middlesex: Penguin Books.

Kellaway, Roger George. 1989. "Geographical Change in Tasmanian Agriculture During the Great Depression." PhD, UTas.

Keneley, Monica. 2002. "Closer Settlement in the Western District of Victoria: A Case Study in Australian Land Use Policy, 1898–1914." *Journal of Historical Geography* 28 (3): 363–79.

Kenyon, C.M. 1971. "Thomas Jefferson." In *Encyclopedia Britannica*, vol. 12, 985–89. Chicago: Chicago University Press.

Kiddle, Margaret. 1961. *Men of Yesterday: A Social History of the Western District of Victoria, 1834–1890.* Melbourne: Melbourne University Press.

King, Margaret 'Margy' nee Peebles. November 14, 2017. Interview.

Kirkendall, Richard S. 1987. "A History of the Family Farm" in *Is there a moral obligation to save the family farm?*, edited by G Comstock, 80–5. Ames, Iowa: Iowa State University Press.

Kitteringham, Jennie. 1975. "Countrywork Girls in Nineteenth Century England." In *Village Life and Labour*, edited by Raphael Samuel, 73–138. London: Routledge & Kegan Paul.

Kociumbas, Jan. 1997. *Australian Childhood: A History.* St Leonards, NSW: Allen & Unwin.

Koller, Andreas. 2010. "The Public Sphere and Comparative Historical Research: An Introduction." *Social Science History* 34 (3): 261–90.

Kremzer, Ed. 2005. "Red Cross." *Companion to Tasmanian History* 302–3.

Lake, Marilyn. 1985. "Helpmeet, Slave, Housewife: Women in Rural Families 1870–1930." In *Families in Colonial Australia*, edited by Patricia Grimshaw, 173–85. Sydney: Unwin & Allen.

Lake, Marilyn. 1987. *The Limits of Hope: Soldier Settlement in Victoria 1915–1938.* Melbourne: Melbourne University Press.

Land Surveys Department (TA69):

AF395-1-22 Map – Exploration Chart 10 – Devon, River Blythe and tributaries (sheet 1); AF395-1-23 (sheet 2); AF395-1-24 (sheet 3) – surveyor James Dooley. 1862.

AF395-1-13 Map – Historic Plan 15 – 'Walsh's New Map of Tasmania', 200722.1868.

AF396-1-668 Map – Devon 57 – Bradworthy, Plan of Lots to McCulloch and Other Landholders – Surveyor Richard Hall (Field Book 289).

AF396-1-671 Map – Devon 60 – Castra, Plan of Lots Including Leven River and Various Landholders – Hall (Field Book 291).

Bibliography 249

AF396-1-672 Map – Devon 61 – Castra. Lots incl Ulverstone to Nietta Tramway. Gawler Rv. Hall (Field Book 292).

AF396-1-673 Map – Devon 62 – Castra. Lots Including Road from Dooleys Plains to Ulverstone. West Gawler River – Hall (Field Book 293).

AF396-1-674 Map – Devon 63 – Abbotsham. Plan of Lots of Various Landholders – Hall (Field Book 348).

AF396-1-675 Map – Devon 64 – North Motton. Rough Plan of Lots of Various Landholders – Hall (No Field Book Noted) 1872.

AF396-1-676 Map – Devon 65 – North Motton. Gawler Rv. Roads from Castra to Ulverstone. to Gunns Plains and Nietta to Ulverstone. Hall (Field Book 295).

AF396/1/702 Map – Devon 90 – Leven River Meets Bass's Strait. Sheet 1. Including Gawler River and Port Fenton – Surveyor James Scott. landholder Clerke. A.

AF396-1-704 Map – Devon 92 – North Motton. Plan Under the *Closer Settlement Act* of the Isandula Estate. Gawler River and Road to Ulverstone – Surveyor A. C. Hall (Field Book 304). 1909.

AF396-1-709 Map – Devon 97 – Upper Castra. Castra Settlement Subdivision for Closer Settlement Purposes Including Ulverstone to Nietta Road and Various Landholders – Hall.

AF396-1-710 – Devon 98 – Parish of Castra. Werona Estate Subdivided Under Closer Settlement Act Including Leven Rv. Road to Gunns Plains. A. C. Hall (Field Book 319).

AF396-1-719 – Devon 106 – Parish of Castra. Parts of Lots 7425 and 7426 Including Baxters Road. Main Road and Various Landholders.

AF398/1/676 Map – Devon Roads 43 – Township of Ulverstone – Dooley. 1865.

AF398-1-731 Map – Devon Roads – County of Devon New Road Through Castra & Nietta. Hall. 1886.

AF721/1/735 Map – U/5 – Town of Ulverstone. various landowners. surveyor Dooley (Field Book 1240). 1861.

AF819-1-45 Castra C62.

AF819-1-60 Map – Crawford C49 [now Central Castra].

AF819-1-176 Map – Leven L24.

Applications from returned soldiers featured in chapter 6: LSD190/1/18. LSD190/1/138. LSD190/1/286. LSD190/1/340. LSD190/1/503. LSD190/1/667. LSD190/1/734. LSD190/1/788. LSD190/1/929. LSD190/1/1014. LSD190/1/1184. LSD190/1/1298. LSD190/1/1237. LSD190/1/1297. LSD190/1/1342. LSD190/1/1419. LSD190/1/1420. LSD190/1/1453. LSD190/1/1454. LSD190/1/1472. LSD190/1/1473. LSD190/1/1557. LSD190/1/1746. LSD190/1/1582. LSD190/1/1845. LSD190/1/1875.

LSD166-1-496. p. 1. Soldiers' Free Selections – Draft Calculations. December 14. 1922.

LSD166/1/434 522/SS Ira Stanley Charles Cullen. 1922–1928.

LSD 190 Applications to Lease Land Under the Returned Soldiers Settlement Act 1916.

LS2480 – Road – Gunns Plains to Nietta Tram. 1919. LSD35/1/1573. Notices of Acquisition of Land.

Surveyor General's Letterbook LSD72-1-3 Colonial Secretary and Under-Treasurer.

Lang. J.D. 1892. *Queensland Parliamentary Debates*. Vol. 65.

Large. Tony. 2004. *Ulverstone: Sunshine and Storm, 1920–1940*. Ulverstone. Tasmania: Author.

Laverty. J.R. 1995. "The Study of City and Regional History in Australia." *Australian Journal of Politics & History* 41 (s1): 103–38.

Lawrence. G.A. 1987. *Capitalism and the Countryside: The Rural Crisis in Australia*. Sydney: Pluto Press.

250   Bibliography

Learmonth, Alex. 185-. *Collection of Materials Relating to St Andrew's Immigration Society*. Launceston: St Andrew's Immigration Society.

Legislation – Tasmania:

Administration and Probate Act. 1935.
Administration and Probate Act (No. 2). 1935.
Closer Settlement Act. 1906.
Closer Settlement Act. 1911.
Council of Agriculture Act. 1891.
Crown Lands Amendment Act. 1895.
Dairy Produce Act. 1932, 1935.
Dairy Products Act. 1933, 1934 Amendment.
Department of Agriculture Act. 1897.
Immigration Act. 1867.
Land for Settlers from India Act. 1867.
Lands for Settlement Act. 1901.
Manure Adulteration Acts. 1893, 1898.
The Potato Disease Act. 1909.
Potato Diseases Amendment Act. 1909.
Potato Diseases Amendment Act (No. 49). 1909.
Potato Marketing Board Establishment Act. 1952.
Potato Rate Reduction Act. 1909–10.
Probate Duties Act. 1868.
The Public Schools Act. 1868.
The Public Schools Amendment Act. 1873.
The Public Works Act. 1865.
Returned Soldiers Settlement Act. 1916.
State Advances Act. 1907.
The Succession Duty Act. 1865.
Waste Lands Act. 1858.
Waste Lands Act. 1859.
Waste Lands Act. 1863.
Waste Lands Act No. 3. 1865.
Waste Lands Act No. 4. 1867.

Lees, Jim. 1997. "The Origins of the Legacy." In *A Legacy Under Threat? Family Farming in Australia*, edited by Jim Lees, 1–13. Armidale, NSW: University of New England.

Leonard, Susan Hautaniemi, Glenn D. Deane, and Myron P. Gutmann. 2011. "Household and Farm Transitions in Environmental Context." *Population and Environment* 32 (4): 287–317.

Lewis Family File. UHM.

Linn, Rob. 1999. *Battling the Land: 200 Years of Rural Australia*. St Leonards, NSW: Allen & Unwin.

Lloyd, Alan, and Bill Malcolm. 1997. "Agriculture and the Family in the Economy." In *A Legacy Under Threat? Family Farming in Australia*, edited by Jim Lees, 59–80. Armidale: University of New England.

Lohrey, Jeanie nee Johnson. February 27, 2019, March 13, 2019. Interviews.

Longman, Phillip. 2009. "A Return to Yeomanry. Break out Your Mulching Fork: Jeffersonian Farmers are Back!" *Foreign Policy* 173 (July–August): 29.

Lopatin, Nancy. 1998. "Refining the Limits of Political Reporting: The Provincial Press, Political Unions and the Great Reform Act." *Victorian Periodicals Review* 31 (4): 337–55.

Bibliography 251

Lower. Arthur R.M.. and Harold Adams Innis. 1936. *Settlement and the Forest Frontier in Eastern Canada*. Vol. 9. Toronto: Palgrave Macmillan.

Lundie. Rob. and Dr Joy McCann. 2015. "Executive Summary." *Commonwealth Parliament from 1901 to World War 1*. May 4. Accessed May 2. 2019. www.aph.gov.au/About_Parliament/.

MacKellar. Maggie. 2004. *Core of My Heart, My Country: Women's Sense of Place and the Land in Australia & Canada*. Carlton: Melbourne University Press.

MacKenzie. Eneas. 1853. *The Emigrant's Guide to Australia. with a Memoir of Mrs. Chisholm*. London: Clark Beeton & Co.

MacKintosh. W.A. 1940. "Foreword." In *Pioneering in the Prairie Provinces: The Social Side of the Settlement Process*. edited by Carl Dawson and Eva Younge. ix.Toronto: Palgrave Macmillan.

MacIntyre. Stuart. 1986. "The Succeeding Age 1901–1942." In *Oxford History of Australia*. Vol. 4. Melbourne: Oxford University Press.

Macmillan. David S. 1967. *Scotland and Australia 1788–1850: Emigration, Commerce and Investment*. Oxford: Clarendon Press.

Martin. Alan. 2001. "Immigration Policy Before Federation." In *The Australian People*. edited by James Jupp. 39–44. Cambridge: Cambridge University Press.

Martin. Christopher. 1992. "War and After War: The Great War and its Aftermath in a Tasmanian Region: The Huon. 1914–1926. Master of Arts. University of Tasmania.

Matheson. John. 1838. *Counsel for Emigrants*. Aberdeen.

Mathias. Peter. 1969. *The First Industrial Nation: An Economical History of Britain 1700–1914*. London: Methuen & Co.

Matthews. Hugh. Mark Taylor. Kenneth Sherwood. Faith Tucker. and Melanie Limb. 2000. "Growing-Up in the Countryside: Children and the Rural Idyll." *Journal of Rural Studies* 16 (2): 141–53.

Matthews. Jill. 1984. *All Her Labours: Working It Out*. Sydney: Hale & Iremonger.

Mauss. Marcel. 1925. *The Gift: The Form and Reason for Exchanges in Archaic Societies*. London: Routledge. reprint 2001.

May. Andrew. 2009. "Ideas From Australian Cities: Relocating Urban and Suburban History." *Australian Economic History Review* 49 (1): 70–86.

Mayne. Alan and Stephen Atkinson. eds. *Beyond the Black Stump: Histories of Outback Australia*. Kent Town. SA: Wakefield Press. 2008.

Mayne. Alan and Stephen Atkinson. eds. *Outside Country: Histories of Inland Australia*. Kent Town. SA: Wakefield Press. 2011.

Mays. Herbert J. 1981. "A Place to Stand: Families. Land and Permanence in Toronto Gore Township 1820–1890." *Canadian Historical Papers* 15 (1): 185–211.

McAloon. Jim. 2002. *No Idle Rich: the Wealthy in Canterbury and Otago, 1840–1914*. Otago. NZ: University of Otago Press.

McCarty. J.W. 1978. "Australian Regional History." *Australian Historical Studies* 18 (70): 88–105.

McCarty. J.W. 1980. "The Inland Corridor." *Australians: 1888: Bicentennial History Bulletin* 5: 33–48.

McCulloch. Clarence. 1998. *Past by Distance Softened*. UHM. Tasmania. Unpublished Memoir.

McEwen. Ellen. 1985. 'Family History in Australia: Some Observations on a New Field." In *Families in Colonial Australia*. edited by Grimshaw et al.. 186–197. Sydney: Allen & Unwin.

252   *Bibliography*

McIntyre, W. David, and W.J. Gardner. 1971. *Speeches and Documents on New Zealand History*. Oxford: Oxford University Press.

McKay, Anne. 1962. *Journals of the Land Commissioners for Van Diemen's Land 1826–28*. Hobart: UTas & THRA.

McMurry, Sally. 1992. "Women's Work in Agriculture: Divergent Trends in England and America, 1800 to 1930." *Comparative Studies in Society and History* 34 (2): 248–70.

McMurry, Sally. 1994. "American Rural Women and the Transformation of Dairy Processing, 1820–80." *Rural History* 5 (2): 143–53.

McQuilton, John. 1993. "Comparative Frontiers: Australia and the United States." *Australasian Journal of American Studies* 12 (1): 26–46.

Meikle, Bronwyn. 2011. "Squatters and Selectors: The Waste Lands Acts of Tasmania, 1858–1868." *THS* 16: 1–23.

Meikle, Bronwyn. 2014. "Cronyism, Muddle and Money: Land Allocation in Tasmania under the Waste Lands Acts, 1856–1889." PhD, UTas.

Melville, Henry. 1833. *Van Diemen's Land: Information Likely to be Interesting to the Emigrant*. London: Smith, Elder and Co.

Mercer, Peter. 1978. "From Raj to Rustic." *THRAPP* 25 (3): 71–95.

Meredith, Louisa. 1852. *My Home in Tasmania*. London: John Murray.

Metcalf, Bill. 2008. "The Encyclopedia of Australian Utopian Communalism." *Arena* 31: 47–61. Accessed June 27, 2017.

Metcalf, William. 2008. "Utopian Communal Experiments in Tasmania: A Litany of Failure?" *Communal Societies* 28 (1): 1–26.

Methodist Church in Tasmania, NG499:

NS499-1-2643 Ulverstone Circuit – Preston Home Mission Station – Church Leaders Meetings 1927–1948.

NS499-1-2644 Ibid – Ladies Church Aid Minute Book. 1937–42.

NS499-1-3213 Ibid – Ladies Guild Minutes. 1935–45.

NS499-1-3214 Ibid – Ladies Guild Minutes. 1946–53.

NS499-1-3218 Ibid – Minutes of Ladies Guild Meetings. 1966–74.

NS499-1-3219 Ibid – Minutes of Ladies Guild Meetings. 1974–77.

NS499-1-3220 Ibid – Minutes of Ladies Guild Meetings. 1977–1986.

NS499-1-3222 Ibid – Office Bearers, Ladies Fellowship. 1936–1986.

NS499-1-3233 Ibid – a) Christian Endeavour Roll Book 1937–47 b) Christian Endeavour Minute Book. 1939–48.

NS499-1-3277 Ibid – Members Roll. 1966–9.

Milton, E. 1968. "Soldier Settlement in Queensland After World War I." BA Hons diss., University of Queensland.

Moore, Gloria J. 1988. "Anglo Indians." In *The Australian People*, edited by James Jupp, 434–38. Cambridge: Cambridge University Press.

Morell, Lionel. 2011. "The Influence of India on Colonial Tasmanian Architecture and Artifacts." *Launceston Historical Society P&P* 23: 25–38.

Morgan, Sharon. 1991. *Land Settlement in Early Tasmania: Creating an Antipodean England*. Cambridge: Cambridge University Press.

Moyle, Helen. 2015. "The Fall of Fertility in Tasmania in the Late 19th and Early 20th Centuries." PhD, Demographic and Social Research Institute, Australian National University.

Moyle, Helen. 2020. *Australia's Fertility Transition: A Study of 19th-Century Tasmania*. Canberra: ANU Press.

Bibliography 253

Murchie. Robert Welch. William Allen. and John Franklin Booth. 1936. *Agricultural Progress on the Prairie Frontier*. Vol. 5. Toronto: Palgrave Macmillan.

Murphy. Kate. 2005. "Rural Womanhood and the 'Embellishment' of Rural Life in Urban Australia." In *Struggle Country*. 2.1–2.15. Melbourne: Monash University ePress.

Murphy. Kate. 2010. *Fears and Fantasies: Modernity. Gender and the Rural-Urban Divide*. New York: Peter Lang.

Neale. R.S. 1981. *Class in English History 1680–1850*. Oxford: Blackwell.

Neth. Mary. 1988. "Building the Base: Farm Women. the Rural Community. and Farm Organizations in the Mid-West. 1900–1940." In *Women and Farming*. 339–55. Boulder: Westview.

Neth. Mary. 1994. "Gender and the Family Labor System: Defining Work in the Rural Midwest." *Journal of Social History* 27 (3): 563–77.

Neth. Mary. 1995. *Preserving the Family Farm: Women, Community and the Foundations of Agribusiness in the Mid-West, 1900–1940*. Baltimore: Johns Hopkins University Press.

Newby. Howard. 1987. *Country Life: a Social History of Rural England*. London: Cardinal.

News. 1837. "Hobart Town Arrivals." *Hobart Town Courier*. July 14: 2.

1854a. "Immigration Information." *Manchester Weekly Times*. February 18: 11.

1854b. "Dowling. Launceston Immigration Aid Society. Letter." *LEx*. June 22: 3.

1860a. "Immigration." *Cornwall Chronicle*. April 21: 5.

1860b. "The Mersey and the Leven." *LEx*. September 20: 3.

1866a. "Cholera in Bengal and Calcutta." *Madras Times*. March 14. in *Queenslander*. April 28: 10.

1866b. "Letter from the Englishman." *Madras Times*. May 11. in *Mercury*. August 11: 4.

1866c. "Letter from Crawford." *Mercury*. August 21: 2.

1866d. "Immigration Information." *Manchester Weekly Times*. September 8: 7.

1867a. "Immigration Information." *Manchester Weekly Times*. September 7: 2.

1867b. "Editorial." *Mercury*. October 2: 2: October 8: 3.

1868a. "Castra Tramway Tenders." *LEx*. July 30: 3.

1868b. "Editorial Re Public Education." *Mercury*. August 17: 2.

1869a. "Castra Tramway Tenders." *LEx*. February 2: 2: February 11: 3.

1869b. "Dumbleton to Castra & Co. Then to Editor." *Times of India*. October 6.

1869c. "Castra & Co. Letter to Editor." same problem as above. *Times of India*. December 3.

1870. "J.D. Lang." *Clarence and Richmond Examiner*. March 29: 2.

1871. "Yeoman Class of Settlers." *Clarence and Richmond Examiner*. November 28: 2.

1872. "Young. Letter to Castra & Co." *Times of India*. July 9.

1874. "Launceston-Westbury Railway." *Weekly Examiner*. April 18: 10 and June 27: 3.

1876. "Anglo-Indian. 'Tasmania for Anglo-Indians'." *Times of India*. December 5.

1877a. "Editorial." *Clarence and Richmond Examiner*. October 23: 2: November 13: 2.

1877b. Crawford. "Letter to the Editor." *Times of India*. December 21.

1880a. "A Year's Residence in Tasmania and Australia." *Bombay Gazette*. July 24. in *Devon Herald*. September 9: 2.

1880b. "Ulverstone Agricultural Show." *LEx*. December 6: 4.

1881. "Ulverstone Agricultural Show." *Tasmanian*. December 10: 1167.

1884a. "Crown Lands Guide." *Mercury*. April 24: 2.

1884b. "Crawford Brothers. Advert." *LEx*. July 14: 1.

1885. "Crawford Brothers. Land for Sale." *LEx*. March 25: 1.

1886. "Braddon. House of Assembly." *Mercury*. September 3: 3.

254 Bibliography

1887a. "Robert Robson, Advert." *LEx*, February 5: 1.

1887b. "Castra IOOF Lodge Meeting." *NWP*, April 16: 2 and April 21: 2.

1887c. "J. Sturzaker, Castra, Land Agency." *NWP*, April 19: 3.

1887d. "Castra IOOF Lodge Meeting." *Tasmanian*, July 23: 13.

1887e. "C.A. Jarvis & Co., Land Agency." *Examiner*, August 22: 1; September 22: 1.

1887f. "Crawford Brothers, Advert." *NWP*, August 30: 3.

1887g. "Crawford Brothers, Business Notices." *Examiner*, September 22: 1.

1888a. "A Trip to the Interior." *NWP*, May 15: 4.

1888b. "S Aust Land Comm., Crown Lands for Sale." *Launceston Examiner*, June 2: 1.

1888c. "Sports at Castra." *NWP*, December 22: 4.

1889a. "Marriage, Robert Crawford to Helen." *NWP*, January 3: 3.

1889b. "Meeting, Castra." *NWP*, June 21: 2.

1889c. "Castra News: By a Former Splitter." *NWP*, November 28: 2.

1890a. "Life in Tasmania." *Manchester Weekly Times*, March 1: 4; March 8: 4; March 15: 4.

1890b. "Rifle Balls – Dancing Till Daybreak." *NWP*, April 24: 4.

1890c. "Dairymen's Assn." *Mercury*, May 21: 2.

1890d. "Ulverstone." *Tasmanian*, October 25: 25.

1890e. "Gala at Castra." *NWP*, November 6: 4.

1890f. "Dedicating New Sprent Church of England." *Tasmanian*, November 8: 25.

1891a. "What Shall We Do with Our Sons?" *Wagga Advertiser*, March 12, April 4: 5.

1891b. "Dairymen's Assn. Tasmania." *Tasmanian*, February 28: 10.

1892. "Ulverstone Local Directory. Finch." *NWP*, March 5: 8.

1894a. "Deyrah Cheese, G. & A. Ellis of Ulverstone." *Mercury*, July 10: 2.

1894b. "Upper Castra Notes." *LEx*, September 26: 7.

1895a. "Road Construction in West Devon." *NWP*, March 21: 4.

1895b. *NWP*, July 18: 2.

1896. "Council of Agriculture Visit." *NWP*, October 10: 2.

1897. "Peter Pry, Castra Correspondent." *NWP*, July 29: 3.

1898a. "President Fincham's Address." *The Surveyor*, January.

1898b. "A Trip to Gunns Plains." *NWP*, March 3: 4.

1898c. "Out and About." *NWP*, March 17: 4.

1898d. "Eliza Fulton, Death Notice." *NWP*, April 19: 2.

1899a. "The Late Colonel Crawford: His Life." *NWAEBT*, February 17: 3.

1899b. "Crown Lands for Sale." *NWAEBT*, March 27: 4.

1899c. "Out and About." *NWP*, June 8: 4.

1899d. "Out and About." *NWP*, June 15: 4.

1899e. "Sports at Preston." *NWP*, December 9: 2.

1900a. "School at Preston." *NWAEBT*, February 6: 2.

1900b. "Church of England, Gunns Plains." *NWAEBT*, June 22: 2.

1900c. "Parliament, 11 July." *Mercury*, July 12: 4.

1900d. "Inter-State Settlement." *Mercury*, July 13: 2; *Mercury*, August 11: 2.

1900e. "Leven Road Trust." *NWAEBT*, September 4: 4.

1901a. "Land for Settlement." *Mercury*, August 30: 4.

1901b. "Parliamentary Onlookers." *Mercury*, September 4: 2.

1902a. "Union of Wesleyan Branches." *NWP*, February 25: 2.

1902b. "Land for Settlement Act." *Mercury*, June 18: 3.

1903a. "Preston Meeting Re Potatoes." *NWP*, January 16: 3.

1903b. "Editorial." *Mercury*, April 17: 4.

1903c. "W.C. Lewis. Letter." *NWAEBT.* December 24: 4.

1903d. "W. Delaney. Letter." *NWAEBT.* December 30: 4.

1904a. "George H. Wing and W.C. Lewis. Letters." *NWAEBT.* January 4: 4.

1904b. "Sports at Preston." *NWAEBT.* March 21: 3.

1904c. "Business Notices." *NWAEBT.* August 17: 4.

1904d. "Round the Farms: Preston District." *NWP.* October 2: 4.

1904e. "Death of Mrs. Guest." October 29: 2.

1904f. "Accident." *NWAEBT.* November 18: 2.

1904g. Rockliff. "Tenders to Clear and Timber Purchase." *NWAEBT.* December 24: 2.

1905a. "Victoria." *Mercury.* May 17: 4.

1905b. William Redmond. "Irish Issues." Sydney *Telegraph,* in *Mercury.* May 29: 8.

1905c. "The Northern Agitation. Available Crown Land." *NWAEBT.* October 7: 8.

1906a. "Leven Road Trust." *NWP.* April 14: 2.

1906b. "Closer Settlement Bill." *Examiner.* July 14: 8 and *NWAEBT.* July 14: 5.

1906c. "Round the Farms – Preston District." *NWP.* October 2: 4.

1906d. "State Parliament." *Examiner.* November 2: 6.

1907a. *Express and Telegraph.* Adelaide. September 20: 4.

1907b. "Commercial' Report." *NWP.* May 8: 2.

1907c. "Preston Athletic Assn." *NWAEBT.* September 26: 2.

1907d. Cheshunt Estate. "On the Land." *Farmer and Settler,* May 10: 6.

1908a. "Hilder. NW Agricultural Progress. No. 6." *NWAEBT.* May 20: 4.

1908b. "Reps. Chosen." *NWP.* February 25: 3.

1908c. "Public Works Railway Meetings." *NWAEBT.* March 7: 4 and March 11: 2.

1908d. "Railway Report." *Mercury.* May 30: 5: *NWAEBT,* May 30: 6 and June 1: 3: *NWP.* April 4: 5.

1908e. "Church and School at Lowana." *NWP.* May 28: 2.

1908f. "Potato Diseases: Opinion in the North-West." *Mercury.* August 20: 6.

1908g. "Council of Agriculture Annual Report." *NWAEBT.* September 30: 2.

1908h. "West Devon Ag. Socy. Nichols Delegate." *Examiner.* March 27: 4.

1908i. "Dairymen's Assn." *Daily Post.* September 29: 4.

1909a. "Sick Babies in Summer." *NWEBT.* March 29: 4.

1909b. "The Potato Industry: Threatened by Disease." *NWP.* May 21: 3.

1909c. "Potato Diseases: Resolutions Endorsed." *NWP.* July 29: 4.

1909d. "Isandula Applicants." *Daily Post.* June 25: 4.

1909e. "Cooperative Dairying: Go in For Dairying." *NWAEBT.* June 30: 4.

1909f. "Dairymen's Conference." *NWP.* July 15: 4.

1909g. "Commercial." *NWP.* September 29: 2.

1909h. Irish Town. "Potatoes and Dairying." *NWAEBT.* October 4: 2.

1909i. "Council of Agriculture Report." *Daily Telegraph.* October 27: 3.

1910a. "Preston Crop Yields." *NWAEBT.* January 31: 2.

1910b. "The Potato Tax: An Upper Castra Protest." *NWP.* April 20: 3.

1910a. "Closer Settlement – Isandula." *Daily Telegraph* (Launceston). May 2: 3.

1910b. "Compulsory Purchase Debate. 2nd Reading." *Tasmanian News.* July 27: 1.

1910c. "Dairy Conference at Burnie." *NWAEBT.* August 4: 4.

1910d. George Henry Wing. "In Memoriam." *NWAEBT.* October 28: 2.

1910e. "Infant Diarrhoea." *NWAEBT.* December 24: 2.

1911a. "Preston." *NWAEBT.* August 17: 2.

1911b. "Impressions of the Dairy School." *NWAEBT.* August 21: 2.

1911c. "Upper Castra and Nietta Teams." *NWP.* August 30: 2.

256   *Bibliography*

1911d. "Colonel Bernard. Obituary." *Mercury*, September 1: 6.

1911e. "Butter Production." *NWP*, November 23: 2.

1911f. "Dr. Purdy's Annual Summary of Public Health." *NWAEBT*, December 5: 1.

1913a. "Mother's Union." *NWAEBT*, February 15: 4.

1913b. "Upper Castra Diphtheria." *NWAEBT*, February 13: 3.

1913c. "Isandula Estate." *Examiner*, February 20: 6.

1915a. "Werona for Closer Settlement." *NWAEBT*, March 4: 2 and March 9: 2.

1915b. *NWAEBT*, May 29: 4.

1915c. "Rail Use, Opening." *NWAEBT*, June 18: 2; *NWP*, December 14: 2.

1915d. "Red Cross." *NWAEBT*, March 9: 3 and July 21: 5.

1915e. "Ellis Nominations." *NWAEBT*, April 16: 3 and *Examiner*, November 15: 3.

1915f. "Empire Day at Preston." *Examiner*, May 28: 6.

1915g. "Closer Settlement in Tasmania." *NWAEBT*, October 28: 6.

1916a. "Editorial." *Daily Telegraph*, February 12: 8.

1916b. "Ballarat." *Evening Echo*, February 15: 4.

1916c. "Hotels Closed, Sydney, 14 February." Adelaide's *Express*, February 15: 4.

1916d. "Liverpool Mutiny, Quiet Restored." *Melbourne's Argus*, (Melbourne) February 16: 9.

1916e. "Interstate Conference Commenced." *Herald* (Melbourne), February 17: 10.

1916f. "Recommendations Approved." *Argus* (Melbourne), February 18: 6.

1916g. "Settling Soldiers." *Herald* (Melbourne), February 19: 3.

1916h. "Another Gunns Plains Purchase." *North Western Advocate*, May 20: 4.

1916i. "Government Land Settlement Scheme." *Mercury*, September 21: 4.

1916j. "Parliament." *Mercury*, September 28: 7–8; *Advocate*, September 27: 6.

1917a. "George Johnson Rejoins Unit." *NWAEBT*, February 17: 2.

1917b. "Alexander Peebles Home on Final Leave." *NWAEBT*, March 12: 2.

1917c. "O.A.S. Ulverstone Branch." *NWAEBT*, March 9: 2.

1917d. "Closer Settlement – Annual Report of the Board." *Mercury*, October 3: 8.

1917e. "Land for Soldiers: Serious Allegations." *Mercury*, October 5: 6.

1917f. "Preston O.A.S." *NWAEBT*, November 23: 2.

1917g. "Looking for Land." *Mercury*, December 1: 4.

1918a. "Nichols Shield." *NWAEBT*, January 12: 4.

1918b. "Gunns Plains to Preston Road." *NWAEBT*, March 5: 2.

1918c. "Roll of Honour." Andrew Peebles Killed in France. *NWAEBT*, April 20: 4.

1918d. "O.A.S. Collections." *NWAEBT*, July 13: 2.

1919a. "Concern Over Decisions." *Advocate*, January 15: 2; April 14: 3; August 29: 2.

1919b. "Chamberlain." *Advocate*, August 29: 2.

1919c. "Estates for Closer Settlement: Land for Soldiers." *Mercury*, October 25: 3.

1919d. "Butter Factories." *Advocate*, October 1: 2.

1920a. "Objection to CSB: Overcrowded School." *Advocate*, February 18: 1, 4.

1920b. "Nietta Progress Assn." *Advocate*, May 17: 3.

1921a. "Road from Gunns Plains to Preston." *Advocate*, March 16: 3.

1921b. "The Minster's Statement: Soldier Settlers." *Mercury*, October 24: 3.

1922a. "Soldiers' Concerns." *Advocate*, March 17: 3 and May 30: 5.

1922b. "Policy Explained at Preston: Address to Electors." *Advocate*, April 26: 5.

1922c. "Memorial Ward." *Advocate*, May 25: 2 and May 31: 3.

1922d. "Football Matches." *Northern Standard*, May 10: 1.

1922e. "Preston Returned Soldiers." *Advocate*, May 30: 5.

1922f. "Upper Castra Sports." *Advocate*, August 11: 4.

1922g. "Rationalisation." *Mercury*, September 9: 6.

Bibliography 257

1922h. "Preston Recreation Ground." *Advocate*. November 2: 4.
1923a. "Kirkland Marriage." *Advocate*. June 2: 2.
1923b. "Premiership." *Advocate*. August 9: 4.
1923c. "Farmers' Co-op." *Advocate*. June 6: 8.
1924a. "USA Moisture Article." *Examiner*. March 8: 4.
1924b. "Potato Market: Disastrous Slump." *Land*. September 26: 2.
1925a. "Zeehan Peace Ward." *Advocate*. January 24: 4.
1925b. "New Preston Hall: Official Opening." *Advocate*. August 27: 2.
1926a. "Agricultural Bureau Progressing Satisfactorily." *Mercury*. April 30: 2.
1926b. "Case for Revaluation." *Advocate*. May 8: 14.
1926c. "Soldier Settlement. Department's Losses." *Advocate*. June 15: 3.
1926d. "Preston Rifle Club." *Advocate*. July 3: 3.
1926e. "Preston Meeting: Gillam Hospitalised." *Advocate*. August 6: 4.
1926f. "Riana Meeting." *Mercury*. October 14: 8.
1926g. "Preston's History: Trials of the Pioneers." *Advocate*. December 4: 11.
1927a. "Potato Marketing Board." *Advocate*. January 20: 3.
1927b. "A Soldier's Wife. Ulverstone. Letter to Editor." *Advocate*. April 1: 2.
1927c. "Soldier Farmers' Grievances: Deputation to Cabinet." *Advocate*. May 26: 6.
1927d. "Deputation." *Advocate*. June 1: 5.
1927e. "CSB Report for Werona in 1926." *Advocate*. June 20: 8.
1927f. "Sewing Machine Funds Raised." *Advocate*. June 29: 4.
1928a. "Preston Sports." *Advocate*. January 14: 3.
1928b. "Gillam Operation." *Advocate*. June 7: 4.
1928c. "South Leven Branch." *Advocate*. June 9: 8.
1928d. "School Productions." *Advocate*. December 22: 4.
1930a. "Preston Methodist Church." *Advocate*. February 13: 4.
1930b. "Preston Sports." *Advocate*. March 10: 4.
1930c. "South Leven Branch: Broken Promise." *Advocate*. July 12: 8.
1930d. "South Leven Branch." *Advocate*. November 6: 4.
1931a. "Carnival at Ulverstone." *Advocate*. March 18: 6.
1931b. "Outspoken complaints." *Advocate*. April 14: 4.
1931c. "Depression in Canada." *Examiner*. May 2: 2.
1931d. "Future of the Nietta Railway Rests with People." *Advocate*. August 6: 4.
1931e. "Nietta Railway: Uncomplimentary References." *Advocate*. October 30: 6.
1932a. "Castra Potatoes." *Advocate*. January 23: 5.
1932b. "Nietta Railway: Mr. Nichol's Allegations." *Advocate*. April 20: 6.
1932c. "G.W.E. Leven Pioneering Days." *Advocate*. April 2: 4.
1932d. "Preston Meeting: Satisfactory Explanations." *Advocate*. July 27: 2.
1932e. "New Butter Factory." *Advocate*. September 30: 7.
1933a. "Embargo on N.Z. Potatoes: Ulverstone Protest." *Advocate*. April 4: 2.
1933b. "Preston Badminton." *Advocate*. May 24: 6.
1935a. "FSOA." *Advocate*. February 2: 12.
1935b. "District School Sports." *Advocate*. April 26: 6.
1935c. "Calf Club at Preston." *Advocate*. November 6: 12.
1935d. "Women's' Forum." *Advocate*. November 13: 4.
1935e. "Mrs Cannon CWA." *Mercury*. December 7: 3.
1936a. "South Leven F.S.O.A." *Advocate*. March 12: 10 and August 26. 1937: 6.
1936b. "Potato Trials." *Advocate*. January 20: 10.
1936c. "CWA in Tasmania." *Advocate*. July 9: 8.

258   *Bibliography*

1936d. "Preston – Potato Crop Competition." *Advocate*, June 13: 8 and June 18: 9.

1936e. "Stan Wing President." *Advocate*, September 16: 8 and August 4: 6.

1936f. "Obituary, Mrs. Jessie Peebles." *Advocate*, November 28: 2.

1937. "Potato Show." *Advocate*, May 12: 8.

1939a. "Nichols Remembers." *Advocate*, May 11: 8.

1939b. "Preston Competition." *Advocate*, July 19: 6.

1939c. "Abbotsham Red Cross." *Advocate*, October 3: 6.

1939d. "Girl Winners, Calf Club." *Advocate*, November 27: 9.

1940a. "CWA Branches' News." *Advocate*, May 7: 7.

1940b. "Upper Castra Red Cross Funds." *Advocate*, July 3: 6.

1940c. "Preston CWA." *Advocate*, June 25: 7.

1940d. "Frank Tongs, 'Obituary.' and Funeral." *Advocate*, August 13 and 15: 2.

1940e. "Obituary, Mr. H.A. Nichols: Public Personality." *Advocate*, August 22: 2.

1941a. La Donna, "C.W.A. Juvenile Ballette at Preston." *Advocate*, May 6: 8.

1941b. "Obituary, Henry Johnson." *Advocate*, December 10: 2.

1942. "Tree Planting Ceremony, Preston CWA." *Advocate*, September 8: 6.

1943. "Farmers Harassed: Too Many Regulations." *Advocate*, August 4: 6.

1944a. "Potato Payments Adjusted." *Advocate*, August 15: 6.

1944b. "Membership Growth of CWA Continues." *Advocate*, September 5: 6.

1944c. "Electric Power at Preston: Official Opening." *Advocate*, October 23: 4.

1946. "Potatoes Railed from Castra." *Advocate*, July 31: 8 and August 21: 8.

1947. "AGM of CWA." *Mercury*, September 10: 5.

1948a. "Obituary, Sydney Johns." *Advocate*, January 13: 2.

1948b. "Thirteen CWA Branches Reported." *Advocate*, November 16: 11.

1949a. "Preston School Opens." *Advocate*, February 11: 13.

1949b. "Nietta CWA." *Advocate*, February 12: 12.

1949c. "We Must Grade Up Dairy Herds." *Advocate*, August 27: 9.

1949d. "Ulverstone's Early Days." *Advocate*, September 3: 15.

1950a. "Potato Freight, 50 Years School in Preston." *Advocate*, March 17: 22, 24.

1950b. "Mrs Cannon, CWA." *Advocate*, December 12: 13.

1951. "Field Day at Cressy." *Advocate*, December 6: 5.

1953a. "Koala Club." Radio. *Advocate*, September 28: 8.

1953b. "Preston Premiers." *Advocate*, October 2: 14.

1953c. "Rural Youth Clubs." *Advocate*, December 9: 14.

1954. "The Tiller, Calf Club." *Advocate*, December 3: 19.

1981. Stanley Wing. "Noted NW Identity Dies." *Advocate*, April 18: 3.

1999a. "Preston a Draw for Settlers." History Column, *Advocate*, 4 May: 8–10.

1999b. "Hard Times for Preston Pioneers." *Advocate*, May 11: 2.

2012. Gill Vowles, "Tassie Towns." Saturday Magazine, *Advocate*, August 25: 7–10.

New Zealand Electoral Rolls 1853–1981, re: Ira and Millicent Cullen, Manawatu-Wanganui, 1935.

New Zealand Death Index, 1848–1966. Re: Ira Cullen.

Nicholls, Mr Justice H. 1926. *Royal Commission into Soldier Settlement 1926 (Tasmania)*. Hobart: Parliament of Tasmania.

Office of the Status of Women and CWA. 1988. *Life has Never Been Easy: Report of the Survey of Women in Rural Australia*. Canberra: AGPS.

Opie, Iona, and Peter Opie. 1970. *Children's Games in Street and Playground*. Oxford: Clarendon Press.

Orme, Nicholas. 2001. *Medieval Children*. New Haven: Yale University Press.

Bibliography 259

Orwin, Christabel Susan Lowry, and Edith Holt Whetham. 1964. *History of British Agriculture, 1846–1914*. London: Longmans.

Ostergren, Robert C. 1981. "Land and Family in Rural Immigrant Communities." *Annals of the Association of American Geographers* 71 (3): 400–11.

Osterud, Nancy Grey. 1988. "Land, Identity, and Agency in the Oral Autobiographies of Farm Women." In *Women in Farming*, edited by Haney and Knowles, 73–87. Boulder: Westview.

Osterud, Nancy Grey. 1991. *Bonds of Community: The Lives of Farm Women in Nineteenth-Century*. Ithaca: Cornell University Press.

Osterud, Nancy Grey. 1993. "Gender and the Transition to Capitalism in Rural America." *Agricultural History* 67 (2): 14–29.

Osterud, Nancy Grey. 2012. *Putting the Barn Before the House: Women and Family Farming in Early Twentieth-Century New York*. Ithaca: Cornell University Press.

Osterud, Nancy Grey. 2015. "The Meanings of Independence in the Oral Autobiographies of Rural Women in Twentieth-Century New York." *Agricultural History* 89 (3): 426–43.

Oughton Papers. UHM.

Parker, D. 1982. "An Assessment of Stanthorpe Soldier Settlement 1915–1930." BA hons diss., University of New England.

Parker, Stanley R. 1976. *The Sociology of Leisure*. New York: International Publications Service.

Pascoe, Carla. 2009. "Be Home Before Dark: Childhood Freedoms and Adult Fears in 1950s Victoria." *Australian Historical Studies* 40 (2): 215–31.

Pascoe, Carla. 2010. "The History of Children in Australia: An Interdisciplinary Historiography." *History Compass* 8 (10): 1142–64.

Pearce, Margaret nee Archer. September 27, 2015. Interview.

Pearce, Ian, and Clare Cowling. 1975. "Records Relating to Free Immigration." *Guide to the Public Records of Tasmania*. https://catalogue.nla.gov.au/Record/1180559.

Pearn, John. 2012. "Where There Is No Doctor: Self-Help and Pre-Hospital Care in Colonial Australia." *Health and History* 14 (2): 162–80.

Peebles Family File. UHM.

Peebles, George Henry Robert. Army Records, Series B883. Personnel no. TX14416. National Archives of Australia.

Peebles, June. November 11, 2017. May 26, 2018. June 16, 2018. Interviews.

Peebles, Rob, and Bub. July 13, 2018. Interview.

Petrow, Stefan. 2001. " 'Discontent and Habits of Evasion'." *Australian Historical Studies* 32 (117): 240–56.

Petrow, Stefan. 1992. "Knocking Down the House: Introduction of the Torrens' System to Tasmania." *UTas Law Review* 11: 167–81.

Phillips, Derek. 1985. *Making More Adequate Provision: State Education in Tasmania, 1839–1985*. Hobart: Education Department of Tasmania.

Pickard, John. 2005. "Post and Rail Fences: Derivation, Development, and Demise of Rural Technology in Colonial Australia." *Agricultural History* 79 (1): 27–49.

Pike, Mr Justice George Herbert. 1929. "Report on Losses Due to Soldier Settlement." In *Commonwealth Parliamentary Papers*, vol. II, no. 46, pp. 1901–59. Canberra: Govt. Printer.

Pike, Douglas. 1957. *Paradise of Dissent: South Australia 1829–1857*. Melbourne: Melbourne University Press.

Pike, Douglas. 1962. "The Smallholder's Place in the Australian Tradition." *THRAPP* 10 (2): 28–33.

260   *Bibliography*

Pink, Kerry. 1990. *And Wealth for Toil: A History of North-West and Western Tasmania, 1825–1900*. Burnie: Advocate Marketing.

Pink, Kerry. 2001. *Edward Braddon: Adventurer, Farmer, Statesman*. Devonport, Tasmania: Sid Sidebottom MHA.

Pleck, Elizabeth H. 1976. "Two Worlds in One: Work and Family." *Journal of Social History* 10 (2): 178–95.

Poiner, Gretchen. 1990. *The Good Old Rule: Gender and Other Power Relationships in a Rural Community*. Sydney: University Press.

Pooley, Sian. 2013. "Parenthood, Child-Rearing and Fertility in England, 1850–1914." *The History of the Family* 18 (1): 83–106.

Pos, Margaretta. 2014. *Mrs Fenton's Journey: India and Tasmania 1826–1876*. Hobart: Author.

Powell, J.M. 1970. *The Public Lands of Australia Felix: Settlement and Land Appraisal in Victoria 1834–91 with Special Reference to the Western Plains*. Melbourne: Oxford University Press.

Powell, J. M. 1971. "Soldier Settlement in New Zealand, 1915-1923." *Geographical Research* 9 (2): 144–16 0. 160.

Powell, J.M. 1973. "Arcadia and Back: 'Village Settlement' in Victoria 1894–1913." *Australian Geographical Studies* 11 (2): 134–49.

Powell, J.M. 1981. "The Debt of Honour: Soldier Settlement in the Dominions, 1915–1940." *Journal of Australian Studies* 5 (8): 64–87.

Powell, J.M. 1985. "Australia's 'Failed' Soldier Settlers, 1914–23: Towards a Demographic Profile." *Australian Geographer* 16 (3): 225–29.

Powell, J.M. 1988. *An Historical Geography of Modern Australia: The Restive Fringe*. Cambridge: Cambridge University Press.

Powell, J.M. 1997. "Resource Development, Environmental Planning and the Family Farm: An Historical Interpretation." In *A Legacy Under Threat?* edited by Jim Lees, 147–73. Armidale, NSW: University of New England.

Powell, Mary Ann, Nicola Taylor, and Anne B. Smith. 2013. "Constructions of Rural Childhood: Challenging Dominant Perspectives." *Children's Geographies* 11 (1): 117–31.

Prinsep, A., and Elizabeth. 1833. *The Journal of a Voyage from Calcutta to Van Diemen's Land*. London.

Pritchard, Bill, David Burch, and Geoffrey Lawrence. 2007. "Neither 'Family' nor 'Corporate' Farming: Australian Tomato Growers as Farm Family Entrepreneurs." *Journal of Rural Studies* 23: 75–87.

Probate Registry TA1574:

Peebles, Allan. AD963/1/1, Will 941.

Peebles, James Robert. AD960/1/21, Will 4622.

Peebles, James Robert. AD960/1/54, Will 17623.

Tongs, Frank Allan. AD960-1-65, Will 23987.

Wing, Roy William Diaper. AD960/1/92, Will 41979.

Public Works Department TA24:

PWD18-1-14253 7 Geo. 5. Item 431 – Road: Central Castra to Preston Railway Station.

PWD219-1-1 Public Works Commissioners Reports on Prosed Railway Facilities for the Castra District and Sheffield District, 1908–11. Parliamentary Reports Numbered 82 and 83, Minister for Lands and Works.

Quiggin, Pat. 1988. *No Rising Generation: Women & Fertility in Late Nineteenth Century Australia*. Australian Family Formation Project Monograph No. 10. Canberra: Australian National University.

Bibliography 261

Raby. Geoff. 1996. *Making Rural Australia: An Economic History of Technical and Institutional Creativity, 1788–1860*. Melbourne: Oxford University Press.

Rae. John. 1883. "Why have the Yeomanry Perished?" *Contemporary Review, 1866–1900* (44): 546–65.

Ramsay. Charles. 1980. *With the Pioneers*. 2nd Ed. Devonport: Latrobe Group. National Trust of Australia (Tasmania).

Reay. Barry. 1996. *Microhistories: Demography, Society, and Culture in Rural England, 1800–1930*. Cambridge: Cambridge University Press.

Reeves. William Pember. 1902. *State Experiments in Australia and New Zealand*. Vol. I–II. Melbourne: Palgrave Macmillan. reissued 1969.

Register of Births, Deaths and Marriages RG35:

RGD3-1-47. No. 886. Marriage of James Robert Peebles and Margaret Mason.

RGD37-1-20. No. 339. Marriage of Robert Peebles and Jane Mong.

Reynolds. Henry. 1969a. " 'Men of Substance and Deservedly Good Repute': The Tasmanian Gentry 1856–1875." *Australian Journal of Politics & History* 15 (3): 61–72.

Reynolds. Henry. 1969b. "Regionalism in Nineteenth Century Tasmania." *THRAPP* 17 (1): 14–28.

Reynolds. Henry. 2005. "Identity." In *Companion to Tasmanian History*. edited by Alison Alexander. 457–62. Hobart: THS. UTas.

Reynolds. Henry. 2012. *A History of Tasmania*. Melbourne: Cambridge University Press.

Reynolds. John. 1956. "Premiers and Political Leaders." In *A Century of Responsible Government*. edited by F.C. Green. 115–240. Hobart: Shea. Govt. Printer.

Reynolds. Margaret. 1982. "The Noble Failure: King Island Soldier Settlement. 1918–1930." B.Ed. diss.. UTas.

Richards. Eric. 1999. "An Australian Map of British and Irish Literacy in 1841." *Population Studies* 53 (3): 345–59.

Richards. Eulalia S. 1939. *The Ladies Handbook of Home Treatment*. Warburton: Signs Publishing.

Richardson. Andrew. 2005. "The Long Road Home: Repatriation in Tasmania. 1916–1929." PhD. UTas.

Richmond. Barbara M. 1957. "Some Aspects of the History of Transportation and Immigration in Van Diemen's Land. 1824–1855." Master of Arts. UTas.

Riley. Glenda. 1977. "Images of the Frontierswoman: Iowa as a Case Study." *Western Historical Quarterly* 8 (2): 189–202.

Riley. Mark. 2009. " 'The Next Link in the Chain': Children. Agri-cultural Practices and the Family Farm." *Children's Geographies* 7 (3): 245–60.

Risjord. Norman K. 1973. *Forging the American Republic 1760–1815*. Reading. MA: Addison-Wesley.

Roake. Albert H. 1928. *Sixty Years of Progress, 1868–1928: Parish of Forth and Leven, Tasmania*. Burnie. Tasmania: Advocate.

Roberts. Brian K. 1977. *Rural Settlement in Britain*. Folkestone: Dawson.

Roberts. Stephen H. 1924. *History of Australian Land Settlement: 1788–1920*. Melbourne: Macmillan. reprint 1968.

Robson. L.L. 1983. *A History of Tasmania: Van Diemen's Land from the Earliest Times to 1855*. Vol. 1. Melbourne: Oxford University Press.

Roche. M. 2002. "Soldier Settlement in New Zealand After World War 1: Two Case Studies." *New Zealand Geographer* 58 (1): 23–32.

Rogers. Susan Carol. and Sonya Salamon. 1983. "Inheritance and Social Organization Among Family Farmers." *American Ethnologist* 10 (3): 529–50.

262 Bibliography

Rollison, David. 1992. *The Local Origins of Modern Society: Gloucestershire 1500–1800*. London: Routledge.

Rootes, Grant L. 2004. "Local Government Reform in Tasmania 1906–1939: With Special Reference to the North West Coast." MA Thesis, UTas.

Rootes, Grant L. 2008. "A Chaotic State of Affairs?: The Permissive System of Local Government in Rural Tasmania 1840–1907." PhD, UTas.

Rootes, Grant. 2009. "'Overstrained and Creaking at Every Joint': Local Government in Rural Tasmania 1945-1969." *Tasmanian Historical Research Association P & P 56* (2): 154–196.

Rosenberg, Charles E., ed. 2003. *Right Living: An Anglo-American Tradition of Self-Help Medicine and Hygiene*. Baltimore: Johns Hopkins University Press.

Ross, Kaz. 2017. "Imagined Futures and Forgotten Pasts: Tasmania's Asian Connections." *Journal of Australian Studies* 41 (3): 296–311.

Rost, Allan. 2008. "World War 1 Soldier Settlement: Government Attempts and Some Private Contributions." *Journal of the Royal Australian Historical Society* 94 (1): 38–56.

Rowe, B. A. 1982. "Effects of limestone on Pasture Yields and the pH of Two Kraznozems in North-Western Tasmania", *AJEA* 22 (115): 100–105.

Royal Society Collection, RS 2448/A260 later RS62. "Colonel Crawford's Settlement in Tasmania." Scrapbook of Clippings, Unknown Compiler. UTas. Library.

Royal Society Collection, RS66.1869. Shaw, Lt. Col. Michael M. Typescript of Letter to W. Boyer. July 7, 1869. UTas. Library.

Rural Reconstruction Commission. 1944. *Settlement and Employment of Returned Men on the Land*. Canberra: Commonwealth of Australia.

Russell, John, Rod Kirkpatrick, Victor Isaacs, and Henry Mayer. 2009. *Australian Newspaper History: A Bibliography*, 2nd ed. Andergrove (Mackay), QLD: Australian Newspaper History Group.

Russell, Peter A. 2012. *How Agriculture Made Canada: Farming in the Nineteenth Century*. Montreal: McGill-Queens University Press.

Sachs, Carolyn E. 1983. *The Invisible Farmers: Women in Agricultural Production*. Totowa, NJ: Rowman and Allanheld.

Sachs, Carolyn E. 1988. "The Participation of Women and Girls in Market and Non-Market Activities on Pennsylvania Farms." In *Women and Farming*, edited by Haney and Knowles, 123–34. Boulder: Westview.

Salamon, Sonya. 1985. "Ethnic Communities and the Structure of Agriculture." *Rural Sociology* 50 (3): 323–40.

Sahlins, Marshall. 1974. *Stone Age Economics*. Chicago: Aldine-Atherton.

Samuel, Raphael. 1975. "Village Labour." In *Village Life and Labour*, edited by R. Samuel, 3–26. London: Routledge Kegan Paul.

Sanson, Ann, and Sarah Wise. 2001. "Children and Parenting." *Family Matters* 60: 36–45.

Saugeres, Lise. 2002a. "'She's Not Really a Woman, She's Half a Man': Gendered Discourses of Embodiment in a French Farming Community." *Women's Studies International Forum* 25 (6): 641–50.

Saugeres, Lise. 2002b. "Of Tractors and Men: Masculinity, Technology and Power in a French Farming Community." *Sociologia Ruralis* 42 (2): 143–59.

Saunders, Kay, and Raymond Evans. 1992. *Gender Relations in Australia: Domination and Negotiation*. Sydney: Harcourt Brace Jovanovich.

Scates, Bruce, and Melanie Oppenheimer. 2014. "'I Intend to Get Justice': The Moral Economy of Soldier Settlement." *Labour History* 106 (June): 229–53.

Bibliography 263

Scates, Bruce, and Melanie Oppenheimer. 2016. *The Last Battle: Soldier Settlement in Australia, 1916–1939*. Pt. Melbourne: Cambridge University Press.

Schafer, Markus H. 2009. "Parental Death and Subjective Age: Indelible Imprints from Early in the Life Course?" *Sociological Inquiry* 79 (1): 75–97.

Schwieder, Dorothy. 1980. *Labor and Economic Farm Roles of Iowa's Farm Wives*. Washington, DC: Howard University Press.

Schwieder, Dorothy. 1986. "Education and Change in the Lives of Iowa Farm Women, 1900–1940" *Agricultural History* 60 (2): 200–215.

Scott, Ernest. 1925. *A Short History of Australia*. Melbourne: Oxford University Press.

Scott, Ernest. 1936. *Australia During the War Vol. XI, the Official History of Australia in the War of 1914–1918*. Sydney: Angus and Robertson.

Shaw, A. G. L. 1961. *The Story of Australia 2nd ed*. London: Faber & Faber Ltd.

Shaw, A.G.L. 1990. "Colonial Settlement 1788–1945." in *Agriculture in the Australian Economy*. edited by D.B. Williams. 3rd ed., 1–18. Melbourne: Sydney University Press.

Skemp, J.F. 1891. "Foreword." In *Bush Life in Tasmania: Fifty Years Ago*. i–xvi. Launceston: Tasmania University Press, reprint 1964.

Skemp, John Rowland. 1952. *Memories of Myrtle Bank: The Bush-farming Experiences of Rowland and Samuel Skemp in North-Eastern Tasmania, 1883–1948*. Carlton: Melbourne University Press.

Slatham, Pamela. 1992. "The Tanner Letters: A Pioneer Saga of Swan River and Tasmania 1831–1845." In *Lifelines*. edited by P. Clarke and D. Spender. Crows Nest, NSW: Allen and Unwin.

Smith, Michael A., Stanley R. Parker, and Cyril S. Smith. 1973. *Leisure and Society in Britain*. London: Allen Lane.

Smith, Patricia 'Pat'. October 13, 2015, August 2, 2017, December 6, 2017. Interviews.

Smith, Philipa Mein. 2017. "Fraction too Much Friction: Tasmanian-New Zealand Tensions Over Apples." *THS* 22: 39–53.

Snell, K.D.M. 1985. *Annals of the Labouring Poor: Social Change and Agrarian England, 1660–1900*. Cambridge: Cambridge University Press.

Solomon, R.J. 1972. *Tasmania*. Sydney: Angus & Robertson.

Spender, Dale. 1985. *Man Made Language*. 2nd Ed. London: Routledge & Kegan Paul.

Spock, Dr. Benjamin. 1945. *The Common Sense Book of Baby and Child Care*. New York: Dual, Sloan & Pearce.

Sprod, M.N. 1984. "'The Old Education': Government Schools in Tasmania 1839–1904." *THRAPP* 31 (2): 18–36.

Stansall, M.E.J. 1975. *Tasmanian Methodism, 1820–1975*. Launceston: Methodist Church of Australasia.

Statistics of Tasmania, 1870 – Agricultural Report.

Stewart, William Downie. 1909a. "Land Tenure and Land Monopoly in New Zealand, Pt.1." *Journal of Political Economy* 17 (2): 82–91.

Stewart, William Downie. 1909b. "Land Tenure and Land Monopoly in New Zealand, Pt.11." *Journal of Political Economy* 17 (3): 144–52.

Stilwell, G.T. 1969. "Crawford, Andrew (1815–1899)." *ADB*. Vol. 3. Melbourne.

Stilwell Research Papers. NS1383/1/1. TA.

Stilwell, G.T. 1992. "The Castra Scheme." In *Tasmanian Insights*, edited by Gillian Winter, 11–30. Hobart: State Library of Tasmania.

Stokes, Henry J.W. 1969. "North West Tasmania 1858–1910: The Establishment of an Agricultural Community." PhD, Australian National University.

264 Bibliography

Stokes, Henry J.W. 1971. *A Century of Tasmanian Railways, 1871–1971*. Hobart: Transport Commission.

Stoney, Captain H. Butler 1856. *A Residence in Tasmania*. London: Smith, Elder & Co.

Stratford, Elaine. 2019. *Home, Nature and the Feminine Ideal*. London: Rowman & Littlefield.

Stubbs, Brett J. 1998. "Land Improvement or Institutionalised Destruction? The Ringbarking Controversy, 1879–1884, and the Emergence of a Conservation Ethic in New South Wales." *Environment and History* 4 (2): 145–65.

Surveyor General and Commissioner for Crown Lands Department AA579:

The Following Information Respecting the Method of Acquiring Land in That Part of Tasmania Known as Castra. 1867. Hobart: Government Printer, 2-page map (Piguenit W. C. (William Charles)). 1836–1914. And Calder, James Erskine, 1808–1882. TL.PE 325.946 TAS.

Sutton-Smith, Brian. 1981. *A History of Children's Play: New Zealand 1840–1950*. Philadelphia: University of Pennsylvania Press.

Symon, J.A. 1859. *Scottish Farming: Past and Present*. Edinburgh.

Szreter, Simon, and Kate Fisher. 2010. *Sex Before the Sexual Revolution: Intimate Life in England, 1918–1963*. Cambridge: Cambridge University Press.

Tasmanian Electoral Rolls. Various Locations and Years.

Tasmanian Government Gazette, September 12, 1916, October 1, 1916, May 21, 1935, Revocation of Original Road on Greenfield's Lot.

Tasmanian Government Railways TA245: 1934. Mr. C. Geale Preston – Potato Loading Ramp. General Correspondence. TC10/1/4422.34/367.

Tasmanian Journal of Agriculture, vol.1-v.52, 1929–1981. Cited Vol. 33, No. 1, 1962; Vol. 34, No. 3, 1963; Vol. 43, No. 2, 1972. RSC, UTas Library.

Tasmanian Parliamentary Papers:

Castra: Letter from Colonel Crawford re Extension of *Indian Settlers Act*, HAJ, 1870. Vol. XX, Paper 106.

Castra Road: Letter and Petition from Lt.-Col. Crawford, HAJ, 1879. Vol. XXXVII, Paper 91.

Collector for Port Sorell. 1870. Agricultural Report, Census. *Statistics of Tasmania*.

Crown Lands Reports: Agricultural Areas in Devon, HAJ, 1864. Vol. IX, Paper 19.

Department of Lands and Surveys, "Report for 1915–16." JPPP (Tas), 1916–17. Vol. LXXV, Paper 23.

Don and Leven Crown Lands, HAJ, 1859. Vol. IV, Paper 89.

Education: Petition from the Benevolent Society, HAJ, 1868. Vol. XVI, Paper 67 and LCJ, 1868. Vol. XIV, Paper 59.

Exports and Imports: Circular Head and River Mersey, Report of Customs Collector, HAJ, 1856. Vol. I, Paper 28.

Exploration of Northern Country, HAJ, 1860. Vol. V, Paper 11.

Free Education: Statement in Connection with the Proposal to Abolish Payment of Fees in State Schools, JPPP, 1900. Vol. XLII, Paper 65.

Lieut.-Colonel J. R. Fulton – Request for Grant of Land – Immigration Board, HAJ, 1868. Vol. XVI, Paper 54.

Parliamentary Standing Committee on Public Works: Gunn's Plains Road Proposal, JPPP (Tas), 1918. Vol. LXXLX, Paper 8.

Pre-Emptive Rights – Devon and Wellington, HAJ, 1864. Vol. XI, Paper 104.

Progress Report from Select Committee on the workings of the *Waste Lands Act*, HAJ. Vol. VII, Paper 161 (1861): 4–19.

Bibliography 265

R. C. Gunn's Exploration of North-Western Country. LCJ. 1860. Vol. V. Paper 14.

Report and Evidence to the Select Committee on *Waste Lands Act* 1861. HAJ. Vol. VIII. Paper 111 (1862): 4–37.

Report of Joint Committee into the Council of Agriculture with Minutes of Proceedings. Evidence. and Appendices. JPPP (Tas). 1902. Vol. XLVII. Paper 49.

Report of Joint Committee of both Houses of Parliament. *Farmers Relief Bill*. 1935 (No. 24). JPPP (Tas). 1935. Vol. CXIII. Paper 15 and 20.

Report of the Public Works Commission: Railway Facilities for the Castra District. JPPP (Tas). 1908. Vol. LIX. Paper 18. pp. 1–4.

Report of the Royal Commission on Public Education. HAJ. Vol. XV. 1867. Paper 31.

Report of Select Committee and Minutes re: Bill Regulating the Sale and Disposal of Lands of the Crown. HAJ. 1883. Vol. XLIV. Paper 130. And Ibid. LCJ. 1883. Vol. XXXV. Paper 112.

Report of Select Committee re: The Road Trust System of the Colony. JPPP (Tas). 1886. Vol. II. Paper 160.

Report of Select Committee into Closer Settlement with Minutes of Proceedings. and Evidence. JPPP (Tas). 1909. Vol. LX. Paper 18.

Report of Select Committee of Legislative Council re: Dairy Produce Bill 1950 (No. 10) JPPP (Tas). Vol. CXXXVI. Paper 12.

Report of Select Committee. Potato Marketing Board Bill. 1952 (No. 98. Private). JPPP (Tas). 1952. Vol. 138. Paper 62.

Report of a Select Committee into Returned Soldiers' Settlement. JPPP (Tas). 1921–1922. Vol. LXXXV Paper 61.

Report of a Select Committee into Returned Soldiers' Settlement. JPPP (Tas). 1922–23. Vol. LXXXVI. Paper 60.

Report of a Select Committee into the Rural Industries Bill. 1943 (No. 15). JPPP (Tas). 1943. Vol. CXXIX. Paper 3.

Report of Standing Committee on Public Works: Gunn's Plains to Riana 1943 JPPP (Tas). Vol. CXXIX. Paper 4.

Road Accommodation: Petition from Inhabitants of Castra. HAJ. 1880. Vol. XXXIX. Paper 68.

Road Policy: Petition from East and West Devon. and Wellington. HAJ. 1873. Vol. XXVI. Paper 60.

Tasmanian Towns Directory. 1929.

Taylor. Tracey. ed. 2003. *Tasmania's Potato History 1803–2003*. Launceston: DPIPWE.

Tebbutt. Melanie. 1995. *Women's Talk?: A Social History of "Gossip" in Working-class Neighbourhoods, 1880–1960*. Aldershot: Scolar Press.

Templeton. Jacqueline. 1988. "Set Up to Fail?: Soldier Settlers in Victoria. Rv: Marilyn Lake. *The Limits of Hope*." *Victorian Historical Journal* 59 (1): 42–50.

Thirsk. Joan. 1957. *English Peasant Farming: The Agrarian History of Lincolnshire from Tudor to Recent Times. London:* Routledge Kegan Paul.

Thompson. E.P. 1967. "Time. Work-Discipline and Industrial Capitalism." *Past and Present* 38 (1): 56–97.

Thompson. Flora. 1939. *Lark Rise to Candleford*. Bath: BBC Audiobooks. reprint 2008.

Tongs Family File. NG2314. TA.

Tonnies. Ferdinand. 1887. *Community and Society*. Edited and Translated by Charles A. Loomis. East Lansing: Michigan State University Press. reprint 1957.

Tonts. Matthew. 2002. "State Policy and the Yeoman Ideal: Agricultural Development in Western Australia. 1890–1914." *Landscape Research* 27 (1): 103–15.

266   Bibliography

Tonts, Matthew. 2005. "Competitive Sport and Social Capital in Rural Australia." *Journal of Rural Studies* 21 (2): 137–49.

Townsley, W.A. 1955. "Tasmania and the Great Economic Depression, 1858–1872." *THRAPP* 4 (2): 36.

Townsley, W.A. 1956. "The Parliament of Tasmania." In *A Century of Responsible Government 1856–1956*, edited by F.C. Green, 1–112. Hobart: Shea, Govt. Printer.

Trevelyan, G.M. 1973 (1926). *History of England*. New Illustrated Ed. London: Longman.

Ulverstone District Hospital TA466:

CSD22/99/187, Ulverstone Benevolent Society Hospital.

CSD22/144/157, Ulverstone Hospital (State Government).

LSD35-1-5294. Levenbank Maternity Hospital.

Ulverstone Show Society. 1996. Centenary Brochure, 1896–1996. Accessed at Libraries Tasmania, Ulverstone, November 16, 2017.

Valenze, Deborah. 1991. "The Art of Women and the Business of Men: Women's Work and the Dairy Industry c. 1740–1840." *Past & Present* 130 (1): 142–69.

Valuation Rolls: Castra Parish. 1871–1895.

Valuation Rolls: Castra Paris. 1923–1929.

Valuation Rolls: Forrabury Parish. 1859, 1860–1861.

Valuation Rolls, Road District of Leven. 1905, 1906, 1907, 1908.

Vanclay, Frank. 2016. "The Impacts of Deregulation and Agricultural Restructuring for Rural Australia." *Australian Journal of Social Issues* 38 (1): 81–94.

van Krieken, Robert. 2000. "Sociological Theory." *Sociology: Themes and Perspectives* 631–80.

Voyce, Malcolm. 1994. "Testamentary Freedom, Patriarchy and Inheritance of the Family Farm in Australia." *Sociologia Ruralis* 34 (1): 71–83.

Wadham, S.M. 1935. "Some Aspects of the Problem of Rural Development Today." *The Australian Quarterly* 7 (28): 62–69.

Wadham, S.M. 1967. *Australian Farming 1788–1965*. Melbourne: F.W. Cheshire.

Wakefield, Edward Gibbon. 1849. *A View of the Art of Colonization, in Letters Between a Statesman and a Colonist*. Oxford: Clarendon Press, reprint 1914.

Walch's Map of Tasmania. 1868. Extract, 200722. TA.

Walch's Map of Tasmania. 1883. Item 1446–6513. TA.

Walch's Tasmanian Guide Book: A Handbook of Information for all Parts of the Colony. 1871. Hobart: Walch & Sons.

Walch, J. & Sons. 1901, 1911. *Walch's Tasmanian Almanac*. Hobart: Walch & Sons.

Walker, Marion. 2011. "Sanitorium of India: Climate and Tourism in Nineteenth and Twentieth Century Tasmania." *Launceston Historical Society P & P* 23: 39–50.

Walker, R.B. 1966. *Old New England*. Sydney: Sydney University Press.

Wall, Richard. 2002. "Elderly Widows and Widowers and Their Coresidents in Late 19th- and 20th-Century England and Wales." *History of the Family* 7 (1): 139–55.

Ward, Colin. 1988. *The Child in the Country*. London: Robert Hale Ltd.

Ward, Russel. 1992. "The Australian Legend." In *Images of Australia*, 179–190. eds. Gillian Whitlock and David Carter. St Lucia: UQ Press.

Warner-Smith, Penny, and Peter Brown. 2002. " 'The Town Dictates What I Do': The Leisure, Health and Well-Being of Women in a Small Australian Country Town." *Leisure Studies* 21 (1): 39–56.

Waterhouse, Richard. 2004. "The Yeoman Ideal and Australian Experience, 1860–1960." In *Exploring the British World: Identity, Cultural Production, Institutions*, edited by K.

Bibliography   267

Darian-Smith, P. Grimshaw, K. Lindsey, and S. Macintyre. 440–59. Melbourne: RMIT Publishing.

Waterhouse, Richard. 2005. *The Vision Splendid: A Social and Cultural History of Rural Australia*. Fremantle, WA: Curtin University Books.

Waterson, D.B. 1968. *Squatter, Selector and Storekeeper: A History of the Darling Downs, 1859–93*. Sydney: Sydney University Press.

Waugh, John. 1838. *Three Years Practical Experience as a Settler in New South Wales*. Edinburgh.

Webster's *Dictionary*. 1828.

West, Elliot. 1989. *Growing Up with the Country: Childhood on the Far West Frontier*. Albuquerque: University of New Mexico Press.

West, John. 1852. *The History of Tasmania*. Vol. 1–2. Charleston, SC: BiblioBazaar, reprint 2008.

Westripp, Joyce, and Peggy Holroyde. 2010. *Colonial Cousins: A Surprising History of Connections Between India and Australia*. Adelaide: Wakefield Press.

Widowson, Henry. 1829. *Present State of Van Diemen's Land; Comprising an Account of Its Agricultural Capabilities, and Other Important Matters Connected with Emigration*. St. Paul's and London: S. Robinson.

Wilkison, Kyle. 2008. *Yeomen, Sharecroppers, and Socialists: Plain Folk Protest in Texas, 1870–1914*. College Station, TX: Texas A & M University Press.

Williams, D. B. ed. 1990. *Agriculture in the Australian Economy* 3rd ed. Sydney: Sydney University Press.

Williams, Julie. 1992. *The Invisible Farmer – A Report on Australian Farm Women*. Canberra: Commonwealth Department of Primary Industries.

Williams, Raymond. 1973. *The Country and the City*. London: Chatto and Windus.

Williams, Michael. 1975. "More and Smaller Is Better: Australian Rural Settlement 1788–1914." In *Australian Space, Australian Time: Geographical Perspectives*, edited by J. M. Powell and M. Williams. 61–103. Melbourne: Oxford University Press.

Wilson, Elisabeth. 2011. "'Wandering Stars': The Impact of British Evangelists in Australia, 1870s–1900." PhD, UTas.

Wimshurst, Kerry. 1981. "Child Labour and School Attendance in South Australia 1890–1915." *Australian Historical Studies* 19 (76): 388–411.

Winstanley, Michael. 1996. "Industrialization and the Small Farm: Family and Household Economy in Nineteenth-Century Lancashire." *Past & Present* 152 (1): 157–95.

Wing, George Henry Snr. November 1, 1873–November 25, 1875. Diary. Photocopy of Handritten Original. UHM.

Winter, Jay. 2016. "Foreword." In *The Last Battle: Soldier Settlement in Australia, 1916–1939*, edited by Bruce Scates and Melanie Oppenheimer, vii–ix. Pt. Melbourne: Cambridge University Press.

Wise's *Post Office and Town Directories*. 1890–1, 1900, 1914, 1921, 1931 and 1941. Hobart: TA.

Wood, G.L. 1923. *The Tasmanian Environment: A Human and Economic Geography of Tasmania*. Adelaide: Rigby.

Wood, Karen Grace. 1997. "Home Sweet Home: Women and Domesticity in Rural Australia 1930–1970." Master of Fine Arts, UTas.

Wood, L. J. 1981. *Rural Accessibility: The Case of School Transport in Tasmania*. Department of Geography, University of Tasmania.

Wood, Vaughan, and Eric Pawson. 2008. "Information Exchange and the Making of the Colonial Farm: Agricultural Periodicals in Late Nineteenth-Century New Zealand." *Agricultural History* 82 (3): 337–65.

268 Bibliography

Woodley, Peter. 2017. "RV: The Last Battle, Scates and Oppenheimer." *Journal of the Royal Australian Historical Society* 103 (1): 97–99.

Woods, John. 1822. *Two Years' Residence in the Settlement on the English Prairie, in the Illinois Country, United States*. Chicago: Lakeside Press, reprinted 1968.

Zelizer, Viviana A. 1985. *Pricing the Priceless Child: The Changing Social Value of Children*. New York: Princeton Paperbacks.

Zutinic, Durdica, and Ivo Grgic. 2010. "Family Farm Inheritance in Slavonia Region, Croatia." *Czech Academy of Agricultual Sciences: Agricultural Economics* 56 (11): 522–31.

Index

Abbotsham 28, 60, 65, 72, 80, 130, 175, 178, 183, 225
adolescence 16, 146, 156, 164, 176–9, 231
agrarianism 12, 67, 91, 109, 158, 192, 206; agrarian ideal 7, 48
Agricultural Bank of Tasmania 98, 102, 123, 211
agricultural heritage 65–8
Agriculture, Department of 90, 163, 178, 205, 218
America (USA) 1, 4, 10–15, 70, 73, 93, 156, 161, 179, 188, 195–6, 205, 233; Illinois 45, 141, 202; Iowa 183; Minnesota 142; New England USA 6, 11; Wisconsin 202
American historians 11–14, 140–2, 151, 156, 181–2, 185, 191
Anglican Church 171, 185; see also Church of England
Anglo-Indian(s): definition 18; as a group 16, 20, 27, 35, 37–8, 41–4; in Tasmania 18–19, 49–62, 73, 85, 94
Arthur, Lt. Governor George 20, 46, 159
Australian Pulp and Paper Mill 221
Australian Rules football 173–4, 186

badminton 168, 171, 174
Baptist church/goers 76, 81, 84, 123
Beveridge, Robert 66, 67, 74
Bigge, Commissioner John Thomas 18–19, 47, 106
Bingham, John 201, 204
Bingham, Thomas (Tom) 73, 134, 204, 208, 213, 219, 222
Bonney, Joseph 71
Bounty Scheme/system/ticket 71, 74, 77
Braddon, Sir Edward Nichols Coventry and Alice 27, 38, 40, 42, 48, 59, 69, 79

Brett family: Isaac and Elizabeth 77–8; William and Mary Ann 77
Britain 4, 10, 23, 65, 68–9, 70–3, 91, 99, 105, 109, 159, 191, 215; see also England; Scotland
brotherhood 127, 135, 230
brothers 122, 127–9, 148, 151, 161, 196, 216, 229
Brown, Harold (Bal) and Irene 153, 173
Brown, Max 174, 184
Brown family early migrants: William and Elizabeth nee Brett 71, 77–8, 138
Brown family second generation: Arthur William and Ada Annie nee Porter 63, 77–8, 138, 151; William Alfred 77–8
Brown family third generation: Albert Hedley (Joe) and Gladys nee Smith 152, 155, 173, 225
Brown family fourth generation: Kenneth Albert (Ken) and Josephine (Josie) 152–3, 161, 174, 193, 225
Brown family fifth generation: John 152; Paul 152, 229
Brown family sixth generation: Joe 152–3; Travis 152
Burgess brothers: Ambrose and Elizabeth nee Butler 135, 146; Samuel and Ada nee Johnson 146; William 146
Burnie 94, 118, 128, 168, 177–8, 185, 209, 210, 215; see also Emu Bay
butter 95, 156, 157–8, 167, 191, 196, 202, 213, 215, 216

Calder, Surveyor General James 23, 24–5, 27, 32, 48, 54
Canada 14, 15, 39, 45, 67, 88–9, 107, 143, 187, 202; Manitoba 88–9; Ontario 88, 140, 202

270   *Index*

Cannon, Capt. Samuel and Mrs Joan
  Cannon 212, 215, 216
Carter, Peter 163, 166
Castra, Upper 57−9, 80−2, 93, 104−5,
  127, 168, 177, 187, 208
Castra & Co. 32, 33, 34, 41, 60
Castra Association 18−44, 45, 49−54,
  57−8, 94, 231
Castra Parish/District 45−62, 78−87, 100,
  120, 132, 140, 220−1
Chamberlain, John Hartley and Ada Sarah
  118−19, 123, 126, 187, 205, 210, 221−2
Chamberlain, Philip(Phil) and wife 129,
  147, 149, 177, 228
cheese-making 61, 101, 213, 218
children 16, 27, 42, 67, 71, 83−4, 119,
  135, 137−8, 156−79, 182−3, 190, 193,
  204
Chilcott, Charles T. 131−2; Leonard D.
  121, 133
Chisholm, Allan 80; Frank 81; John 210
Church of England 39, 81, 82, 84, 87
climate 3, 8, 27, 35, 39−40, 42, 61, 68, 78,
  94−5, 97, 120, 192, 218; snow 46, 78,
  163, 167−8
Closer Settlement Board *see* Tasmanian
  Closer Settlement Board (CSB)
Coastal Dairy Co. Pty. Ltd 215
Commissioners of Survey and Valuation,
  Journals of 46
Commodore Perry 71, 74
Conlon, Augustus 213−15
convicts, ex-convicts *see* emancipists ('old
  hands')
Council of Agriculture 61, 201, 209
Country Women's Association (CWA)
  186−7, 216, 231
Crawford, Lt. Col. Andrew and Matilda
  Frederica 15, 18, 26−31, 34−6, 38, 43, 52,
  57, 61, 82, 86, 109, 137, 203, 219, 230
Crawford Brothers of Redbourne 64−5
Crawford family: Alexander 38, 65,
  122−3, 177, 204, 219; Ernest Henry
  Kinleside 59; Hugh Sewell 59; Robert
  St. John 59, 85
cream production 61, 169, 191, 194, 196,
  205, 213, 215; cream cheques 118
cricket 38, 166, 169, 174−5
Crown Land(s) 8, 18, 23, 28, 37, 45−8,
  63, 70, 85, 88, 96−7, 98, 100, 114, 133,
  151, 221
Cullen family: Ira Stanley Charles and
  Millicent 128−9; Allan Lindsay 128−9;

Thomas (Tom) and Ada nee Tongs 82,
  85, 86, 171, 184, 203, 204

Delaney family: Edward 80−1; Frank 171;
  William 51, 54, 82, 83, 86, 87, 171, 201,
  202−4, 219
Deloraine 8, 24, 28, 66, 68, 72, 76, 98, 125
Denison, Lt. Governor William 70
depression: 1870s 43, 47, 73; 1890s 85,
  91−3, 219; 1920s-30s 5, 135, 153, 168,
  177, 179, 182, 206, 211, 215, 220−1
Devon, County of, Tasmania 2, 4, 16, 22,
  23, 30, 37, 38, 63, 66
Devon, East: West Devon 2, 61, 177, 220
Devonport (prev. Formby and Torquay)
  Tasmania 2, 59, 60, 68, 146, 168, 206
Deyrah 35, 43, 57, 65, 76, 151, 205
Dooley, James Monahan 23−6, 71
Dooley's Plains 25, 36, 49, 52, 60, 63, 74,
  78, 81, 84, 133
Dry, Richard 31, 32
Dumbleton, Major Arthur Vincent 34, 37,
  38, 57
Dunham family: John Jnr. 129, 177; John
  Snr. and Mary Ann 85, 86, 129, 130;
  Thomas 129

East India Company 26, 27
education 9, 38, 48, 71, 87, 118, 143, 160,
  178, 215
Edwards, Inspector George 118, 126,
  134−5
Ellis, G. & A.: site for school 83;
  storekeepers/landowners 60, 61, 80,
  151, 169, 186, 192, 195, 206, 212, 219,
  223−4
emancipists ('old hands') 24, 27, 47
Emu Bay 2, 21; *see also* Burnie
England 1, 10, 12, 15, 27, 34, 39, 60,
  67−70, 106, 143, 156−7, 175; *see also*
  Britain
Eustace, Lance and Flora 138
Ewington brothers: George and Henry
  128, 153; Thomas and (1) Jane
  Elizabeth nee Peebles 128, 184, 190,
  212, 221; and (2) Effie nee Cullen
  187, 190

family(ies) 5, 15, 74−8, 120, 125, 129−31,
  137−55, 156−98, 223−9
Fenton, Elizabeth and Michael 42, 79
Fenton, James 21, 27, 38
football *see* Australian Rules football

Index 271

Forth (Hamilton-on-Forth) 22–3. 25. 34–5. 38. 42. 53. 57. 68. 72. 172
Fulton. Lt. Col. James Robert 33. 34. 38. 42. 53–4

Geale. Clarence 129
Gillam: Stanley Roy and Annie 130–1: William Edward 84
Gillam. Walter 219
Gollan. Dr. Lachlan 204
Gunn. Ronald 24. 25. 54
Gunns Plains 4. 34. 59. 80–1. 100. 120. 133. 162. 173. 187. 216. 219. 232

Hall: Arthur Caplan 102. 219: Richard 23. 28. 34. 49–52. 54. 65
Hall. Edward Swarbreck 160. 189
Harding family first Preston generation: Harry 128. 138. 153. 173: Herbert H. 153
Harding family second generation: Herbert. Thomas 173: William Henry and Melvie nee Smith 153. 173. 174. 193. 223
Harding family third generation: Denzil and Margaret nee Anderson 152. 153. 174. 186. 193: sisters Wilma and Beryl 153
Harding family fourth generation: brothers Kelvin 154. 229: Desmond 229: Selwyn 154. 174. 229
Harrop. Marie nee Johnson *see* Johnson family
health. healthiness 3. 37. 39. 75. 100. 125. 126–32. 146. 147. 154. 160. 172. 181. 188–91
Henry brothers Frederick 82. 100–1: William 82. 100–1. 185. 203. 219
Hilder. Richard 64. 75. 80. 81. 85. 200
Hobbs. Edward 220. 221
Hudson: James and Maria. John and Ellen 77

immigrants 4. 14. 20. 35. 37. 39. 47. 48. 51. 66–70. 71–3. 105. 152. 156
Immigration Act 31. 37. 59
Indiana 74
Indian Mutiny 27
"Indian Settlers Act" or *Land for Settlers from India Act* 1867 49. 51–3
inheritance 16. 65. 75. 137–55. 180. 199. 230: *see also* succession
inspectors. closer and soldier settlement 105. 106. 116–17. 120–1. 134–5

Ireland 4. 42. 65. 67–8. 69. 71. 72–3. 96. 139. 144. 172
Isandula Estate 100. 102–4. 105. 135. 153. 218

Jefferson. Thomas (USA) 1. 12. 14
Johns brothers: George Reginald and Jessie 127–8: Robert Roy and Alice nee Kirkland 127–8: Sydney Rupert 127–8
Johnson family first Preston generation: Henry and Sarah Ann nee Burgess 63. 69. 75–6. 82. 123. 138. 145. 148. 171
Johnson family second generation: Albert and Florence 138: Ambrose (Amby) and Alice Victoria nee Stevens 138. 146–7: Harty John and Mary 76. 146–7: George and Dulcie nee Stevens 138. 146–7. 162. 173. 192: Henry (Harry) and Elsie 129: John (Jack) and Jane Elizabeth nee Stevens 138. 146–7. 148. 209: Phoebe (*see* Marshall. Ernest): Sarah (*see* Marshall. Peter J.): William and Rose nee Lunson 76. 146–7. 166
Johnson Preston family third generation: Alice (*see* Peebles): Amby (Tas) and Merle Winifred nee Stewart 168. 169. 173. 189. 190. 203. 215: Aubrey(Aub) and Lily 183: Denzil 148: Edis (Ned) and Ruth 174. 188–9. 224: Gollan/Georgie and Iris nee Stewart 148. 149. 169. 183. 184–5. 188. 190. 191. 196–7. 218. 224: Gordon (Bill) 148. 224: Jeanie Loughrey 148–9. 166: Johnny and Valerie 148: Keith (Kate) and Marie 148: photo 226: Sidney and Joan nee Reid 148–9. 183. 192. 196. 224
Johnson Preston family fourth generation: Ian and Hilda 164: Kevin and Gillian nee Chilcott 149. 175. 179. 222. 223: Marie Harrop 169–70. 175. 183. 193
Johnson (Upper Castra) family: Albert (Bert) and Thelma nee Marshall 147. 175: daughter Glennys 168–9. 171. 175
Jupp: Peter and Elizabeth 123. 138: Peter Jnr. and Ellen nee Brown 138. 151. 171

Kindred 28. 153. 154. 171. 219
King. Murray 161. 174. 212. 215
King Island 3. 116. 134
kinship 5. 16. 139. 147. 154. 171. 180. 182. 183. 186. 199. 216. 223–7. 231–2
Kirkland. Robert W. 133. 177. 187. 209. 212

272　*Index*

land agents 64–5, 114, 115, 204
landscape/countryside 7, 22, 42, 46, 59,
    155, 163, 168, 204, 215, 218, 231
Lands Department (aka Surveys and Lands
    Dept.) 25, 54, 56, 113
Lang, Archbishop John Dunmore 9
Last, Clarence and Dorothy 122, 133;
    William 161
Latrobe 23, 28, 35, 37, 60, 123, 172, 175,
    207
Launceston 20, 21, 22, 23, 54, 70–1, 77,
    94, 184, 186, 211, 213
Launceston Immigration Aid Society 70
Lea, Arthur Mills 207
leases 47, 90, 93, 101, 104–5, 106, 109,
    115, 116, 125, 127, 220, 230
Legge, Lt. Col. William Vincent 35
lessees 16, 23, 66, 97, 100–1, 102, 104,
    105, 114, 117, 134
Leven 53, 57, 63, 64, 65, 72–3, 79, 82,
    100, 115–18, 134, 166, 189, 203, 206;
    see also Ulverstone
Leven River 38, 49, 51, 52, 57, 105, 122,
    133, 166, 219–20
Lewis brothers: George Alfred 56, 65, 80,
    94, 137, 201, 204, 224; James and Sarah
    65, 80, 82, 83, 84–5, 87, 180, 204;
    William E. 65, 80, 103, 204
Lyons, Minister and Premier Joseph 116,
    119, 209

mainland Australia 8, 87, 91–3, 120, 232;
    see also New South Wales; Queensland;
    South Australia; Victoria; Western
    Australia
manures, fertilisers 191, 201
Marshall, Ernest: and Phoebe nee Johnson
    138
Marshall, Peter J.: and Sarah nee Johnson
    82, 138, 148
Marshall, William S.J. 133
McCall, Dr John 82, 85, 201, 204, 206, 219
McCulloch, James 72, 73
McCulloch family in Preston: Ernest and
    Elsie nee Tongs 82, 124, 175, 179, 184,
    194, 224; their children Athol 173, 177,
    186; Clarence(Clarrie) 159, 166, 167,
    174, 189, 194; Edis and Sheila 163,
    177, 184, 186
McKenzie, Lands Minister John (NZ) 89,
    90, 93, 143
McPherson: Angus 204; Burns Thompson
    and Fanny 130

Melrose, Surveyor George 23
Methodism/Methodists 71, 139, 164–5
Methodist church(es) 76, 77, 81, 82, 83,
    86–7, 146, 171, 177, 184–5
Mong, Alexander 66, 67; David 71, 74;
    Jane (*see* Robert Peebles Snr)

New Holland 45
New South Wales 9, 19, 32, 40, 44, 95, 96,
    98, 112, 120, 127, 232
newspapers 20, 26, 33, 64–5, 78, 81–2,
    84, 95, 100, 104, 110, 135, 163, 172,
    183, 189, 199–201, 203, 208, 219, 229
New Zealand 6, 14, 15, 17, 30, 48, 67,
    73, 108, 110, 129, 145, 165; closer
    settlement 88–90, 91, 93, 96–7, 107,
    143; comparisons with 39–40, 41, 143,
    158–9, 169, 177, 181, 201, 209, 213,
    228, 232–3
Nichols, Hubert Allen 86, 93, 103, 114,
    118, 122, 172, 177, 201–2, 204, 206–7,
    209, 210, 212, 219, 221–2
Nietta 78, 85, 93–4, 114, 123, 128, 131–2,
    135, 162, 173–5, 178, 185, 207, 210,
    219–20, 223–4
Norfolk UK 68, 70–1, 72, 77, 152;
    Norfolk four-course sequence 68
North Motton 4, 25, 37, 50, 59–60, 63,
    71–2, 77–8, 80–5, 109, 170, 178, 180,
    204, 210, 220–1, 216
North Western Butter Factories
    Association 215

Ocean Chief 71
Ogilvy, Captain David 26–7, 39
On Active Service Fund (OAS) 186

pastoralists/pastoralism 15, 21, 43, 46–7,
    55, 62, 68, 72, 95, 106
patriarchs/patriarchy 63, 66, 77, 87, 137,
    144, 145, 146, 152, 180–1, 222
peas 193, 206, 220, 223, 225, 227
Peebles family first immigrants: Robert
    Snr and Jane nee Mong 66, 67, 71, 74
Peebles family first Preston generation:
    James Robert and Margaret nee Mason
    50, 63, 74–5, 82, 87, 138, 150–1,
    155, 190
Peebles family second generation (their
    children): Alexander James and Eva
    May 150; Allan and Marion Jessie nee
    Dick 150; Andrew Henderson 150;
    David Mason and Alice nee Johnson

Index 273

129. 145. 150–1. 155. 173. 174. 184.
193. 218. 222; Henry Robert and Louie
150–1. 184. 190; Jane Elizabeth (*see*
Ewington brothers); Ruby Allison Fisher
74. 150
Peebles family third generation: George
Henry 150; Gilbert (Snow) 150; Gordon
(Bub) and June nee Buxton 151. 163.
170. 171. 174–5. 184. 193. 197. 213;
Margaret (Margy) King 151. 169. 174.
193. 228; Neville 151. 163. 174. 186;
Robert (Rob) 75. 151. 224
Peebles family fourth generation: siblings
Mark and Sharon 151. 170. 174. 229
Penguin 38. 58. 72. 82. 100. 177. 203. 206
pigs 71. 80. 101. 141. 161. 162. 191–2.
192. 193. 196. 213. 218. 220. 225. 233
Pike. Mr Justice George Herbert 112. 113.
117. 119. 132
pioneers 22–3. 30. 36. 39. 59. 61. 63. 67.
70–1. 73. 85. 87. 132. 154. 159. 161.
175. 180. 191
Plank Road 26. 29. 63. 72. 93; *see also*
tramway
Porter. John 78. 80. 151; son John Hogben
151. 152
Port Phillip 22
Port Sorell 22. 23. 24. 28. 36. 66. 71. 76
post offices 4. 61. 64. 78. 84. 85. 87. 100.
112. 130. 149. 167. 172. 195. 197. 204
potatoes 58. 69. 75. 80. 95. 97. 101. 104.
129–33. 148. 152–5. 169. 192. 196.
205–10. 211. 217. 220. 224–5
Potato Marketing Board 205. 208. 217
pre-emptive land rights 22. 24. 26. 46. 50.
66. 89. 106
Preston 63. 70. 74. 78. 84. 99. 118. 120.
133. 145. 168. 170. 183. 216
Preston Farmers' and Stockowners'
Association (FSOA) 209. 212
Preston (South Leven) Agricultural
Bureau 205
public sphere 17. 199–201. 202. 203. 228

Queensland 30. 40. 48. 91. 93. 96. 160. 206

radio programmes. stations 7AD and 7BU
168–9. 171. 179
Red Cross 185. 187. 231
Returned Sailors and Soldiers Imperial
League of Australia. RSL 116. 117–18.
120. 127. 130
ringbarking 21. 28. 46. 79

Rockliff. Peter 75
Rockliff. William and Matilda 123
Rockliff brothers: Francis 68; George 66.
68. 76; Henry 23–4. 28. 38. 66. 68. 76;
John 68
Robertson. John 72–3. 201
Royal Society of Tasmania 30. 31
ruralism. rural life/settlement 7. 8. 17. 92.
93. 99. 105. 110. 170. 176. 180–1
rural population 91. 110. 113. 139.
194. 212

Sassafras 28. 36. 60. 63. 65. 66–7. 69. 74.
76. 81. 146. 165
schools/schooling 20. 30. 46. 61. 64. 75.
81. 83–4. 133. 159–60. 162. 179
Scotland 3. 65. 70. 72. 100; Fife 71;
Highlands 71. 89; Lothians and
Perthshire 66–8. 71
Scott. Surveyor James 5. 23
Scott. J.R. 'Anglo-Indian' 43. 60
Shaw. Lt. Col. Michael Maxwell 33. 34–5.
37. 39. 41. 51
Skemp. Samuel and Rowland 66. 72. 94.
161
smallholder farmers 99. 136
Smith family of South Preston: Henry
(Harry) and Elizabeth Sarah 126. 138.
153. 155; son Mervyn John 121. 126;
daughters Gladys (*see* Brown family);
and Melvie (*see* Harding family)
Smith family of Waringa: Alan 225; Vernon
John 125. 161; Edward (Ted) 225; Ernest
and Betty Hazel 225. 228; Patricia (Pat)
161. 163. 169. 178; Peter 125. 126.
147. 228
Smith family soldier settlers: Bernard
Horace and Lillian Annie 121; Harry
Andrew Harford 125; William
Joseph 125
soils: description of 3. 21. 25. 27. 51–2.
60. 78. 122. 206. 233; potential 8. 36.
46. 65–6. 68. 80. 104. 115. 120. 132
soldier settlers. soldier settlement 16.
108–36. 186. 204
South Australia 6. 7. 8. 14. 39. 48. 54. 65.
72. 97. 112. 157. 160
Southern Eagle 70. 77
Sprent (Castra pre-1891) 57. 60. 62. 65.
80. 82. 93. 148. 160–3. 171–2. 187.
210–12. 216. 225
Sprent. Surveyor-General Charles 54. 81
St. Andrews Immigration Society 71. 74

274 *Index*

Stevens, John and Mary Ann 138, 192;
  daughters (*see* Johnson family)
Stuart: Don and Ruth nee Bucis 184
Stirling, Governor James 157
Stockley, Col. Henry Watts 57, 58, 103
succession 5, 137–55, 166; *see also*
  inheritance
surveys 10, 23, 54, 55–6, 90, 113
surveyors 16, 21, 46–7, 65, 230

Tasmanian Closer Settlement Board (CSB)
  58, 98–135, 205, 211
Tasmanian Countrywoman 187
Tasmanian Dairymen's Association
  213
Tasmanian Football Hall of Fame 174
tenant farmers 22, 66, 68, 72, 78, 204
Tewkesbury Potato Research Station
  209
timber, timber products 22–3, 36, 57, 75,
  85, 94, 218, 220–1
Tongs brothers in Preston: Allan Lorenzo
  127, 216; Frank Allan and Minnie 167,
  171, 177, 190, 206, 215, 216; their son
  Mervyn E. 138, 153; grandson Fred 148
Tongs family in North Motton: Alfred
  D.W. 203, 204, 206, 216; Frederick and
  Rosina nee Brett 138, 206, 216
Torrens system 54
tramway (plank/ed road) 26, 28, 29, 31,
  36, 203

Ulverstone 24, 34, 38, 57, 81, 86, 130,
  185, 186, 212
Ulverstone Benevolent Society Hospital
  130, 187, 191
Ulverstone Butter Factory 213, 215
Ulverstone Farmers' Club 38, 83, 85
Ulverstone-Nietta Railway 218–22
Ulverstone Show Society (later Agricultural
  and Pastoral Society) 85, 216
United Australian Axemen's Association
  86, 172, 204

United Kingdom *see* Britain
Upper Castra *see* Castra, Upper

Van Diemen's Land (VDL) 19–21, 42,
  46–7, 69, 106
Victoria 8–9, 23, 40, 48, 73, 91, 95–6,
  111, 158, 196, 199, 224

Wakefield, Ernest Gibbon 1, 20
Wales 46, 65, 67
Warner, Col. A.H. 85
water supply 175, 192
Werona Estate 100–2, 122, 134
Wesley, John 165, 227
Western Australia 7, 21, 70, 92, 112, 174
Whirlwind 70, 77
widows and widowers 117, 142, 145, 148
Wilmot 25, 163, 168, 171
Wing, Raymond Alfred 121, 133
Wing family early settlers: George Henry
  72, 84–5, 86
Wing family in Preston: Ebenezer 73;
  George Henry Jun. 73, 79, 80, 87, 137,
  192, 201, 203, 206; Stanley (Stan) 209,
  210, 216–18
Wing family in Waringa: Donald (Don)
  George 126; Roy William Diaper and
  Ruby 121, 125–6
women 16, 42, 67, 121, 138–40, 180–98,
  213, 215, 231
Wright, John Forsyth Snr and Emma nee
  Lewis 94, 137
Wright, Thomas William Snr and Sara 137,
  201
Wright, Warden John Forsyth Jnr 172, 205,
  212, 221
Wynyard 94, 120, 178, 190

Yaxley, J.W. 84
yeomanry characteristics 9–15, 17, 63, 71,
  91, 106, 140, 144, 154, 181, 230
Yorkshire 10, 23–4, 68, 156–7
Young, Dr. Arthur 38, 60